Sexual Victimization

D1608987

*I would like to dedicate this book to my nephews: Landon,
Chase, and Wesley. Each of you continually surprise and amaze me.*

—Tara N. Richards

*I would like to dedicate this book to my goddaughters, Lydia and Katie.
I look forward to seeing you grow and mature into beautiful and
strong young women—I love you and am proud of you.*

—Catherine D. Marcum

Sexual Victimization
Then and Now

Tara N. Richards
University of Baltimore

Catherine D. Marcum
Appalachian State University

Editors

Los Angeles | London | New Delhi
Singapore | Washington DC

Los Angeles | London | New Delhi
Singapore | Washington DC

FOR INFORMATION:

SAGE Publications, Inc.
2455 Teller Road
Thousand Oaks, California 91320
E-mail: order@sagepub.com

SAGE Publications Ltd.
1 Oliver's Yard
55 City Road
London EC1Y 1SP
United Kingdom

SAGE Publications India Pvt. Ltd.
B 1/I 1 Mohan Cooperative Industrial Area
Mathura Road, New Delhi 110 044
India

SAGE Publications Asia-Pacific Pte. Ltd.
3 Church Street
#10-04 Samsung Hub
Singapore 049483

Acquisitions Editor: Jerry Westby
Editorial Assistant: MaryAnn Vail
Production Editor: Melanie Birdsall
Copy Editor: Paula L. Fleming
Typesetter: C&M Digitals (P) Ltd.
Proofreader: Jeff Bryant
Indexer: Sue Nedrow
Cover Designer: Anupama Krishnan
Marketing Manager: Terra Schultz

Printed in the United States of America

Library of Congress Cataloging-in-Publication Data

Sexual victimization : then and now / [edited by]
Tara N. Richards, University of Baltimore, Catherine D. Marcum, Appalachian State University.

pages cm
Includes bibliographical references and index.

ISBN 978-1-4833-0817-3 (pbk.)

1. Sex crimes—United States. 2. Sexual abuse victims—United States. 3. Criminal justice, Administration of—United States. I. Richards, Tara N. II. Marcum, Catherine Davis

HV6592.S4864 2015
362.8830973—dc23   2013036560

This book is printed on acid-free paper.

MIX
Paper from
responsible sources
FSC® C014174

14 15 16 17 18 10 9 8 7 6 5 4 3 2 1

Brief Contents

Detailed Contents

Preface

After almost three decades of activism and legal reform, the criminal justice system, with the help of non–criminal justice system partners, has made great strides regarding the handling of cases of sexual victimization, including how sexual victimization is defined, how evidence is collected, and how cases are prosecuted as well as how victims are treated by criminal justice system actors. Every state now includes rape and sexual assault in its penal code, and many states' definitions of forcible rape include language pertaining to diverse groups of victims, including special populations of victims such as prisoners and the elderly. In addition, many police departments now assist in the facilitation of victims' court advocates and counseling services post–sexual assault. However, there are still ways in which criminal justice practitioners, activists, and scholars could advance their understandings of sexual victimization and improve the treatment of victims as they move through the criminal justice process. This continuum of change, as well as the lack thereof, was inspiration for the development of this book. We as the editors felt as if the academic community, as well as practitioners, could benefit from a text that outlined the various facets of "then and now" in regard to sexual victimization as a whole.

The purpose of this project is to produce a book that provides scholars easy access to information that specifically examines the continuum of change in the sexual victimization field. It is the desire of the editors to educate and enlighten a wide audience, from those who are completely unfamiliar with the topic to individuals who need more specific information on a particular type of sexual victimization. This text should be a useful guide to students, academics, and practitioners alike.

Acknowledgments

We would like to extend a huge thank you to all the contributors of this book. Your expertise in the field will provide enlightenment and insight to academics and students alike. All your hard work is appreciated.

Thank you to Jerry Westby, MaryAnn Vail, and the staff at SAGE for their assistance and patience with the preparation of this manuscript. It was wonderful to work with a group of individuals who shared the same vision for this book. We hope it is a great success.

Finally, thank you very much to the following reviewers of this text for their thoughts and insight on improving the book:

Kelley Christopher, University of West Georgia

Wendy Perkins Gilbert, Urbana University

Sheri Jenkins Keenan, Cameron University

Rebecca Loftus, Arizona State University

Stephanie P. Manzi, Roger Williams University

Christine L. McClure, Cape Cod Community College

Elizabeth Quinn, Fayetteville State University

Bradford W. Reyns, Weber State University

We hope you are pleased with the finished product.

1

State Variations on Definition of Sexual Assault

*Amanda Burgess-Proctor
and Christopher G. Urban*

The task of evaluating state sexual assault statutes is more complicated than it might appear at first. States have long ago abandoned a solitary "rape" law in favor of more nuanced and multilayered sets of laws. Even a cursory exploration of sexual assault legislation demonstrates that these laws address a wide variety of proscribed behaviors, including (but not limited to) child sexual assault; adult sexual assault; statutory rape; rape occurring within correctional, educational, and other specific populations; sodomy; and bestiality. There is also tremendous variation in the terminology states use to describe sexual assault ("sexual abuse," "criminal sexual conduct," "sexual battery," "sexual torture," etc.), and there likewise exists no necessary consistency in the definitions of these terms across states. Even the language states use to define "consent" varies considerably, as does the standard by which consent (or lack thereof) is measured.

Thus, a tidy summary of state legislative definitions of rape and sexual assault remains elusive, particularly within the context of this brief essay. In addition, we elected to focus solely on adult offenses, as child sexual assault brings with it a category of offenses (child pornography, pedophilia, incest, and so on) that would broaden our analysis beyond the intended scope of this essay. As a result, we do not address statutory rape or the development of age-of-consent laws, though analyses of these laws are readily available elsewhere (see Davis & Twombly, 2000; NIC, 2006; Oberman, 1994).

With those caveats offered, this chapter presents a general overview of the current status of sexual assault legislation in the United States. First, we begin by summarizing U.S. rape law reform over the last three decades. We then examine how states define sexual assault in the contemporary era. We do so by examining four important targets of rape law reform: force, non-consent, and corroboration requirements; rape shield laws; gender-neutral language; and marital exemptions. Ours is not an exhaustive legal analysis (for that, see AEquitas, 2012; and Decker & Baroni, 2011) but instead is intended to provide a "state of the statutes" summary along these four dimensions. As a counterexample to statutory definitions, we also examine definitions of sexual assault used in federal legislation and in national sources of crime data. Next, we consider the importance of legal definitions of rape and sexual assault and their impact on reporting, arrest, and prosecution patterns, and we briefly assess the extent to which rape law reforms have been fully achieved. Finally, we offer suggestions for continued advancement in states' responses to sexual assault.

Overview of Rape Law Reform: Evolving Definitions and Legal Standards in State Statutes

At common law, rape was defined as "carnal knowledge of a female, by a man, not his wife, forcibly and against her will" (Caringella, 2009, p. 12), where the term *carnal knowledge* refers to penile–vaginal penetration (Spohn & Horney, 1992). Historically, then, the legal definition of rape considered only male perpetrators and female victims; excluded digital, object, oral, and anal penetration, as well as contact offenses such as kissing, fondling, or frottage; excluded spouses; and required both that the perpetrator use force and that the victim withhold consent. Thus, the legal standard defining "rape" was sufficiently narrow as to exclude a whole host of behaviors involving intimate partners, male victims (and/or female perpetrators), nonpenile vaginal penetration, and the like. Moreover, Lord Chief Justice Sir Matthew Hale suggested that rape was "an accusation easy to be made, hard to be proved, and harder to be defended by the party accused though ever so innocent" (as quoted in Bachman & Paternoster, 1993, p. 558; Caringella, p. 16) cultivated a social response to rape that was reflexively protective of the accused (Bachman & Paternoster). As a result, victims' moral character and sexual history often were presented as mitigating evidence. This climate of suspicion and skepticism persisted for centuries, as accusers routinely were questioned at trial about their previous sexual encounters well into the mid-20th century.

Beginning in 1970s, reformers and activists began agitating for legal reform that would make state rape statutes both more progressive and more inclusive (Caringella, 2009). These reform efforts had two separate but aligned sources: feminist groups, for whom legal reform was intended to serve a largely ideological function aimed at dispelling popularly held rape myths and reducing victim stereotyping and stigmatization, and victims' rights and "law and order" groups, for whom legal reform was intended to serve a more instrumental function aimed at increasing the processing and adjudication of perpetrators (Bachman & Paternoster, 1993, p. 555). Despite their somewhat divergent orientations, both groups hoped legal reform would, among other advances, broaden definitions of rape beyond the narrow, antiquated common-law standard.

Over the decades that followed, a series of legal reforms did indeed occur. Some of the most important of these reforms were (a) expansion of the terminology used from *rape* to *sexual assault* or *criminal sexual conduct*, (b) inclusion of additional offenses beyond penile–vaginal penetration, (c) removal of requirements for corroborating evidence (which existed only for rape) and statutory requirements of resistance and non-consent, (d) forbiddance of accusers' sexual history or character evidence at trial (i.e., "rape shield" laws), (e) elimination of the marital/spousal exemption, (f) adoption of gender-neutral language for victims and offenders, and (g) creation of age-of-consent laws (Caringella, 2009; Horney & Spohn, 1991; Koss, 1996).

Michigan enacted the first and most comprehensive rape reform legislation with the creation of its Criminal Sexual Conduct statute (Bachman & Paternoster, 1993), which replaced the existing "carnal knowledge" rape statute in 1975. Indeed, Michigan's statute was regarded as a model for state sexual assault legislation (Caringella, 2009). In addition to creating a four-pronged statute that considered penetration and contact offenses as well as a victim's capacity to consent, it also included the nation's first rape shield law (Anderson, 2002).

Throughout the 1970s and 1980s, other states followed Michigan's lead, albeit to varying degrees and with varying speed. For example, while most states had adopted rape shield laws by the mid-1980s (Anderson, 2002), it was not until 1993 that all 50 states had included some statutory recognition of marital rape, whether through repeal of spousal exemptions or through creation of statutes explicitly allowing spouses to be prosecuted (AEquitas, 2012).

Examining Statutory Definitions Past and Present Using Four Targets of Rape Law Reform

Given the tremendous breadth and complexity of state rape and sexual assault statutes, we have selected four issues targeted by early rape law reformers to serve as examples for use in evaluating statutory definitions of rape both past and present. Below, we discuss four of the most prominent targets of rape law reform—force, non-consent, and corroboration requirements; rape shield laws; gender-neutral language; and marital exemptions—and we evaluate the evolution of statutory definitions and standards for each of those targets over the last three decades.

FORCE, NON-CONSENT, AND CORROBORATION

Historically, sexual offenses were categorized as "rapes" only when the perpetrator used force and the victim actively resisted the attack; moreover, successful prosecution for rape generally required corroborating evidence to demonstrate that the offense occurred against the victim's will (Caringella, 2009; Decker & Baroni, 2011). First, most U.S. jurisdictions adopted a definition of rape that included a "forcible compulsion" requirement, and a successful conviction could occur only when the victim withheld consent (e.g., "against her will"; Decker & Baroni). Is it important to observe that the standards to which victims were expected to resist the attack were extremely high: "to the utmost," "throughout the duration of the attack," etc. (Caringella). Similarly, drawing upon the "hue and cry" standard, corroborating evidence of the victim's lack of consent was required for successful conviction for rape (Decker & Baroni). This corroboration requirement existed for no crime other than rape (Caringella). However, as the force and non-consent requirements slowly became obsolete, many states began abandoning corroboration requirements. "Today, for the most part, testimony of an alleged rape victim is sufficient to uphold a conviction for rape without the need for corroborating evidence" (Decker & Baroni, p. 1148).

That said, a careful reading of contemporary state statutes reveals that the force, non-consent, and corroboration requirements have not been completely eliminated in practice. For example, only 28 states currently criminalize nonconsensual sex acts, including both contact and penetration offenses, committed without force (AEquitas, 2012). Decker and Baroni (2011) called these "true non-consent states," in which a defendant can be convicted on the basis of victim non-consent alone. However, of those 28 states, only 17 have non-consent provisions for penetration offenses; in the other 11 states, the non-consent language applies only to contact offenses, and, therefore, they "still require a showing of 'forcible compulsion' or 'incapacity to consent' for sexual penetration offenses" (Decker & Baroni, pp. 1084–1085). The remaining 22 states have statutory definitions that conflict with non-consent standards. Some of those states ("contradictory non-consent states") have statutory definitions that require a lack of capacity to consent, while others ("force states") lack non-consent statutes altogether (Decker & Baroni). As for corroboration, it appears that much of the advancement in this arena has actually occurred in the judiciary through case law, as only 17 states have statutorily dismissed or otherwise addressed common-law corroboration requirements (Decker & Baroni).

RAPE SHIELD LAWS

The criminal justice processing of rape cases historically focused not on the actions of the accused, but on the actions of the victim. For example, offenses in which victims did not resist "to the utmost" and/or "throughout the entire duration of the attack" (Caringella, 2009; Horney & Spohn, 1991) did not meet original statutory definitions of rape, so victims who could not demonstrate that level of resistance were unlikely to receive legal protection and have their cases prosecuted. This view shifted during the 1970s, but as legislation caught up with these more progressive views, new methods of victim blaming emerged—and with them new legal practices aimed at discrediting victims.

While statutory resistance requirements were losing traction, victim blaming shifted to the personal and sexual history of the victim. Unchaste women were considered untrustworthy and less likely to make "legitimate" claims of rape because universal consent to sex was inferred on the basis of their impurity, therefore making them less worthy of legal protection (Anderson, 2002; Spohn & Horney, 1991). Thus, information about an accuser's previous sexual partners and relationships was admissible at trial as it was believed relevant to establishing consent, and as such, it was readily used as a defense tactic in order to discredit accusations of rape (Anderson; Spohn & Horney). Rape law reformers raised concerns about this practice, prompting states and the federal government to develop new rules meant to protect character evidence from being used against victims at trial. In the late 1970s, states began to create what would later be termed "rape shield" laws. While not uniform in content, the basic intent of these laws was to protect rape victims from being questioned about their sexual histories at trial (Anderson; Spohn & Horney).

At present, most states have some type of rape shield law forbidding or otherwise governing the admissibility of evidence about complainants' past sexual history (AEquitas, 2012). In spite of these laws, however, details about victims' prior sexual relationships—particularly with the accused—are still "routinely worked into case proceedings" as they are believed relevant to issues of consent (Caringella, 2009, p. 32). Indeed, all states make exceptions for the admissibility of evidence pertaining to a past sexual relationship between the complainant and the defendant, which serve in practice to dismantle the protection the rape shield laws are purported to offer (Anderson, 2002). In Colorado (C.R.S. § 18-3-407, 2005), for example, evidence of a victim's past sexual conduct and other "opinion" or "reputation" evidence is presumed irrelevant and therefore inadmissible at trial, except when it pertains to the victim's "prior sexual conduct with the actor [defendant]." These exceptions therefore undermine the intended protections for victims.

GENDER NEUTRALITY AND SAME-SEX RELATIONSHIPS

Rape laws originally were written in gender-specific language that used female pronouns for victims and male pronouns for perpetrators. Gendered statutes therefore excluded male victims and female perpetrators, as well as same-sex victim/ perpetrator combinations. These limitations became especially problematic during the late 1980s and early 1990s as scholarly recognition of gay and lesbian relationship violence began to grow (Morrow & Hawxhurst, 1989; Renzetti, 1992). Out of a desire to protect male victims and to enable the prosecution of female perpetrators—as well as to address sexual assault between same-sex individuals—in the 1970s and 1980s, states began revising their statutes to use gender-neutral terminology (Caringella, 2009). According to Rumney (2007),

Across dozens of jurisdictions, gender-neutral reforms have been adopted as part of a wider law reform agenda in an attempt to reflect a more modern understanding of the purpose of rape law—the protection of sexual autonomy from the harm of non-consensual penetrative sex acts. (pp. 482–483)

Currently, only six states require opposite-sex parties or that the victim be female for there to be a chargeable sexual assault offense. As a result, most states use gender-neutral language in at least one of their statutes (AEquitas, 2012). Examples of gender-neutral language include referring to the attacker or victim as *he or she*, using the generic term *actor* or *perpetrator*, or otherwise avoiding gendered references altogether. Alternatively, some states retain gender-specific language but define the terms broadly. For example, while New Jersey does not have a gender-neutral sexual assault statute, a logical reading of the law reveals that the word *he* does not necessarily refer only to males because *actor* is defined as "the person" (not "the man") committing the offense (N.J.S.A. § 2C:14-3b, 2012). Likewise, Delaware's statute uses the word *he* but qualifies this use by stating, "The male pronoun shall be deemed to refer to both male and female" (11 Del. C. § 762[b], 1953). Other states use inconsistent language across statutes, which can lead to confusion. For example, Alabama's statutes use gender-neutral language to define the crime of rape (Code of Alabama § 13A-6-61, 1977) but use the pronoun *he* when defining the crimes of sodomy (Code of Alabama § 13A-6-63, 1977) and sexual abuse (Code of Alabama § 13A-6-66, 1977). Other states struggle to consistently utilize gender-neutral language.

One important issue to note here is concern that the adoption of gender-neutral language for the purpose of expanding the applicability of rape statutes to broad populations actually conceals or diminishes the truly gendered nature of sexual assault:

> In addition to achieving gender neutrality in the statutes, rape law reform accomplished several other changes, including expansion of the definition of the crime to include a range of sexual contacts. Thus, where rape before was understood to mean penile-vaginal intercourse, the crime now encompasses other sexual acts involving penetration by objects other than the penis and of orifices other than the vagina. These two accomplishments of rape law reform may in turn have accomplished something unintended. . . . Specifically, to the extent the feminist challenge rightly and necessarily intended its beneficiaries to be female, has it been undermined by a rising tide of male victims? By gender-neutralizing the victim position, have we gained or lost ground in the struggle against sexual assault and harassment? (Novotny, 2003, p. 745)

MARITAL EXEMPTIONS

Wives were believed to be "unrapeable" at common law because submitting to sex at their husbands' request was considered an inherent part of wifely duties. The origins of this marital exemption for rape likely rest with 17th-century jurist Sir Matthew Hale, who stated, "The husband cannot be guilty of rape committed by himself upon his lawful wife, for by their mutual matrimonial consent and contract, the wife have given up herself in this kind unto the husband which she cannot retract" (Caringella, 2009, p. 20). Reform activists vigorously challenged this view as both antiquated and insufficiently protective of women, and they advocated for the dismissal of marital exemptions.

> By July 1993, the rape or sexual assault of one's spouse had become a crime, *to some degree*, in all 50 states. This means that each state in the country has some provision within its law allowing for the prosecution of a husband for the rape or sexual assault of or lewd conduct against his wife. (AEquitas, 2012, p. 103)

Thus, in no state are spouses entirely exempt from rape prosecution, but as with the force/non-consent and corroboration requirements, substantial variations remain.

Only 14 states have completely discarded marital exemptions for rape; the remaining states still offer some degree of marital immunity, albeit to varying degrees (Decker & Baroni, 2011). For example, some states might forbid spousal rape involving force or bodily harm but fail to outlaw less serious assaultive behaviors such as threatening one's spouse in order to procure sex (Decker & Baroni, p. 1156). In Nevada (NRS 200.373, 1967) for example, "It is no defense to a charge of sexual assault that the perpetrator was, at the time of the assault, married to the victim, *if the assault was committed by force or by the threat of force* [emphasis ours]." Thus, "significant hurdles" to prosecution for marital rape still exist in many states (AEquitas, 2012, p. 103).

Beyond State Statutes: Evolving Definitions at the Federal Level and in National Sources of Crime Data

DEFINING RAPE IN THE FEDERAL STATUTE AND MODEL PENAL CODE

The arguments presented by rape law reformers had an impact on federal definitions of rape as well. In keeping with changes occurring at the state level, the federal rape statute was revised as part of the Sexual Abuse Act of 1986 to expand definitions of sexual assault:

> The intent of the legislation is described in these points: (1) defining offenses in gender-neutral terms; (2) defining offenses so that a trial focuses on the conduct of the defendant, instead of the conduct of the victim; (3) expanding the offenses to reach all forms of sexual abuse; (4) abandoning the doctrines of resistance and spousal immunity; and (5) expanding the federal jurisdiction to include all federal prisons. (U.S. Congress, 1986)

However, this reform was predated by more than two decades by the Model Penal Code (MPC), which is intended to serve as a guide to states for criminal statutes. As early as 1962, the MPC sought to move away from the common law approach by downplaying—but not eliminating—the [victim] resistance requirement. Although it removed "against her will" from the definition of rape, it included a requirement that the [defendant] had "compelled her to submit." Most states did not follow the MPC's recommendation to eliminate a resistance requirement and instead followed the MPC's emphasis on force instead of the victim's non-consent. Thus, the victim's resistance remained an explicit element in most states' rape statutes as an indicator of the defendant's use of force and the victim's non-consent. (Decker & Baroni, 2011, pp. 1102–1103)

This was true at least until the 1970s and 1980s, when states began revisiting this standard, as described previously.

DEFINING RAPE IN THE NATIONAL CRIME VICTIMIZATION SURVEY

The arena of state statutes was not the only one in which definitions of sexual assault began to shift and change following the reform movement of the 1970s. Take, for example, the National Crime Victimization Survey (NCVS), which is administered annually by the Bureau of Justice Statistics and serves as the primary source of victimization data in the United States. The NCVS underwent an extensive redesign in the 1980s, partly in an effort to produce more reliable estimates of rape and sexual assault (Bachman & Saltzman, 1995; Bachman & Taylor, 1994). Prior to the redesign, there was concern that respondents who did not interpret their sexual victimization experiences as "rape" (for example, if the assailant was an intimate partner or if the offense did not involve physical force) would fail to respond affirmatively to screening questions designed to assess rape victimization. Recognizing the potential for underreporting, the criminal justice terminology (e.g., "rape") was replaced with more behavior-specific language (e.g., "forced or coerced sexual intercourse"; Bachman & Saltzman; Bachman & Taylor) intended to prompt respondents to recognize and report their sexual assault victimization experiences.

By 1992, the NCVS interviewer's manual stated:

Rape is forced sexual intercourse and includes both psychological coercion as well as physical force. Forced sexual intercourse means vaginal, anal, or oral penetration by the offender(s). This category also includes incidents where the penetration is from a foreign object such as a bottle. (Bachman & Saltzman, 1995, p. 6)

Note the relative breadth of this definition. Like the reformed state statutes that were commonplace by the mid-1990s, the post-redesign NCVS definition of rape recognized other types of force beyond physical aggression, included many types of penetration, and was gender neutral. Thus, the current NCVS operational definition of rape reflects many of the legal changes that occurred at the state statutory level in the 1970s and 1980s.

DEFINING RAPE IN THE UNIFORM CRIME REPORT

A counterexample to the NCVS exists in the Uniform Crime Report (UCR). The UCR, compiled annually by the Federal Bureau of Investigation (FBI), is the primary source of official offending data in the United States. Given its prominence as a data source from which crime rates are calculated, definitions of crime used in the UCR have sizeable importance for generating accurate crime statistics. Despite the extensive statutory reforms of the 1970s and 1980s and the revised wording adopted by the NCVS in the early 1990s, the UCR maintained the common law definition of rape—"the carnal knowledge of a female forcibly and against her will"—until December 2011. Until recently, the FBI had declined legal advocates' requests for change, citing the existence of broader definitions of sexual assault in the National Incident-Based Reporting System (NIBRS) and the perceived investment costs of expanding the UCR system (see Saltzman, 2004, p. 1240). Thus, the UCR definition of rape that retained the force requirement, applied only to penile-vaginal penetration, and covered only male-to-female assaults went unchanged for 80 years. In contrast, the new definition of rape adopted in 2011 is much more consistent with the language that has been used in contemporary state statutes and by the NCVS since the mid-1990s: "penetration, no matter how slight, of the vagina or anus with any body part or object, or oral penetration by a sex organ of another person, without the consent of the victim" (FBI, 2012).

Importantly, rape statistics generated from UCR data using the new definition will become more comprehensive as broader operational definitions give rise to larger estimates (see Kilpatrick, 2004, for a review). For example, for the first time, offenses involving sodomy or same-sex sexual assault will be counted and included in rape statistics (FBI, 2012). As with the NCVS, the primary outcome of the revised UCR definition of rape is an increase in reporting—specifically, an increase in the number of reported rapes as a function of the broadened definition.

Impact of Rape Law Reforms on Reporting, Arrest, Prosecution, and Conviction Rates for Sexual Assault

In the decades since rape law reform was first enacted, state statutes have undergone significant changes, as described in the previous section. Exhaustive legal analyses of current state statutes are available elsewhere (see AEquitas, 2012; Decker & Baroni, 2011), so we will not attempt to replicate those here. We can, however, draw some general conclusions about components of state rape laws that were the targets of reformers in the 1970s.

One primary goal of the statutory reforms described above was to increase both the number of reported rapes and the adjudication of perpetrators. It was widely understood that rape was among the most underreported crimes and that arrest and conviction rates were correspondingly low as well. Reformers "suggested that the laws and rules of evidence unique to rape were at least partially responsible for the unwillingness of victims to report rapes and for the low rates of arrest, prosecution, and conviction" (Horney & Spohn, 1991, p. 117). Thus, beyond symbolic and ideological gains such as dispelling myths and dismantling stereotypes, legal reforms were intended to increase criminal justice processing of sexual assaults (Bachman & Paternoster, 1993).

Evidence about the extent to which reforms have actually resulted in the intended changes is unclear at best and disheartening at worst. Throughout the 1980s, results of the few empirical evaluations of rape law reforms that existed were inconclusive. By the early 1990s, investigators continued to see little tangible change in victim reporting or in offender processing (Bachman & Paternoster, 1993; Horney & Spohn, 1991) and also encountered continued problems with the ways in which rape and sexual assault were captured in national crime statistics (Koss, 1996). However, some recent evidence offers hope by demonstrating concrete improvement in rape case processing resulting from legal reform:

> The effects of reform have not been limited to the symbolic ones achieved through changes in legal doctrine. This study shows that changes in rape law have had real, instrumental effects. Our statistical analysis shows that defining sex crimes on a single continuum, subjecting spouses and cohabitants to prosecution, limiting the admissibility at trial about the victim's past sexual history with the defendant or about the victim's past sexual history on cross-examination, and denying a mistake of incapacity defense all significantly increased the number of "actual rapes." (Futter & Mebane, 2001, p. 111)

Despite these gains, problematic issues persist with nominally "reformed" state statutes, which in many jurisdictions remain contradictory and "fundamentally flawed," particularly as they relate to non-consent and coercion (Decker & Baroni, 2011, p. 1167).

While the broadening of rape definitions and other legal reforms have had some positive impact, they clearly have not yielded the wholesale restructuring of rape processing that reformers envisioned. Several explanations exist for the modesty of these gains. One explanation is that statutory changes may be insufficient to overcome the discretion of individual criminal justice system decision makers, who may or may not endorse the goals of these reforms (Horney & Spohn, 1991; Spohn & Horney, 1991). Or, as the focal movement of grassroots women's groups shifted in the 1990s from rape to domestic violence, activists may have felt that reformed rape laws offered evidence that the problem had been sufficiently addressed (Caringella, 2006). Alternatively, lingering acceptance of rape myths perpetuated by the media and endorsed by criminal justice practitioners may mean that, despite broader definitions, only those "strongest cases" meeting original definitions and standards of rape are most likely to result in conviction (Caringella, 2009, p. 61). Finally, acceptance of rape myths also may play a role in creating societal resistance to rape law reform, as when it is believed that obtaining positive assent from a partner before engaging in sexual activity will "de-romanticize adult sexual relationships" (Decker & Baroni, 2011, p. 1168).

Moving Forward: Areas for Continued Advancement

It is clear that significant advances have occurred where rape law reform is concerned. The repeal of the "carnal knowledge" standard to include sexual acts beyond penile–vaginal penetration; the abolition of force, consent, and corroboration requirements and the marital exemption; the adoption of gender-neutral language; and the passage of rape shield laws all mark gains made since the rape law reform movement began in the 1970s. However, even this cursory evaluation of state sexual assault statutes makes it clear that improvements are still needed. Below, we outline two concerns that future reformers might address.

First, state sexual assault statutes are a thicket of complex, convoluted, and sometimes contradictory laws that resist easy navigation. An obvious solution to this problem would be for states to carefully examine their sexual assault legislation to identify contradictory terms, definitions, and standards and correct them accordingly. One strategy for states to "clean house" with their sexual assault legislation is to identify and adopt model statutory language. This might come from other states like Michigan, which has passed progressive and comprehensive legislation, or from the Model Penal Code, which is designed to serve as a guiding template for state law.

Second, some state laws continue to include worrisome exceptions and loopholes, such as marital exemptions for nonviolent sexual offenses and rape shield exemptions that permit information about past sexual encounters between victims and defendants to be admitted at trial. This reality is particularly problematic in light of the prevalence of sexual assault between intimate partners. For example, the most recent estimates from the NCVS reveal that approximately 34% of all rapes and sexual assaults involved current or former intimate partners (Planty, Langton, Krebs, Berzofsky, & Smiley-McDonald, 2013). Therefore, state statutes that include spousal exemptions or that otherwise present obstacles for sexual assault victims to receive protection from their current or former intimate partners are worthy of review.

Conclusion

It is clear that state definitions of rape and sexual assault have evolved considerably over the last 40 years. However, a review of the literature and a careful reading of state statutes reveal that a myriad of problems remain, suggesting that rape law reform efforts may not have been as fruitful as advocates had hoped. As a result, it is imperative that scholars and legal experts continue to direct their attention toward rape and sexual assault and especially to the reporting and processing of these crimes irrespective of improved statutory definitions. In particular, creating laws that are free from confusing language and contradictory standards and that are responsive to the unique circumstances of sexual assault between intimate partners might be especially worthy of future research and reform efforts. Hopefully, the gains achieved by the first wave of rape law reformers will be matched in coming years by additional successes that continue to protect and empower victims of rape and sexual assault.

Discussion Questions

1. To what extent do you believe the legal reforms championed by activists in the 1970s have been achieved today? In other words, do you think those early reformers would be satisfied with the status of state rape laws today? Why or why not?

2. What legal definition of rape do you think is most useful? In your view, should all states adopt the same definition? If so, which one, and why?

3. If you were a reformer, what changes to state rape laws would you want to see enacted? What do you think are the most important issues activists should address in the coming years, and why?

References

11 Del. C. (Delaware Code Annotated) § 762(b). (1953). *Provisions generally applicable to sexual offenses.* Retrieved from http://delcode.delaware.gov/title11/c005/sc02/index.shtml#762

AEquitas: The Prosecutors' Resource on Violence Against Women. (2012). *Rape and sexual assault analyses and laws.* Retrieved from http://www.aequitasresource.org/Rape_and_Sexual_Assault_Analyses_and_Laws.pdf

Anderson, M. J. (2002). From chastity requirement to sexuality license: Sexual consent and a new rape shield law. *George Washington Law Review, 70,* 51–165.

Bachman, R., & Paternoster, R. (1993). A contemporary look at rape law reform: How far have we really come? *The Journal of Criminal Law & Criminology, 84*(3), 554–574.

Bachman, R., & Saltzman, L. E. (1995). *Violence against women: Estimates from the redesigned survey.* Washington, DC: U.S. Department of Justice.

Bachman, R., & Taylor, B. H. (1994). The measurement of family violence and rape by the redesigned National Crime Victimization Survey. *Justice Quarterly, 11*(3), 499–512.

Caringella, S. (2006). Sexual assault reforms: Thirty years and counting. In C. M. Renzetti, L. Goodstein & S. L. Miller (Eds.), *Rethinking gender, crime, and justice: Feminist readings* (pp. 155–167). New York, NY: Oxford University Press.

Caringella, S. (2009). *Addressing rape law reform in law and practice.* New York, NY: Columbia University Press.

Code of Alabama § 13A-6-61. (1977). *Rape in the first degree.* Retrieved from http://www.legislature.state.al.us/codeofalabama/1975/13A-6-61.htm

Code of Alabama § 13A-6-63. (1977). *Sodomy in the first degree.* Retrieved from http://www.legislature.state.al.us/codeofalabama/1975/13A-6-63.htm

Code of Alabama § 13A-6-66. (1977). *Sexual abuse in the first degree.* Retrieved from http://www.legislature.state.al.us/codeofalabama/1975/13A-6-66.htm

C.R.S. (Colorado Revised Statutes) § 18-3-407. (2005). *Colorado rape shield law.* Retrieved from http://www.boulder-bar.org/bar_media_manual/offenses/6.7.html

Davis, N. S., & Twombly, J. (2000). *State legislators' handbook for statutory rape issues.* Washington, DC: American Bar Association, Center on Children and the Law; U.S. Department of Justice, Office for Victims of Crime.

Decker, J. F., & Baroni, P. G. (2011). "No" still means "yes": The failure of the "non-consent" reform movement in American rape and sexual assault law. *Journal of Criminal Law & Criminology, 101*(4), 1081–1169.

Federal Bureau of Investigation (FBI). (2012). *UCR program changes definition of rape: Includes all victims and omits requirement of physical force.* Retrieved from http://www.fbi.gov/about-us/cjis/cjis-link/march-2012/ucr-program-changes-definition-of-rape/

Futter, S., & Mebane, W. R. (2001). The effects of rape law reform on rape case processing. *Berkeley Women's Law Journal, 16*, 72–139.

Horney, J., & Spohn, C. (1991). Rape law reform and instrumental change in six urban jurisdictions. *Law & Society Review, 25*(1), 117–154.

Kilpatrick, D. G. (2004). What is violence against women: Defining and measuring the problem. *Journal of Interpersonal Violence, 19*(11), 1209–1234.

Koss, M. P. (1996). The measurement of rape victimization in crime surveys. *Criminal Justice and Behavior, 23*(1), 55–69.

Morrow, S. L., & Hawxhurst, D. M. (1989). Lesbian partner abuse: Implications for therapists. *Journal of Counseling & Development, 68*, 58–62.

National Institute of Corrections (NIC). (2006). *50 state survey of sexual offenses against children (statutory rape).* Retrieved from http://static.nicic.gov/Library/021769.pdf

N.J.S.A. (New Jersey Statues Annotated) § 2C:14-3b. (2012). *Criminal sexual contact.* Retrieved from http://www.judiciary.state.nj.us/criminal/charges/sexual014.pdf

Novotny, P. (2003). Rape victims in the (gender) neutral zone: The assimilation of resistance? *Seattle Journal for Social Justice, 1*(3), 743–751. Retrieved from http://digitalcommons.law.seattleu.edu/sjsj/vol1/iss3/62/

NRS (Nevada Revised Statutes) 200.373. (1967). *Sexual assault of spouse by spouse.* Retrieved from http://www.leg.state.nv.us/nrs/nrs-200.html#NRS200Sec373

Oberman, M. (1994). Turning girls into women: Re-evaluating modern statutory rape law. *Journal of Criminal Law & Criminology, 85*(1), 15–79.

Planty, M., Langton, L., Krebs, C., Berzofsky, M., & Smiley-McDonald, H. (2013). *Female victims of sexual violence, 1994–2010* (NCJ Publication No. 240655). Washington, DC: Bureau of Justice Statistics. Retrieved from http://www.bjs.gov/content/pub/pdf/fvsv9410.pdf

Renzetti, C. M. (1992). *Violent betrayal: Partner abuse in lesbian relationships.* Newbury Park, CA: Sage.

Rumney, P. N. S. (2007). In defence of gender neutrality within rape. *Seattle Journal for Social Justice, 6*, 481–512.

Saltzman, L. E. (2004). Issues related to defining and measuring violence against women: Response to Kilpatrick. *Journal of Interpersonal Violence, 19*(11), 1235–1243.

Spohn, C., & Horney, J. (1991). "The law's the law, but fair is fair": Rape shield laws and officials' assessments of sexual history evidence. *Criminology, 29*(1), 137–161.

Spohn, C., & Horney, J. (1992). *Rape law reform: A grassroots revolution and its impact.* New York, NY: Plenum Press.

U.S. Congress, House of Representatives, 99th Congress. (1986). *Sexual Abuse Act of 1986.* Retrieved from http://www.gpo.gov/fdsys/pkg/STATUTE-100/pdf/STATUTE-100-Pg3660.pdf

2

Legislative Origins, Reforms, and Future Directions

Lane Kirkland Gillespie and Laura King

Throughout history, criminal laws have been created in order to control as well as to protect members of society. As public sentiment and the definitions of crime have changed throughout time, so too have the laws meant to control criminal behavior and alleviate some of the difficulties experienced by crime victims. Sexual victimization is one such category of crime that has been marked by drastic changes in public sentiment and legislation. These changes have affected not only the manner in which offenders are handled by the criminal justice system but the response to survivors of sexual victimization as well.

The purpose of this chapter is to provide a general overview of the development of legislative reform pertaining to rape and sexual victimization. In the United States, there have been two prominent avenues of reform: those aimed at revising rape statutes[1] and those aimed at controlling sex offenders. Therefore, this chapter begins by addressing the historical evolution of sexual-victimization legislation and the evolving legal definition of rape and sexual assault. The most influential legislative reforms regarding rape began in the 1970s and resulted in what is commonly referred to as the "rape reform movement." Following a discussion of the rape reform movement, this chapter addresses legislative reform pertaining to the control of sex offenders—in particular, the sexual psychopath laws that developed in the early to mid-1900s and the sexually violent predator laws that evolved primarily in the 1990s. This chapter's discussion of the historical evolution of these laws also touches on evaluations of their effectiveness.

The Emergence of Sex Crimes Legislation

Dating back to the beginning of the social order, rape was viewed as a property crime. The Code of Hammurabi described rape as "the theft of virginity, an embezzlement of his daughter's fair price on the market" (Brownmiller, 1975, p. 18). According to this ancient set of laws, rape was defined as an offense in which the theft of a woman's virginity represented a crime against her father in that his daughter's marketability had been devalued (Belknap, 2007; Pistono, 1988). Pursuant to this code, if an innocent virgin were raped, she was not culpable. However, if a married woman were raped, she was believed to have somehow precipitated the attack, and both the married rape victim and her rapist were bound and thrown into the river (Brownmiller). In ancient Hebrew culture, any woman who was raped was held responsible for contributing to the attack and was subsequently stoned to death at the side of her rapist (Pistono).

According to Brownmiller (1975), 10th-century English law reflected a similar sentiment regarding sex crimes. During this era, a man who raped a virgin was sentenced to death, and his land and money were given to the victim. Again, rape was viewed as a property crime contingent upon the victim's virginity. However, the rapist could evade this punishment if his victim agreed to marry him. In fact, "bride capture" was a common practice in which a man raped a woman in order to declare her his property (Belknap, 2007). During this time, the issue of socioeconomic class was also apparent in several laws regarding sex crimes, as the punishment of death and dismemberment was only applicable "to the man who raped a highborn, propertied virgin who lived under the protection of a powerful lord" (Brownmiller, p. 24).

It was not until the 12th and 13th centuries that considerable advances were made in legislation regarding sex crimes (Pistono, 1988). The first advancement enabled a raped virgin to file a civil suit against her attacker, which resulted in a trial by jury (Brownmiller, 1975). Later, during the 13th century, the criminal definition of rape was expanded to include the rape of matrons, nuns, widows, concubines, and prostitutes, as well as the statutory rape of children. After hundreds of years of being viewed as a property crime, rape was finally considered a public safety issue in which survivors had some system of resources available to them (Brownmiller; Pistono). Though this era was marked by some advancement in terms of responding to sexual victimization, several significant changes affecting both sex offenders and survivors of sexual violence remained on the horizon.

Rape Statutes in the United States

Early American rape statutes were heavily influenced by the English common-law definition of rape, which described the offense as "illicit carnal knowledge of a female by force and against her will" (Allison & Wrightsman, as cited in Reddington, 2009, p. 319). Common-law rape consisted of five elements that had to be proven in a court of law: The act had to be criminal, involve carnal knowledge, victimize a woman, and be committed using force, and the force had to be against the will of the victim. Thus, under common law, the definition of rape was narrow and limited to sexual intercourse between a man and a woman (to the exclusion of spouses), and proving rape centered on the degree of resistance provided by the victim. Evidence of physical harm and corroboration of the victim's claim were requirements for the prosecution of rape offenses.

Legal statutes rooted in common law were the standard from 1642 through the mid-1900s, with the next attempt at modernization occurring in the publication of the Model Penal Code (MPC) in 1962. The MPC provided this revised definition of rape:

> A male who has sexual intercourse with a female not his wife is guilty of rape if: (a) he compels her to submit by force or by threat of imminent death, serious bodily injury, extreme pain or kidnapping, to be inflicted on anyone; or (b) he has substantially impaired her power to appraise or control her conduct by administering or employing without her knowledge drugs, intoxicants or other means for the purpose of preventing resistance; or (c) the female is unconscious; or (d) the female is less than 10 years old. (American Law Institute, 1962, p. 142)

The MPC's definition was a conservative revision of the common-law statute. It included a slightly expanded definition of rape and slightly reduced the burden of resistance, but it retained the corroboration requirement and the use of the victim's sexual past as evidence. Thus, the MPC statutes retained many of the elements that future reformers would aim to change (Seidman & Vickers, 2005). While the MPC's definition was adopted in some states, common-law statutes remained intact in the majority of states for another decade.

Rooted in concerns about increasing rates of rape and criticisms of traditional rape laws, reformers in the 1970s lobbied to revise the definition of rape and revise the procedures for handling rape cases, particularly in reference to victim treatment (Spohn, 1999). Women's groups, crime control advocates, and crime victim advocates came together in an effort to change rape laws (Futter & Mebane, 2001; Spohn). Commonly referred to as the "anti–sexual assault revolution" or the "rape reform movement," this effort led to pronounced growth and development in sexual assault legislation as well as victim services between 1970 and 2000. Rape statutes in every state were redrafted with a variety of goals, including improving the experiences of rape victims with the criminal justice system, increasing the likelihood of reporting, deterring the commission of rape, and increasing prosecution and conviction rates (Seidman & Vickers, 2005; Spohn). Some state legislatures adopted completely revised rape statutes that addressed all areas of reform, while others adopted piecemeal changes. The result was that specific reforms varied greatly across states. As Dripps (2010) stated, "The United States thus does not have a single set of rape laws or a single system for enforcement, but instead 51 different rape statutes and 51 different procedural systems" (p. 224).

In spite of this variation, several changes that are reflective of reformers' goals have been widely adopted in some form. These goals centered on enacting change in four areas: (1) redefining the offense of rape, (2) changing the evidentiary rules, (3) addressing the statutory age of consent, and (4) creating a penalty structure (Berger, Seals, & Neuman, 1988; Futter & Mebane, 2001). Each area of reform resulted in several legislative changes, summarized below.

DEFINITIONAL REFORMS

Under common law and the MPC definitions, the act of rape required nonconsensual penile–vaginal intercourse between a man and a woman who were not married. This definition excluded the rape of men, rape committed by women, and the rape of spouses, as well as oral assaults, anal assaults, and assaults conducted with objects (Spohn, 1999). Therefore, the primary goal of definitional reforms was to broaden the acts and circumstances that constituted the crime of rape. Through reform efforts, the majority of legal statutes became sex neutral, no longer excluding males from victim status or females from perpetrator status. The marital exception to rape was eliminated in all states, but not without controversy and resistance (Reddington, 2009).

A third definitional reform had to do with the term *rape* itself. Feminist reformers argued that changing the terminology to reflect the violent, assaultive nature of the crime over the sexual component was crucial to defining and treating the act appropriately (and to move away from historical images associated with *rape*; Berger et al., 1988). Furthermore, using different terms assisted in broadening the definition to include acts other than penile-vaginal penetration (Berger et al.). Many revised statutes removed *rape* verbiage and replaced it with terms such as *sexual assault* or *sexual battery*. States that retained the offense term *rape* added additional offenses, such as *sodomy*, to distinguish between different forms of sexual assault (Futter & Mebane, 2001).

Accompanying changes in terminology was the establishment of graded sexual offense definitions that recognized variation in assaults (e.g., the use of a weapon, the amount of coercion, and the degree of injury; Berger et al., 1988; Spohn, 1999). This led to a distinction between simple and aggravated sexual assault, in a similar manner to nonsexual assault, and a definition of degrees of sexual assault. Emphasis on describing a continuum of offenses was also intended to eliminate consent language by defining the circumstances under which consent would be inherently absent (e.g., in the presence of a weapon; Berger et al.). The primary goal of minimizing consent language was to limit the use of a consent defense that might be based upon arguments that the victim did not resist or did not resist enough. Consent and resistance issues were also addressed through evidentiary reforms.

EVIDENTIARY REFORMS

For reformers, the rules of evidence in rape cases raised numerous concerns, including the emphasis on victims in order to prove consent, resistance requirements for victims, corroboration requirements, and cautionary jury instructions. Certain definitional reforms mentioned above were aimed at minimizing consent language and, by extension, the use of consent as a defense (Berger et al., 1988). Rape trials commonly included extensive discussion of the victim's character, past sexual history, chastity, dress, and/or recreational activities, all commonly intended to suggest that the victim was likely to have consented or that consent was at least possible. Reformers were concerned that, aside from being improper, scrutiny of the victim was also reducing the willingness of victims to report rape offenses (Reddington, 2009).

Addressing this issue led to the development of "rape shield" laws. Rape shield laws placed restrictions on the admissibility of the victim's sexual history and personal life (Reddington; Spohn, 1999). Among the most prominently discussed reforms of this era, the enactment of these laws has been championed as a success for victim's rights, but it has also been criticized by legal scholars who argue that the laws erode the defendant's rights to due process (see Klein, 2008). In part due to this debate, rape shield laws vary greatly across the states. Some states do not allow any discussion of prior sexual history, while other states allow discussion under certain circumstances (e.g., to illustrate that the victim and defendant had prior consensual sexual contact; Futter & Mebane, 2001; Klein).

By meeting the requirement to resist, presumably physically, rape victim were supposedly proving non-consent. Thus, in conjunction with minimizing consent language and revising evidentiary rules pertaining to discussion of the victim's sexual history, reforms addressed the requirement to show resistance/non-consent (Reddington, 2009). Initially, the "utmost" resistance requirement of common law was replaced by a "reasonable" resistance standard (Reddington). The requirement to display physical resistance was relaxed even further in some states and was removed from the definition or explicitly not required in others (Dripps, 2010; Spohn, 1999). In some states that retained a more serious offense with a resistance requirement, a non-consent rape without physical resistance was included as a lesser offense (Dripps).

In addition to resisting the attack, rape victims historically had to provide corroborating evidence that the attack had occurred. The inclusion of a corroboration requirement reflected long-held beliefs about the propensity for women to lie about rape experiences, using them as a means to explain pregnancies or sexually transmitted diseases resulting from a consensual affair or as a reaction to regretted sexual encounters (Futter & Mebane, 2001; Spohn, 1999). However, research on false reporting has consistently indicated that few women lie about rape experiences. For example, Lonsway, Archambault, and Lisak (2009) analyzed 2,059 rape cases from eight U.S. communities and found that only 7% were classified as false reports. Beyond evidence that false reporting is uncommon, the corroboration requirement was often difficult to meet because rapes tend to occur in private settings. The impact of the corroboration requirement in practice was a reduction in the number of prosecutions (Reddington, 2009). Over time, however, all states that required corroboration eliminated the requirement from their statutes (Reddington).

Finally, evidentiary reforms also aimed to address the implementation of cautionary jury instructions unique to rape trials. These instructions often reminded the jury of the difficulty of both proving and defending rape charges and were therefore prejudicial against the victim (Reddington, 2009). While the elimination of these jury instructions was one of the slower changes to take place, all states have now eliminated them through law or practice (Futter & Mebane, 2001; Reddington). In sum, evidentiary reforms were meant to eliminate differences in the rules of evidence between rape trials and all other types of violent crime trials.

AGE REFORMS

Age-related reforms were made in an attempt to allow sexual activity among consenting teenagers while still protecting children (Berger et al., 1988; Futter & Mebane, 2001). Statutory rape laws were revised in many states, leading to the establishment of specific age differentials required for statutory rape charges. For example, some states created a graded offense scale with harsher penalties for the statutory rape of younger victims and less harsh penalties for the statutory rape of older teenagers still below the age of consent (Berger et al.). In addition, age reforms led to the elimination of the mistake-of-age defense in most states, though some jurisdictions retain a reasonable-mistake defense applied to questions of age and consent (Dripps, 2010; Futter & Mebane).

PENALTY REFORMS

The fourth primary area of reform addresses the punishments for rape. A vestige of the historical treatment of rape as a serious property crime remained evident in the penalties for rape prior to the 1970s, which included the death penalty in many states. In 1977, the Supreme Court ruled in *Coker v. Georgia* that the death penalty was unconstitutional for the offense of rape. Even with the death penalty off the table, there was much debate about how to reform the penalty structure for rape and for the newly developing sexual assault and battery offenses (Berger et al., 1988). Some reformers were concerned that severe punishments might reduce a jury's willingness to convict the offender (Berger et al.). Other reformers were concerned that reducing the penalties would send the message that rape was not a serious offense. In an attempt to find middle ground, most states enacted legislation that both reduced penalties for sexual assault offenses while also establishing mandatory minimums (Futter & Mebane, 2001; Spohn, 1999).

These reforms (definitional, evidentiary, age, and penalty) were intended to have instrumental and symbolic impacts on the handling and treatment of rape cases (Bachman & Paternoster, 1993; Spohn & Horney, 1992). In terms of instrumental impacts, reforms were intended to increase reporting by victims, increase prosecutions, and increase convictions (Reddington, 2009). While evaluations have been somewhat limited, those that have been conducted indicate mixed results but have generally found little evidence of effects on case outcomes (Bachman &

Paternoster; Marsh, Geist, & Caplan, 1982; Reddington; Spohn, 1999; Spohn & Horney). However, some studies have found that criminal justice actors view legal changes favorably, leading Spohn (1999) to conclude that "passage of the reforms sent an important symbolic message regarding the seriousness of rape cases and the treatment of rape victims. In the long run, this symbolic message may be more important than the instrumental change that was anticipated" (pp. 129–130).

Legislative Reforms and the Sex Offender

While many reforms in the late 20th century emphasized changing the handling of rape cases and the treatment of the victims, legal reforms have also been directed at offenders. Two prominent sets of legal reforms are sexual psychopath laws and sexually violent predator (SVP) laws. Sexual psychopath laws were introduced in the early to mid-1900s, predating the rape reform movement. In comparison, many SVP laws were enacted in the 1990s, coming on the heels of crime control demands in response to rising violent crime from the late 1980s through the early 1990s. These laws have influenced the handling of sexual assault cases and led to the creation of punishment outcomes unique to sex crimes. Whereas the driving force behind the rape reform movement was an attempt to acknowledge the victimization experience of rape and the unique, often negative, treatment of (adult) rape victims by the criminal justice system, public outcry regarding the sexual abuse of children was the driving force behind the development of sexual psychopath and SVP laws.

SEXUAL PSYCHOPATH LAWS

During the 20th century, sex crimes legislation in the United States was marked by three periods of moral panic that resulted from a number of highly publicized cases of child sexual abuse (Tonry, 2004). Of particular relevance to this discussion is the second period of moral panic, which began in the late 1930s and resulted in the enactment of sexual psychopath laws in 26 states (Tonry). These laws, enacted between 1937 and 1960, were intended to protect children from uncontrollable sexual psychopaths (Pratt, 1998; Sutherland, 1950). Similar laws were enacted by Canada, New Zealand, and Australia throughout the 1940s (Pratt). The belief was that sex crimes were increasing at a rate faster than that of any other type of crime (Sutherland).

The main provision in this legislation was the involuntary commitment of the "sexual psychopath" to a mental health facility until such time that his "malady" had been cured (Reinhardt & Fisher, 1949; Sutherland, 1950). In the District of Columbia, for example, a sexual psychopath was defined as follows:

> any person, not insane, who by course of repeated misconduct in sexual matters has evidenced such lack of power to control his sexual impulses as to be dangerous

to other persons because he is likely to attack or otherwise inflict injury, loss, pain, or other evil on the objects of his desire. (Reinhardt & Fisher, p. 737)

Similar verbiage was utilized in other states to define sexual psychopaths (Reinhardt & Fisher, 1949). As can be seen in the definition above, these laws directly targeted males and suggested that all sex offenders were dangerous, uncontrollable predators. In most jurisdictions, qualified experts (e.g., psychiatrists) performed the diagnosis (Reinhardt & Fisher; Sutherland, 1950). However, it is important to note that assessments of sexual psychopathy during this time were based on the subjective opinions of mental health professionals, not the empirically tested instruments available today (e.g., Psychopathy Checklist [PCL-R]; Static-99). Moreover, the definition of sexual psychopath used in many states suggested that any offender who committed more than one serious sex crime was a mentally ill person eligible for commitment to a mental health facility (Sutherland). The presence of this sentiment in sex crimes legislation became apparent in civil-commitment statutes enacted several decades later.

SEXUALLY VIOLENT PREDATOR LAWS

During the latter half of the 20th century, another set of laws targeting sex offenders—commonly referred to as sexually violent predator (SVP) laws—were enacted in the United States. In large part, the impetus for these laws can be traced to a number of horrific sex crimes involving children (e.g., Polly Klaas) and the ensuing public outcry to protect society's most vulnerable members. Although these laws were perceived to be innovative responses to sexual victimization, many states had had similar laws in force for several years (Levenson, 2003). Thus, it is possible that this legislation was primarily symbolic rather than evidence based (Brown, 2009; Harris & Lurigio, 2010). In fact, although the perception was that sex crimes rates were on the rise in the United States, several data sources reveal that sex crimes rates were decreasing during this time and have continued that downward trend since (BJS, 2012; FBI, 2011). It is important to note, however, that underreporting of crimes is endemic and that sexual offenses are one of the most consistently and grossly underreported crimes (BJS, 2003).

The first of the federal SVP laws was the Jacob Wetterling Act of 1994, which was enacted in response to the kidnapping of 11-year-old Jacob Wetterling (Levenson, 2003). Although Jacob was never found, the similarity of his abduction to the case of a boy who was abducted and sexually assaulted in a neighboring town led to the assumption that Jacob was a victim of the same offender (Sample & Bray, 2003). This act mandated that law enforcement in all states create sex offender registries to monitor the whereabouts of released sex offenders (Levenson). All individuals convicted of a qualifying sexual offense—the definition of which varies by state—are required to register with their local law enforcement agency within a specified number of days following their release (Scholle, 2000). Offenders are typically required to provide their name, address, date of birth, Social Security number, photograph, fingerprints, and (in some states) a DNA sample (Scholle). In addition, they are required to update the information as needed throughout the duration of registration, which typically ranges from 10 years to lifetime (Scholle).

Although the Jacob Wetterling Act was initially intended to protect children from predatory, repeat sex offenders, all individuals convicted of a qualifying sexual offense are now required to register regardless of risk assessment (Levenson, 2003). It could be surmised that requiring such a large portion of sex offenders to register contributes to the perception that all sex offenders are highly recidivistic, untreatable predators who prey on children (Levenson; Quinn, Forsyth, & Mullen-Quinn, 2004; Sample & Bray, 2003). On the contrary, empirical evidence suggests that sex offenders are not a homogeneous group (CSOM, 2001). That is, assumptions made about "sex offenders" as a whole are not necessarily accurate and are often based primarily on the characteristics of the highest-risk offenders (Quinn et al., 2004). It is also important to note that no other group of offenders, including convicted murderers, is subjected to monitoring of this caliber (Sample & Bray). As such, this legislation suggests that convicted sex offenders are more dangerous than any other type of offender. It also suggests that known sex offenders represent the greatest risk when, in fact, statistics show that perpetrators are more likely to be first-time offenders than be listed on the registry (Craun, Simmons, & Reeves, 2011; Quinn et al., 2004).

The second SVP legislation, an amendment to the Jacob Wetterling Act often referred to as "Megan's Law," was enacted in 1996 in response to the rape and murder of 7-year-old Megan Kanka by a convicted sex offender living near her home (Scholle, 2000). Megan's Law required all states to develop a notification policy to alert the community of sex offenders living in the area, and it offered states financial incentives for compliance (Levenson, 2003). In fact, a state's failure to develop registration and notification policies resulted in a 10% decrease in federal crime funds (Wright, 2003). As with registration policies, notification practices vary by state and can include flyers, phone calls, door-to-door notification, neighborhood meetings, or an online database (Levenson). In some states, the community is notified of all sex offenders in the area, while in others, notification is required only for high-risk offenders (ATSA, 2008).

In addition to registration and community notification legislation, several states enacted civil commitment statutes for sex offenders in the early 1990s, although similar provisions (as discussed above) had been enacted under the sexual psychopath laws in many states decades prior. Current civil commitment policy involves the involuntary, potentially indefinite confinement of sexually violent predators in a psychiatric facility following their release from prison (Levenson, 2003). *Sexually violent predator* is a legal term encompassing dangerous offenders who are likely to recidivate. Once again, the definition of a sexually violent predator and the eligibility requirements for civil commitment vary by state. It is important to note that one of the main differences between the sexual psychopath laws of the early 20th century and the SVP laws is the point at which they impose civil commitment. The sexual psychopath laws imposed commitment in lieu of a criminal sentence, while current legislation imposes commitment after the sentence has been served (Levenson; Reinhardt & Fisher, 1949; Sutherland, 1950).

Residency restrictions for sex offenders have also been implemented in several states to promote public safety (Cohen & Jeglic, 2007). These policies prohibit convicted sex offenders from being within a certain number of feet of schools or day care centers. Offenders are not permitted to live, work, or set foot within these boundaries. It is important to note, however, that such restrictions have been shown to adversely affect offenders' ability to gain employment and reintegrate into society (Willis, Levenson, & Ward, 2010). For instance, in a recent study of sex offender reintegration, Brown, Spencer, and Deakin (2007) found that sex offenders have even more difficulty reintegrating into society and gaining employment than other offenders because of the negative stigma associated with sexual offending. Interviews with employers confirmed this, as more than half indicated they would not employ a convicted sex offender. As such, residency restrictions seem to exacerbate the myriad reintegration barriers that already exist for sex offenders, thus potentially contributing to recidivism and further sexual victimization.

While the bulk of sex offender management legislation was passed in the 1990s, additional legislation continues to appear. For example, in 2006, the Adam Walsh Child Protection and Safety Act (AWA) introduced federal standards to regulate state registration and notification programs and made the failure to register as a sex offender a federal offense (Harris, Lobanov-Robansky, & Levenson, 2010). However, researchers have discovered that the new classification rules under this legislation have elevated many offenders previously assessed as low risk to a high-risk classification. This has the potential to affect the criminal justice agents charged with monitoring sex offenders in their jurisdiction, most notably by giving them increased caseloads that could make it more difficult for them to monitor dangerous offenders.

In terms of public opinion regarding SVP laws, researchers generally find strong support (Kernsmith, Craun, & Foster, 2009; Mears, Mancini, Gertz, & Bratton, 2008; Phillips, 1998; Willis et al., 2010). A number of researchers have also examined the extent to which these laws have reduced sex offender recidivism. In 2010, Zandbergen, Levenson, and Hart examined the impact of sex offender residency restrictions in Florida. Their findings indicated that proximity to schools or day care centers had no effect on sexual recidivism. Tewksbury and Jennings (2010) examined sex offender recidivism in Iowa before and after the passage of sex offender management policies, and they found no effect. Similarly, Letourneau, Levenson, Bandyopadhyay, Armstrong, and Sinha (2010) assessed the impact of sex offender registration and community notification in South Carolina. Registration laws were found to exert a general deterrent effect for first-time offenders only, while notification laws had no effect. Although additional policy evaluations are warranted to examine the effectiveness of this type of legislation, the aforementioned studies suggest it may not serve its intended purpose.

The SVP laws have also been criticized for the messages they convey to the public. Since the focus is on convicted offenders (i.e., those known to authorities), SVP laws suggest that detected sex offenders are more dangerous than undetected offenders, which is not necessarily accurate (Wright, 2003). The net-widening effect that has occurred in recent years has also been a source of contention because it affirms the myth that all sex offenders are equally dangerous, thus diverting attention away from the high-risk sex offenders who should be more closely monitored (ATSA, 2008). Another criticism of this type of legislation is that it obscures the fact that most offenders are known to their victims (Wright). Despite these criticisms, SVP laws seem to make the public feel safer. However, many have argued that this is a false sense of security that masks the fact that the majority of perpetrators are first-time offenders (i.e., not on the registry) who are known to their victims (Quinn et al., 2004). Protecting society from victimization is undoubtedly a laudable goal. However, when the assumptions upon which these protective behaviors are based are inaccurate, the results are unlikely to do much in the way of reducing sexual victimization.

PUNISHMENT

In addition to the management of sex offenders in the community, several laws have been enacted to increase the severity of punishment for convicted sex offenders. Despite the Supreme Court's ruling in *Coker v. Georgia* (1977) regarding the use of capital punishment for the crime of rape, several states expanded their use of the death penalty in the 1990s to include offenders convicted of child rape (Mancini & Mears, 2010). This legislation was considered drastic by many since the use of the death penalty has typically been reserved for convicted murderers. Nevertheless, a 1997 CNN poll found that 47% of the public supported the use of the death penalty for rapists and that 65% supported it for child molesters. However, following the case of *Kennedy v. Louisiana* (2008)—in which the defendant was convicted of raping an 8-year-old girl—the U.S. Supreme Court ruled that the imposition of the death penalty for cases of child rape not involving murder violates the Eighth Amendment.

Another method of punishment for sex offenders, the use of which dates back to the Middle Ages, is surgical castration. According to Weinberger, Sreenivasan, Garrick, and Osran (2005), surgical castration was legalized in many European countries during the beginning of the 20th century because it was believed to reduce the sexual urges that lead to criminal sexual behavior. Between 1934 and 1944, approximately 2,800 castrations were performed in Germany as a result of the Nazi German Act of 1933, which allowed for the involuntary castration of sex offenders. Similarly, in Denmark, approximately 1,100 sex offenders were castrated between 1929 and 1973 in an effort to protect society from recidivist rapists. While surgical castration was also used for sex offenders in the United States at the beginning of the 20th century, its legality came under scrutiny in the case of *Weems v. United States* (1910), in which the Supreme Court held that castration was a "barbaric" punishment (Miller, 2008, p. 179). Likewise, in the case of *State v. Brown* (1985), the South Carolina Supreme Court referred to surgical castration as cruel and unusual punishment as outlined in the Eighth Amendment.

Though surgical castration is rarely used as a modern-day punishment for sex offenders, the use of chemical castration began to gain popularity in the 20th century. The procedure involves periodic injections of a female contraceptive (e.g., Depo-Provera), which is believed to reduce sexual urges in males by lowering testosterone levels (Meisenkothen, 1999). This form of punishment, which is also considered treatment, was first legalized in the United States in California in 1996 for all paroled two-time sex offenders. Similar legislation was later passed in several other states (Miller, 2008). Critics of chemical castration argue its unconstitutionality, most notably in reference to First and Eighth Amendment protections. A handful of studies have been conducted to examine the effectiveness of reducing sex offender recidivism via this treatment. The findings often appear promising, though many of the studies are plagued by methodological issues, most notably small sample sizes (Kutcher, 2010; Miller). Nevertheless, many argue that chemical castration is a more cost-effective and possibly more humane method of dealing with repeat sex offenders than incarceration (Harrison, 2007; Meisenkothen). It is important to note that chemical castration has been found to be useful primarily among male paraphiliacs, who are those plagued by uncontrollable fantasies and urges. As such, sex offenders who are motivated by power and control, anger, or violence or who are female may not be affected by this treatment.

Conclusion

Legislative responses to sexual victimization have been present in society for millennia. Though the specific provisions of these responses have varied considerably over time and and by location, it is clear that sexual victimization has been a prominent focus of societal concern, legislative action, and criminal justice system response. As discussed in the previous sections, the United States has experienced a rape reform revolution since the 1970s, resulting in substantial changes to the definition of rape and the handling of rape cases in the criminal justice system (Spohn, 1999). While many of these changes have been heralded as successful reforms, they have also been met with varying degrees of resistance and skepticism, particularly regarding the balance between victim and offender rights (Klein, 2008). A similar dichotomy in opinion has characterized discussion of sex offender laws. The most recent legislation in the United States targeting offenders who sexually victimize others is the conglomeration of SVP laws that emerged in the 1990s. These laws include sex offender registration and notification, and in many states, they include residency restrictions and civil commitment statutes as well. Historically, these laws are arguably the most stringent in terms of the management of sex offenders in the community. Individuals convicted of a qualifying sexual offense must remain on the registry for a considerable amount of time, their names and addresses are made available to the public, and some may be confined indefinitely after serving their sentence. It could be surmised that society and legislators alike have progressed to a veritable war on sex offenders akin to the war on crime in the 1960s and the war on drugs in the 1980s.

Sexual victimization is a serious offense deserving of appropriately serious treatment and response. Survivors of sexual victimization often experience extensive trauma such as physical injury, psychological difficulties, and rape trauma syndrome. Thus, a swift and appropriate response from the criminal justice system is indeed warranted to punish the offender, provide support for the victim, and protect society from future victimization. Theoretically, rape reform legislation and the SVP laws were enacted to meet some of these ends. As discussed previously, rape reform may have had a more symbolic impact than an instrumental one. Seidman and Vickers (2005) asserted that for rape law reform to progress and have its desired outcomes, reformers' focus must broaden to the treatment of victims beyond the criminal justice system. In particular, the accessibility of civil remedies must improve and should perhaps be disentangled from the criminal justice system.

The 1994 Violence Against Women Act (VAWA) was the first legislation that attempted to provide a civil rights remedy for victims of domestic and sexual violence (Goldscheid, 2005). Specifically, the VAWA provided women with the civil right to be protected from crimes of violence based on their gender and provided female victims of gender-motivated sexual assaults with access to a civil cause of action in federal courts (Goldscheid; Reddington, 2009). However, the civil rights provision of the 1994 VAWA was declared unconstitutional by the Supreme Court in *United States v. Morrison* (2000). In response to this decision, many states passed their own civil rights provisions for victims of domestic and sexual violence. The provision of the VAWA and the influence it has had on state legislation is one example of broadening the focus of reforms beyond procedural criminal justice reforms.

In addition to reforms that move beyond the criminal justice system, criminal justice reforms have been broadened through federal legislation. Examples of such reforms include the Jeanne Clery Disclosure of Campus Security Policy and Campus Crime Statistics Act of 1990 (Clery Act), the Cruise Vessel Security and Safety Act of 2010 (CVSSA), the Debbie Smith Act of 2004, and the Sexual Assault Forensic Evidence Reporting Act (SAFER Act) of 2013. While these acts address crime victims and services in a variety of ways, each contains provisions directed at sexual assault victims in particular. The Clery Act, originally signed into law in 1990 and amended several times since, is intended to provide protections for crime victims on college campuses. In particular, the act has been amended to include basic rights for campus sexual assault victims, protection for victims from retaliation, and provisions for registered sex offender notification (Clery Center for Security on Campus, 2012a, 2012b). Also extending recognition to a specific group of potential victims, the CVSSA of 2010 aimed to improve the safety and security of passengers aboard cruise ships and included emphasis on ensuring availability of resources for sexual assault victims. The Debbie Smith Act, originally passed in 2004 and reauthorized in 2008, provides funding for grant programs specifically aimed at processing rape kits and DNA evidence associated with sexual victimizations (Debbie Smith Reauthorization Act, 2008; RAINN, 2009). The provisions of the SAFER Act (passed as a component of the reauthorization of the VAWA in 2013) authorize the Attorney General to make Debbie Smith grants to state and/or local governments to assist in auditing sexual assault evidence backlogs and to ensure appropriate and timely processing of DNA evidence (SAFER Act, 2013; Violence Against Women Reauthorization Act, 2013).

The aforementioned legislative reforms illustrate new and continued efforts to develop methods and resources for combating rape and sexual assault. Acts such as Clery and CVSSA illustrate recognition of vulnerable populations (e.g. college students, cruise passengers), while acts such as Debbie Smith and SAFER emphasize the importance of funding forensic science in an effort to assist in apprehending and convicting sex offenders. While the tangible impact of federal legislation requires additional and continued evaluation, reforms such as these have kept rape and sexual assault on the national agenda.

In regard to SVP laws, the majority of research on public opinion finds strong support, yet empirical evidence suggests that SVP laws may not be achieving their main goal of reducing sex offender recidivism and sexual victimization. What's more, although they seem to make much of society feel safer, these laws appear to promote a number of misconceptions regarding sexual victimization risk. One of the most damaging of these is the misconception that sex offenders on the registry pose the greatest risk. Empirical evidence suggests not only that first-time offenders (i.e., offenders not known to authorities) pose the greatest risk, but that 80% to 90% of sexually abused children are molested by a friend or family member and more than 75% of adult rape/sexual assault survivors are victimized by someone with whom they had a previous relationship (ATSA, 2008; CSOM, 2000).

Overall, in terms of what is known about sexual victimization, more effective, evidence-based responses than those currently in place may be in order. These could include educating the public about how to best protect themselves and their loved ones from sexual victimization, encouraging reporting to police, streamlining civil resources (e.g., victim compensation), reserving registry and community notification for high-risk offenders, and improving reintegration and treatment programs for convicted sex offenders. Furthermore, continued evaluation of the instrumental impacts of rape legislation is needed to bridge the gap between symbolic outcomes and instrumental ones. Based on the fervor with which sexual victimization has been regarded throughout history, (a) legislation pertaining to rape and sexual assault should benefit from continued evaluations of existing reforms, as well as from consideration of non–criminal justice remedies that may increase the success of enacted legislative reform, and (b) legislation pertaining to the treatment of offenders should be firmly based on empirical evidence to effectively address and, ideally, reduce the occurrence of sexual victimization.

Discussion Questions

1. The common-law definition of rape consisted of five elements. List these five elements and describe how they have evolved since the 1970s. What future reforms, if any, should legislators consider?

2. One of the overarching, and often difficult, goals of criminal justice is to balance the rights of offenders (i.e., due process) with the goal of protecting society from victimization (i.e., crime control). Do you believe the sexually violent predator (SVP) laws achieve this balance? Why or why not?

3. Some reformers have argued for changing the term *rape* in legal statutes to *sexual assault* or *sexual battery*. Do your home state's legal statutes use the term *rape*, or has the verbiage changed to *sexual battery*, *sexual assault*, or something else? What is the definition of rape, sexual assault, and/or sexual battery used in your home state? What types of SVP laws are in your state's legal statutes?

4. Overall, do you think that rape reforms have had a more instrumental or symbolic impact? Why? What about SVP laws? Why?

5. Reformers have suggested that efforts need to reach beyond the criminal justice system. For example, civil remedies have been suggested as an alternative, or in addition to, criminal justice processes. Develop one or two additional alternatives (beyond direct criminal justice system responses and civil remedies) that could assist in reforming the handling and treatment of sexual assault cases, their victims, and/or perpetrators.

Note

1. By *rape statutes*, we mean those laws that define and criminalize the acts that legally constitute "rape." In general, discussion of rape statutes and legislative change has centered on the victims. In fact, the impetus for reforming rape laws was the desire to change the status quo of rape trials, which focused more on the victim and the victim's behavior than on the defendant (Spohn & Horney, 1992).

References

Adam Walsh Child Protection and Safety Act (AWA), 42 U.S.C. § 16911 (2006).

Allison, J. A., & Wrightsman, L. S. (1993). *Rape: The misunderstood crime*. Thousand Oaks, CA: Sage.

American Law Institute. (1962). *Model penal code*. Philadelphia, PA: The American Law Institute.

Association for the Treatment of Sexual Abusers (ATSA). (2008). Research and statistics debunk common misconceptions. In L. Zott (Ed.), *Sex offenders and public policy* (pp. 43–53). Detroit, MI: Greenhaven Press.

Bachman, R. & Paternoster, R. (1993). A contemporary look at the effects of rape law reform: How far have we really come? *The Journal of Criminal Law & Criminology, 84*(3), 554–574.

Belknap, J. (2007). *The invisible woman: Gender, crime and justice* (3rd ed.). Belmont, CA: Thomson/ Wadsworth.

Berger, R. J., Searles, P., & Neuman, W. L. (1988). The dimensions of rape reform legislation. *Law & Society Review, 22*(2), 329–358.

Brown, S. (2009). Attitudes towards sexual offenders and their rehabilitation: A special case? In J. Wood & T. A. Gannon (Eds.), *Public opinion and criminal justice* (pp. 187–213). Portland, OR: Willan.

Brown, K., Spencer, J., & Deakin, J. (2007). The reintegration of sex offenders: Barriers and opportunities for employment. *Howard Journal of Criminal Justice, 46*(1), 32–42.

Brownmiller, S. (1975). *Against our will: Men, women and rape.* New York, NY: Bantam.

Bureau of Justice Statistics (BJS). (2003). *Reporting crime to the police, 1993–2000* (NCJ Publication No. 195710). Retrieved from http://bjs.ojp.usdoj.gov/content/pub/pdf/rcp00.pdf

Bureau of Justice Statistics (BJS). (2012). *Criminal victimization, 2011* (NCJ Publication No. 239437). Retrieved from http://www.bjs.gov/content/pub/pdf/cv11.pdf

Center for Sex Offender Management (CSOM). (2000). *Myths and facts about sex offenders.* Retrieved from http://www.csom.org/pubs/mythsfacts.pdf

Center for Sex Offender Management (CSOM). (2001). *Recidivism of sex offenders.* Retrieved from http://www.csom.org/pubs/recidsexof.pdf

Clery Center for Security on Campus. (2012a). *Jeanne Clery Act.* Retrieved from http://clerycenter .org/node/38/

Clery Center for Security on Campus. (2012b). *Summary of the Jeanne Clery Act.* Retrieved from http://clerycenter.org/summary-jeanne-clery-act/

Cohen, M., & Jeglic, E. L. (2007). Sex offender legislation in the United States: What do we know? *International Journal of Offender Therapy and Comparative Criminology, 51*(4), 369–383.

Coker v. Georgia, 433 U.S. 584 (1977).

Craun, S. W., Simmons, C. A., & Reeves, K. (2011). Percentage of named offenders on the registry at the time of the assault: Reports from sexual assault survivors. *Violence Against Women, 17*(11), 1374–1382.

Cruise Vessel Security and Safety Act (CVSSA), 46 U.S.C. 3507–3508 (2010).

Debbie Smith Act, 42 U.S.C. § 13701 (2004).

Debbie Smith Reauthorization Act of 2008, 42 U.S.C. § 13701 (2008).

Dripps, D. (2010). Rape, law and American society. In F. P. Reddington & B. W. Kreisel (Eds.), *Rethinking rape law: International and comparative perspectives* (pp. 224–236). New York, NY: Routledge.

Federal Bureau of Investigation (FBI). (2011). *Crime in the United States 2011.* Retrieved from http://www.fbi.gov/about-us/cjis/ucr/crime-in-the-u.s/2011/crime-in-the-u.s.-2011/tables/table-1/

Futter, S., & Mebane, W. R., Jr. (2001). The effects of rape law reform on rape case processing. *Berkley Women's Law Journal, 16,* 72–139.

Goldscheid, J. (2005). The civil rights remedy of the 1994 Violence Against Women Act: Struck down but not ruled out. *Family Law Quarterly, 39*(1), 157–180.

Harris, A. J., Lobanov-Rostovsky, C., & Levenson, J. S. (2010). Widening the net: The effects of transitioning to the Adam Walsh Act's federally mandated sex offender classification system. *Criminal Justice and Behavior, 37*(5), 503–519.

Harris, A. J., & Lurigio, A. J. (2010). Introduction to special issue on sex offenses and offenders: Toward evidence based public policy. *Criminal Justice and Behavior, 37*(5), 477–481.

Harrison, K. (2007). The high-risk sex offender strategy in England and Wales: Is chemical castration an option? *The Howard Journal of Criminal Justice, 46*(1), 16–31.

Jacob Wetterling Crimes Against Children and Sexually Violent Offender Registration Act (Jacob Wetterling Act), 42 U.S.C. § 14071 (1994).

Jeanne Clery Disclosure of Campus Security Policy and Campus Crime Statistics Act (Clery Act), 20 U.S.C. § 1092(f) (1990).

Kennedy v. Louisiana, 554 U.S. 407 (2008).

Kernsmith, P. D., Craun, S. W., & Foster, J. (2009). Public attitudes toward sexual offenders and sex offender registration. *Journal of Child Sexual Abuse, 18*(3), 290–301.

Klein, R. (2008). An analysis of thirty-five years of rape reform: A frustrating search for fundamental fairness. *Akron Law Review, 41,* 981–1057.

Kutcher, M. R. (2010). The chemical castration of recidivist sex offenders in Canada: A matter of faith. *Dalhousie Law Journal, 33*(2), 193–216.

Letourneau, E. J., Levenson, J. S., Bandyopadhyay, D., Armstrong, K. S., & Sinha, D. (2010). Effects of South Carolina's sex offender registration and notification policy on deterrence of adult sex crimes. *Criminal Justice and Behavior, 37*(5), 537–552.

Levenson, J. S. (2003). Policy interventions designed to combat sexual violence: Community notification and civil commitment. *Journal of Child Sexual Abuse, 12*(3/4), 17–52.

Lonsway, K. A., Archambault, J., & Lisak, D. (2009). False reports: Moving beyond the issue to successfully investigate and prosecute non-stranger sexual assault. *The Voice, 3*(1). Retrieved from http://www .ndaa.org/pdf/the_voice_vol_3_no_1_2009.pdf

Mancini, C., & Mears, D. P. (2010). To execute or not to execute? Examining public support for capital punishment of sex offenders. *Journal of Criminal Justice, 38*(5), 959–968.

Marsh, J. C., Geist, A., & Caplan, N. S. (1982). *Rape policy: The limits of law reform.* Boston, MA: Auburn House.

Mears, D. P., Mancini, C., Gertz, M., & Bratton, J. (2008). Sex crimes, children, and pornography: Public views and public policy. *Crime & Delinquency, 54*(4), 532–559.

Meisenkothen, C. (1999). Chemical castration: Breaking the cycle of paraphiliac recidivism. *Social Justice, 26*(1), 139–154.

Miller, R. D. (1998). Forced administration of sex-drive reducing medication to sex offenders: Treatment or punishment? *Psychology, Public Policy, and Law, 4*(1/2), 175–199.

Phillips, D. M. (1998). *Community notification as viewed by Washington's citizens.* Retrieved from http://www.wsipp.wa.gov/rptfiles/CnSurvey.pdf

Pistono, S. P. (1988). Susan Brownmiller and the history of rape. *Women's Studies, 14*(3), 265–276.

Pratt, J. (1998). The rise and fall of homophobia and sexual psychopath legislation in postwar society. *Psychology, Public Policy, and Law, 4*(1/2), 25–49.

Quinn, J. F., Forsyth, C. J., & Mullen-Quinn, C. (2004). Societal reaction to sex offenders: A review of the origins and results of the myths surrounding their crime and treatment amenability. *Deviant Behavior, 25*(3), 215–232.

Rape, Abuse, and Incest National Network (RAINN). (2008). *Congress passes important anti-rape legislation.* Retrieved from http://www.rainn.org/news-room/sexual-assault-news/Debbie-Smith-Act-reauthorization/

Reddington, F. P. (2009). A brief history of rape law and rape law reform in the United States. In F. P. Reddington & B. W. Kreisel (Eds.), *Sexual assault: The victims, the perpetrators, and the criminal justice system* (2nd ed., pp. 319–333). Durham, NC: Carolina Academic Press.

Reinhardt, J. M., & Fisher, E. C. (1949). The sexual psychopath and the law. *Journal of Criminal Law & Criminology, 39*(5), 734–742.

Sample, L. L., & Bray, T. M. (2003). Are sex offenders dangerous? *Criminology & Public Policy, 3*(1), 59–82.

Scholle, A. (2000). Sex offender registration. *FBI Law Enforcement Bulletin, 69*(7), 17–25.

Seidman, I., & Vickers, S. H. (2005). The second wave: An agenda for the next thirty years of rape law reform. *Suffolk University Law Review, 38,* 467–491.

Sexual Assault Forensic Evidence Reporting Act of 2013 (SAFER Act), Pub. L. 113-4, title X, § 1001, 127 Stat. 127 (2013).

Spohn, C. C. (1999). The rape reform movement: The traditional common law and rape law reforms. *Jurimetrics, 39,* 119–130.

Spohn, C., & Horney, J. (1992). *Rape law reform: A grassroots revolution and its impact.* New York, NY: Plenum Press.

State v. Brown, 284 S.C. 407, 326 S.E.2d 410 (1985).

Sutherland, E. H. (1950). The sexual psychopath laws. *Journal of Criminal Law and Criminology, 40*(5), 543–554.

Tewksbury, R., & Jennings, W. G. (2010). Assessing the impact of sex offender registration and community notification on sex-offending trajectories. *Criminal Justice and Behavior, 37*(5), 570–582.

Tonry, M. (2004). *Thinking about crime: Sense and sensibility in American penal culture.* New York, NY: Oxford University Press.

United States v. Morrison, 529 U.S. 598 (2000).

Violence Against Women Act (VAWA), 42 U.S.C. § 14039, (1994).

Violence Against Women Reauthorization Act of 2013, S. 47, 113th Cong., 1st Sess. (2013). Retrieved from http://www.govtrack.us/congress/bills/113/s47/text/

Weems v. United States, 217 U.S. 349 (1910).

Weinberger, L. E., Sreenivasan, S., Garrick, T., & Osran, H. (2005). The impact of surgical castration on sexual recidivism risk among sexually violent predatory offenders. *The Journal of the American Academy of Psychiatry and the Law, 33,* 16–36.

Willis, G. M., Levenson, J. S., & Ward, T. (2010). Desistance and attitudes towards sex offenders: Facilitation or hindrance? *Journal of Family Violence, 25*(6), 545–556.

Wright, R. G. (2003). Sex offender registration and notification: Public attention, political emphasis, and fear. *Criminology & Public Policy, 3*(1), 97–104.

Zandbergen, P. A., Levenson, J. S., & Hart, T. C. (2010). Residential proximity to schools and daycares: An empirical analysis of sex offense recidivism. *Criminal Justice and Behavior, 37*(5), 482–502.

3

Criminal Justice System Treatment Approaches for Sexual Assault Victims

Shelly Clevenger

The criminal justice system's treatment of victims has changed over time to include mechanisms for victim involvement in prosecution. However, crime victims—and victims of sexual crimes in particular—do not always experience the best treatment by criminal justice system personnel. One of the common problems crime victims report is that they feel blamed and/or are treated with insensitivity by criminal justice officials. In addition, victims of sexual crimes often report that they do not feel that justice was served in their case. A sexual assault victim's involvement in the system is arguably a bit different from that of the victim who experiences other types of crime due to the nature of the crime. Sexual assault victims must endure painful and oftentimes embarrassing medical exams and questions. Also, they may be treated with disrespect or insensitivity by those individuals who are in place to assist victims, such as medical personnel, police officers, and legal professionals. However, strides have been made to improve upon historical treatment of victims, specifically sexual assault victims. This chapter will describe the evolution of the criminal justice system's treatment of victims of sexual crimes and the implementation of legislation and programs aimed at improving victims' experiences.

Law Enforcement Treatment
of Victims of Sexual Assault

Historically, sexual assault victims reported negative interactions with police, including experiencing disrespect, suspicion, and contempt on the part of law enforcement officers. Victims were often only seen as a means to an end for police to make a case and secure a conviction. Victims frequently were treated as inconsequential, and some victims' reports of sexual assault were dismissed without a written report. For example, in many jurisdictions in the 1950s, the 1960s, and even the early 1970s, victims who reported a sexual assault committed by someone whom they were romantically involved with or married to and/ or who reported an incident of domestic violence were often sent away by law enforcement because (typically male) police officers viewed the incident as a "personal problem" or a "lovers' quarrel." During that same time period, law enforcement officers often asked victims who reported sexual assault a list of questions about their sexual history, their character, and the clothing they were wearing during the attack. In addition, victims may have been required to provide proof of their attack before law enforcement would move forward with an investigation or file charges. Also, during that time, the only sexual act that was considered rape was vaginal intercourse between a woman and a man. Other forms of rape (e.g., rape between two men or women) would not have been charged as such given that many states' definition of rape included the term *vaginal intercourse* and specifically defined the victim as a woman. Progress in the victim's rights movement and implementation of federal and state legislation has improved victim treatment by law enforcement and has broadened the definitions of rape and sexual assault. However, victims of sexual crimes often still report poor treatment by law enforcement.

Current research reveals that the antiquated treatment of sexual assault victims by law enforcement may still linger in many jurisdictions. For example, several studies report that law enforcement officers may still discourage many victims of sexual assault from filing police reports (Campbell, 2005, 2006; Campbell & Raja, 2005). Such actions on the part of law enforcement officers are often linked to attitudes or stereotypes that police officers hold regarding what they consider a "real" sexual assault victim who is worthy of their time. To be a real or "worthy" victim, the individual must have reported the crime in a timely fashion; the offender must not be a friend, acquaintance, or present/past intimate of the victim; and the offender must have used physical force or a weapon in the commission of the assault (Archambault & Lindsay, 2001; Estrich, 1987; LaFree, 1989; Madigan & Gamble, 1991). Victims who have not experienced this stereotypical assault, meaning those who were not raped by a stranger who threatened them with physical force or a weapon, are less likely than other victims to receive criminal justice system assistance (Campbell, Wasco, Ahrens, Sefl, & Barnes, 2001; Patterson, Greeson, & Campbell, 2009; Starzynski, Ullman, Filipas, & Townsend, 2005). However, most victims of sex crimes know the person who sexually assaulted them (Logan, Cole, & Capillo, 2007), and many offenders do not use weapons and/or physical force. Law enforcement officers may also insinuate that the victim is to blame or partially to blame for his or her assault; they may do this by asking questions about the victim's attire, asking about the use of drugs and/or alcohol prior to the assault, and making inquiries as to whether the victim had a prior sexual relationship with the offender. Also, law enforcement officers often revictimize victims of sex crimes by repeatedly questioning them about the details of their victimization to ensure that the victim's account of the crime remains the same.

Police are concerned with building strong cases against offenders, which means that they need to obtain physical evidence and consistent interview testimony from witnesses. These priorities often supersede the needs and welfare of victims (Martin, 2005), and while victims may feel that they are treated insensitively by law enforcement, police officers often report that such treatment is normal and that they are just doing their job (Campbell, 2005). At the same time, when victims feel revictimized by law enforcement officers, they are less likely to cooperate with police or the prosecution, and other individuals who hear about the insensitive treatment of victims may be unlikely to report their own victimization experiences.

SEX CRIMES UNITS

In an effort to deal with the concerns of victims and to promote a more positive image of law enforcement officers, many police departments are establishing sex crimes units. These units consist of officers who are specifically trained to deal with crimes of a sexual nature, as working with individuals who have been sexually victimized is often much different from working with victims of other types of crime (e.g., property crime). Such training may consist of special investigatory techniques as well as training in crisis intervention and sensitive interviewing. These units aim to provide the best assistance to victims of sexual crimes and also, concurrently, the best investigation possible to help ensure a strong case against the offender. Satisfactory victim treatment is a priority for law enforcement given that it encourages victim cooperation with investigations and leads to solid cases (Meyers, 2002). Sex crimes units may house programs such as referral processes for victim compensation. They may also offer specialized services such as victim assistance and witness assistance, in which one or more individuals help the victim to navigate the entire criminal justice process.

Scholars suggest that specialized units create an environment in which cases of intimate partner violence are a priority, meaning such cases do not have to compete with the interests of other types of cases. Sex crimes units also allow victims to work with one or two people who handle their case until final deposition, limiting the number of times they need to repeat and relive their stories (Fagan, 1996). In addition, scholars assert that specialized units may also increase the chances of arrests and prosecution; however, there has been limited research on sex crimes units. Two investigations by LaFree (1989) and Beichner and Spohn (2005) did not find evidence that specialized units result in higher rates of arrest or prosecution compared to traditional law enforcement operations. At the same time, LaFree concluded that officers employed in sex crimes units displayed lower rates of victim-blaming attitudes than did other officers.

Victims of Sexual Assault and the Legal System

After experiencing questioning and reporting to the police, a victim may be fearful about experiencing blame or insensitive treatment by the prosecutor, judge, or jury, or about having to retell his or her story in public at a trial (Konradi, 2007). Victims may actually delay reporting a sexual assault to the police because they are apprehensive concerning the treatment they will receive from the prosecutor and, during the cross-examination, from the defense. Many victims are especially fearful that they will go through a painful and/or humiliating trial and then, in the end, not receive what they consider to be justice (Konradi & Burger, 2000). For example, victims may feel justice was not served when no charges are filed against the offender (Campbell et al., 1999; Frazier & Haney, 1996), when continuances are granted, or when plea bargains and reduced sentences are negotiated. These occurrences often incite anger in victims and cause them to feel revictimized (Konradi).

NATIONAL CRIME VICTIM LAW INSTITUTE (NCVLI)

The National Crime Victim Law Institute (NCVLI) is one initiative aimed at improving the experience of victims within the legal system. This program is designed to educate legal professionals, victim advocates, law enforcement, and law students about the legal process for crime victims. The NCVLI provides legal clinics for victims and practitioners focused on victims' rights. The organization also promotes public policy, with the goal of ensuring victims' rights in the future (NCVLI, 2013). In association with the NCVLI, the National Alliance of Victims' Rights Attorneys (NAVRA) is a professional nonprofit organization aimed at creating and maintaining a network of attorneys who are knowledgeable in legal advocacy so that they can promote and protect victims' rights and represent victims' cases nationwide (NAVRA, 2013). Both of these groups are working to ensure that victims' rights and victims' experiences within the criminal justice system continue to improve.

RAPE SHIELD LAWS

Rape shield laws have been enacted to assist in improving sexual assault victims' experience in the legal system. The first rape shield laws were enacted in the early 1970s, and they had spread to almost every state by the 1980s. Prior to the implementation of these laws, sexual assault victims' past sexual history—including their sexual partners—could be introduced during trial and used as evidence regarding their credibility. The court rationalized that if a rape victim had previously consented to sex with an individual, she was more likely to have consented to later sexual acts (i.e., including her rape). The use of a victim's past sexual history often discouraged victims from coming forward and reporting. As a result of the implementation of rape shield laws, a victim's past cannot be used in the trial. Some information may be used to establish the facts of the case or a past relationship between the defendant and the victim, but the passage of these laws has limited the breadth of information that is admissible in court.

Victims of Sexual Assault and the Medical System

Historically, rape victims who sought medical attention or were sent to medical professionals by law enforcement for evidence collection were often seen as a low priority at hospitals (Martin, 2005) and were forced to wait for long periods (sometimes as long as 4 to 10 hours) before being seen (Littel, 2001). During this waiting period, a victim would not be able to eat, drink or urinate until the examination was completed. This requirement was designed to keep the victim from tampering with any evidence that may have been on her person. Also, medical personnel were typically untrained regarding how to treat a victim of a sexual assault and/or how to properly collect forensic evidence (Campbell, Patterson, & Lichty, 2005). Some medical professionals reported feeling that completing a rape exam was not something that required their medical skills (Martin), which contributed to the insensitive treatment of victims by medical staff (Littel). Many times, as did law enforcement officers, medical staff asked questions that led victims to blame themselves for their attack. These included questions such as inquiries about their sexual history, their clothing, and why they were with the offender (if they knew their assailant). As a result of such negative contact with doctors or nurses, victims frequently reported self-blame and guilt and reluctance to seek further help (Campbell, 2005). These negative experiences by sexual assault victims have been referred to as a "secondary victimization" (Campbell & Raja, 1999; Williams, 1984), "second rape" (Madigan & Gamble, 1991), or "the second assault" (Martin & Powell, 1994), as the people who are there to help the victim after a traumatic event instead make them feel worse about their victimization.

SEXUAL ASSAULT NURSE EXAMINER (SANE)

Sexual Assault Nurse Examiner (SANE) programs were enacted in an attempt to remedy the poor treatment that sexual assault victims frequently experienced from medical personnel (Ledray, 1999). The first such program was established in Memphis, Tennessee, in 1976 (Ledray & Arndt, 1994), and since then, SANE programs have become widespread in the United States (Campbell, Patterson,

& Lichty, 2005). Most SANE programs are hospital based, but some are located at rape crisis centers or private medical offices (Ledray, 1997). The SANE program's goal is to improve the experiences of sexual assault victims and to advance the collection and presentation of evidence for a more successful outcome in the case. The program produces registered forensic nurses or nurse practitioners who complete extensive classroom training (usually 40 hours) and clinical training (40–96 hours). In the clinical training, they learn techniques of evidence collection, how to use specialized equipment, injury identification and treatment, how to screen for sexually transmitted diseases (STDs) and pregnancy, and the protocol regarding the chain of evidence. Also, they learn how to identify rape trauma syndrome as well as how to intervene in a crisis and treat trauma victims. The SANE program also provides training for SANEs on how to provide expert testimony in court pertaining to the evidence they collect (IAFN, 2013). It is important to note that although SANEs are trained to better assist sexual assault victims regarding the collection of evidence and presentation of evidence in court, they are not advocates for victims (Ledray & Barry, 1998).

Research demonstrates that SANE programs are beneficial to victims of sex crimes. Evidence demonstrates that victims treated by SANEs have reduced waiting times (DiNitto Martin, Norton, & Maxwell, 1986; Girardin, 2005; Littel, 2001) and that SANEs spend more time with victims than do emergency room doctors or nurses (Girardin). Victims treated by SANEs report feeling that they were treated with sensitivity (Campbell et al., 2001; Campbell, Patterson, et al., 2005), that they were able to ask questions and pause the exam if needed (Campbell, Patterson, Adams, Diegel, & Coats, 2008), and that they often left the exam feeling more informed and in control (Ericksen et al., 2002). Given that SANEs are specially trained to collect physical evidence of sex crimes, SANEs assist victims by collecting more accurate and complete evidence kits than those collected by non-SANEs (Ledray & Simmelink, 1997), thus increasing the likelihood of securing the conviction of offenders (McGregor, DuMont, & Myhr, 2002).

The increased use and presence of SANE programs is a step forward in reducing the revictimization of sexual assault victims and improving their experience with medical personnel when seeking medical attention post assault. However, interviews with SANEs reveal that they believe that even while their presence has improved the treatment of victims, police, medical personnel, and the legal system may still be contributing to the revictimization of sexual assault victims (Maier, 2012).

Correctional Supervision and Sexual Assault Victimization

Historically, the correctional arm of the criminal justice system was generally unconcerned with victims, their rights, or their treatment by the criminal justice system. This was due to the fact that the focus of corrections was on the offender and his or her supervision and punishment. However, in light of the victims' rights movement, over the past few decades the correctional system has begun to emphasize the importance of victims. In the 1980s, the American Correctional Association (ACA) published a document that stated that victims had the right to be treated with dignity and respect and to be updated on the status of the offender, such as parole hearings and the granting or revocation of parole. Additionally, victims were afforded the right to be present at all hearings and to read a victim impact statement if they so desired. The ACA also published a list of recommendations to improve the services offered to victims, recognizing that victims were a key part of the criminal justice system (NCVC, 2013).

In the 1990s, the correctional system began training personnel to improve the services offered to victims and to develop programs aimed at addressing the needs of victims. The Office for Victims of Crime (OVC) provided resources to train and assist federal and military correctional systems in more than 40 states. The U.S. Parole Commission has established a victim/witness coordinator to assist victims in navigating the corrections system. The coordinator also has the responsibilities of scheduling hearings, answering victims' questions, providing referrals, and keeping victims up-to-date on changes.

VICTIM–OFFENDER MEDIATION (VOM)

Victims may want to be more involved in the prosecution of the offender and to take a more proactive approach in dealing with their own victimization. One way to accomplish this is through victim–offender mediation (VOM), in which the victim and the offender meet face-to-face and discuss the crime in the presence of a mediator. During VOM, the victim may express how the victimization impacted his or her life, and the offender may acknowledge the harm he or she caused. A mediator is there as a neutral third party to direct and facilitate dialogue. The decision to participate in mediation is voluntary on both parts, but it is ultimately up to the victim. Victims who are given the opportunity to participate in VOM usually do so (Umbreit & Greenwood, 2000). VOM is often offered to offenders as a diversion program, in that if the offender cooperates and completes the program, he or she will not be formally charged and prosecuted. Mediation can also occur as a conditional part of probation or after the offender has been incarcerated for a period of time. VOM has been successful in reducing the fear that victims have of their offenders (Umbreit, Coates, & Kalanj, 1994) and in reducing symptoms of posttraumatic stress (Angel, 2005). Research also indicates that both offenders and victims report fulfillment from the VOM process (Umbreit & Greenwood). Finally, evidence suggests that when VOM occurs, there are greater rates of restitution payments to victims (VORP Information and Resource Center, 2013) and a reduction in recidivism by offenders.

Victims' Rights

The victims' rights movement began in the 1970s on the heels of both the civil rights and women's rights movements. Victims' rights advocates rallied against the inadequate treatment of victims in the system and victims' lack of representation in the prosecution of offenders who harmed them. The victims' rights movement developed alongside the law-and-order movement, as U.S. politicians began calling on the criminal justice system to "get tough on crime." Likewise, Martinson's (1974) highly publicized manuscript, which deemed that "nothing works" in rehabilitating and treating offenders and documented societal attitudes that offenders were "getting off easy," aided in the success of the victims' rights movement.

Prior to the initiation and eventual successes of the victims' rights movement, victims lacked rights in a criminal proceeding. They were seen as just another form of evidence; they were there to testify and assist the police and prosecution in building a strong case against a suspect. The first step for victims' rights was a test pilot of what is now the National Crime and Victimization Survey (NCVS), launched in 1965 (Smith, 1988). This was the first government-sponsored crime survey that captured the perspective of victims. Prior to the NCVS, the only official source of crime statistics was the Uniform Crime Report (UCR), a compilation of law enforcement data. The NCVS allowed crimes left unreported to police to be accounted for. This was especially impactful in developing statistics on crimes of a sexual nature, given that these crimes are consistently underreported to law enforcement.

The first rape crisis centers were established in 1972 in San Francisco, Washington, DC, and Ann Arbor, Michigan. They were staffed by former victims and were dedicated to helping victims recover from their trauma. This was an important step toward assisting crime victims. Then in 1974, the first victim/witness assistance programs were established in New York and Wisconsin. They were designed to assist victims in dealing with the process of the criminal justice system. These early programs paved the way for the creation and expansion of other victims' programs in the United States throughout the next decades (Young & Stein, 2004).

Legislation

In the eyes of the criminal justice system, when a crime is committed, it is committed against the state—not an individual victim. As such, the state (or federal government) brings the case against the offender on behalf of the victim. The victim's name is not even included in the name of a case: Cases are referred to as *"The People"* or *"The State of* [insert state name here] *v.* [insert offender name here]." Historically, the rationale for using the state in lieu of the individual victim in the prosecution of offenders was to discourage vigilante justice and blood feuds between the families of victims and those of offenders. Nowadays, this process encourages the extension of due process rights to offenders. While constitutional amendments do outline specific protections for those accused of a crime, the U.S. Constitution does not extend specific protections to crime victims. Some argue that victims' rights overburden the already overworked criminal justice system. However, victims' rights groups contend that victims' voices should be recognized, and legislation has been enacted at the state and federal levels to provide remedies to crime victims. In addition, many states have passed constitutional amendments delineating the rights afforded to victims in the state and ensuring those rights are extended to victims.

Two pieces of early legislation established the victim as a party to the crime who deserved to be recognized and treated with dignity. The first piece of federal legislation addressing victims' rights was the Federal Victim Witness Protection Act, passed in 1982. This law required that the Attorney General create and implement guidelines for how crime victims should be treated, as well as for how officials in the system should respond to victims. In 1984, the government enacted the Victims of Crime Act (VOCA), which provided funds for state crime victim compensation programs through the establishment of the Office for Victims of Crime.

The Child Victims' Bill of Rights, passed in 1990, expanded the rights of victims to include children and gave them the followings rights: to initiate proceedings and receive answers to questions in language that they can understand, to have a victim advocate present with them, and to have a secure waiting area during court proceedings. It also gave child witnesses and victims the right to have their information kept private unless a parent or guardian requested otherwise. In 1990, the Crime Control Act and the Victims' Rights and Restitution Act were also implemented. These laws created a federal bill of rights for victims, outlining their rights and guaranteeing that victims have the right to restitution under the law. The rights that this legislation expressly gave to victims include protection from the accused; notification in a timely fashion about changes in the case; inclusion in proceedings; and the right to be reasonably heard at public proceedings involving release, plea, or sentencing. Victims were also afforded protections against unreasonable delay in their case proceedings, which is similar to the right to a speedy trial afforded to individuals who are accused of a crime.

The victims' rights movement gained momentum in the 1990s with legislation specifically targeted to assist female victims. The 1994 Violent Crime Control and Law Enforcement Act provided over $1 billion for victim's services and advocates, as well for rape education and prevention programs. Also in 1994, the Violence Against Women Act provided money for victim compensation programs, funds to establish a national sex offender registry, and funds for programs designed to respond to and prevent acts of violence against women. This act was further modified in 2000 to include protections for immigrant, disabled, and elderly women.

The next essential piece of legislation pertaining to victim's rights came in 1996 with the passage of the Antiterrorism and Effective Death Penalty Act, which made restitution mandatory in the sentences of offenders who committed a violent crime and extended victim assistance and compensation to the victims of terrorism. The Justice for All Act, passed in 2004, provided funds to test DNA samples that had been collected but had not yet been tested, as well as providing additional protections for crime victims.

As a result of the aforementioned federal legislation, all states currently have provisions pertaining to the rights of victims; however, victims' rights vary by jurisdiction. Some states have passed very rigorous legislation; for example, California has passed the Victims' Bill of Rights Act of 2008: Marsy's Law (Marsy's Law), one of the most comprehensive pieces of law pertaining to victims' rights. The legislation, passed in 2008, is named after Marsalee (Marsy) Nicholas, who was stalked and murdered by her ex-boyfriend. A week after his apprehension, her mother ran into her daughter's killer in a grocery store. She was not notified of his release, as the state was under no obligation to inform her of his status. Marsy's Law requires that the victim and/or the victim's family be notified of changes in the case, be given the opportunity to speak at different phases in the process, and be able to view the presentence investigation report (except for any items on the report that are deemed to be confidential by law) once it is available to the defendant. The law also mandates that every prosecutor in the state go through victim's rights training. Furthermore, the law requires the courts to factor in the safety of the victims, as well as of their families, when establishing whether the accused will be released and under what conditions. Marsy's Law also makes restitution mandatory in every case in which a victim suffers a loss, and the law requires the return of property once it is no longer needed for evidence. Other states have begun to follow suit by passing versions of Marsy's Law (Marsy's Law for All, 2013).

VICTIM ADVOCACY GROUPS

The first programs aimed at assisting witnesses and victims of crimes were created in the 1970s. These programs initially were grassroots efforts of former victims and their friends, who would visit with victims and offer their support. The first government-sponsored programs were established in Brooklyn, New York, and Milwaukee, Wisconsin. In 1982, President Ronald W. Reagan signed an executive order establishing the Task Force on Victims of Crime with the goal of conducting a national study to assess the treatment of crime victims by the criminal justice system. This task force traveled across the United States interviewing victims about their experiences with the criminal justice system and determining which needs of victims criminal justice personnel were and were not meeting. In addition to speaking with victims, task force members also interviewed criminal justice personnel and other victim service professionals. Based on the data collected, the task force recommended that the criminal justice system implement additional services to assist victims. As a result, victim assistance programs proliferated in the United States.

Currently, victim advocacy and support programs are in place nationwide. Victim advocacy programs may be funded by nonprofit groups and housed in privately run facilities, such as rape crisis centers or domestic violence shelters, or they may be run by the prosecutor's office or police department. Victim advocacy programs can be found through the National Center for Victims of Crime (www.victimsofcrime.org), which promotes victims' rights and assists organizations in providing training for those supplying victim services or advocacy programs. In general, victim advocacy programs aim to inform victims about their rights and to offer support and guidance as victims navigate the criminal justice process. These programs also provide information and assistance regarding how to apply for victim compensation programs and write victim impact statements. Some programs also provide an advocate to attend hearings and the trial with the victim and to relay updates on cases between the court and the victim. Programs may also employ advocates with specialized skills, such as a legal advocate, who may assist victims with legal issues and/or with the trial, or a medical advocate, who may assist victims at the emergency room or accompany them to doctor's appointments and procedures.

One example of a current victim advocacy program is Stepping Stones, part of the larger nonprofit, statewide organization Illinois Coalition Against Sexual Assault, which is dedicated to assisting victims of sexual assault. Stepping Stones is a local community program in Bloomington, Illinois, that provides free counseling to victims of sexual assault and to their significant others. Stepping Stones also provides free medical, legal advocacy, and general advocacy services for sexual assault victims. If a victim requests a medical advocate, a trained Stepping Stones medical advocate will accompany a victim to the hospital or medical office to provide advocacy and support. A legal advocate will work on behalf of the needs and/or rights of the victim with police, with the state's attorney's office, and/or during criminal justice proceedings such as the trial. In addition, victim advocates at Stepping Stones aid victims with filing for civil or no-contact orders; applying for crime victim compensation; and operating the Illinois Automated Victim Notification System (AVN), which notifies victims of changes in their case. The victim advocates at Stepping Stones assist victims from the initial request until the victims feel that their needs have been met, which may be after the case has been tried and the offender sentenced.

VICTIM COMPENSATION PROGRAMS

The first victim compensation program in the United States was established in California in 1966; however, crime victim compensation programs have roots dating back to ancient Rome and Greece, where families of victims received food and clothes from the community. The Victims of Crime Act of 1984 was a federal law authorizing a regular allocation of funds for state crime victim compensation and assistance programs. This act covers all U.S. citizens but not all crimes or crime victims. Specific requirements must be met for a victim to receive compensation under VOCA. A person must have reported the crime to the police within 72 hours or have a "good" cause or valid reason as to why they did not report it. They must cooperate with law enforcement and prosecution, and their victimization must not be a result of their own criminal activity. Victims also must submit an application for compensation with evidence of expenses and show that these expenses are not covered by other funding sources, such as insurance. The total amount of victim compensation that a person may apply for varies by state, but typically, the total ranges from $10,000 to $25,000 per criminal incident. Victims may apply to have a variety of crime-related expenses covered, such as medical and dental costs, eyeglasses, crime scene cleanup, moving expenses, and compensation for damaged or stolen property. Most states also allow for a victim's family to apply for coverage of funeral expenses (Klein, 2010).

Additionally, under VOCA, there is a Son of Sam (or "notoriety-for-profit") provision that prohibits offenders from profiting from books written about their crime. This provision of the law ensures that criminals will not profit while their victims suffer financially. Any profits are to be held in escrow for 5 years to satisfy any civil suits made by the victim (Parent, Auerbach, & Carlson, 1992). Most states also have the requirement that if any profits do not go to a victim through a civil claim, the profits must go into the state crime victim compensation fund.

RESTITUTION

Restitution is typically court-ordered payment from the offender to the victim and is often ordered in conjunction with the sentence or punishment that the offender receives. Restitution may be ordered as a conditional part of probation or parole or in tandem with a sentence in jail or prison. In cases where restitution is considered, the judge will review the financial losses suffered by the victim as well as the finances and earning potential of the offender and his or her dependents. This information is often contained in the pre-sentence investigation report collected by the probation department prior to the sentencing hearing. The goal of restitution is to make the offender aware of the financial effects and suffering that the crime had on the victim, while trying to restore the victim to the financial condition he or she was in before the crime occurred. Restitution can be ordered to pay for medical or dental expenses, lost wages, child care, and other expenses relating to attending court and to the crime itself. Typically, a third party, such as a probation officer, disperses the funds to the victim.

The Mandatory Victims Restitution Act of 1996 expanded restitution and required that restitution be ordered if there is an identifiable victim who suffered from physical and/or financial harm as a result of the crime. This act required the court to mandate restitution, regardless of the ability of the offender to pay, if the offender pled or was found guilty of a crime of violence, a property crime (including fraud and telemarketing fraud), sexual abuse, sexual exploitation and abuse of children, domestic violence, or tampering with consumer products. One exception to this act occurs in cases where the number of victims is so large that it makes the collection of restitution for each victim impractical; another exception occurs when restitution would infringe upon and prolong the sentencing of the offender.

When restitution is ordered, payments are commonly split up, allowing the offender to pay over a period of time, as with repayment of a loan. To ensure that restitution is paid, the court may garner the wages of the offender if he or she is under community supervision or may garner the offender's prison wage if he or she is incarcerated. However, there can be issues with offenders failing to pay restitution, and since restitution is a condition of the offender's sentence, failure to pay may result in the revocation of probation or parole. Additionally, victims may file a civil suit against the offender for failure to pay restitution (NCVC, 2013).

In addition to the failure to pay restitution, some other issues can arise with the use of restitution in criminal cases. Until restitution is paid to the victim, the victim must cover his or her own costs. The process of receiving restitution also can be slow, and restitution payments can be small, meaning they may not provide much ongoing support to the victim. The time it takes an offender to pay restitution varies with each case and the total amount of restitution, but it can take up to 20 years or even until the death of the offender before the victim receives the full amount of restitution. In addition, the victims of offenders who are not apprehended and/or convicted have no recourse regarding restitution since restitution is a condition of a criminal sentence. Although a guilty verdict is necessary for a victim to receive restitution from an offender, a victim may sue an offender in civil court even if a criminal court does not find the individual guilty. Civil court has a burden of proof that is different from and lower than that of the criminal court. For a plaintiff to be successful in civil court, he or she only needs to prove the defendant's guilt beyond a preponderance of evidence, whereas in a criminal case, a prosecutor must prove guilt beyond a reasonable doubt.

Restitution is also problematic in cases where there are multiple victims and a single offender, given that the money ordered for restitution must be spread among all the victims and it therefore often takes longer for each victim to recoup the losses he or she suffered. Likewise, if there are multiple offenders and a single victim, and if one of the offenders makes a deal for immunity in exchange for testimony against the others, then the victim cannot seek restitution against the person who made the deal. That may diminish the amount of restitution the victim may receive. Finally, while the intent of restitution is to assist in making the victim whole again, many victims are reminded of the crime each time they receive a restitution payment (An Abuse, Rape & Domestic Violence Aid & Resource Collection, www.aardvarc.org).

NOTIFICATION AND PRESENTATION

Victims have the right to be notified about events or happenings regarding their case. This can include the arrest of the offender, the offender's release from custody, bail, court proceedings, parole hearings, and release of the offender on parole. The responsibility of notification may fall upon the court, law enforcement, the prosecutor's office, corrections personnel (such as a parole board), or a victim advocate assigned to the case. The party responsible for notifying the victim of changes varies by jurisdiction, but more and more jurisdictions are converting to an automated system of notification. Automatic notifications may entail that an email, recorded phone message, text message, or letter be automatically generated and sent to the victim, alerting him or her that there has been a change in status. The automatic systems allows the victim to be notified quickly and efficiently. Some jurisdictions allow a victim to consult with judges or prosecutors before some changes are made regarding a plea bargain, bail, or parole; in these jurisdictions, a victim would be notified that a change may occur, and he or she would be able to offer input on the matter before a decision is made (Davis & Mulford, 2008).

VICTIM IMPACT STATEMENTS

Victim impact statements were first implemented in Fresno, California, in 1976, and over time, they have been widely integrated into state and federal legislation regarding victims' rights. Victim impact statements provide an opportunity for victims to explain how the victimization affected their life. Typically, the statement describes the physical, psychological, or financial harm the victim experienced as a result of the crime. Victims may also include a sentencing recommendation for the offender in their statement. Victim impact statements may be written and read aloud in court by the victims themselves, a family member, or a representative such as a victim advocate. Victims may also send the statement to the judge directly. A victim impact statement is usually read at the sentencing stage or at an offender's parole hearing; however, some jurisdictions may allow the victim to read a statement at a bail hearing (NCVC, 2013).

There are benefits to the use of victim impact statements. These statements allow victims to be heard and to express the pain they felt and the harm they suffered as a result of the victimization. This is often therapeutic and empowering for victims, as they feel their voice is being heard in the process. Impact statements also allow judges and jurors to understand the crime from a victim's point of view, rather than just hearing the facts of the case presented by the prosecution and defense. However, victim impact statements may also be problematic for victims. For example, in cases where the victim knows the offender, as is often true in cases of sexual victimization, the victim may be fearful of expressing himself or herself to the offender for fear of future retaliation. Additionally, writing the statement forces the victim to relive the victimization experience, often causing pain and trauma (Bandes, 1999). Victims may also be dissatisfied and feel as if justice has not been served if the sentencing recommendation suggested in the impact statement is not implemented by the court (Davis, Henley, & Smith, 1990). Some critics assert that victim impact statements are unduly prejudicial against offenders and lead to more severe punishment than is warranted by the evidence. However, the U.S. Supreme Court ruled in *Payne v. Tennessee* (1991) that victim impact statements are admissible and do not violate a defendant's right to freedom from cruel and unusual punishment.

COMPLIANCE PROGRAMS

The use of compliance programs is one way to ensure that victims are informed about their rights and actually receive the protections they are afforded. Compliance programs currently exist in several states as a result of state legislation or an amendment to the state's constitution. They are often run by the governor's office or the state's Department of Justice. Compliance programs also exist at the federal level and are housed within the U.S. Department of Justice's Offices of the U.S. Attorneys. Compliance programs investigate complaints regarding violations of a victim's rights. Any victim who feels that his or her rights have been violated can file a complaint against an agency. The compliance program would then be responsible for investigating the violation and, if the violation is sustained, taking the appropriate action. Remedies usually entail educating the agency regarding the specific victim's rights in question, with the goal of preventing future violations. Agencies may also incur penalties, depending on both the jurisdiction and the offense (U.S. Department of Justice, 2013).

SEXUAL ASSAULT RESPONSE TEAMS (SARTS)

A final mechanism aimed at improving the treatment of victims of sexual violence by the criminal justice system is the sexual assault response team. The use of SARTs is a holistic and collaborative approach to treating victims of sex crimes in that SARTs usually include individuals from different criminal justice system agencies such as law enforcement officers, victim advocates, forensic nurse examiners, and prosecutors. When a rape or sexual assault occurs in a jurisdiction that has a SART, the SART is notified, and the team members begin to carry out their respective responsibilities simultaneously. SARTs work together as a group for the welfare and benefit of the victim in an attempt to eliminate confusion, anxiety, and negative experiences (Howton, 2010). The SART works to ensure that victims receive all the services they need (from the initial report to the final disposition of the case) and that victims are treated with dignity and respect. Also, many SARTs offer culturally specific assistance to victims and provide services that meet the specific needs of mentally or physically disabled victims.

Conclusion

Since the beginning of the victims' rights movement in the 1970s, victims have won many successes regarding their treatment by the criminal justice system. Legislation has been passed, policies have been implemented, and sweeping changes have been realized for the betterment of crime victims, especially victims of sexual offenses. Two major victories for victims of sex crimes include the proliferation of Sexual Assault Nurse Examiners and sexual assault response teams. These resources were created wholly for victims and consider the victim's needs to be their highest priority.

However, as previously noted, there are continuing limitations regarding the treatment of victims by the criminal justice system. Many victims remain unaware of their rights and the services that are available to them. Too few victims receive compensation or restitution because they are not encouraged to seek these services from criminal justice personnel. Even in states that have strong victims' rights legislation and policies in place, victims are not always notified of changes in their case (Kilpatrick, Beatty, & Howley, 1998). There is still much work to be done with regard to victims' rights, but the implementation and creation of new victim-centered programs engender hope for victims of sexual assault, as well as for victims across the criminal justice system as a whole.

Discussion Questions

1. Which piece of legislation mentioned in this chapter do you believe has had the greatest impact on the treatment of sexual assault victims in the criminal justice system? Please explain your choice.

2. Do you think that the programs that have been put in place to assist sexual assault victims will encourage victims to initially report and/or become involved with the criminal justice system? Why or why not?

3. Although there has been progress made in the treatment of sexual assault victims by the criminal justice system, what else would you suggest be done to improve the experience of victims? Please explain your answer.

References

An Abuse, Rape & Domestic Violence Aid & Resource Collection. http://www.aardvarc.org

Angel, C. M. (2005). *Crime victims meet their offenders: Testing the impact restorative justice on victims' post-traumatic stress symptoms* (Unpublished doctoral dissertation). University of Pennsylvania.

Antiterrorism and Effective Death Penalty Act, Pub. L. No. 104-132, 110 Stat. 1214 (1996).

Archambault, J., & Lindsay, S. (2001). Responding to non-stranger sexual assault. In M. M. Reuland, C. S. Brito, & L. Carroll (Eds.), *Solving crime and disorder problems: Current issues, police strategies, and organizational tactics* (pp. 21–42). Washington, DC: Police Executive Research Forum.

Bandes, S. (1999). Victim standing. *Utah Law Review*, 331.

Beichner, D., & Spohn, C. (2005). Prosecutors' charging decisions in sexual assault cases: Examining the impact of a specialized unit. *Criminal Justice Police Review, 16*, 461–498.

Campbell, R. (2005). What really happened? A validation study of rape survivors' help-seeking experiences with the legal and medical systems. *Violence & Victims 20*(1), 55–68.

Campbell, R. (2006). Rape survivors' experiences with the legal and medical systems: Do rape victim advocates make a difference? *Violence Against Women, 12*(1), 30–45.

Campbell, R., Patterson, D., & Lichty, L. F. (2005). The effectiveness of Sexual Assault Nurse Examiner (SANE) programs: A review of psychological, medical, legal, and community programs. *Trauma, Violence and Abuse, 6*(4), 313–329.

Campbell, R., Patterson, D., Adams, A. E., Diegel, R., & Coats, S. (2008). A participatory evaluation project to measure SANE nursing practice and adult sexual assault patients psychological well-being. *Journal of Forensic Nursing, 4*(1), 19–28.

Campbell, R., & Raja, S. (1999). Secondary victimization of rape victims: Insights from mental health professionals who treat survivors of violence. *Violence and Victims, 14*(3), 261–275.

Campbell, R., & Raja, S. (2005). The sexual assault and secondary victimization of female veterans: Help-seeking experiences in military and civilian social systems. *Psychology of Women Quarterly, 29*(1), 97–106.

Campbell, R., Sefl, T., Barnes, H. E., Ahrens, C. E., Wasco, S. M., & Zaragoza-Diesfeld, Y. (1999). Community services for rape survivors: Enhancing psychological well-being or increasing trauma? *Journal of Consulting and Clinical Psychology, 67*(6), 847–858.

Campbell, R., Wasco, S. M., Ahrens, C. E., Sefl, T., & Barnes, H. E. (2001). Preventing the "second rape." Rape survivors' experiences with community service providers. *Journal of Interpersonal Violence, 16*(12), 1239–1259.

Child Victims' Bill of Rights, 18 U.S.C. §3509 (1990).

Crime Control Act, Pub. L. 101-647, § 1, 104 Stat. 4789 (1990).

Davis, R. C., Henley, M., & Smith, B. E. (1990). *Victim impact statements: Their effects on court outcomes and victim satisfaction.* New York, NY: New York City Victim Service Agency.

Davis, R. C., & Mulford, C. (2008). Victim rights and new remedies: Finally getting the victims their due. *Journal of Contemporary Criminal Justice, 24*(2). 198–208.

DiNitto, D., Martin, P. Y., Norton, D., & Maxwell, M. (1986). After sexual assault: Who should examine sexual assault survivors? *American Journal of Nursing, 86*, 538–540.

Ericksen, J., Dudley, C., McIntosh, G., Ritch, L., Shumay, S., & Simpson, M. (2002). Clients' experiences with a specialized sexual assault service. *Journal of Emergency Nursing, 28*(1), 86–90.

Estrich, S. (1987). *Real rape.* Cambridge, MA: Harvard University Press.

Fagan, J. (1996). The criminalization of domestic violence: Promises and limits. *National Institute of Justice: Research report.* Retrieved from https://www.ncjrs.gov/pdffiles/crimdom.pdf

Federal Victim Witness Protection Act, Pub. L. No. 97-291, 96 Stat. 1248 (1982).

Frazier, P. A., & Haney, B. (1996). Sexual assault cases in the legal system: Police, prosecutor, and victim perspectives. *Law and Human Behavior, 20*(6), 607–628.

Girardin, B. W. (2005). The Sexual Assault Nurse Examiner: A win-win solution. *Topics in Emergency Medicine, 27*(2). 124–131.

Howton, A. J. (2010). Sexual assault response team (SART). In B. S. Fisher & S. P. Lab (Eds.), *Encyclopedia of victimology and crime prevention* (Vol. 2, pp. 855–856). Los Angeles, CA: Sage.

International Association of Forensic Nurses (IAFN). (2013). *Database of the International Association of Forensic Nurses.* Retrieved from http://forensicnurse.org

Justice for All Act, 18 U.S.C. § 3771 (2004).

Kilpatrick, D. G., Beatty, D., & Howley, S. S. (1998). *The rights of crime victims: Does legal protection make a difference?* Washington, DC: U.S. Department of Justice, National Institute of Justice. Retrieved from https://www.ncjrs.gov/pdffiles/173839.pdf

Klein, L. (2010). Victim compensation. In B. S. Fisher & S. P. Lab (Eds.), *Encyclopedia of victimology and crime prevention* (Vol. 2, pp. 971–974). Los Angeles, CA: Sage.

Konradi, A. (2007). *Taking the stand: Rape survivors and the prosecution of rapists.* Westport, CT: Praeger.

Konradi, A., & Burger, T. (2000). Having the last word: An examination of rape survivors' participating in sentencing. *Violence Against Women, 6*(4), 351–395.

Lafree, G. (1989). *Rape and criminal justice: The social construction of sexual assault.* Belmont, CA: Wadsworth.

Ledray, L. E. (1997). SANE program locations: Pros and cons; Sexual Assault Nurse Examiner. *Journal of Emergency Nursing, 23*(2), 182–186.

Ledray, L. E. (1999). *Sexual assault nurse examiner, SANE: Development and operations guide.* Washington, DC: U.S. Department of Justice, Office for Victims of Crime.

Ledray, L. E., & Arndt, S. (1994). Examining the sexual assault victim: A new model for nursing care. *Journal of Psychosocial Nursing and Mental Health Services, 32*(2), 7–12.

Ledray, L. E., & Barry, L. (1998). SANE expert and factual testimony. *Journal of Emergency Nursing, 24*(3), 284–287.

Ledray, L. E., & Simmelink, K. (1997). Efficacy of SANE evidence collection: A Minnesota study. *Journal of Emergency Nursing, 23*(1), 75–77.

Littel, K. (2001). *Sexual Assault Nurse Examiners (SANE) programs: Improving the community response to sexual assault victims.* Washington, DC: U.S. Department of Justice, Office for Victims of Crime.

Logan, T. K., Cole, J., & Capillo, A. (2007). Differential characteristics of intimate partner, acquaintance, and stranger rape survivors examined by a Sexual Assault Nurse Examiner (SANE). *Journal of Interpersonal Violence, 22*(8), 1066–1076.

Maier, S. L. (2012). Sexual assault nurse examiners' perceptions of the revictimization of rape victims. *Journal of Interpersonal Violence, 27*(2), 287–315.

Madigan, L., & Gamble, N. C. (1991). *The second rape: Society's continued betrayal of the* victims. New York, NY: Lexington Books.

Mandatory Victims Restitution Act of 1996, 18 U.S.C. § 3663 (1996).

Marsy's Law for All. (2013). *Marsy's law for all*. Retrieved from http://www.marsyslawforall.org

Martin, P. Y. (2005). *Rape work: Victims, gender, and organizations in community context*. New York, NY: Routledge.

Martin, P. Y., & Powell, R. M. (1994). Accounting for the "second assault": Legal organizations' framing of rape victims. *Law & Social Inquiry, 19*(4), 853–890.

Martinson, R. (1974, spring). What works? Questions and answers about prison reform. *The Public Interest, 35*, 22–54.

McGregor, M. J., DuMont, J., & Myhr, T. L. (2002). Sexual assault forensic medical examination: Is evidence related to successful prosecution? *Annals of Emergency Medicine, 39*(6), 639–647.

Meyers, T. W. (2002). Policing and sexual assault: Strategies for successful victim interviews. In L. J. Moriarty (Ed.), *Policing and victims* (pp. 57–73). Upper Saddle River, NJ: Pearson.

National Alliance of Victim's Rights Attorneys (NAVRA). (2013). *NAVRA website*. Retrieved from http://navra.org

National Center for Victims of Crime (NCVC). (2013). *Victim impact statements*. Retrieved from http://www.victimsofcrime.org/help-for-crime-victims/get-help-bulletins-for-crime-victims/victim-impact-statements/

National Crime Victim Law Institute (NCVLI). (2013). *NCLVI website*. Retrieved from http://law.lclark.edu/centers/national_crime_victim_law_institute/

Office for Victims of Crime. (2013).

Parent, D. G., Auerbach, B., Carlson, K. E. (1992). *Compensating crime victims: A summary of policies and practices*. Washington, DC: U.S. Department of Justice, National Institute of Justice.

Patterson, D., Greeson, M., & Campbell, R. (2009). Protect thyself: Understanding rape survivors' decisions not to seek help from formal social systems. *Health & Social Work, 34*(2), 127–136.

Payne v. Tennessee, 501 U.S. 808 (1991).

Smith, B. L. (1988). Victims and victim rights activists: Attitudes toward criminal justice officials and victim-related issues. *Criminal Justice Review, 13*(1), 21–27.

Starzynski, L. L, Ullman, S. E., Filipas, H. H., & Townsend, S. M. (2005). Correlates of women's sexual assault disclosure to informal and formal support sources. *Violence and Victims, 20*(4), 417–432.

Umbreit, M. S. (with R. B. Coates & B. Kalanj). (1994). *Victims meets offender: The impact of restorative justice and mediation*. Monsey, NY: Criminal Justice Press.

Umbreit, M. S., & Greenwood, J. (2000). *Guidelines for victim-sensitive victim offender mediation: Restorative justice through dialogue*. Washington, DC: U.S. Department of Justice, Office for Victims of Crime.

U.S. Department of Justice, Office for Victims of Crime. (2013). *Crime victims' rights: Victim rights' compliance*. Retrieved from http://www.ojp.usdoj.gov/ovc/rights/compliance.html/

Victim-Offender Reconciliation Program (VORP) Information and Resource Center. (2013). *About victim-offender mediation and reconciliation*. Retrieved from http://www.vorp.com

Victims' Bill of Rights Act of 2008: Marsy's Law (Marsy's Law), California Constitution, Art. 1, § 28 (2008).

Victims of Crime Act (VOCA), 42 U.S.C. § 10601–10604 (1984).

Victims' Rights and Restitution Act, 42 U.S.C. § 10607 (1990).

Violence Against Women Act (VAWA), 42 U.S.C. § 14039 (1994).

Violent Crime Control and Law Enforcement Act, Pub. L. 103-322, §1, 108 Stat. 1796 (1994).

Williams, J. E. (1984). Secondary victimization: Confronting public attitudes about rape. *Victimology, 9*(1), 66–81.

Young, M., & Stein, J. (2004). *The history of the crime victims' movement in the United States*. Washington, DC: U.S. Department of Justice, Office for Victims of Crime. Retrieved from https://www.ncjrs.gov/ovc_archives/ncvrw/2005/pdf/historyofcrime.pdf

4

Sexual Harassment

Tammatha L. Clodfelter

S exual harassment has been extensively studied over the past 30 years across a wide variety of contexts such as the workplace, the military, academic settings, on the streets, and among peers (e.g., Bursik & Gefter, 2011; Cortina, Swan, Fitzgerald, & Waldo, 1998; Firestone, Miller, & Harris, 2012; Lipson, 2001; Macmillan, Nierobisz, & Welsh, 2000; McDonald, 2012; O'Leary-Kelly, Bowes-Sperry, Bates, & Lean, 2009; Rock, Lipari, Cook, & Hale, 2011). More recent studies have addressed topics such as factors that influence case outcomes (Hershcovis & Barling, 2010; Kulik, Perry, & Pepper, 2003), juror decision making (Huntley & Constanzo, 2003), compensatory awards (Cass, Levett, & Kovera, 2010; Sharkey, 2006), and organizational culture and trust (Vijayasiri, 2008). However, much of the attention has been paid to workplace sexual harassment.

A result of the vast attention to sexual harassment is the plethora of definitions utilized to examine sexual harassment (Birdeau, Somers, & Lenihan, 2005; Fitzgerald, Swan, & O'Donohue, 1997). However, several key factors are consistently present across the various descriptions, regardless of whether the harassment occurs at work, school, or among peers. First, the behavior must be sexual in nature (Charmaraman, Jones, Stein, & Espelage, 2013). A few examples of such behaviors include sexual coercion to retain employment (quid pro quo), spreading rumors about a person's alleged sexual activities on social media sites (hostile environment), or derogatory remarks and attitudes related to one's sex (gender harassment). A second important aspect of the behavior is that it must be unwanted or unwelcomed. In addition, to hold an employer or a school responsible, the victim must demonstrate that such behaviors diminished the victim's ability to continue his or her employment or education in the environment due to the organization's ineffective response to the harassment (U.S. DOE, 2010; U.S. EEOC, n.d.).

Previously understudied populations are now garnering attention from researchers. For example, a growing body of literature is investigating the experiences of adolescents and young adults. Further, topics such as same-sex sexual harassment and sexual harassment that occurs by text messaging and various types of social media are gaining interest. In addition to sexual harassment between known parties, sexual harassment that occurs in public and is committed by strangers is also being more frequently addressed. Therefore, this review aims to provide a comprehensive overview of each topic and offer suggestions to further expand the existing knowledge of this complex and pervasive type of sexual victimization.

Peer Sexual Harassment
Among Adolescents and Young Adults

Rates of peer sexual harassment among adolescents and young adults are staggering. Recent estimates suggest that middle and high school students are just as likely to experience sexual harassment as college students, with a few studies reporting victimization rates higher than 90% (Chiodo, Wolfe, Crooks, Hughes, & Jaffe, 2009; Fineran & Bennett, 1999; Hill & Kearl, 2011; Hill & Silva, 2005; Lacasse & Mendelson, 2006; Lichty & Campbell, 2012; Ormerod, Collinsworth, & Perry, 2008; Yoon, Funk, & Kropf, 2010). Even though students are legally protected against sexually harassing behaviors, the overwhelming frequency implies that such occurrences may be interpreted as acceptable behavior.

While estimates of sexual harassment are available, understanding the full scope of this type of sexual victimization may be more problematic for young peers than for adults, for numerous reasons. An issue discussed by Ormerod et al. (2008) is the lack of a comprehensive measure that captures the range of behaviors in a manner that will prompt a valid response from the participant. Ormerod et al. suggested that individuals are less likely to label their experiences in a negative way and that, therefore, measurements should focus on specific behaviors rather than on vague definitions. However, some studies do ask a broad array of questions to assess specific sexual harassment behaviors. These studies use either the American Association of Women instrument (Chiodo et al., 2009; Fineran & Bennett, 1999; Hand & Sanchez, 2000; Hill & Kearl, 2011; Hill & Silva, 2005; Miller et al., 2013) or a modified version of the Sexual Experiences Questionnaire (Boivin, Lavoie, Hébert, & Gagné, 2012; Lacasse & Mendelson, 2006; Lichty & Campbell, 2012; Ormerod et al.; Yoon et al., 2010).

Second, the term *sexual harassment* is used interchangeably with *bullying*, particularly when referring to behavior among adolescents (Charmaraman et al., 2013; Hill & Kearl, 2011). A commonly used definition of bullying describes repeated and targeted behaviors that are intended to cause harm to others and are considered to be a form of harassment (Hill & Kearl). Yet, recently the U.S. Department of Education Office for Civil Rights (2010) indicated that bullying or harassment does not have to be intentional or directed at a certain individual; rather the behavior need only create such a negative environment that it interferes with the student's ability to learn and participate. While sexual harassment falls under the umbrella of harassment, the behaviors are specifically sexual in nature (Charmaraman et al.). Other research suggests that the term *sexual bullying* may appropriately describe bullying behaviors that are intended to harm a person and that are sexual in nature (Shute, Owens, & Slee, 2008). Overall, without clear definitions, it is difficult to ascertain valid estimates of the breadth of this type of victimization.

Third, the intent of the behavior has not been as thoroughly investigated for peer harassment as it has with respect to adult workplace harassment or teacher-student sexual harassment. For adults and those in superior–subordinate relationships, sexual harassment is traditionally considered to be related to power, yet studies among younger populations often do not fully explore this dynamic (Fineran & Bennett, 1999). Hand and Sanchez (2000) argued that children are taught gender roles early in life and that their view of power is inherently tied to this socialization. Hand and Sanchez suggested that this key construct should not be overlooked. Of the limited research that has investigated why students sexually harass other students, the most frequently given reasons dismiss the students' own actions as being normal, funny, or stupid (Hill & Kearl, 2011).

Notwithstanding the concerns of defining and measuring peer sexual harassment, studies have provided insight into the various dynamics, risk factors, and ramifications of experiencing peer sexual harassment. Similar to victims of workplace harassment, victims of peer sexual harassment are predominantly female, while most perpetrators are male (Chiodo et al., 2009; Clodfelter, Turner, Hartman, & Kuhns, 2010; Fineran & Bennett, 1999; Hill & Kearl, 2011; Hill & Silva, 2005). Incidents are more likely to occur in locations where victims spend more time (Clodfelter et al.; Hill & Silva) without the presence of a teacher or potential guardian (Lichty & Campbell, 2012). Also, the nature of the harassing behavior differs across gender, as males most frequently report being called homophobic names and having their perceived or actual sexual orientation targeted (Fineran & Bennett, 1999), whereas females are repeatedly subjected to unwelcome sexual comments, jokes, or gestures (Chiodo et al.; Hill & Kearl; Hill & Silva). Additionally, perpetrators of sexual harassment often engage in other types of behaviors such as bullying and dating violence (Miller et al., 2013).

Another significant finding is that adolescent and young adult females suffer more negative consequences from being sexually harassed compared to males (Boivin et al., 2012; Chiodo et al., 2009; Hand & Sanchez, 2000; Hill & Kearl, 2011; Hill & Silva, 2005). For example, Chiodo et al. found that females who were sexually harassed by the ninth grade were more likely to have suicidal thoughts and engage in self-destructive behaviors. Goldstein, Malanchuk, Davis-Kean, and Eccles (2007) suggested that victimization among females may increase substance use, lower self-esteem, and lead to various mental health issues. The general finding that the effects of sexual harassment are more serious for females supports the belief that females are more cognizant of and sensitive to sexual harassment.

Various studies have explored risk factors and correlates of peer sexual harassment victimization (Boivin et al., 2012; Goldstein et al., 2007; Miller et al., 2013; Ormerod et al., 2008). Prevalent factors include low self-esteem (Ormerod et al.), early pubertal development (Goldstein et al.; Hill & Kearl, 2011), involvement with problem behaviors (Goldstein et al.), sexual orientation (Hill & Silva, 2005), and an environment perceived to condone sexual harassment (Ormerod et al., 2008). Additionally, prior sexual harassment has been shown to be related to future incidents of sexual harassment and other types of victimization and perpetration (Boivin et al.; Chiodo et al., 2009; Clodfelter et al., 2010). More specifically, Boivin et al. concluded that being the victim of both peer sexual harassment and dating violence increased hostility among females and influenced the perpetration of physical dating violence. Meanwhile, Chiodo et al. suggested that both males and females sexually harassed in ninth grade were significantly more likely to be revictimized later in high school and had increased risk of dating-violence victimization. Also, both studies found that prior victimization increased emotional distress, more so for males, which may influence future behaviors (Boivin et al.; Chiodo et al.).

The current understanding of peer sexual harassment among adolescents and young adults indicates that young individuals experience sexual harassment in similar ways as do adults. Females are predominantly targeted, and males are most commonly the perpetrators. Differences across gender emerge beyond the role of victim or perpetrator. The nature of the victimization is distinctly different for females. Further, females incur more consequences than males. Additionally, the prevalent risk factors (e.g., physical features, self-esteem, perceived sexual orientation) are present across other groups of sexual harassment victims.

Moving forward, ample opportunities exist to contribute to the overall understanding of adolescent and young-adult sexual harassment. The body of research would greatly benefit from prospective studies that measure attitudes, experiences, and consequences over a longer period of time. Such studies would be further valuable when framed in a theoretical context. For example, some studies have tested whether routine activities theory is applicable to sexual harassment among emerging adults in person (Clodfelter et al., 2010) as well as online (Marcum, Higgins, & Ricketts, 2010). Additionally, it is vital to explore the existence and effectiveness of sexual harassment awareness and prevention programs that may be offered in secondary schools.

Sexual Harassment via Social Media

Contemporary culture, especially among adolescents and young adults, has embraced the plethora of social media options that are available to communicate with others. This is evidenced by the popularity of text messaging, Facebook, and Twitter. This rapid growth in utilization may have challenged the ability of social science to swiftly and systematically assess the influence of social media on sexual harassment perpetration and victimization. However, the body of literature specifically addressing sexual harassment across different types of social media has grown (e.g., Barak, 2005; Hill & Kearl, 2011; Mainiero & Jones, 2013; Marcum et al., 2010).

Exploration of this avenue of sexual harassment has typically focused on specific behaviors such as unwanted sexual solicitation and/or receipt of unwanted sexually explicit materials, including pornography (Finn, 2004; Marcum et al., 2010; Mitchell, Finkelhor, Wolak, Ybarra, & Turner, 2011; Mitchell, Wolak, & Finkelhor, 2007, 2008; Ybarra & Mitchell, 2008). Few studies have used a more exhaustive measure of sexual harassment (Biber, Doverspike, Baznik, Cober, & Ritter, 2002; Hill & Kearl, 2011). Furthermore, other research has examined online harassment but has not specified whether the nature of the harassment was sexual or nonsexual (Priebe & Svedin, 2012; Ybarra & Mitchell, 2004).

Of the available estimates, most were obtained from a limited number of data sources. Most recently, Mitchell et al. (2011) utilized the National Survey of Children's Exposure to Violence that surveyed the experiences of 10- to 17-year-olds in 2008. Comparing incidents of online and offline sexual harassment, Mitchell et al. reported that 3% of students had received unwanted online sexual solicitations in the past year (5% lifetime), while 6% had been sexually harassed offline in the past year (9% lifetime). Earlier, Mitchell and her various colleagues analyzed the Youth Internet Safety Survey that focused on 10- to 17-year-olds in 2000 and 2005. Those results indicated that the receipt of unwanted sexual solicitation declined from 19% in 2000 to 13% in 2005, while unwanted exposure to explicit materials increased from 25% to 34% (Mitchell et al., 2007, 2008). Meanwhile, Ybarra and her collaborators assessed the Growing Up With Media Survey, which targeted 10- to 15-year-olds in 2006. Unwanted sexual solicitation was received by 15% of the students in the past year, and 3% of the respondents reported perpetrating the solicitations (Ybarra et al., 2007, 2008).

Aside from those primary sources of data, Finn (2004) found that among college students, the prevalence of receiving unwanted explicit materials, specifically pornography, was 58.7%. Additionally, Hill and Kearl (2011) reported that approximately 30% of students indicated that they were subjected to various types of online sexual harassment, not including unwanted sexual solicitation or exposure to explicit materials. Overall, one can glean from this limited body of literature that the prevalence of receiving unwanted sexual solicitation ranged from 3% to 15%, while more students reported receiving unwanted sexually explicit materials, with estimates ranging from 25% to 58.7%. Upward of 30% of students were also victimized by other types of online sexual harassment. It must be highlighted that these studies only focused on a few select types of behaviors.

In addition to prevalence estimates, various studies examined the different types of social media to explore whether their use increased a person's risk of victimization. As may be expected, those considered to be extensive online users in general were more likely to be victimized than less frequent Internet users (Marcum et al., 2010; Mitchell et al., 2008). However, some types of interaction increased the risk. For example, Ybarra and Mitchell (2008) found that sexual harassment, particularly unwanted sexual solicitation, more frequently occurred in chat rooms and through instant messaging (IM) compared to on social networking sites. Ybarra and Mitchell also found that among those who reported frequent unwanted solicitations, email was the most common means of communication. Mitchell and her colleagues (2008) also questioned whether blogging specifically increased the risk of victimization. They found that online users who blogged were no more likely to receive unwanted sexual solicitations but were more likely to be targeted for nonsexual harassment.

Some research closely examines the overlap between victimization and perpetration (Ybarra, Espelage, & Mitchell, 2007) as well as between online and offline victimization (Hill & Kearl, 2011; Mitchell et al., 2011) across different types of behaviors. In conformance to crime patterns among the general population, perpetrators do not seem to specialize in certain types of behaviors; for instance, they do not engage only in unwanted sexual solicitations (Piquero, Jennings, & Barnes, 2012). Ybarra et al. indicated that perpetrators of online sexual harassment are also engaged in other types of online victimization and were recipients of various unwanted online behaviors as well. This finding is consistent with other research that suggests that perpetrators are often also victims (Fagan & Mazerolle, 2011).

When Mitchell et al. (2011) further explored the overlap of victimization, they found that online victims (i.e., victims of nonsexual harassment and unwanted sexual solicitation) more often experienced offline sexual victimization compared to other types of offline victimizations. More clearly, those who were sexually victimized offline were more likely to be targets online (Mitchell et al.). This evidence is supported by Hill and Kearl's (2011) study of high school students, as they also found a considerable overlap among cyber victims and in-person victims. Together, these findings further demonstrate the widely accepted belief that once a person is victimized, particularly as an adolescent or young adult, he or she is at greater risk of being victimized again by the same or a different offense (Fagan & Mazerolle, 2011; Lauritsen & Quinet, 1995; Tseloni & Pease, 2003).

Research has also applied different theoretical perspectives to sexual harassment that occurs online or through methods such as text messaging (Barak, 2005; Marcum et al., 2010). Using social media as a conduit to perpetrating harassment is attractive for many reasons. According to routine activities theory, motivated offenders will select targets who are attractive and lack protection (Cohen & Felson, 1979). A recent study utilizing this theoretical perspective specific to online sexual harassment highlights that high school seniors and college freshmen are more susceptible to unwanted sexual solicitation and sexually explicit material (i.e., pornography) when engaged in various computer-mediated communication (CMC) methods (Marcum et al.). More specifically, for high school students, the risk of receiving both unwanted sexual solicitations and pornography is significantly related to their use of chat rooms (Marcum et al.). Meanwhile, college freshmen are at greater risk for both types of harassment when they engage in online communication. Other behaviors, such as providing information to online contacts, also increase students' likelihood of victimization. Individuals of this age may be less capable of identifying and responding to unwanted online sexual advances. In addition, social media is more likely to be used by adolescents and young adults. Taken together, harassers have greater access to victims who may be perceived as easier targets.

A second theoretical perspective specifically addresses why perpetrators may find online forums more appealing. In this phenomenon, known as the online disinhibition effect (Barak, 2005), some perpetrators become their true selves when interacting online because they have less fear of identification, can enter and leave communication forums (e.g., chat rooms, social media networks) quickly, and can more easily treat people with disregard than when engaged in face-to-face communications. The perceived ability to interact more freely online may increase motivation to engage in unwanted sexual behaviors. Theories such as routine activities theory generally assume the offender's motivation, so less scholarly attention is devoted to understanding this aspect of the victimization or criminal event (Maxfield, 1987). Therefore, study of the online disinhibition effect may lend insight into why an offender decides to engage in this particular type of behavior.

The online disinhibition effect may also relate to deterrence theory, which posits that individuals weigh the consequences of their actions (i.e., formal and informal sanctions) before engaging in behavior and that the perceived certainty of being apprehended is a vital factor in the decision-making process (Nagin & Pogarsky, 2006). Thus, offenders who have less fear of being caught may not be deterred by sanctions. Furthermore, the fear of formal sanctioning may be irrelevant to an online sexual harasser, as few laws currently address online harassment, particularly across differing national and international jurisdictions (Barak, 2005).

Due to the abundant usage of texting and various social media, it is logical that individuals use these outlets to engage in sexually harassing behaviors. While many of the impacts of and influences on this behavior are still left to be explored, the available research contributes a considerable amount of empirical insight. First, even after only examining a few behaviors consistent with the general definition of sexual harassment, the prevalence of sexual harassment is concerning. Second, only certain types of social media (i.e., chat rooms and instant messaging) are significantly related to victimization. Particularly with chat rooms, a lack of face-to-face contact and, possibly, unknown identity contribute to this type of victimization. Further, there is overlap across online and offline victimization as well as perpetrator and victim roles.

Future research can expand upon existing studies in numerous ways. A valuable avenue would be to implement a prospective design that compares the onset, frequency, and desistance of sexual harassment experiences to those of other types of behaviors consistent with the developmental period. Furthermore, information should be collected for an exhaustive list of behaviors that are delineated as online and offline. Also, the responses to sexual harassment victimization and perpetration should be thoroughly examined in the context of personal attitudes and beliefs about sexual harassment. In sum, research efforts should seek to uncover the process of socialization that accepts such online and offline behaviors.

Same-Sex Harassment

The pervasiveness of same-sex sexual harassment (SSSH) is not as well known compared to the more studied realm of cross-sex sexual harassment (CSSH). Many factors contribute to the previously scant attention paid to SSSH. First, traditional views maintained that sexual harassment was predominantly experienced by female victims and was perpetrated by males in an attempt to maintain male dominance (Maass, Cadinu, Guarnieri, & Grasselli, 2003). Males who were victimized by other males were unsuccessful in seeking legal recourse, as the courts argued that unwanted sexual behaviors between males did not meet the sexual harassment criteria (Fineran, 2002). Furthermore, harassment that was sexual in nature but occurred between gay or lesbian parties was also rejected, as sexual orientation was not considered a protected class (Waldo, Berdahl, & Fitzgerald, 1998). However, in 1998, the Supreme Court rebuked the exclusions previously applied to victims of SSSH in the landmark case *Oncale v. Sundowner Offshore Services, Inc.,* 523 U.S. 75. Specifically, the Supreme Court ruled that SSSH is sexual harassment, regardless of whether the harasser is motivated by sexual desire, and that victims of sexual harassment are protected by Title VII. Furthermore, the Court's decision mandated that the harassing behaviors in question meet the definition of sex discrimination, regardless of the sexual orientation of the harasser or the victim, and that the context of the situation must be carefully evaluated.

Another limitation of SSSH research is the fact that until recently, empirical studies did not investigate SSSH to the same extent as CSSH (DeSouza & Solberg, 2004; DuBois, Knapp, Faley, & Kustis, 1998; Waldo et al., 1998). Earlier studies often only examined female experiences with CSSH in academic and workplace contexts, and as a by-product of this limited perspective, measurement instruments were not readily available to study male experiences, whether they were same-sex or cross-sex (Waldo et al.). However, SSSH research began appearing more frequently around the same time as *Oncale v. Sundowner,* and contemporary investigations not only ascertain prevalence estimates but also seek to understand the similarities and differences between SSSH and CSSH (Castillo, Muscarella, & Szuchman, 2011; DeSouza, Solberg, & Elder, 2007; Goldberg & Zhang, 2004; Hill & Silva, 2005; Rock et al., 2011).

Not only do society and the courts tend not to acknowledge victims of SSSH and the social sciences have limited ability to study SSSH, but SSSH incidents are underreported. It is commonly known that sexual victimization is generally grossly underreported (Fisher, Cullen, & Turner, 2000). A lack of reporting stems from factors such as a lack of understanding among victims of the nature of the incident, a belief among victims that the authorities will not believe them or take them seriously, or embarrassment (Fisher et al.). Furthermore, the perception of being a victim strongly influences whether one will report an encounter. In regard to sexual harassment, females are more likely to report incidents than are males, as females are believed to be more sensitized to this particular form of victimization and are more likely to identify unwelcome behaviors as harassment (DeSouza et al, 2007; Wilson, 2000). However, females are less likely to report minor forms of sexual harassment (Fitzgerald & Ormerod, 1991) and often endure harassment for a period of time before reporting it (Hébert, 2007). When males report sexual harassment, particularly SSSH, it is often in relation to their actual or perceived sexual orientation (Hill & Silva, 2005).

Several similarities emerge between SSSH and CSSH from the growing body of research. A common finding is that men are most commonly the perpetrator of sexual harassment, regardless of whether their victim is male or female (Hill & Silva, 2005; Rock et al., 2011; Waldo et al., 1998). Moreover, the concept of power is attributed to male-perpetrated SSSH as well as CSSH (DuBois et al., 1998). For example, DuBois and her colleagues investigated the differing circumstances of female and male workplace victimization across male and female perpetrators. They concluded that male victims of SSSH were often targeted by older males in positions of greater power and were more likely to not report in order to avoid being given negative labels by their superiors. Other harassers use their perceived power to retain the traditional hierarchy of heterosexual male dominance and their beliefs regarding the appropriate roles of males and females (Maass et al., 2003). For example, male SSSH victims most frequently report incidents of homophobic name-calling and the use of homophobic slurs due to their perceived sexual orientation, even if they are not homosexual (Hill & Kearl, 2011; Hill & Silva). The dynamic of female-to-female sexual harassment has yet to be fully explored, but it may also be informed by the explanations offered by Maass et al.

Another interesting commonality between SSSH and CSSH is the perception of victimization when accounting for physical attractiveness. When an alleged perpetrator is perceived as attractive, he or she is seen as less likely to engage in harassing behaviors (Wuensch & Moore, 2004). Furthermore, if the victim is seen as unattractive, the belief that harassment occurred declines (Wuensch & Moore). Similarly, in recent research conducted by Castillo et al. (2011), SSSH perpetrators were less likely to be perceived as harassing when observers considered the perpetrator to be attractive, and the effect was greater for male observers compared to female observers.

Overall, the expansion of same-sex sexual harassment literature in recent years has broadened the unique understanding of sexual harassment that occurs between members of the same sex. However, major gaps still exist. For example, female-to-female sexual harassment is understudied, as most of the attention is paid to males. Further, sexual harassment among same-sex sexual minorities, defined as those who are attracted to the same sex or who identify as gay, lesbian, or bisexual (Berlan, Corliss, Field, Goodman, & Austin, 2010), is currently insufficient. Future research would benefit tremendously by exploring these additional dynamics.

Stranger Harassment

While perpetrators and victims of sexual harassment often know each other, harassing behavior is also committed by strangers (Wesselman & Kelly, 2010), and evidence suggests that stranger harassment may be more prevalent than non-stranger harassment (Fairchild & Rudman, 2008; Macmillan et al., 2000). And yet, research regarding unwanted public sexual advances by strangers as a form of sexual harassment is limited. Fairchild and Rudman argued that the lack of attention to this type of victimization is due to its perceived social acceptability and the lack of formal consequences should a victim want to pursue any type of recourse.

Early research considers sexual objectification as a form of sexual harassment (Gruber, 1992), whereas more recent studies view objectification as a component of both stranger harassment and sexual harassment (Fairchild & Rudman, 2008). Objectification is summarized as the treatment of a person as merely a sexual object that is to be used for the enjoyment of others (Fredrickson & Roberts, 1997). Fredrickson and Roberts described objectification as gazing or visually inspecting another's body, and they contended that the victim may internalize the underlying intention of the behavior and eventually view himself or herself in this sexualized manner. More simply, victims may begin to accept and embrace the bestowed sexual status and further perpetuate the perception, even if they are not consciously aware of their actions (Fredrickson & Roberts).

Although it is beyond the scope of this review to thoroughly discuss the manifestation of sexual objectification across many facets of contemporary culture, it is vital to explore how sexual objectification may influence sexual harassment and other forms of sexual violence. Blame, an important aspect of victimization, is directly and indirectly related to sexual objectification (Calogero, 2013; Fredrickson & Roberts, 1997; Loughnan, Pina, Vasquez, & Puvia, 2013). Loughnan et al. (2013) explored conditions in which observers place blame on rape victims and concluded that victims who are sexualized or who are defined as physically attractive or dressed provocatively are treated differently than nonsexualized victims. More specifically, male and female observers demonstrate less concern about the objectified victim's well-being or suffering than about the well-being or suffering of the nonobjectified victim (Loughnan et al.). Further, Loughnan et al. found that observers blame the objectified victim more than the nonobjectified victim. Although the topic of rape victim blame has been extensively studied, this particular study reminds readers how observers can minimize the blame that should be placed on the perpetrator and transfer it to victims who are viewed as relatively sexual.

Blame is placed on victims not only by outsiders/observers of situations of sexual harassment but also by themselves (Fairchild & Rudman, 2008; Fredrickson & Roberts, 1997). As stated previously, victim blaming is not a novel area of research. However, understanding the process in which sexual objectification leads to self-objectification and ultimately self-blame is important in the realm of sexual harassment, whether the perpetrator is a stranger or known to the victim. Fairchild and Rudman suggested that because objectification by strangers is commonplace and dismissed as a trivial aspect of life, the detrimental effects of the behavior are little understood. Their study concludes that victims of sexual harassment by strangers are more likely than victims of non-stranger sexual harassment to internalize the sexualized treatment and are more likely to blame themselves or react passively to the behaviors. This reaction commonly reduces the likelihood that the victim will report the incident. Self-objectification may also be related to other negative outcomes such as anxiety, depression, eating disorders, and sexual dysfunction (Fredrickson & Roberts) that may add further complexity to the understanding of sexual harassment. Moreover, other research argues that self-objectification hinders efforts to advance social equity if victims internalize and ultimately embrace the sexual status assigned to them by society (Calogero, 2013). This act of perceived acceptance may bolster the belief that objectification and stranger harassment are simply a part of life.

Various studies suggest that stranger harassment and objectification have considerable influence on victims' perception of safety and safety anxiety (Fairchild & Rudman, 2008; Fredrickson & Roberts, 1997; Macmillan et al., 2000). For example, Macmillan et al. compared victims' accounts of stranger harassment to accounts of non-stranger harassment. Victims of stranger harassment report experiencing a higher frequency of incidents and types of behaviors, resulting in a greater fear of sexual victimization, than do victims of non-stranger harassment. Fairchild and Rudman extended this finding by exploring the types of coping strategies in relation to self-objectification and concluded that victims who internalize and self-blame are more likely to fear sexual victimization, particularly rape. On the other hand, victims who actively confront their harassers are less likely internalize objectification and to fear rape or sexual victimization.

An important aspect of stranger harassment research is the repeated finding that sexual advances by strangers are not always viewed as harassment (Fairchild, 2010; Fairchild & Rudman, 2008; Fredrickson & Roberts, 1997). Specifically, the victim's perception of behavior is key, given that behaviors that are considered unwanted by some may be welcomed by others. Further, the same behavior committed by different people may be not be perceived similarly by the same person (Fairchild). Fairchild argued that context is important in shaping a victim's perception of stranger harassment. For example, her study asked participants to reflect upon their own experiences as well as to envision themselves as the victim in a hypothetical situation. She concluded that behaviors are more likely to be seen as harassing if the stranger is unattractive and older; if the incident occurs at night and in a public place such as a street, on public transportation, or in a public park; and if the victim is alone. However, if the behavior occurs in the daytime in a bar or restaurant and the perpetrator is young and attractive, it is considered a more enjoyable interaction related to flirting.

Fairchild's (2010) study, as well as the other findings presented herein, reinforces the applicability of routine activities theory in understanding the occurrence of stranger harassment. According to routine activities theory, victimization is more likely to occur when the target is viewed as suitable and does not have proper guardianship (Cohen & Felson, 1979). Particularly important in this conceptual framework is the perception of vulnerability and how it relates to target suitability and guardianship. Stranger harassment occurs in public places when the victim is most likely alone (Fairchild & Rudman, 2008; Fredrickson & Roberts, 1997; Macmillan et al., 2000). Further, the victim must perceive the actions of the stranger as unwanted, as in the case of lewd comments made by an older or unattractive man (Fairchild). How a victim copes with harassment may influence the aggressor's perception of vulnerability, in that those who actively respond to the harasser may seem less susceptible and more capable of defending themselves. Yet, those who do not respond or passively respond to sexual advances may increase their risk for further and perhaps escalated forms of harassment if the perpetrator views them as weak or an easy target (Fairchild & Rudman). This is particularly concerning if nonresponse is due to safety anxiety related to objectification. According to Campbell (2005), safety anxiety is specifically capitalized on in crime prevention efforts to induce potential victims to change their behaviors to avoid what otherwise could result in an inevitable sexual victimization. For example, a common recommendation on college campuses is to walk in pairs at night or in remote areas. By adopting this crime prevention technique, intended targets may be able to dissuade an offender from engaging in sexually harassing behaviors.

Other research examining the role of the harasser has found support for routine activities theory. For example, Wesselmann and Kelly (2010) found that college males were more likely to perpetrate stranger harassment when they were in a group. The group dynamic provided a sense of anonymity as well as support from the other group members. This situational context could increase an individual's motivation to engage in the behavior when the individual(s) might not engage in such behavior when alone. Furthermore, the intended target might decline to actively react to a group and thus increase the perception of vulnerability.

In sum, sexual harassment committed by strangers is estimated to be more prevalent than harassment occurring between known parties. However, this type of behavior has been generally overlooked by society as just a part of life. This is reflected in a lack of laws to protect victims or allow them to seek recourse. Stranger harassment is argued to have an effect on victims that is equal to if not more severe than that of traditional sexual harassment. An area of exploration distinct to stranger harassment is its relationship to perceived safety and safety anxiety. Studies investigating victimization by perpetrators known to victims generally do not inquire about victims' level of fear of other types of sexual victimization.

Researchers are urged to fully explore stranger harassment within the context of sexual harassment. Numerous existing studies (such as Clodfelter et al., 2010) are likely to have captured the relationship between the victim and perpetrator without focusing on the comparison of known offenders and unknown offenders. Within the context of this review, exploration of stranger harassment across adolescents and young adults, social media, and same-sex interactions would be highly informative in determining whether perceptions and reactions differ according to the status of the offender. Further, stranger harassment should be explored from developmental and situational perspectives to discern whether victims respond differently across time periods and contexts.

Discussion

Until recently, sexual harassment that occurs in the workplace and academia has dominated the overall body of literature. Meanwhile, harassment that occurs among peers and online and that is committed by members of the same sex and by strangers has been less extensively studied. Therefore, this review has aimed to provide a comprehensive overview of these specific topics and to draw parallels with what is commonly understood about traditional perspectives of sexual harassment.

The various dynamics reviewed herein are not mutually exclusive, and advancing knowledge in one realm will further expand understanding of another. For example, continued exploration of sexual harassment that occurs in chat rooms is likely to reveal a considerable percentage of perpetrators who are not known to the victim. Given that adolescents commonly use chat rooms and other types of social media, their risk for online victimization by strangers increases. Likewise, how they respond to these situations may shape their reactions if they experience face-to-face or offline victimization. For example, if the adolescent casually dismisses such behaviors or internalizes self-blame, then a level of acceptance may influence passivity toward more serious types of sexual harassment or sexual victimization.

Also, advancing research in these areas is vital given the overwhelming access youths have to both social media and sexualized materials. If acceptance of such behaviors is due to socialization, it is imperative to seek a broader understanding of the age-related and situational context of the transmission of beliefs about gender roles and acceptable treatment of others based on gender. This insight could assist in the development and implementation of awareness and prevention programs aimed at reducing the motivation to sexually harass others and increase active responses against victimization. Further, because it is now understood that stranger harassment has a detrimental impact on victims, educational programs should expand their discussion to include this dynamic, as strangers now have greater access to youth than ever before.

Numerous recommendations can be made for future research across these topics. First, to determine any causal relationships, researchers must strive to engage in longitudinal studies that fully measure the concept(s) in question. Currently, studies are limited by cross-sectional data that often measure only a subset of behaviors. Furthermore, studies should expand their focus to examine the various relationship dynamics between victim and perpetrator across gender and sexual orientation. Improvements can also be made by investigating the overlap of online and offline victimization involved in not only sexual harassment but also other, related behaviors (e.g., sexual assault, stalking and cyberstalking, dating violence). Additionally, a better understanding of the potential overlap of victims and perpetrators is warranted. A final recommendation is to explore the applicability of various theoretical perspectives to sexual harassment victimization and perpetration across the multiple types of sexual harassment.

Conclusion

Considerable attention is paid to sexual harassment that occurs in the workplace and in academia. The types of sexual harassment commonly recognized are quid pro quo and hostile work environment. However, less is understood about the nature and extent of sexual harassment as well as the negative consequences associated with peer sexual harassment among adolescents and young adults, stranger harassment, and sexual harassment committed by those of the same sex.

As the use of social media rapidly increases, the body of literature regarding the potentially negative consequences of online consumption is also expanding. Prevalent concerns are the ease of navigation across different online forums, the ability to remain anonymous and avoid detection, and the ability to target young and potentially naïve users. Although existing research demonstrates that online sexual harassment is prevalent, more comprehensive and rigorous exploration is needed.

Populations often overlooked in the body of sexual harassment research have recently become the focus of numerous avenues of research. For example, greater interest is being given to adolescent sexual harassment and its distinction from bullying. However, explanations of the intent of individuals of this age to engage in this type of sexual aggression are sparse. Furthermore, how being sexually harassed at an early age can lead to serious outcomes such as poor self-esteem, self-objectification, and self-inflicted physical harm is not fully understood.

Other realms of emerging research include sexual harassment committed by strangers and those of the same sex regardless of the sexual orientation of the victim and harasser. Some research suggests that victimization by a stranger can potentially cause greater harm than unwanted behaviors committed by someone known to the victim. However, this limited body of research also recognizes the importance of factors such as victim perception in determining whether the sexually aggressive behavior is deemed unwanted or desirable. Meanwhile, even less is known about same-sex sexual harassment, as this type of harassment was not legally recognized until 15 years ago. Therefore, expanding this avenue of research is critical. Overall, as previously overlooked populations are garnering interest, it is imperative for researchers to engage in thorough and innovative investigations to broaden the overall understanding of sexual harassment.

Discussion Questions

1. Among adolescents and young adults, how can the intent of sexually harassing behaviors be adequately examined?

2. Research suggests that experiencing sexual harassment from peers reduces self-esteem and leads to other negative consequences, particularly for young females. What are some types of initiatives that could appropriately address this type of victimization?

3. The use of social media is rapidly growing and provides greater opportunities for victimization of youth and adults alike. In a society that generally accepts some degree of unwanted sexual attention and behaviors, how can awareness be raised to inform social media users of the seriousness of this type of behavior?

References

Barak, A. (2005). Sexual harassment on the Internet. *Social Science Computer Review, 23*(1), 77–92. doi:10.1177/0894439304271540

Berlan, E. D., Corliss, H. L., Field, A. E., Goodman, E., & Bryn Austin, S. (2010). Sexual orientation and bullying among adolescents in the Growing Up Today Study. *Journal of Adolescent Health, 46*(4), 366–371. doi:10.1016.j.jadohealth.2009.10.015

Biber, J. K., Doverspike, D., Baznik, D., Cober, A., & Ritter, B. A. (2002). Sexual harassment in online communications: Effects of gender and discourse medium. *CyberPsychology & Behavior, 5*(1), 33–42.

Birdeau, D. R., Somers, C. L., & Lenihan, G. O. (2005). Effects of educational strategies on college students' identification of sexual harassment. *Education, 125*(3), 496–510.

Boivin, S., Lavoie, F., Hébert, M., & Gagné, M-H. (2012). Past victimizations and dating violence perpetration in adolescence: The mediating role of emotional distress and hostility. *Journal of Interpersonal Violence, 27*(4), 662–684. doi:10.1177/0886260511423245

Bursik, K., & Gefter, J. (2011). Still stable after all these years: Perceptions of sexual harassment in academic contexts. *The Journal of Social Psychology, 151*(3), 331–349.

Calogero, R. M. (2013). Objects don't object: Evidence that self-objectification disrupts women's social activism. *Psychological Science.* Advance online publication. doi:10.1177/0956797612452574

Campbell, A. (2005). Keeping the "lady" safe: The regulation of femininity through crime prevention literature. *Critical Criminology, 13*, 119–140. doi:10.1007/s10612-005-2390-z

Cass, S. A., Levett, L. M., & Kovera, M. B. (2010). The effects of harassment severity and organizational behavior on damage awards in a hostile work environmental sexual harassment case. *Behavioral Sciences and the Law, 28*, 303–321. doi:10.1002/bsl.886

Castillo, Y., Muscarella, F., & Szuchman, L. T. (2011). Gender differences in college students' perceptions of same-sex sexual harassment: The influence of physical attractiveness and attitudes toward lesbians and gay men. *Journal of College Student Development, 52*(5), 511–522. doi:1353/csd.2011.0070

Charmaraman, L., Jones, A. E., Stein, N., & Espelage, D. L. (2013). Is it bullying or sexual harassment? Knowledge, attitudes, and professional development experiences in middle school staff. *Journal of School Health, 83*(6), 438–444. doi:10.1111/josh.12048

Chiodo, D., Wolfe, D. A., Crooks, C., Hughes, R., & Jaffe, P. (2009). Impact of sexual harassment victimization by peers on subsequent adolescent victimization and adjustment: A longitudinal study. *Journal of Adolescent Health, 45*(3), 246–252. doi:10.1016.j.jado health.2009.01.006

Clodfelter, T. A., Turner, M. G., Hartman, J. L., & Kuhns, J. B. (2010). Sexual harassment victimization during emerging adulthood: A test of routine activities theory and a general theory of crime. *Crime & Delinquency, 56*(3), 455–481. doi:10.1177/0011128708324665

Cohen, L. E., & Felson, M. (1979). Social change and crime rate trends: A routine activity approach. *American Sociological Review, 44*(4), 588–608.

Cortina, L. M., Swan, S., Fitzgerald, L. F., & Waldo, C. (1998). Sexual harassment and assault: Chilling the climate for women in academia. *Psychology of Women Quarterly, 22*(3), 419–441.

DeSouza, E., & Solberg, J. (2004). Women's and men's reactions to man-to-man sexual harassment: Does the sexual orientation of the victim matter? *Sex Roles, 50*(9/10), 623–639.

DeSouza, E. R., Solberg, J., & Elder, C. (2007). A cross-cultural perspective on judgments of woman-to-woman sexual harassment: Does orientation matter? *Sex Roles, 56*(7), 457–471. doi:10.1007/s11199-007-9184-6

DuBois, C. L. Z., Knapp, D. E., Faley, R. H., & Kustis, G. A. (1998). An empirical examination of same- and other-gender sexual harassment in the workplace. *Sex Roles, 39*(9/10), 731–749.

Fagan, A. A., & Mazerolle, P. (2011). Repeat offending and repeat victimization: Assessing similarities and differences in psychosocial risk factors. *Crime & Delinquency, 57*(5), 732–755. doi:10.1177/0011128708321322

Fairchild, K. (2010). Context effects on women's perceptions of stranger harassment. *Sexuality & Culture, 14,* 191–216. doi:10.1007/s12119-010-9070-1

Fairchild, K., & Rudman, L. A. (2008). Everyday stranger harassment and women's objectification. *Social Justice Research, 21,* 338–357. doi:10.1007/s11211-008-0073-0

Fineran, S. (2002). Sexual harassment between same-sex peers: Intersection of mental health, homophobia, and sexual violence in schools. *Social Work, 47*(1), 65–74.

Fineran, S., & Bennett, L. (1999). Gender and power issues of peer sexual harassment among teenagers. *Journal of Interpersonal Violence, 14*(6), 626–641. doi:10.1177/088626099014006004

Finn, J. (2004). A survey of online harassment at a university campus. *Journal of Interpersonal Violence, 19*(4), 468–483. doi:10.1177/0886260503262083

Firestone, J. M., Miller, J. M., & Harris, R. (2012). Implications for criminal justice from the 2002 and 2006 Department of Defense Gender Relations and Sexual Harassment surveys. *American Journal of Criminal Justice, 37*(3), 432–451. doi:10.1007/s12103-010-9085-z

Fisher, B. S., Cullen, F. T., & Turner, M. G. (2000). *The sexual victimization of college women.* Washington, DC: U.S. Department of Justice, National Institute of Justice. Retrieved from https://www.ncjrs.gov/pdffiles1/nij/182369.pdf

Fitzgerald, L. F., & Ormerod, A. J. (1991). Perceptions of sexual harassment: The influence of gender and academic context. *Psychology of Women Quarterly, 15*(2), 281–294.

Fitzgerald, L., Swan, S., & O'Donohue, W. (1997). But was it really sexual harassment? Legal, behavioral, and psychological definitions of the workplace victimization of women. In W. O'Donohue (Ed.), *Sexual harassment: Theory, research, and treatment* (pp. 5–28). Boston, MA: Allyn & Bacon.

Fredrickson, B. L., & Roberts, T. (1997). Objectification theory: Toward understanding women's lived experiences and mental health risks. *Psychology of Women Quarterly, 21*(2), 173–206. doi:10.1111/j.1471-6402.1997.tb00108.x

Goldberg, C., & Zhang, L. (2004). Simple and joint effects of gender and self-esteem on responses to same-sex sexual harassment. *Sex Roles, 50*(11/12), 823–833.

Goldstein, S. E., Malanchuk, O., Davis-Kean, P. E., & Eccles, J. S. (2007). Risk factors of sexual harassment by peers: A longitudinal investigation of African American and European American adolescents. *Journal of Research on Adolescence, 17*(2), 285–300.

Gruber, J. E. (1992). A typology of personal and environmental sexual harassment: Research and policy implications for the 1990s. *Sex Roles, 26*(11/12), 447–464.

Hand, J. Z., & Sanchez, L. (2000). Badgering or bantering? Gender differences in experience of, and reactions to, sexual harassment among U.S. high school students. *Gender & Society, 14*(6), 718–746. doi:10.1177/089124300014006002

Hébert, L. C. (2007). Why don't "reasonable women" complain about sexual harassment? *Indiana Law Journal, 82*(3), 711–743.

Hershcovis, M. S., & Barling, J. (2010). Comparing victim attributions and outcomes for workplace aggression and sexual harassment. *Journal of Applied Psychology, 95*(5), 874–888. doi:10.1037/a0020070

Hill, C. A., & Kearl, H. (2011). *Crossing the line: Sexual harassment at school.* Washington, DC: AAUW Education Foundation.

Hill, C., & Silva, E. M. (2005). *Drawing the line: Sexual harassment on campus.* Washington, DC: AAUW Educational Foundation.

Huntley, J. E., & Constanzo, M. (2003). Sexual harassment stories: Testing a story-mediated model of juror decision-making in civil litigation. *Law and Human Behavior, 27*(1), 29–51.

Kulik, C. T., Perry, E. L., & Pepper, M. B. (2003). Here comes the judge: The influence of judge personal characteristics on federal sexual harassment case outcomes. *Law and Human Behavior, 27*(1), 69–86.

Lacasse, A., & Mendelson, M. J. (2006). The perceived intent of potentially offensive sexual behaviors among adolescents. *Journal of Research on Adolescence, 16*(2), 229–238.

Lauritsen, J. L., & Quinet, K. F. D. (1995). Repeat victimization among adolescents and young adults. *Journal of Quantitative Criminology, 11*(2), 143–166. doi:10.1007/BF02221121

Lichty, L. F., & Campbell, R. (2012). Targets and witnesses: Middle school students' sexual harassment experiences. *The Journal of Early Adolescence, 32*(3), 414–430. doi:10.1177/0272431610396090

Lipson, J. (2001). *Hostile hallways: Bullying, teasing, and sexual harassment in school.* Washington, DC: AAUW Educational Foundation.

Loughnan, S., Pina, A., Vasquez, E. A., & Puvia, E. (2013). Sexual objectification increases rape victim blame and decreases perceived suffering. *Psychology of Women Quarterly.* Advanced online publication. doi:10.1177/0361684313485718

Maass, A., Cadinu, M., Guarnieri, G., & Grasselli, A. (2003). Sexual harassment under social identity threat: The computer harassment paradigm. *Journal of Personality and Social Psychology, 85*(5), 853–870. doi:10.1037/0022-514.85.5.853

Macmillan, R., Nierobisz, A., & Welsh, S. (2000). Experiencing the streets: Harassment and perceptions of safety among women. *Journal of Research in Crime and Delinquency, 37*(3), 306–322. doi:10.1177/0022427800037003003

Mainiero, L. A., & Jones, K. J. (2013). Workplace romance 2.0: Developing a communication ethics model to address potential sexual harassment from inappropriate social media contacts between coworkers. *Journal of Business Ethics, 114*(2), 367–379. doi:10.1007/s10551-012-1349-8

Marcum, C. D., Higgins, G. E., & Ricketts, M. L. (2010). Potential factors of online victimization of youth: An examination of adolescent online behaviors utilizing routine activity theory. *Deviant Behavior, 31*(5), 381–410. doi:10.1080/01639620903004903

Maxfield, M. G. (1987). Lifestyle and routine activity theories of crime: Empirical studies of victimization, delinquency, and offender decision-making. *Journal of Quantitative Criminology, 3*(4), 275–282.

McDonald, P. (2012). Workplace sexual harassment 30 years on: A review of the literature. *International Journal of Management Reviews, 14*(1), 1–17. doi:10.1111/j.1468-2370.2011.00300.x

Miller, S., Williams, J., Cutbush, S., Gibbs, D., Clinton-Sherrod, M., & Jones, S. (2013). Dating violence, bullying, and sexual harassment: Longitudinal profiles and transitions over time. *Journal of Youth and Adolescence, 42*(4), 607–618. doi:10.1007/s10964-013-9914-8

Mitchell, K. J., Finkelhor, D., Wolak, J., Ybarra, M. L., & Turner, H. (2011). Youth internet victimization in a broader victimization context. *Journal of Adolescent Health, 48*(2), 128–134. doi:10.1016/j.jadohealth.2010.06.009

Mitchell, K. J., Wolak, J., & Finkelhor, D. (2007). Trends in youth reports of sexual solicitations, harassment, and unwanted exposure to pornography on the internet. *Journal of Adolescent Health, 40*(2), 116–126. doi:10.1016/j.jadohealth.2006.05.021

Mitchell, K. J., Wolak, J., & Finkelhor, D. (2008). Are blogs putting youth at risk for online sexual solicitation or harassment? *Child Abuse & Neglect, 32*(2), 277–294. doi:10.1016/j.chiabu.2007.04.015

Nagin, D. S., & Pogarsky, G. (2006). Integrating celerity, impulsivity, and extralegal sanction threats into a model of general deterrence: Theory and evidence. *Criminology, 39*(4), 865–892. doi:10.1111/j.1745-9125.2001.tb00943.x

O'Leary-Kelly, A. M., Bowes-Sperry, L., Bates, C. A., & Lean, E. R. (2009). Sexual harassment at work: A decade (plus) of progress. *Journal of Management, 35*(3), 503–536. doi:10.1177/0149206308330555

Oncale v. Sundowner Offshore Services, Inc., 523 U.S. 75 (1998).

Ormerod, A. J., Collinsworth, L. L., & Perry, L. A. (2008). Critical climate: Relations among sexual harassment, climate, and outcomes for high school girls and boys. *Psychology of Women Quarterly, 32*(2), 113–125. doi:10.1111/j.1471-6402.2008.00417.x

Piquero, A. R., Jennings, W. G., & Barnes, J. C. (2012). Violence in criminal careers: A review of the literature from a developmental life-course perspective. *Aggression and Violent Behavior, 17*(3), 171–179. doi:10.1016/j.avb.2012.02.008

Priebe, G., & Svedin, C. G. (2012). Online or off-line victimisation and psychological well-being: A comparison of sexual-minority and heterosexual youth. *European Child and Adolescent Psychiatry,* (21)*10*, 569–582. doi:10.1007/s00787-012-0294-5

Rock, L. M., Lipari, R. N., Cook, P. J., & Hale, A. D. (2011). *2010 Workplace and Gender Relations Survey of Active Duty Members: Overview report on sexual harassment.* Arlington, VA: Defense Manpower Data Center. Retrieved from http://www.dtic.mil/cgi-bin/GetTRDoc?AD=ADA541045

Sharkey, C. M. (2006). Dissecting damages: An empirical exploration of sexual harassment awards. *Journal of Empirical Legal Studies, 3*(1), 1–45.

Shute, R., Owens, L., & Slee, P. (2012). Everyday victimization of adolescent girls by boys: Sexual harassment, bullying or aggression? *Sex Roles, 58*(7), 477–489. doi:10.1007/s11199-007-9363-5

Tseloni, A., & Pease, K. (2003). Repeat personal victimization: "Boosts" or "Flags"? *British Journal of Criminology, 43*(1), 196–212. doi:10.1093/bjc/43.1.196

U.S. Department of Education (U.S. DOE), Office for Civil Rights. (2010). *Dear colleague letter.* Retrieved from http://www2.ed.gov/about/offices/list/ocr/letters/colleague-201010.pdf

U.S. Equal Employment Opportunity Commission (U.S. EEOC) (n.d.). Sexual Harassment. Retrieved from http://www.eeoc.gov/laws/types/sexual_harassment.cfm

Vijayasiri, G. (2008). Reporting sexual harassment: The importance of organizational culture and trust. *Gender Issues, 25*(1), 43–61. doi:10. 1007/s12147-008-9049-5

Waldo, C. R., Berdahl, J. L., & Fitzgerald, L. F. (1998). Are men sexually harassed? If so, by whom? *Law and Human Behavior, 22*(1), 59–79.

Wesselmann, E. D., & Kelly, J. R. (2010). Cat-calls and culpability: Investigating the frequency and function of stranger harassment. *Sex Roles, 63*(7–8), 451–462. doi:10.1007/s11199-010-9830-2

Wilson, F. (2000). The social construction of sexual harassment and assault of university students. *Journal of Gender Studies 9*(2), 171–187.

Wuensch, K. L., & Moore, C. H. (2004). Effects of physical attractiveness on evaluations of male employee's allegation of sexual harassment by his female employer. *The Journal of Social Psychology, 144*(2), 207–217.

Ybarra, M. L., Espelage, D. L., & Mitchell, K. J. (2007). The co-occurrence of Internet harassment and unwanted sexual solicitation victimization and perpetration: Associations with psychosocial indicators. *Journal of Adolescent health, 41*, 31–41. doi:10.1016/j.jadohealth.2007.09.010

Ybarra, M. L., & Mitchell, K. J. (2004). Online aggressor/targets, aggressors, and targets: A comparison of associated youth characteristics. *Journal of Child Psychology and Psychiatry, 45*(7), 1308–1316. doi:10.1111/j.1469-7610.2004.00328.x

Ybarra, M. L., & Mitchell, K. J. (2008). How risky are social networking sites? A comparison of places online where youth sexual solicitation and harassment occurs. *Pediatrics, 121*(2), 350–357. doi:10.1542/peds.2007-0693

Yoon, E., Funk, R. S., & Kropf, N. P. (2010). Sexual harassment experiences and their psychological correlates among a diverse sample of college women. *Affilia, 25*(1), 8–18. doi:10.1177/ 0886109909354979

5

Sexual Victimization Among Intimates

Tara N. Richards and Lauren Restivo

Prevalence of Sexual Violence Between Intimate Partners

Decades of research have demonstrated that intimate-partner violence, including sexual violence, is a pervasive problem (Tjaden & Thoennes, 2006). Although few studies have measured the prevalence of sexual violence between intimates separately from physical violence, the limited research has suggested that 40% to 50% of battered women also experience sexual assault (Bergen, 1996; Campbell & Soeken, 1999). Also, 18.3% of women in a recent nationally representative community sample reported rape, and 5.6% reported sexual assault victimization (other than rape; Black et al., 2011). Additionally, data from the National Violence Against Women survey indicate that 62% of adult women who reported being raped also reported that an intimate partner had perpetrated the rape (Tjaden & Thoennes).

Intimate-partner sexual violence may include a myriad of acts that may or may not involve physical force, such as completed or attempted forced vaginal, anal, or oral sex (rape or attempted rape), injury to the breasts or genitals, and coercive sexual acts (e.g., invoking "spousal duty," threatening to end the relationship) as well as noncontact acts such as forcing a partner to view pornographic material (Basile & Smith, 2011). In addition, some researchers have developed continuums to assist in understanding the breadth of intimate sexual violence. In their study of assaults between dating partners, Koss, Leonard, Beezeley, and Oras (1985) advanced a spectrum of sexual violence that included sexually nonaggressive, sexually coercive, sexually abusive, and sexually assaultive behaviors. Likewise, Finkelhor and Yllö (1985) identified four categorizations of sexual violence by husbands toward their wives ranging from social coercion (e.g., wifely duty), interpersonal coercion (e.g., threats of cheating or withholding money), threatened physical force, and use of physical force. Building upon these early studies, Basile (2002) utilized a nationally representative sample to determine the prevalence of coercive and physically forced sex among married women. Specifically, she examined seven circumstances surrounding the sexual coercion of women by their husbands or heterosexual partners (ranging from feeling that sex was expected after he had spent money on her to forcible rape). Basile determined that 34% of sampled women reported having unwanted sex with a current or former partner. Of the women who reported having unwanted sex, 48% reported having sex with a current husband/partner because they felt it was their duty, 29% after a romantic situation, 26% after he begged or pleaded with her, and 24% after he spent money on her. Additionally, 9% of women reported having unwanted sex with their current husband/partner after he bullied or humiliated her, 7% after he used physical force, and 3% after he threatened to physically hurt her. Overall, findings indicated that 13% of married women and 10% of all women sampled reported rape (physically forced sex) by an intimate partner.

Sexual violence between intimates often occurs alongside other forms of violence such as physical or emotional abuse. For example, Coker, Smith, McKeown, and King (2000) examined intimate-partner violence (IPV) in a large sample of adult women in South Carolina who reported ever being in a heterosexual relationship for 3 months or longer. Findings demonstrated that 5% of women reported experiencing only sexual violence in a current or former relationship while 18.1% reported sexual and physical violence and 17.3% reported sexual, physical, and emotional violence by a current or former partner. Additionally, research has demonstrated a significant relationship between intimate sexual violence and *more frequent and severe* physical abuse and psychological abuse, stalking, and intimate-partner homicide (Campbell et al., 2003; Coker et al.).

Sexual violence between intimates is often reoccurring within a relationship, with victims reporting ongoing sexual violence for the length of their relationship with their partner. Walker (1979), who developed the concept of a "cycle of violence," observed that these cycles may occur hundreds of times over the span of a relationship, with each cycle ranging from a few months to a year. The British Crime Survey found a high prevalence of repeat domestic-violence victimization over a year, with 56% of women reporting one repeat incident, 21% reporting two assaults, and 23% reporting three or more repeat assaults (Simmons & Dodd, 2004). Research from Tjaden and Thoennes (2006) examining 16,000 individuals (8,000 males and 8,000 females) in the National Violence Against Women Survey from 1995 to 1996 showed that women reported intimate sexual and physical violence occurring for an average of 3.8 years with an average of 7.1 assaults during the relationship, while men reported violence occurring over an average of 3.3 years with 4.7 assaults during the course of the relationship. Likewise, McFarlane and colleagues found that the majority of abused women in their sample had experienced four or more rapes during the course of their relationship with their abusive partner and that 55% reported that the second assault was perpetrated within 30 days of the first assault (McFarlane, Malecha, Watson, et al., 2005). In addition, individuals who have sexual victimization histories often have increased probabilities for sexual victimization in future relationships (Coker et al., 2000). Over the past 30 years, victimization self-reporting surveys have documented that a small proportion of respondents experience a disproportionate number of victimizations, with prior victimization experiences emerging as one of the most prominent predictors of future victimization (Cantor & Lynch, 2000).

Impact of Sexual IPV on Victims and Children

Intimate-partner sexual violence victimization has been linked with multiple mental problems. As Finkelhor and Yllö suggested, "A woman who is raped by a stranger lives with a memory of a horrible attack; a woman who is raped by her husband lives with her rapist" (Finkelhor & Yllö, as cited by Mahoney & Williams, 1998, p. 3). Victims of intimate sexual violence often experience depression and/or anxiety as a result of the attack(s). Research from McCauley and colleagues (1995) and Saunders, Hamberger, and Hovey (1993) and co-authors demonstrated that separate from physical assault, intimate sexual assault is associated with high rates of depression in victims. Intimate sexual abuse has also been linked to posttraumatic stress disorder (PTSD) among victims. Bennice, Resick, Mechanic, and Astin (2003) examined sexual abuse independently from physical abuse among victims of IPV and found that, even after controlling for the severity of physical abuse, victims of sexual abuse were significantly more likely to experience PTSD. Likewise, in a recent study of abused women, women who had been raped by an intimate partner reported significantly more symptoms of PTSD and an increased likelihood of having threatened or attempted suicide than did women who were physically but not sexually abused (McFarlane, Malecha, Watson, et al., 2005).

Intimate sexual violence victimization has also been linked to physical health problems. Research demonstrates that victims of sexual violence that is perpetrated by an intimate sustain greater rates of physical injury than do victims of non-intimate assault (Kilpatrick, Best, Saunders, & Veronen, 1988). Additionally, as mentioned above, women who are sexually assaulted by their intimate partner are also at a greater risk of experiencing extreme physical violence from their partner (Bergen, 1996; Campbell & Alford, 1989). Severe physical abuse may include being kicked, burned, or hit during sex (Campbell & Alford). Victims of intimate sexual abuse also report sustaining injuries at the hands of their partners such as broken bones, black eyes, and head wounds (Bergen); oftentimes, perpetrators will rape victims directly after a severe beating (Bergen; Campell & Alford; Russell, 1990). Victims may also suffer from sleeping and eating disorders and substance abuse (Goodman, Koss, & Russo, 1993; Kilpatrick et al.; McFarlane, Malecha, Gist, et al., 2005).

Intimate sexual violence has also been linked to a myriad of sexual health problems such as bladder infections, vaginal and anal tearing, sexual dysfunction, pelvic pain, urinary tract infections (Campbell & Alford, 1989), and sexually transmitted diseases (STDs) including HIV/AIDS (Campbell & Alford; Eby, Campbell, Sullivan,

& Davidson, 1995). In addition, male perpetrators of intimate sexual violence often maintain sole control over the use of contraception, leading to unintended pregnancies. For example, McFarlane, Malecha, Watson, and colleagues' (2005) examination of women who had been abused by their intimate partners found that 26% of sampled women reported pregnancies as a result of wife rape. Unintended pregnancies are often associated with negative outcomes for both the mother and child, including increased complications during and after pregnancy (Conde-Agudelo & Belizan, 2000; King, 2003), and low birth weight and failure to thrive (Bustan & Coker, 1994; Gadow et al., 1998).

Extant research has also revealed a significant, negative impact of intimate-partner sexual abuse on children who are exposed to violence in their home. Prior studies have revealed that children who see or hear the sexual assault or rape of their mother demonstrate greater rates of depression, anxiety, and behavior problems than do children who witness their mothers being physically but not sexually abused (McFarlane & Malecha, 2005; McFarlane et al., 2007). Many children who witness the sexual abuse of their mother internalize trauma to the extent that they experience symptoms of posttraumatic risk disorder (Pynoos & Nader, 1988). In addition, children who are exposed to intimate-partner sexual violence may grow to adopt unhealthy views of sexual intimacy and violence and may demonstrate sexual aggression in their own intimate relationships. Finally, perpetrators of intimate-partner sexual violence are also more likely to sexually abuse children in the home.

Criminal Justice System Response to Intimate Sexual Violence: Marital Exemptions

For centuries, marital exemption laws, which precluded states from charging husbands for raping their wives, legitimized violence against married women (Schelong, 1994; Siegel, 1998). The origin of marital exemption laws is often linked to English Chief Justice Sir William Hale as well as to William Blackstone. According to Hale, upon marriage, a wife unequivocally submitted "herself" to her husband and thus forfeited her own right to autonomy in both person and property (Hale, 1736/1971). This ideal, which became known as the Hale doctrine, surmised that under the matrimonial contract, a husband had an undisputed right to his wife's paid and unpaid labor, her property, and her body. The Hale doctrine was utilized as precedent for the legal acceptance of marital exemptions in the United States in the case of *Commonwealth v. Fogerty* (1857, as cited in Bennice & Resick, 2003). Likewise, Blackstone espoused the "unities theory," which held that upon marriage, man and woman were joined as one and a woman's legal rights were suspended to her husband. Under the unities theory, the rape of a married woman by a man other than her husband was legally viewed as a crime against the husband's property—his wife.

During the mid-19th century, the women's movement advanced progressive ideals regarding the individual and autonomous rights of women. Then, with the passage of the Married Women's Property Acts in various states in the early 1900s, married women won the right to own property, the right to their wages, and the right to file legal suit and tort damages without their husband's consent (Siegel, 1998). However, it was not until the late 1970s and 1980s that the women's movement attained significant reforms regarding marital exemption laws. The first successful prosecution of a rape by a husband against his wife in the United States was *Commonwealth v. Chretien* in 1981 (Pagelow, 1988). In *Chretien*, the victim had filed for divorce from her husband (who was also living separately from his wife) prior to the rape. As such, the judge ruled that the divorce action nullified the perpetrator's right to marital exemption, and, therefore, the court convicted him of the forcible rape of his wife. Then, finally, in *People v. Liberta* (1984) the court ruled that allowing married men the right to rape their wife was a denial of equal protection. In effect, *People v. Liberta* was the first case to overturn marital exemption laws. The ruling judge argued that rape is "not simply a sexual act . . . Rather [it] is a degrading, violent act which violates the bodily integrity of the victim" (as cited in Ryan, 1995, p. 989). He denounced any "implied consent" to such an act based on marital status and argued that to justify wife rape as a private matter was to say that the law turns its face from violent and degrading acts that would be a contradiction to the very goals and purposes of our justice system (Ryan). Mahoney and Williams (1998) suggested that in *Liberta*, the court made clear the following regarding the rights and privileges of marriage and marital privacy:

(1) Marital privacy is meant to provide privacy of acts that both husband and wife find agreeable; it is not meant to shield abuse; (2) labeling all wives potentially vindictive is a poor stereotype not supported by any evidence; (3) many crimes without witnesses are hard to prove, yet this is no reason for making a crime "unprosecutable"; (4) making rape in marriage a crime does not make marriage more difficult; it is rather a rape which would make a marriage more difficult. (p. 5)

People v. Liberta (1984) proved to be a major force of change regarding marital privilege, and by 1993, each state had revisited its marital exemption law; however, many states still allow some spousal exemptions under some circumstances. As of 2005, 30 states allowed for exemptions from prosecution for marital rape; allowances usually pertain to the degree of force that can be legally used and/or the ability of a wife to consent due to physical or mental impairment. In several states, such exemptions are also extended to cohabitating, nonmarried couples.

Victim Reporting

Evidence suggests that sexual victimization is a severely underreported crime. Examinations of data from the National Violence Against Women Survey found that only 19.1% of adult women who reported on the survey that they had been raped also reported the crime to law enforcement (Tjaden & Thoennes, 2006). Likewise, multiple analyses of the National Crime Victimization Survey (NCVS) have demonstrated that rape/sexual assault is the least reported of all violent crimes (BJS, 2003, 2007). Studies further indicate that sexual victimizations that involve strangers are more frequently reported to police than those that involve intimates, friends, or acquaintances (Chen & Ullman, 2010; Felson & Paré, 2005; Fisher, Daigle, Cullen, & Turner, 2003; Ruback & Ménard, 2001; Russell & Bolen, 2000).

Barriers to reporting sexual victimization are numerous, especially when the victimization is perpetrated by an intimate partner. Victims often report feeling ashamed and embarrassed by their assault. They fear negative reactions from law enforcement officers and prosecuting attorneys (Bachman, 1998) and feel trepidation about whether law enforcement officers will believe them (Campbell, 2005). Victims also fear retaliation from the perpetrator and are fearful about what a prosecution will do to their children and/or extended families. Furthermore, some victims are reluctant to label their assault as rape if they believe that physical force or a weapon are essential elements of a sexual assault (Fisher et al., 2003), and others may believe that their victimization is not serious enough to warrant police attention (Muehlenhard, Friedman, & Thomas, 1985). At the same time, victims who experience assaults that include physical force (Bachman, 1993; Russell & Bolen, 2000), the use of a weapon (Fisher et al.; Russell & Bolen), victim injuries (Bachman), and completed rapes (Bachman; Russell & Bolen) are more likely to report these crimes to law enforcement.

Law Enforcement Response

Given the legal history of intimate sexual violence, it is no surprise that service calls of a domestic nature were traditionally viewed as low priorities by law enforcement officers (Sparks, 1997). Across the United States, both formal and informal policies discouraged police involvement in disputes between intimate partners, which were seen as private family matters (Reuland, Morabito, Preston, & Cheney, 2006). For example, the 1975 Training Bulletin on Techniques of Dispute Intervention in California stated that in domestic situations, law enforcement officers should "act as a mediator rather than an enforcer of the law" (cited in Siegel, 1998, p. 39). Similarly, when restraining orders were issued to wives for protection against their husbands, law enforcement officers regularly failed to enforce them (Fagan, 1996).

The dismissive treatment of intimate-partner violence by law enforcement is especially problematic given that law enforcement officers serve as the "gatekeepers" to the criminal justice system. Although some strides have been made regarding law enforcement response to IPV in general, such as formal arrest and protection order policies (Sparks, 1997), evidence suggests that sexual violence between intimates is rarely treated as seriously as sexual victimization perpetrated by a stranger. Specifically, research reveals that sexual assaults perpetrated by strangers are more likely to be investigated thoroughly (Bachman, 1998; Spohn & Spears, 1996) and are less likely to be treated as unfounded by law enforcement (Bouffard, 2000; Kerstetter, 1990; Tellis & Spohn, 2008) than are cases including intimates. Such differential treatment is most likely related to stereotypical notions held by officers regarding what constitutes a "real rape." Real rapes are often defined as assaults that occur between strangers and that include the use of force and/or weapons by the perpetrator and the sustainment of injuries by the victim. Additionally, Martin, Taft, and Resick (2007) suggested that law enforcement officers often act in the interest of clearance rates, such that officers do not make an arrest in cases where there is no clear-cut evidence or where the victim may not be willing to cooperate in the future. Victims of intimate sexual crimes may unintentionally destroy evidence by immediately showering or washing clothing or sheets in an attempt to hide the assault from their children or other family members. Likewise, evidence suggests that law enforcement officers often question the victim's truthfulness in cases of sexual assault and are expressly concerned with verifying the credibility of sexual assault claims. Lord and Rassel's (2000) examination of nine North Carolina counties found that polygraph tests were still being utilized to prove victims' reports. Additionally, a victim may be reluctant to participate in the prosecution because of the inherent involvement of the perpetrator in her life. Perpetrators of intimate sexual violence are also victim's husbands and partners as well as the fathers of their children. Victims may depend on the perpetrator for financial support, or they may be pressured by other family members to forego criminal charges for the good of the family.

Prosecutorial Decision Making

As with law enforcement, prosecutors exercise great discretion in choosing the cases that will move forward in the criminal justice system as well as in allocating time and resources to specific cases. Prosecutorial decisions can have widespread consequences regarding the outcomes of cases of intimate-partner sexual violence as well as the way in which victims of such violence view the criminal justice system at large. Evidence suggests that historical views characterizing IPV as a private matter instead of as criminal activity worthy of legal intervention have not completely dissolved (Belknap & Potter, 2006). Research reveals that rape and sexual assault cases between strangers are more likely to proceed through the criminal justice system than are cases involving intimate partners and that they have greater rates of successful prosecutorial outcomes (Alderden & Ullman, 2012; Bouffard, 2000; Frazier & Haney, 1996; Spohn & Spears, 1996; but see also Spohn & Holleran, 2001). For example, Bouffard (2000) found that cases of sexual violence involving strangers were more likely to result in an arrest and were more heavily sanctioned than were cases involving intimate partners and acquaintances.

Decisions regarding whether or not to prosecute a case are influenced by the prosecutor's beliefs regarding the odds of securing a conviction for that case. Often beliefs about the likelihood of conviction are intrinsically tied to the credibility or believability of a victim. Victim credibility becomes even more important in cases of sexual assault, where the victim is either the key witness or the only witness as well as the literal crime scene. As such, the ability of the victim to articulate the details of the victimization in court and to do so in a convincing way is vital to the case. In cases of intimate sexual violence, where the victim and offender have had a previous intimate and/or sexual relationship, prosecutors may question whether the victim's story will "hold up" in court. In addition, victim credibility is influenced by personal characteristics, including whether the victim has a history of criminal activity or problems with drugs or alcohol or was engaging in other activities at the time of the assault that could be construed as contributing to his or her victimization. Evidence demonstrates that cases including "blameless" victims are more likely to be prosecuted than cases including victims who are seen as risky (Spohn & Spears, 1996). More specifically, research by Spohn and Holleran (2001) found that risky victim behavior negatively impacted the likelihood of prosecution for cases of sexual assault between intimates but not between strangers.

Moving Forward

In 2009, President Obama declared April as Sexual Assault Awareness Month (U.S. Department of Justice [U.S.DOJ], n.d.). In addition, evidence suggests that rates of reporting for sexual assault, especially assaults between known victims and offenders, has increased in recent years (Baumer, Felson, & Messner, 2003; Clay-Warner & Burt, 2005). Furthermore, all states now issue protective orders to victims of domestic violence that prohibit perpetrators from engaging in abusive behavior such as harassment, stalking, or showing up at a victim's home or place of work. Importantly, research indicates that women who contact the police, apply for a protective order, or seek medical help after an intimate sexual assault are less likely to be reassaulted than women who do not seek help (McFarlane, Malecha, Watson, et al., 2005).

At the same time, policies and practices for responding to victims of sexual victimization still fall short. Surveys demonstrate that law enforcement officers continue to significantly underestimate the level of distress their interactions cause victims (Campbell, 2005), and the limited research on sex crimes units does not provide evidence that such units produce more positive outcomes for victims than do to standard law enforcement units. Furthermore, Coker (2000) asserted that certain populations of victims, including women of color and poor victims, are at a greater disadvantage when seeking help than are their white, middle- or upper-class counterparts. Importantly, there must be adequate material resources—including available housing, food, money, and other resources such as job training and child care—to provide meaningful assistance to victims (Coker). Recognizing that some victims stay in an abusive relationship out of necessity communicates the grave need to make adequate state and county resources available to increase the likelihood of success for victims. According to a 2012 National Alliance to End Sexual Violence (NAESV) study of rape crisis centers around the country, 65% reported waiting lists for counseling, while 30% reported a waiting list for support groups (NAESV, 2012).

Finally, at present, there is a paucity of research examining the prosecution or the disposition of reported rape and sexual assault specifically between intimate partners (Bergen, 2004; Spohn & Tellis, 2012). Given the prevalence of intimate-partner violence that includes sexual victimization and the reported longevity and frequent brutality of such violence, it is imperative that we understand the contextual factors regarding when and how such cases are reported and processed through the criminal justice system. Specific work must include investigations of the different phases of the decision-making process and the multiple actors involved, including victims, law enforcement, prosecutors, judges, and juries as well as victims' advocates and medical personnel.

Conclusion

Despite public perception, research suggests that the majority of sexual violence victimizations are in fact perpetrated by intimates—husbands, partners, and boyfriends—not strangers (Schelong, 1994; Tjaden & Thoennes, 2006). In addition, existing studies have documented that intimate sexual violence is often more severe than sexual violence between strangers and is marked by repeat victimizations over the course of the intimate relationship. Victims are also at higher risks for victimization in future relationships. Short- and long-term consequences of intimate sexual violence include a myriad of physical health and mental health problems for victims (Bennice, Resick, Mechanic, & Austin, 2003; Bergen, 1996; Saunders, Hamberger, & Hover, 1993) as well as, many times, for their children (McFarlane & Malecha, 2005; McFarlane et al., 2007; Pynoos & Nader, 1988). Thus, rape and sexual assault among intimates is considered a grave public health issue worthy of social and political attention (Martin, Taft, & Resick, 2007).

This chapter provides a general explanation of the types of behaviors included in definitions of intimate sexual violence and presents the scope of the problem and the impact of such acts on victims and their children. A historical account of norms and laws pertaining to domestic violence illustrates, however, that marital rape specifically, and intimate sexual violence generally, was long considered unworthy of criminal justice system attention. It has only been since the mid-20th century that criminal justice system actors have treated this violence as criminal behavior. Although significant strides have been made to provide postassault services and improve criminal justice system response to victims of intimate sexual violence, increased efforts are still needed to ensure that we continue to advance both research and services for this historically underserved population.

Discussion Questions

1. In what ways are children affected when their mother suffers intimate sexual violence victimization?

2. What "barriers" do victims experience when deciding whether to report intimate sexual violence?

3. What is a "real rape," and how do stereotypes regarding "real rape" affect the treatment of victims (and offenders) of intimate sexual violence in the criminal justice system?

References

Alderden, M. A., & Ullman, S. E. (2012). Creating a more complete and current picture: Examining police and prosecutor decision-making when processing sexual assault cases. *Violence Against Women, 18*(5), 525–551. doi:10.1177/1077801212453867

Bachman, R. (1993). Predicting the reporting of rape victimizations: Have rape reforms made a difference? *Criminal Justice and Behavior, 20*(3), 254–270. doi:10.1177/0093854893020003003

Bachman, R. (1998). The factors related to rape reporting behavior and arrest: New evidence from the National Crime Victimization Survey. *Criminal Justice and Behavior, 25*(1), 8–29. doi:10.1177/0093854898025001002

Basile, K. C. (2002). Prevalence of wife rape and other intimate partner sexual coercion in a nationally representative sample of women. *Violence and Victims, 17*(5), 511–524.

Basile, K. C., & Smith, S. G. (2011). Sexual violence victimization of women: Prevalence, characteristics, and the role of public health and prevention. *America Journal of Lifestyle Medicine, 5*(5), 407–417. doi:10.1177/1559827611409512

Baumer, E. P., Felson, R. B., & Messner, S. F. (2003). Changes in police notification for rape, 1973–2000. *Criminology, 41*(3), 841–872.

Belknap, J., & Potter, H. (2006). Intimate partner abuse. In C. M. Renzetti, L. Goodstein, & S. L. Miller (Eds.), *Rethinking gender, crime, and justice: Feminist readings* (pp. 155–167). Los Angeles, CA: Roxbury.

Bennice, J. A., & Resick, P. A. (2003). Marital rape: History, research, and practice. *Trauma Violence Abuse, 4*(3), 228–246.

Bennice, J. A., Resick, P. A., Mechanic, M., & Astin, M. (2003). The relative effects of intimate partner physical and sexual violence on posttraumatic stress disorder symptomatology. *Violence & Victims, 18*(1), 87–94.

Bergen, R. K. (1996). *Wife rape: Understanding the responses of survivors and service providers.* Thousand Oaks, CA: Sage.

Bergen, R. K. (2004). Studying wife rape: Reflections on the past, present and future. *Violence Against Women, 10*(12), 1407–1416. doi: 10.1177/1077801204270557

Black, M. C., Basile, K. C., Breiding, M. J., Smith, S. G., Walters, M. L., Merrick, M. T., . . . Stevens, M. R. (2011). *The national intimate partner and sexual violence survey (NISVS): 2010 Summary report*. Atlanta, GA: National Center for Injury Prevention and Control, Centers for Disease Control and Prevention. Retrieved from http://www.cdc.gov/violenceprevention/nisvs/

Bouffard, J. A. (2000). Predicting type of sexual assault case closure from victim, suspect, and case characteristics. *Journal of Criminal Justice, 28*(6), 527–542.

Bureau of Justice Statistics (BJS). (2003). *Reporting crime to the police, 1992–2000* (NCJ 195710). Retrieved from http://www.bjs.gov/content/pub/pdf/rcp00.pdf

Bureau of Justice Statistics (BJS). (2007). *Criminal victimization, 2006* (NCJ 219413). Retrieved from http://www.bjs.gov/content/pub/pdf/cv06.pdf

Bustan, M. N., & Coker, A. L. (1994). Maternal attitude toward pregnancy and the risk of neonatal death. *American Journal of Public Health, 84(3),* 411–414.

Campbell, R. (2005). What really happened? A validation study of rape survivors' help-seeking experiences with the legal and medical systems. *Violence and Victims, 20*(1), 55–68.

Campbell, J. C., & Alford, P. (1989). The dark consequences of marital rape. *American Journal of Nursing, 89*(7), 946–949.

Campbell, J. C., & Soeken, K. L. (1999). Forced sex and intimate partner violence: Effects on women's risk and women's health. *Violence Against Women, 5*(9), 1017–1035. doi:10.1177/1077801299005009003

Campbell, J. C., Webster, D., Koziol-McLain, J., Block, C. R., Campbell, D., Curry, M. A., . . . Wilt, S. A. (2003). Assessing risk factors for intimate partner homicide. *National Institute of Justice Journal, 250,* 14–19.

Cantor, D., & Lynch, J. P. (2000). Self-report surveys as measures of crime and criminal victimization. In *Measurement and analysis of crime and justice* (Vol. 4, pp. 85–138). Washington, DC: U.S. Department of Justice, National Institute of Justice.

Chen, Y., & Ullman, S. E. (2010). Women's reporting of sexual and physical assaults to police in the National Violence Against Women Survey. *Violence Against Women, 16*(3), 262–279. doi:10.1177/1077801209360861

Clay-Warner, J., & Burt, C. H. (2005). Rape reporting after reforms: Have times really changed? *Violence Against Women, 11*(2), 150–176. doi:10.1177/1077801204271566

Coker, D. (2000). Shifting power for battered women: Law, material resources, and poor women of color. *UC Davis Law Review, 33,* 1009–1055.

Coker, A. L., Smith, P. H., McKeown, R. E., & King, M. J. (2000). Frequency and correlates of intimate partner violence by type: Physical, sexual, and psychological battering. *American Journal of Public Health, 90*(4), 553–559.

Commonwealth v. Chretien, 417 N.E.2d 1203 (Mass., 1981).

Commonwealth v. Fogerty, 74 Mass. (8 Gray) 489, 491(1857).

Conde-Agudelo, A., & Belizan, J. M. (2000). Maternal morbidity and mortality associated with interpregnancy interval: Cross sectional study. *British Medical Journal, 321,* 1255–1259.

Eby, K. K., Campbell, J. C., Sullivan, C. M., & Davidson, W. S. II. (1995). Health effects of experiences of sexual violence for women with abusive partners. *Health Care for Women International, 16*(6), 563–576. doi: 10.1080/07399339509516210

Fagan, J. (1996). The criminalization of domestic violence: Promises and limits. *National Institute of Justice: Research report.* Retrieved from https://www.ncjrs.gov/pdffiles/crimdom.pdf

Felson, R. B., & Paré, P-P. (2005). The reporting of domestic violence and sexual assault by nonstrangers to the police. *Journal of Marriage and Family, 67,* 597–610.

Finkelhor, D., & Yllö, K. (1983). Rape in marriage: A sociological view. In D. Finkelhor, R. J. Gelles, G. T. Hotaling, & M. A. Straus (Eds.), *The dark side of families* (pp. 119–130). Beverly Hills, CA: Sage.

Finkelhor, D., & Yllö, K. (1985). *License to rape: Sexual abuse of wives.* New York: Holt, Rinehart, & Winston.

Fisher, B. S., Daigle, L. E., Cullen, F. T., & Turner, M. G. (2003). Reporting sexual victimization to the police and others: Results from a national-level study of college women. *Criminal Justice and Behavior, 30*(1), 6–38. doi:10.1177/0093854802239161

Frazier, P. A., & Haney, B. (1996). Sexual assault cases in the legal system: Police, prosecutor, and victim perspectives. *Law and Human Behavior, 20*(6), 607–628.

Gadow, E. C., Paz, J. E., Lopez-Camelo, J. S., Dutra, M. G., Queenan, J. T., Simpson, J. L., . . . Castilla, E.E. (1998). Unintended pregnancies in women delivering at 18 South American hospitals. *Human Reproduction, 13*(7), 1991–1995.

Goodman, L. A., Koss, M. P., & Russo, N. F. (1993). Violence against women: Physical and mental health effects. Part I: Research findings. *Applied and Preventive Psychology, 2*(2), 79–89.

Hale, S. M. (1971). *The history of the pleas of the crown.* S. Emlyn (Ed.). London, UK: Professional Books. Originally published 1736.

Kerstetter, W. (1990). Gateway to justice: Police and prosecutorial response to sexual assaults against women. *The Journal of Criminal Law & Criminology, 81*(2), 267–313.

Kilpatrick, D. G., Best, C. L., Saunders, B. E., & Veronen, L. J. (1988). Rape in marriage and in dating relationships: How bad is it for mental health? *Annals of the New York Academy of Sciences, 528,* 335–344. doi: 10.1111/j.1749-6632.1988.tb50875.x

King, J. C. (2003). The risk of maternal nutritional depletion and poor outcomes increases in early or closely spaced pregnancies. *Journal of Nutrition, 133*(5), 1732S–1736S.

Koss, M. P., Leonard, K. E., Beezley, D. A., & Oras, C. J. (1985). Nonstranger sexual aggression: A discriminant analysis of the psychological characteristics of undetected offenders. *Sex Roles, 12*(9–10), 981–992.

Lord, V. B., & Rassel, G. (2000). Law enforcement's response to sexual assault: A comparative study of nine counties in North Carolina. *Women & Criminal Justice, 11*(1), 67–88.

Mahoney, P., & Williams, L.M. (1998). Sexual assault in marriage: Prevalence, consequences, and treatment of wife rape. In J. L. Jasinski & L. M. Williams (Eds.), *Partner violence: A comprehensive review of 20 years of research* (pp. 113–163). Thousand Oaks, CA: Sage.

Martin, E. K., Taft, C. T., & Resick, P. A. (2007). A review of marital rape. *Aggression and Violent Behavior, 12*(3), 329–347.

McCauley, J., Kern, D. E., Kolodner, K., Dill, L., Schroeder, A. F., DeChant, H. K., . . . Derogatis, L. R. (1995). The "battering syndrome": Prevalence and clinical characteristics of domestic violence in primary care internal medicine practices. *Annals of Internal Medicine, 123*(10), 737–746.

McFarlane, J., & Malecha, A. (2005). *Sexual assault among intimates: Frequency, consequences and treatments.* Washington, DC: U.S. Department of Justice. Retrieved from https://www.ncjrs.gov/pdffiles1/nij/grants/211678.pdf

McFarlane, J., Malecha, A., Watson, K., Gist, J., Batten, E., Hall, I., & Smith, S. (2005). Intimate partner sexual assault against women: Frequency, health consequences, and treatment outcomes. *Obstetrics and Gynecology, 105*(1), 99–108

McFarlane, J., Malecha, A., Gist, J. Watson, K., Batten, E., Hall, I., & Smith, S. (2005). Intimate partner sexual assault against women and associated victim substance use, suicidality, and risk factors for femicide. *Issues in Mental Health Nursing, 26*(9), 953–967.

McFarlane, J., Malecha, A., Watson, K. Gist, J., Batten, E., Hall, I., & Smith, S. (2007). Intimate partner physical and sexual assault & child behavior problems. *MCN: The American Journal of Maternal Child Nursing, 32*(2), 74–80.

Muehlenhard, C. L., Friedman, D. E., & Thomas, C. M. (1985). Is date rape justifiable? The effects of dating activity, who initiated, who paid, and men's attitudes towards women. *Psychology of Women Quarterly, 9*(3), 297–310. doi: 10.1111/j.1471-6402.1985.tb00882.x

National Alliance to End Sexual Violence (NAESV). (2012). *2012 rape crisis center survey.* Retrieved from http://endsexualviolence.org/files/2012RCCFundingSurveyResults.pdf

Pagelow, M. D. (1988). Marital rape. In V. B. Van Hasselt, R. L. Morrison, A. S. Bellack, & M. Hersen (Eds.), *Handbook of family violence* (pp. 207–232). New York: Plenum Press.

People v. Liberta, 474 N.E. 2d 567 (N.Y. 1984).

Pynoos, R.S., & Nader, K. (1988). Children who witness the sexual assaults of their mothers. *Journal of the American Academy of Child and Adolescent Psychiatry, 27*(5), 567–572.

Reuland, M., Morabito, M. S., Preston, C., Cheney, J. (2006). *Police-community partnerships to address domestic violence.* Washington, DC: U.S. Department of Justice: Office of Community Oriented Policing Services. Retrieved from http://www.cops.usdoj.gov/files/RIC/Publications/domestic_violence_web3.pdf

Ryan, R. M. (1995). The sex right: A legal history of the marital rape exemption. *Law & Social Inquiry, 20*(4), 941–1001. doi: 10.1111/j.1747-4469.1995.tb00697.x

Ruback, R. B., & Ménard, K. S. (2001). Rural–urban differences in sexual victimization and reporting: Analyses using UCR and crisis center data. *Criminal Justice and Behavior, 28*(2), 131–155.

Russell, D. E. H. (1990). *Rape in marriage.* Bloomington: Indiana University Press.

Russell, D. E. H., & Bolen, R. M. (2000). *The epidemic of rape and child sexual abuse in the United States.* Thousand Oaks, CA: Sage.

Saunders, D. G., Hamberger, L. K., Hovey, M. (1993). Indicators of woman abuse based on a chart review at a family practice center. *Archives of Family Medicine, 2*(5), 537–543. doi: 10.1001/archfami.2.5.537

Schelong, K. M. (1994). Domestic violence and the state: Responses to and rationales for spousal battering, marital rape and stalking. *Marquette Law Review, 78*(1), 79–120.

Simmons, J., and T. Dodd (Eds.). (2004). Crime in England and Wales 2002/2003. London, U.K.: Home Office. Retrieved from http://webarchive.nationalarchives.gov.uk/20110220105210/http:/rds.homeoffice.gov.uk/rds/crimeew0203.html

Siegel, R. B. (1998). Civil rights reform in historical perspective: Regulating marital violence. In N. E. Devins & D. M. Douglas (Eds), *Redefining equality.* New York, NY: Oxford University Press, Inc.

Sparks, A. (1997). Feminists negotiate the executive branch: The policing of male violence. In C. R. Daniels (Ed.), *Feminists negotiate the state: The politics of domestic violence* (pp. 35–52). Lanham, MD: University Press of America.

Spohn, C., & Holleran, D. (2001). Prosecuting sexual assault: A comparison of charging decisions in sexual assault cases involving strangers, acquaintances, and intimate partners. *Justice Quarterly, 18*(3), 651–688. doi:10.1080/07418820100095051

Spohn, C., & Spears, J. (1996). The effect of offender and victim characteristics on sexual assault case processing decisions. *Justice Quarterly, 13*(4), 649–679. doi:10.1080/07418829600093141

Spohn, C., & Tellis, K. (2012). The criminal justice system's response to sexual violence. *Violence Against Women, 18*(2), 169–192. doi: 10.1177/1077801212440020

Tellis, K. M., & Spohn, C. (2008). The sexual stratification hypothesis revisited: Testing assumptions about simple versus aggravate rape. *Journal of Criminal Justice, 36*(3), 252–261.

Tjaden, P., & Thoennes, N. (2006). *Extent, nature, and consequences of rape victimization: Findings from the National Violence Against Women Survey.* Washington, DC: U.S. Department of Justice: Office of Justice Programs Special Report. Retrieved from https://www.ncjrs.gov/pdffiles1/nij/210346.pdf

U.S. Department of Justice (U.S.DOJ) Office on Violence Against Women. (n.d.). *The history of the Violence Against Women Act.* Retrieved from http://www.ovw.usdoj.gov/docs/history-vawa.pdf

Walker, L. E. (1979). *The battered woman.* New York, NY: Harper & Row.

6

Sexual Victimization on College Campuses

Leah E. Daigle, Sadie Mummert,
Bonnie S. Fisher, and Heidi L. Scherer

I n May 2013, Yale University was fined $165,000 for failing to meet its disclosure obligations under the mandates of the Clery Act related to four sexual assaults that had happened on its campus (Sander, 2013). This is one of the most severe penalties enacted to date, and it makes evident the seriousness with which the U.S. Department of Education treats sexual victimization on college campuses. It may seem that this treatment and attention given to sexual victimization on college campuses is relatively new, but that is not the case.

First Studies on College Women's Sexual Victimization: Establishing Measures and Extent

In fact, although research in this area took great strides starting in the 1980s, the first forays into studying sexual victimization among college students began in the 1950s. These first early studies were designed with two particular goals in mind: to define and measure sexual victimization among college women and to identify the extent to which college women experience this form of victimization.

In an early attempt to define and measure erotic offensiveness and erotic aggressiveness in dating or courtship relationships among college students, Kirkpatrick and Kanin (1957) developed their own self-report schedule. Between September 1954 and May 1955, they administered the self-report schedule to 291 female college students who were enrolled in 1 of 22 classes at one university. What Kirkpatrick and

Kanin found was that over half (55.7%) of the women in their sample reported being offended at least once by the level of erotic intimacy over the year and that 6.2% indicated that they had experienced aggressive, forceful attempts at sexual intercourse that involved threats or coercive infliction of physical pain. This early study was important for several key reasons. First, Kirkpatrick and Kanin developed one of the first measurement tools of sexual victimization of college women. Second, they provided an estimate of the extent to which college women are raped in a single academic year.

Not until Koss's work almost 30 years later were additional measurement strategies and national-level estimates produced. First, in a smaller-scale study of one university, Koss developed a measurement tool, the Sexual Experiences Survey (SES), to measure several types of sexual victimization (Koss & Oros, 1982). Later, Koss conducted the first national-level study of college student sexual victimization. For this study, Koss and colleagues revised the SES so that it included 10 behaviorally specific questions designed to measure sexual contact, sexual coercion, attempted rape, and completed rape (Koss, Gidycz, & Wisniewski, 1987). Behaviorally specific questions are those that include descriptive language of the behavior in question (in this instance, various types of sexual victimization) rather than simply asking, for example, "Have you been sexually coerced or have you been raped?" Although these types of questions had been used before in community-based studies (Russell, 1982), Koss's use of these types of questions in the SES for college students was innovative.

Koss's work was also important in that her estimates of the extent of rape and other types of sexual victimization were produced at the national level. She found that over half (53.7%) of the women in her study had experienced a sexual victimization since the age of 14. Rape (attempted or completed) was experienced by 27.5% of college women since age 14. To produce 1-year estimates, she also asked about experiences since the previous academic year. She found that slightly less than half (46.3%) had experienced any type of sexual victimization in the previous year. In addition, 6.5% of women had experienced a completed rape, and 10.1% had experienced an attempted rape.[1]

Koss's research set the stage for other researchers to study sexual victimization among college women. Notably, another national-level study of college women's sexual victimization experiences was conducted during the 1990s. The National College Women's Sexual Victimization (NCWSV) study also had effective measurement of sexual victimization as a primary goal (Fisher, Cullen, & Turner, 1999). Surveying 4,446 college women in the spring of 1997 about sexual victimizations that occurred since school started in the fall of 1996, it used a survey with behaviorally specific questions designed to measure five types of unwanted sexual behaviors: unwanted sexual contact without force, unwanted sexual contact with force, sexual coercion, attempted rape, and completed rape.

A key difference between this study and Koss's is that in the NCWSV study, if a woman said that she had experienced any of these five unwanted sexual behaviors in the initial survey (called screen questions), she then completed an incident report about each separate incident that had occurred. In this way, the NCWSV study used a measurement strategy similar to the one employed in the National Crime Victimization Survey. This incident report had detailed questions about the incident, such as where it occurred; who perpetrated it; and, most importantly, the type of contact, the degree of coercion, and whether the incident was attempted or completed. As such, the incident report was used to classify incidents as to what actually occurred based on criteria of a behavior (e.g., the legal definition of completed rape). An important finding using this measurement strategy was that only 25.2% of the incidents that entered into the incident report via a "yes" answer to a question about rape were ultimately classified as rape. In other words, using this two-step measurement strategy allowed for a more precise way to classify incidents as to the type of sexual victimization involved.

A second major finding from the NCWSV study is that 15.5% of the sample of college women had experienced a sexual victimization other than rape since the fall of 1996. In addition, 2.5% of the sample had experienced either a completed or attempted rape. Extrapolating this finding to the entire year and across the college tenure, between one fifth and one fourth of college women will experience rape during their college years.

These first two national-level studies on sexual victimization of college women were particularly noteworthy for their advancement of how we define and measure sexual victimization. In addition, both studies produced estimates of the extent of sexual victimization and rapes that college women experience. Another important contribution of both Koss et al.'s (1987) and Fisher et al.'s (1999) research is the fact that the studies showed how college women responded during and after their victimization. In particular, these studies and others investigated the use of self-protective action during an incident, as well as the acknowledgment of rape and reporting behaviors of victims after an incident.

College Women's Responses During and After Rape

Many people wonder whether a woman should fight back or offer some type of resistance if an offender is trying to rape her. To empirically assess whether it is beneficial for women to resist an offender during sexual victimization, researchers have asked women whether they have employed what are called resistance or self-protective strategies in an effort to stop the attack. Self-protective actions are typically classified into one of four categories: (1) nonforceful physical, (2) forceful physical, (3) nonforceful verbal, and (4) forceful verbal (Ullman, 1997, 2007). Fisher et al.'s study included measures designed to assess the use of self-protective action among college students. Findings from the research indicate that the vast majority of college women use some form of self-protective action during rape incidents (Fisher, Daigle, Cullen, & Santana, 2007). Further, the most common types of self-protective action used during rapes are forceful physical and nonforceful verbal (Fisher et al., 2007). Another important finding from this literature on college students and their use of self-protective action is that using self-protective actions appears to be beneficial in terms of getting the offender to stop (i.e., having the incident remain an attempt rather than be completed). This benefit is especially pronounced when the victim uses the type of self-protective action that appears to be in line with the type and amount of force the offender is using. Known as the parity thesis, this finding means that if an offender is using force that is physical, it is most beneficial if the victim also uses forceful, physical self-protective strategies (Fisher et al.).

Even if a college woman uses resistance, an incident may still be completed. What is she likely to do then? Research on the responses of college women after rape suggests some patterns. First, college women are very unlikely to report their rape or other sexual victimization to the police (Sloan, Fisher, & Cullen, 1997). Koss et al.'s (1987) study examined reporting behavior. In that study, it was found that only 5% of college women who were raped contacted the police. Results from the NCWSV study, conducted about 10 years later, produced similar results. Only 4.5% of rapes were reported to the police (Fisher, Daigle, Cullen, & Turner, 2003b). Notably, more recent, national-level research on college student victimization shows that 10% of college women who had experienced either a drug- or alcohol-facilitated or incapacitated rape reported their experience to the police and that 18% of college women who experienced a forcible rape reported it to the police (Kilpatrick, Resnick, Ruggiero, Conoscenti, & McCauley, 2007). Although most college women do not report their rape to formal authorities like the police, most college women do tell someone about their experience (Fisher et al.).

Second, even though college women are likely to tell someone—most likely their friends (Fisher et al., 2003b)—about being raped, this does not mean that they necessarily are defining what has happened to them as rape. In the NCWSV study, women who had been sexually victimized were asked if they considered the incident to be a rape. Of those women who had experienced a completed rape, slightly less than half said they considered the incident to be a rape (Fisher, Daigle, Cullen, & Turner, 2003a). Terming this conceptualization of the incident "acknowledgment," Koss (1988) had found that only 27% of college women who were raped acknowledged that what they had experienced was rape. Other research on college women has found that about one third to three fourths of rape victims do not acknowledge that they have been raped (Bondurant, 2001; Botta & Pingree, 1997; Cleere & Lynn, 2013; Frazier & Seales, 1997; Kahn, Mathie, & Torgler, 1994; Layman, Gidycz, & Lynn, 1996; Pitts & Schwartz, 1993). If college women do not acknowledge their rape as such, what do they think happened? Research shows that these incidents are most often labeled miscommunications (Koss, 1988; Layman et al., 1996; Littleton, Axson, Breitkopf, & Berenson, 2006) but may also be seen as a seduction or a crime other than rape (Koss; Layman et al.). Importantly, almost always college women define these incidents in ways that indicate that they see them as inappropriate (Fisher, Daigle, & Cullen, 2010).

This acknowledgment and reporting process may be especially important for several reasons. We know that perpetrators cannot be brought to justice, either through the formal criminal justice system or through the school's judicial procedures, if a victim does not report the incident to formal sources. In addition, research on disclosure suggests that the initial response to a victim is particularly important. Victims are likely to internalize the message that the person gives her. If the person suggests that she is somehow at fault, rather than the offender, she is less likely to report to the police or seek help (Ullman, 2010). Furthermore, research on acknowledgment suggests that doing so may have benefit for victims in that it is linked to more positive postrape adjustment among college women (Botta & Pingree, 1997). Other research has linked acknowledgment, however, to negative outcomes such as negative emotional reactions (Kahn, Jackson, Kully, Badger, & Halvorsen, 2003) and posttraumatic stress disorder (PTSD) symptomology (Layman et al., 1996; Littleton, et al., 2006).

Recurring Sexual Victimization

Not only has research investigated these processes, another process that has been examined among college students is victimization recurrence. Recurring sexual victimization occurs when a person who has experienced a sexual victimization experiences a subsequent incident, or multiple incidents, of sexual victimization (Fisher, Daigle, & Cullen, 2010). Utilizing the National College Women Sexual Victimization (NCWSV) study data, Daigle Fisher, and Cullen (2008) found that 7% of the college women who reported an initial sexual victimization incident had experienced more than one of these incidents since the beginning of the school year. Furthermore, they found that these 7% experienced 72% of the total number of sexual victimizations in the study (Daigle et al.). This recurring victimization phenomenon has been established in other studies of college women. For example, Gidycz, Coble, Latham, and Layman (1993) reported that 18% of their sample of female college students who had experienced an incident of sexual victimization had experienced at least one subsequent sexual victimization incident.

Importantly, an additional finding in Daigle et al.'s (2008) study was that females were at greater risk of experiencing recurring sexual victimization in the time immediately following the initial incident. Approximately half of the recurring rape incidents took place during the same month of the initial sexual victimization (Daigle et al.). Additionally, about one third of recurring sexual coercions and threats were found to occur within the same month. Further, the risk of recurring sexual victimization decreased over time (Daigle et al.).

Drug- and Alcohol-Facilitated Sexual Victimization

Along with establishing that recurring victimization is occurring, recent research on college student victimization has centered on the potential links between alcohol and drug use and sexual victimization. This attention is not surprising, given the widespread use of alcohol among college students and the recognition of its negative consequences for students (Wechsler, Dowdall, Maenner, Gledhill-Hoyt, & Lee, 1998). According to the National Institute on Alcohol Abuse and Alcoholism (NIAAA), approximately 80% of college students drink alcohol, with about half of those students engaging in binge drinking (NIAAA, 2012). In addition, approximately 22% of college students use some form of illicit drugs (Substance Abuse and Mental Health Services Administration [SAMHSA], 2011).

With these high usage rates, it is no surprise that researchers have linked sexual victimization with alcohol (Abbey, Zawacki, Buck, Clinton, & McAuslan, 2001; Combs-Lane & Smith, 2002; Schwartz & Pitts, 1995; Siegel & Williams, 2003; Ullman, Karabatsos, & Koss, 1999) and drug use (Cass, 2007; Fisher & Wilkes, 2003; Mustaine & Tewksbury, 2002). For instance, substance use is linked with sexual victimization when alcohol or drugs provide the opportunity for the incident to occur. This opportunity can occur in several ways. Alcohol- and/or other drug-enabled sexual assault occurs when an individual experiences incapacitation as a result of his or her excessive, voluntary substance use (Krebs, Lindquist, Warner, Fisher, & Martin, 2009). Drug-facilitated sexual assault occurs when an individual is incapacitated by the perpetrator through the use of drugs without the victim's knowledge or consent (Krebs et al., 2009). Krebs and colleagues studied both alcohol- and/or drug-enabled and drug-facilitated sexual assault among college females. They found that approximately 11% of their sample had experienced a sexual assault under these conditions—including alcohol- or other drug-enabled sexual assault (7.8%), certain or suspected drug-facilitated sexual assault (2.3%), or some other form of incapacitated sexual assault (1.0%)—since entering college (Krebs et al., 2009). With regard to rape specifically, in their national study of female college students, Kilpatrick and colleagues (2007) found that just over 2% of college women had reported incidents of rape during the previous 7 months that were incapacitated or drug- or alcohol-facilitated rape[2] (Kilpatrick et al., 2007). Other studies have also identified drug-facilitated and incapacitated rape as occurring to college women (Lawyer, Resnick, Bakanic, Burkett, & Kilpatrick, 2010; Mohler-Kuo, Dowdall, Koss, & Wechsler, 2004; Tyler, Hoyt, & Whitbeck, 1998).

The Use of Technology in Sexual Victimization

In addition to the high levels of alcohol consumption on college campuses, the use of technology has recently captured the interest of sexual-victimization researchers. It seems plausible that technological advances, including easy access to computers and smartphones and an increasing use of social media websites such as Facebook, Twitter, and Instagram, may contribute to incidents of sexual victimization among students. Although these technological developments are designed in part to enable people to keep in touch with one another and to share information, they are sometimes used in ways that may enable unwanted sexual behaviors. One such behavior that has recently emerged, especially among teenagers and young adults, is sexting. Sexting is defined as sending sexually suggestive messages and nude or seminude pictures or videos of oneself through text messaging, email, or some other form of Internet messaging or posting these images on the Internet (DeMitchell & Parker-Magagna, 2011). In a 2008 national study, it was found that 33% of young adults engaged in sexting (National Campaign to Prevent Teen and Unplanned Pregnancy, 2008). Specifically related to college students, one study found that approximately 38% of male and female college students reported participating in sexting (Reyns, Burek, Henson, & Fisher, 2013).

Although the sexting phenomenon is relatively new, research has begun to consider its relationship to sexual victimization. Reyns and colleagues (2013) examined the relationship between sexting and cybervictimization (including being sent unwanted sexual advances) among college students. When comparing those who sexted to those who did not, the researchers found that those who sexted were at an increased risk of experiencing cybervictimization (Reyns et al.). In another study of college females, 27% of those who engaged in sexting reported that they had been sexually coerced or threatened into participating in the sexting (Snell & Englander, 2010). Given the emergency of early evidence of a link between sexting and sexual victimization among college students, researchers should further investigate this relationship.

Consequences of Sexual Victimization of College Students

So far, we have discussed what we know about the nature and extent of sexual victimization and how college students are likely to respond. Also important to consider are the many negative outcomes that result from sexual victimization, especially for college students. Although the psychological effects of sexual victimization—such as the symptomology of posttraumatic stress disorder, depression, and anxiety—have been the most widely studied among college students (see Zinzow et al., 2010), research also has identified negative consequences beyond mental health issues. A growing body of research indicates that sexual victimization can also have lasting impacts on victims' lives, influencing such factors as their perceptions of safety (Culbertson, Vik, & Kooiman, 2001), body image (Billingham & Patterson, 1998; Harned, 2001), sexual practices (Littleton, Grills-Taquechel, Buck, Rosman, & Dodd, 2013; Shapiro & Schwartz, 1997), substance use (Brener, McMahon, Warren, & Douglas, 1999), and success in school (Banyard et al., 2007). Taken together, studies of this population demonstrate that the adverse effects of sexual victimization appear to be multidimensional, impacting many domains of the students' lives.

One of the most commonly identified psychological outcomes of sexual victimization among college students is posttraumatic stress disorder. Studies of a wide range of college student samples indicate that students who report experiencing sexual victimization during their college tenure are significantly more likely than nonvictims to meet the diagnostic criteria for PTSD (Aosved, Long, & Voller, 2011; Archambeau et al., 2010; Frazier et al., 2009; Harned, 2001; Zinzow et al., 2010). Highlighting the severity of the relationship between sexual victimization and PTSD, Frazier and colleagues reported that student victims of sexual assault had higher levels of PTSD than did students who had experienced other serious forms of trauma, including family violence and the unexpected death of a loved one. Depression and anxiety are other mental health outcomes that have been associated with sexual victimization among college students (Frazier et al.; Gidycz et al., 1993; Harned; Littleton et al., 2013; Shapiro & Schwarz, 1997; Zinzow et al., 2010).

In addition to pointing at specific psychological impacts of sexual victimization, research indicates that sexual victimization adversely impacts the general mental and physical health of victims. Aosved et al. (2011) and Archambeau et al. (2010) both reported that students who had experienced sexual assault were more likely than nonvictims to experience poorer overall psychopathology and adjustment. Sexual victimization has also been associated with changes in victims' personalities. For instance, Harned (2001) reported that victims experience lower levels of positive affect and the experience of positive emotions than do nonvictims. McMullin and colleagues claimed that in comparison to nonvictims, those who report experiencing sexual victimization express feeling less nurturing and more self-focused (McMullin, Wirth, & White, 2007). Additionally, Banyard, Ward, Cohn, Plante, Moorhead, and Walsh (2007) found that college students who are victims of unwanted sexual contact are more likely to report changes to their health than are nonvictims, while Zinzow and colleagues (2011) reported that student victims are approximately 2 times as likely as their nonvictim counterparts to report poor health.

Sexual victimization among college students also appears to influence the ways in which victims cope and their likelihood to engage in self-harm behavior or substance abuse. Students who report experiencing a sexual victimization during their college tenure are significantly more likely than nonvictims to express suicidal ideation or to attempt suicide (Brener et al., 1999; Stepakoff, 1998; Stephenson, Pena-Shaff, & Quirk, 2006). Bryan, McNaugton-Cassill, Osman, and Hernandez (2013) reported that victims were over 8 times more likely than their nonvictim counterparts to attempt suicide. Research also indicates that sexual assault victims are more likely than nonvictims to engage in hazardous alcohol use (Brener et al.; Littleton et al., 2013), illicit drug use (Brener et al.; Winfield, George, Swartz, & Blazer, 1990), and the nonmedical use of prescription drugs (McCauley et al., 2011). Further illuminating this relationship, Winfield et al. (1990) found that drug dependency can have an onset subsequent to sexual victimization, supporting the assumption that drugs and alcohol can operate as both antecedents and consequences of victimization.

Although much is known about the immediate psychological impacts of sexual victimization on college students, less is known about how victimization impacts students' lives in the long term. However, a small but significant body of research indicates that the experience of sexual victimization among students can extend into many aspects of their lives, including their education and relationships. For instance, Harned (2001) reported that sexual assault victims experience an elevated risk of withdrawing from school, and Banyard, Ward, Cohn, Plante, Moorhead, and Walsh (2007) found that victims are more likely than nonvictims to express self-reported changes in their approach to their education. Further, Culbertson et al. (2001) found that sexual assault victims experienced decreased perceptions of safety at home, in public, and within personal relationships than did nonvictims. Research also indicates that sexual victimization can adversely influence victims' perceptions of their own bodies and their future intimate relationships (Billingham & Patterson, 1998; Harned, 2001). Evidence also suggests an association between sexual victimization and a victim's future sexuality, including lower sexual self-esteem (Shapiro & Schwartz, 1997), the use of alcohol during sexual intercourse (Brener et al., 1999), and the use of sex to regulate affect (Littleton et al., 2013).

In sum, the findings of studies that examined the negative consequences of sexual victimization among college students highlight that victimization affects the overall mental, physical, and emotional health of students. The findings also underscore how critical it is that college administrators, policy makers, and researchers work to devise strategies for preventing and reducing the occurrence of sexual assault and rape among this population.

Responses to Sexual Victimization Against College Students: Legislation and Prevention

College and university responses to sexual victimization have been largely driven by the findings from numerous studies described throughout this chapter and by federal legislation. National estimates of the percentage of college women who experience rape have remained fairly constant over three decades. One change over these years, however, is the number of women enrolled in postsecondary institutions of higher education. There were just over 7.5 million females enrolled in these schools in 1990. Females' enrollment has steadily increased annually, with a projected female enrollment of 14.2 million in 2020, representing close to a 90% increase in the number of female students on campuses (National Center for Education Statistics, 2013). Hence, it is reasonable to deduce that even though the percentage of college women who have experienced rape during their college tenure has remained stable over three decades, the number of college women who have been raped has increased substantially over this time.

Such a grim conclusion raises many issues that neither researchers nor the authors of this chapter can fully address. One issue that can be discussed with some certainty is the reactions of college and university administrators to the outcry over their students' sexual violence rates. To understand their reactions requires a discussion of the federal government's legislative responses to the problem of sexual victimization of college women.

CONGRESSIONAL ACTIONS REQUIRING INSTITUTIONAL POLICIES AND PROGRAMS

Federal Legislation

In response to the continuing salience of the sexual victimization of college women and the activism of the parents of Jeanne Clery, who was raped and murdered in her residence hall room at Lehigh University in 1986, Congress has passed several acts over the last three decades mandating requirements for postsecondary schools. These include the Student Right-to-Know and Campus Security Act of 1990, renamed in 1998 the Jeanne Clery Disclosure of Campus Security Policy and Campus Crime Statistics Act and now commonly referred to as the Clery Act (see Fisher & Sloan, 2013).

Specific to sexual victimization, the Clery Act requires all postsecondary education institutions under Title IV of the Higher Education Act of 1965 to publish (a) an annual report that includes their sexual offense—forcible and nonforcible—statistics as per the FBI's Uniform Crime Report (UCR) definitions and (b) a description of their sexual assault prevention programs. Noteworthy is the limited usefulness of these statistics, given that a large body of research has found that college women experience a continuum of sexual victimization (including sexual harassment) that is not captured in these statistics and given that the majority of rapes and other forms of sexual violence are not reported to campus police or officials. At best, the Clery Act crime statistics underestimate the amount of campus sexual victimization, and at worst, these statistics communicate a grossly distorted reality of sexual victimization that compromises the safety and well-being of college students, especially women (Fisher et al., 2010).

To help prevent the revictimization of sexual violence victims, Congress amended the Clery Act in 1992 and enacted the Campus Sexual Assault Victims' Bill of Rights as part of the Higher Education Amendments of 1992. This Bill of Rights requires policies, procedures, and services for all victims of sexual assaults that occur at postsecondary schools and that result in a disciplinary proceedings being initiated in the case. The law is designed to ensure that both the accuser and the accused are afforded the same rights throughout the student disciplinary process and that survivors are notified about options to change living and academic institutions, to contact law enforcement and assist the student in doing so, and to seek counseling services.

Passed by Congress and signed by President Obama on March 7, 2013, as part of the reauthorization of the Violence Against Women Act (VAWA), the Campus Sexual Violence Elimination Act (SaVE) explicitly requires counts of "domestic, dating violence, and sexual assault, and stalking" to be disclosed in the annual campus crime statistics report beginning in 2014 and provides procedures victims should follow if a sexual offense, domestic violence, dating violence, sexual assault, or stalking has occurred. SaVE also requires that these crimes be included in the standards for institutional disciplinary procedures and in descriptions of programs to prevent these crimes from being published in the annual report. Schools will receive guidance on primary prevention initiatives and awareness, bystander intervention, and information on risk reduction to recognize warnings of abusive behaviors, including sexual assault. The Departments of Justice, Education, and Health and Human Services also will collect and disseminate to secondary schools best practices for preventing and responding to these four types of crimes (Clery Center for Security on Campus, 2013).

The enforcement of the Clery Act has been delegated to the Department of Education, which can fine schools for violations. The largest fine to date was levied against Eastern Michigan University (EMU) for its violation of the Clery Act when handling the 2006 rape and murder of Laura Dickenson in her residence hall room. EMU agreed to pay $350,000 in fines for 13 separate violations of the Clery Act and settled a state law–based tort case with Dickenson's parents for $2.5 million. Eventually, the university president, vice president for student affairs, and director of public safety were all fired (Cantalupo, 2013).

The Campus Program

In addition to the Clery Act and SaVE, Congress also authorized the Office of Violence Against Women under the VAWA and made reauthorizations to implement the Grants to Reduce Sexual Assault, Domestic Violence, Dating Violence, and Stalking on Campus Program (the Campus Program). The Campus Program encourages a comprehensive, coordinated community approach that

> encourages institutions of higher education to adopt comprehensive, coordinated responses to domestic violence, dating violence, sexual assault, and stalking. Campuses, in partnership with community-based nonprofit victim-advocacy organizations and local criminal justice or civil legal agencies, must adopt protocols and policies that treat violence against women as a serious offense and develop victim service programs that ensure victim safety, offender accountability, and the prevention of such crimes. (Office of Violence Against Women, 2012)

The first Campus Program grant was made in 1999; 186 grants totaling nearly $54 million dollars were awarded to both public and private schools across the United States and in Puerto Rico from 2005 to 2011. The 2007 to 2010 reports to Congress submitted by the 90 grantees showed that the top-priority areas that they addressed were (1) implementing education programs for prevention (18% of schools); (2) supporting improved communication among campus and local law enforcement (18%); (3) developing and implementing campus policies, protocols, and services to effectively identify and respond to crime and training of campus law enforcement and those serving on campus disciplinary boards about such polices and protocols and services (17%); (4) developing, enlarging, and strengthening victims' services programs on campuses (e.g., legal, medical, or psychological) (16%); and (5) creating, disseminating, and otherwise providing assistance with and information about victims' options on and off campus to bring disciplinary and other legal action (14%; Daigle, Scherer, Fisher, & Azimi, forthcoming).

Title IX

Title IX of the Educational Amendments of 1972 (Title IX) prohibits sexual harassment in educational institutions, including postsecondary ones, as a form of sexual discrimination; sexual victimization perpetrated by a peer is "generally considered a case of hostile environment sexual harassment that is so severe, pervasive and objectively offensive that it effectively bars the victim's access to an educational opportunity or benefit" (*Davis v. Monroe County Board of Education*, 1999, p. 632, as cited in Cantalupo, 2013). Under Title IX, federally funded educational institutions are responsible "to take immediate and effective steps to respond to sexual violence in accordance with the requirements of Title IX" (Office for Civil Rights, 2011).

This responsibility includes protecting the rights of survivors of student-on-student sexual violence (rape, sexual assault, sexual battery, and sexual coercion), providing policy and procedure standards for fact-finding investigations and hearings, and investigating schools for violations when a student files a complaint. The Office for Civil Rights (OCR) from time to time offers guidance and/or clarifies Title IX requirements. For example, on April 4, 2011, the OCR issued a 19-page "Dear Colleague" letter in which the assistant secretary for human rights detailed steps to prevent sexual harassment and violence and correct its discriminatory impact on the complainant and others. The letter also provided examples of remedies that schools and the OCR may use to end such conduct, prevent its recurrence, and address its effects (Ali, 2011).

Although very few students seem to be aware of the OCR's complaint process, the courts have settled several high-profile cases. A publicized exemplar is *Simpson v. University of Colorado-Boulder* (2007), in which two college women were gang raped as part of an unsupervised football requirement program. The University of Colorado–Boulder (UC-B) was determined to have evidence that the program was leading to sexual violence. The plaintiffs were awarded $2.85 million dollars. UC-B hired a Title IX specialist and fired several university administrators, including the president and the men's football coach. Arizona State University and the University of Georgia also agreed to pay large settlements as a result of Title IX complaints filed against them (Cantalupo, 2013).

COLLEGE AND UNIVERSITY ADMINISTRATORS' POLICY AND PROGRAM RESPONSES

Colleges and universities either funded by the Campus Program and/or required by the Clery Act have implemented prevention policies and awareness and education programs aimed at reducing sexual violence among their students. Given that over 6,500 schools are Title IV eligible, quite a large number of policies and programs are implemented.

School administrators have taken two general approaches to reducing sexual violence—a criminal justice one and a public health one—and they sometimes have integrated the two approaches. Although the criminal justice approach focuses more on reporting incidents to law enforcement or campus officials and on disciplinary procedures and sanctions, the public health approach focuses on primary, secondary, and tertiary prevention.

Primary prevention takes place *before* sexual violence has occurred to prevent initial victimization or perpetration. Typically targeted at all students, these programs involve educational presentations about a variety of topics, including but not limited to defining sexual violence (especially rape), describing risk factors, challenging sex-role stereotypes and prevailing rape myths and behaviors that support violence toward women, defining consent and coercion, and providing instruction in how to use bystander intervention behaviors to defuse risky situations.

Secondary prevention targets at-risk individuals *before* a rape occurs in an effort to reduce known or suspected risk factors. Acquaintance and date rape prevention programs geared toward groups at high risk for perpetrating sexual violence (such as fraternity members) and those who are at risk for rape victimization (such as first-year undergraduates) are popular. These strategies are often directed at reducing lifestyle risks associated with consumption of alcohol and illegal substances. Preventing recurring victimization, especially among sexual- and dating-violence victims who are known to be at high risk for subsequent incidents, is another example of secondary prevention. Many schools have late-evening escort and/or shuttle services to decrease students' risk of violence, primarily from strangers. Many campuses also promote self-defense training to thwart rape.

Tertiary prevention involves responding to victims' needs *after* a rape has occurred to minimize its lasting consequences and harm. Such responses include psychological counseling and mental and physical health support. Some campuses have established sexual assault response teams (also known as SARTs) to respond to and coordinate addressing victims' needs, including transportation to a Sexual Assault Nurse Examiner (SANE) or to a doctor who collects forensic evidence for legal proceedings and connecting the victim with an advocate who can provide support during school disciplinary or criminal justice procedures.

Bear in mind that although legislative mandates are in place for the development of all criminal justice and public health strategies, these statutes do not require any particular practices and do not describe the exact form (e.g., content, duration) that a program should take. College and university administrators (who may or may not be trained in the area of sexual violence) are faced with having to either choose from an array of existing/prepackaged programs or develop a new program on their own. The only national standards for content can be found in SaVE, which requires primary prevention for all incoming students and new employees, including options for bystander intervention, information on risk reduction, and legal definitions of sexual violence and consent under state law. This is the first step toward standardized prevention across Title IV schools. Perhaps not surprisingly, there is no published inventory of what policies or programs have been implemented to address sexual violence.

ARE CAMPUSES' RESPONSES EFFECTIVE?

Only a scant body of research informs what is known about the effectiveness of campuses' responses to Clery Act and Title IX regulations. At best, little is known about "what works" to prevent sexual violence or reduce it. General recommendations can be gleaned from a review of eight articles. The findings suggest that the effectiveness of campus-based sexual violence prevention programs varies depending on the type of audience (e.g., targeted at single gender), facilitator (e.g., professional facilitated), format (e.g., workshop based or offered as classroom courses with frequent and long sessions), and program content (e.g., gender-role socialization, risk education and rape myths, attitudes and avoidance, dating communication, controlled drinking; Vladutiu, Martin, & Macy, 2011).

The effectiveness of specific types of policies and programs is—at worst—unknown by researchers, policy makers, and campus administrators and—at best—questionable, with a few prevention strategies showing promising results. The overall results are summarized as follows:

- Primary prevention
    - The overall effectiveness of primary prevention programs in reducing the incidence of rape is questionable at best (Fisher et al., 2008).
    - A small body of research shows that while educational programs can increase knowledge about rape and change rape-supportive attitudes, the effects diminish over time (see Breitenbecher, 2000). According to Schewe (2002, p. 112), however, "the clearest message that comes from the evaluation literature is that these programs rarely work."
    - Bystander intervention education programs show promise in increasing students' bystander behaviors in risky situations, with sustained changes (2 months after training) in knowledge, attitudes, and bystander behaviors in both males and females relative to control groups (Banyard, Moynihan, & Plante, 2007; see also Coker et al., 2011).
- Secondary prevention
    - The effectiveness of secondary prevention is mixed.
    - Using forceful physical or verbal resistance enhances rape avoidance, whereas nonforceful verbal resistance is ineffective (Ullman, 2007).
- Tertiary prevention
    - The effectiveness of tertiary prevention has not been widely evaluated.

Conclusion

As can be seen, since first being studied, knowledge about college women's sexual victimization has grown at a rapid pace. Early studies centered on defining and measuring sexual victimization. Importantly, these studies provided for the first time national-level estimates of the extent of sexual victimization among college students. It was discovered that between 1 in 5 and 1 in 4 college women experience rape during their college tenure, and an even greater proportion experience sexual victimizations other than rape.

We now know that college women face a real risk of being sexually victimized once, and often a subsequent time, while enrolled in school. Further, research has found that women often respond in "typical" ways to being raped—they do not report their incidents to the police, they often use self-protective actions, and they do not acknowledge their rape. Being raped has other consequences for college women that can sometimes be long-lasting, which may negatively influence their academic performance, as well as their psychological and physical health, and interpersonal relationships.

In part because of these consequences, colleges and universities have developed programs and policies to try to reduce the number of sexual victimizations that occur as well as their attending harm. Some of these policies and programs are a result of federal legislation, such as the Clery Act, the Violence Against Women Act, Title IX regulations, and SaVE. At their heart, programs that are designed to prevent sexual violence among college students are designed to be either primary prevention, secondary prevention, or tertiary prevention. The effectiveness of most of these programs remains unknown. As such, sexual victimization and prevention researchers should work to determine whether prevention programs work and, if so, what elements of the programs are most effective and for whom they work.

Discussion Questions

1. This chapter has discussed the history and progression of research regarding the sexual victimization of college students. Early studies were concerned with measurement and prevalence. More recent studies have considered sexual revictimization and the role of substance use and technology in these unwanted sexual experiences. Which areas of research might sexual victimization researchers explore next? What are the most pressing questions that still need to be answered?

2. Should colleges and universities be held accountable for not disclosing sexual assaults that take place on their campuses? Would it be possible for colleges and universities to provide a more accurate account of the number of sexual victimizations that occur on their campuses? If so, how?

3. Colleges and universities can take a criminal justice approach, a public health approach, or an integrated approach to the reduction of sexual victimization on their campuses. What does each of these approaches include? Which approach do you think is most appropriate and why?

4. Given the research on the consequences of sexual victimization of college students and campuses' responses and programs for students, are colleges and universities doing an adequate job of addressing sexual victimization among college students? What types of programs seem to be most effective? How could programming be improved, keeping in mind the role of drugs and alcohol as well as of technology in sexual victimization?

Notes

1. This estimate was criticized because two of the questions in the SES that measure rape ask about a man attempting to or having sex with a respondent because he gave her alcohol or drugs (Gilbert, 1997). When "yes" answers to these questions are removed from the estimates, 9.3% of the sample had experienced either a completed or an attempted rape during the previous year.

2. Similar to Krebs et al.'s (2009) *alcohol and/or other drug-enabled sexual assault*, Kilpatrick et al.'s (2007) term *incapacitated rape* refers to a voluntary use of drugs or alcohol by the victim that results in an incident of rape. Kilpatrick et al.'s definition of *drug- and alcohol-facilitated rape* refers to the perpetrator giving the victim drugs or alcohol without the victim's consent in order for the rape to occur. This definition is similar to Krebs et al.'s (2009) term *drug-facilitated sexual assault*.

References

Abbey, A., Zawacki, T., Buck, P. O., Clinton, A. M., & McAuslan, P. (2001). Alcohol and sexual assault. *Alcohol Research & Health, 25,* 43–51.

Ali, R. (2011). *Dear colleague letter: Sexual violence.* Retrieved from http://thefire.org/public/pdfs/0559f332d909e0024ac3bc0d07081e60.pdf?direct

Aosved, A. C., Long, P. J., & Voller, E. K. (2011). Sexual revictimization and adjustment in college men. *Psychology of Men & Masculinity, 12*(3), 285–296.

Archambeau, O. G., Frueh, B. C., Deliramich, A. N., Elhai, J. D., Grubaugh, A. L., Herman, S., & Kim, B. S. K. (2010). Interpersonal violence and mental health outcomes among Asian American and Native Hawaiian/Other Pacific Islander college students. *Psychological Trauma, 2*(4), 273–283.

Banyard, V. L., Moynihan, M. M., & Plante, E. G. (2007). Sexual violence prevention through bystander education: An experimental evaluation. *Journal of Community Psychology, 35*(4), 463–481.

Banyard, V. L., Ward. S., Cohn, E. S., Plante, E. G., Moorhead, C., & Walsh, W. (2007). Unwanted sexual contact on campus: A comparison of women's and men's experiences. *Violence and Victims, 22*(1), 52–70.

Billingham, R. E., & Patterson, J. L. (1998). Body dissatisfaction and sexual victimization among college women. *Psychological Reports, 82*(3 Pt 1), 907–911.

Bondurant, B. (2001). University women's acknowledgement of rape: Individual, situational, and social factors. *Violence Against Women, 7*(3), 294–314.

Botta, R. A., & Pingree, S. (1997). Interpersonal communication and rape: Women acknowledge their assaults. *Journal of Health Communication, 2*(3), 197–212.

Breitenbecher, K. H. (2000). Sexual assault on college campuses: Is an ounce of prevention enough? *Applied and Preventive Psychology, 9*(1), 23–52.

Brener, N. D., McMahon, P. M., Warren, C. W., & Douglas, K. A. (1999). Forced sexual intercourse and associated health-risk behavior among female college students in the United States. *Journal of Consulting and Clinical Psychology, 67*(2), 252–259.

Bryan, C. J., McNaugton-Cassill, M., Osman, A., & Hernandez, A. M. (2013). The associations of physical and sexual assault with suicide risk in nonclinical military and undergraduate samples. *Suicide and Life-Threatening Behavior, 43*(2), 223–234.

Campus Sexual Assault Victims' Bill of Rights, Pub. L. 102-325, § 486(c) (1992).

Campus Sexual Violence Elimination Act (SaVE), Pub. L. 113-134, § 304, 127 Stat. 89 (2013).

Cantalupo, N. (2013). "Decriminalizing" campus institutional responses to peer sexual violence. In B. S. Fisher & J. J. Sloan III (Eds.), *Campus crime: Legal, social and policy perspectives* (3rd ed.). Springfield, IL: Charles C Thomas.

Cass, A. I. (2007). Routine activities and sexual assault: An analysis of individual- and school-level factors. *Violence and Victims, 22*(3), 350–366.

Cleere, C., & Lynn, S. J. (2013). Acknowledged versus unacknowledged sexual assault among college women. *Journal of Interpersonal Violence, 28*(12), 2593–2611.

Clery Center for Security on Campus. (2013). *VAWA reauthorization.* Retrieved from http://clerycenter.org/article/vawa-reauthorization/

Combs-Lane, A. M., & Smith, D. W. (2002). Risk of sexual victimization in college women: The role of behavioral intentions and risk-taking behaviors. *Journal of Interpersonal Violence, 17*(2), 165–183.

Coker, A. L., Cook-Craig, P. G., Williams, C. M., Fisher, B. S., Clear, E. R., Garcia, L. S., & Hegge, L. M. (2011). Evaluation of Green Dot: An active bystander intervention to reduce sexual violence on college campuses. *Violence Against Women, 17,* 777–796.

Culbertson, K. A., Vik, P. W., Kooiman, B. J. (2001). The impact of sexual assault, sexual assault perpetrator type, and location of sexual assault on ratings of perceived safety. *Violence Against Women, 7*(8), 858–875.

Daigle, L. E., Fisher, B. S., & Cullen, F. T. (2008). The violent and sexual victimization of college women: Is repeat victimization a problem? *Journal of Interpersonal Violence, 23*(9), 1296–1313.

Daigle, L. E., Scherer, H., Fisher, B. S., & Azimi, A. (forthcoming). Intimate partner violence among college students: Measurement, risk factors, consequences, and responses. In C. Cuevas and C. M. Renninson (Eds.), *Handbook on the psychology of violence.* Wiley-Blackwell.

Davis v. Monroe County Board of Education, 526 U.S. 629 (1999).

DeMitchell, T. A., & Parker-Magagna, M. (2011). Student victims or student criminals: The bookends of sexting in a cyber world. *Cardozo Public Law, Policy, & Ethics Journal, 10,* 1–41.

Fisher, B. S., Cullen, F. T., & Turner, M. G. (1999). *Extent and nature of the sexual victimization of college women: A national-level analysis* (final report). Washington, DC: U.S. Department of Justice, National Institute of Justice.

Fisher, B. S., Daigle, L. E., & Cullen, F. T. (2008). Rape against women: What can research offer to guide the development of prevention programs and risk reduction interventions? *Journal of Contemporary Criminal Justice, 24*(2), 163–177.

Fisher, B. S., Daigle L. E., & Cullen F. T. (2010). *Unsafe in the ivory tower: The sexual victimization of college women.* Thousand Oaks, CA: Sage.

Fisher, B. S., Daigle, L. E., Cullen, F. T., & Santana, S. A. (2007). Assessing the efficacy of the protective action-sexual victimization completion nexus for sexual victimizations. *Violence and Victims, 22*(1), 18–42.

Fisher, B. S., Daigle, L. E., Cullen, F. T., & Turner, M. G., (2003a). Acknowledging sexual victimization as rape: Results from a national-level study. *Justice Quarterly, 20*(3), 535–574.

Fisher, B. S., Daigle, L. E., Cullen, F. T., & Turner, M. G. (2003b). Reporting sexual victimization to the police and others: Results from a national-level study of college women. *Criminal Justice and Behavior, 30*(1), 6–38.

Fisher, B. S., and Sloan, J. J. III (Eds.). (2013). *Campus crime: Legal, social and policy perspectives* (3rd ed.). Springfield, IL: Charles C Thomas.

Fisher, B. S., & Wilkes, A. R. P. (2003). A tale of two ivory towers. *The British Journal of Criminology, 43*(3), 526–545.

Frazier, P. A., & Seales, L. M. (1997). Acquaintance rape is real rape. In M. D. Schwartz (Ed.), *Researching sexual violence again women: Methodological and personal perspectives* (pp. 54–64). Thousand Oaks, CA: Sage.

Frazier, P., Anders, S., Perera, S., Tomich, P., Tennen, H., Park, C., & Tashiro, T. (2009). Traumatic events among undergraduate students: Prevalence and associated symptoms. *Journal of Counseling Psychology, 56*(3), 450–460.

Gidycz, C. A., Coble, C. N., Latham, L., & Layman, M. J. (1993). Sexual assault experience in adulthood and prior victimization experiences: A prospective analysis. *Psychology of Women Quarterly, 17*(2), 151–168.

Gilbert, N. (1997). Advocacy research and social policy. In M. Tonry (Ed.), *Crime and justice: A review of research* (Vol. 22, pp. 101–148). Chicago, IL: University of Chicago Press.

Harned, M. S. (2001). Abused women or abused men? An examination of the context and outcomes of dating violence. *Violence and Victims, 16*(3), 269–285.

Jeanne Clery Disclosure of Campus Security Policy and Campus Crime Statistics Act (Clery Act), 20 U.S.C. § 1092(f) (1990) (Originally the Student Right-to-Know and Campus Security Act)

Kahn, A. S., Jackson, J., Kully, C., Badger, K., & Halvorsen, J. (2003). Calling it rape: Differences in experiences of women who do or do not label their sexual assault as rape. *Psychology of Women Quarterly, 27*(3), 233–242.

Kahn, A. S., Mathie, V. A., & Torgler, C. (1994). Rape scripts and rape acknowledgement. *Psychology of Women Quarterly, 18*(1), 53–66.

Kilpatrick, D. G., Resnick, H. S., Ruggiero, K. J., Conoscenti, L. M., & McCauley, J. (2007). *Drug-facilitated, incapacitated, and forcible rape: A national study.* Charleston: Medical University of South Carolina, National Crime Victims Research & Treatment Center.

Kirkpatrick, C., & Kanin, E. (1957). Male sex aggression on a university campus. *American Sociological Review, 22*(1), 52–58.

Koss, M. P. (1988). Hidden rape: Sexual aggression and victimization in a national sample of students in higher education. In A. W. Burgess (Ed.), *Rape and sexual assault* (pp. 3–25). New York, NY: Garland.

Koss, M. P., Gidycz, C. A., & Wisniewski, N. (1987). The scope of rape: Incidence and prevalence of sexual aggression and victimization in a national sample of higher education students. *Journal of Consulting and Clinical Psychology, 55*(2), 162–170.

Koss, M. P., & Oros, C. J. (1982). Sexual Experiences Survey: A research instrument investigating sexual aggression and victimization. *Journal of Consulting and Clinical Psychology, 50*(3), 455–457.

Krebs, C. P., Lindquist, C. H., Warner, T. D., Fisher, B. S., & Martin, S. L. (2009). College women's experiences with physically forced, alcohol- or other drug-enabled, and drug-facilitated sexual assault before and since entering college. *Journal of American College Health, 57*(6), 639–649.

Lawyer, S., Resnick, H., Bakanic, V., Burkett, T., & Kilpatrick, D. (2010). Forcible, drug facilitated, and incapacitated rape and sexual assault among undergraduate women. *Journal of American College Health, 58*(5), 453–460.

Layman, M. J., Gidycz, C. A., & Lynn, S. J. (1996). Unacknowledged versus acknowledged rape victims: Situational factors and posttraumatic stress. *Journal of Abnormal Psychology, 105*(1), 124–131.

Littleton, H. L., Axson, D., Breitkopf, C. R., & Berenson, A. (2006). Rape acknowledgement and postassault experiences: How acknowledgement status relates to disclosure, coping, worldview, and reactions received from others. *Violence and Victims, 21*(6), 761–778.

Littleton, H. L., Grills-Taquechel, A. E., Buck, K. S., Rosman, L., & Dodd, J. C. (2013). Health risk behavior and sexual assault among ethnically diverse women. *Psychology of Women Quarterly, 37*(1), 7–21.

McCauley, J. L., Amstadter, A. B., Macdonald, A., Danielson, C. K., Ruggiero, K. J., Resnick, H. S., & Kilpatrick, D. G. (2011). Non-medical use of prescription drugs in a national sample of college women. *Addictive Behaviors, 36*(7), 690–695.

McMullin, D., Wirth, R. J., & White, J. W. (2007). The impact of sexual victimization on personality: A longitudinal study of gendered attributes. *Sex Roles, 56*(7–8), 403–414.

Mohler-Kuo, M., Dowdall, G. W., Koss, M. P., & Wechsler, H. (2004). Correlates of rape while intoxicated in a national sample of college women. *Journal of Studies on Alcohol and Drugs, 65*(1), 37–45.

Mustaine, E. E., & Tewksbury, R. (2002). Sexual assault of college women: A feminist interpretation of a routine activities analysis. *Criminal Justice Review, 27*(1), 89–123.

National Campaign to Prevent Teen and Unplanned Pregnancy. (2008). *Sex and tech: Results from a survey of teens and young adults.* Washington, DC: National Campaign to Prevent Teen and Unplanned Pregnancy.

National Center for Education Statistics. (2013). *Digest of Education Statistics: 2011.* Retrieved from http://nces.ed.gov/programs/digest/d11/tables/dt11_200.asp

National Institute on Alcohol Abuse and Alcoholism (NIAAA). (2012). *College drinking.* Retrieved from http://pubs.niaaa.nih.gov/publications/CollegeFactSheet/CollegeFactSheet.pdf

Office for Civil Rights. (2011). *Dear colleague letter: Sexual violence background, summary, and fast facts.* Retrieved from http://www2.ed.gov/about/offices/list/ocr/docs/dcl-factsheet-201104.html

Office of Violence Against Women. (2012). *Campus grant program.* Retrieved from http://www.ovw.usdoj.gov/ovwgrantprograms.htm#1/

Pitts, V. L., & Schwartz, M. D. (1993). Promoting self-blame in hidden rape cases. *Humanity and Society, 17*(4), 383–398.

Reyns, B. W., Burek, M. W., Henson, B., & Fisher, B. S. (2013). The unintended consequences of digital technology: Exploring the relationship between sexting and cybervictimization. *Journal of Crime and Justice, 36*(1), 1–17.

Russell, D. E. H. (1982). The prevalence and incidence of forcible rape and attempted rape of females. *Victimology, 10*, 81–93.

Sander, L. (2013, August 2). Yale U. is fined $165,000 under crime-reporting law. *The Chronicle of Higher Education.* Retrieved from http://chronicle.com/article/Yale-U-Is-Fined-165000/139343/

Schewe, P. A. (2002). Guidelines for developing rape prevention and risk interventions. In P. A. Schewe (Ed.), *Preventing violence in relationships: Interventions across the life span.* (pp. 107–136). Washington, DC: American Psychological Association.

Schwartz, M. D., & Pitts, V. L. (1995). Exploring a feminist routine activities approach to explaining sexual assault. *Justice Quarterly, 12*(1), 9–31.

Shapiro, B. L., & Schwarz, J. C. (1997). Date rape: Its relationship to trauma symptoms and sexual self-esteem. *Journal of Interpersonal Violence, 12*(3), 407–419.

Siegel, J. A., & Williams, L. M. (2003). Risk factors for sexual victimization of women: Results from a prospective study. *Violence Against Women, 9*(8), 902–930.

Simpson v. University of Colorado–Boulder, 500 F.3d 1170 (10th Cir. 2007).

Sloan, J. J., III, Fisher, B. S., & Cullen, F. T. (1997). Assessing the Student Right-to-Know and Campus Security Act of 1990: An analysis of the victim reporting practices of college and university students. *Crime and Delinquency, 43* (2), 148–168.

Snell, P. A., & Englander, E. K. (2010). Cyberbullying victimization and behaviors among girls: Applying research findings in the field. *Journal of Social Sciences, 6*(4), 508–514.

Stepakoff, S. (1998). Effects of sexual victimization on suicidal ideation and behavior in U.S. college women. *Suicide and Life-Threatening Behavior, 28*(1), 107–126.

Stephenson, H., Pena-Shaff, J., & Quirk, P. (2006). Predictors of college student suicidal ideation: Gender differences. *College Student Journal, 40*(1), 109–117.

Substance Abuse and Mental Health Services Administration (SAMHSA). (2012). *Results from the 2011 national survey on drug use and health: Summary of national findings* (NSDUH Series

H-44, HHS Publication No. [SMA] 12–4713). Retrieved from http://www.samhsa.gov/data/NSDUH/2k11Results/NSDUHresults2011.pdf

Title IX of the Educational Amendments of 1972, 20 U.S.C. § 1681–1688 (1972).

Tyler, K., Hoyt, D. R., & Whitbeck, L. B. (1998). Coercive sexual strategies. *Violence and Victims, 13*(1), 47–61.

Ullman, S. E. (1997). Review and critique of empirical studies of rape avoidance. *Criminal Justice and Behavior, 24*, 177–204.

Ullman, S. E. (2007). A 10-year update of "Review and critique of empirical studies of rape avoidance." *Criminal Justice and Behavior, 34*(3), 411–429.

Ullman, S. E. (2010). *Talking about sexual assault: Society's response to survivors.* Washington, DC: American Psychological Association.

Ullman, S. E., Karabatsos, G., & Koss, M. P. (1999). Alcohol and sexual assault in a national sample of college women. *Journal of Interpersonal Violence, 14*(6), 603–625.

Vladutiu, C. J., Martin, S. L., & Macy, R. J. (2011). College- or university-based sexual assault prevention programs: A review of program outcomes, characteristics, and recommendations. *Trauma, Violence, & Abuse, 12*(2), 67–86.

Wechsler, H., Dowdall, G. W., Maenner, G., Gledhill-Hoyt, J., & Lee, H. (1998). Changes in binge drinking and related problems among American college students between 1993 and 1997: Results of the Harvard School of Public Health College Alcohol Study. *Journal of American College Health, 47*(2), 57–68.

Winfield, I., George, L. K., Swartz, M., & Blazer, D. G. (1990). Sexual assault and psychiatric disorders among a community sample of women. *The American Journal of Psychiatry, 147*(3), 335–341.

Zinzow, H., Amstadter, A. B., McCauley, J. L., Ruggiero, K. J., Resnick, H. S., & Kilpatrick, D. G. (2011). Self-rated health in relation to rape and mental health disorders in a national sample of college women. *Journal of American College Health, 59*(7), 588–594.

Zinzow, H. M., Resnick, H. S., McCauley, J. L., Amstadter, A. B., Ruggerio, K. J., & Kilpatrick, D. G. (2010). The role of rape tactics in risk for posttraumatic stress disorder and major depression: Results from a national sample of college women. *Depression and Anxiety, 27*(8), 708–715.

7

The Fine Line Between Statutory Rape and Consensual Relationships

Sarah Koon-Magnin

V arious forms and experiences of sexual assault and victimization are discussed in this volume, but they share a common theme: a lack of consent from the victim. When an assailant uses physical force, a weapon, a threat of force, or a threat of harm against the victim's loved ones, the law is clear that the sexual act was non-consensual, engaged in against the victim's will, and is thus labeled "forcible." When other tactics are used to overpower a victim and facilitate a sexual assault (e.g., the assailant has sex with an incapacitated or intoxicated victim, drugs the victim, or is verbally coercive), these sexual acts, even in the absence of physical injury or threat of physical injury, are also legally recognized as assaults because of the lack of consent provided by the victim. However, there is one type of sexual assault that is recognized by the legal system as a crime, regardless of whether or not a victim consents: statutory rape.

Statutory rape is a legally defined crime (hence, "statutory") based on the age of the individuals involved in the sexual act. If at least one of the individuals falls below a state's determined age of consent, the sexual act is defined as a crime regardless of the intentions of the sexual actors. Just as a 15-year-old cannot legally take out a personal loan, purchase a vehicle, or consume alcohol in the United States, the state has determined that minors cannot make the decision to engage in sexual activity, a choice with many potential short- and long-term consequences. That is, the legal system does not recognize any consent provided by individuals below the state-defined age of consent. As a result, there is a very fine line between consensual relationships among adolescents and the crime of statutory rape.

Statutory rape is a strict liability crime, which means that engaging in sex with an individual below the legally defined age of consent is viewed as so harmful and detrimental that no *mens rea*, "guilty mind," is necessary to establish guilt. The act itself is sufficient proof that a crime occurred to result in prosecution and punishment for the offender. Statutory rape laws are unique in that they apply only to consensual (i.e., not forcible) sexual encounters. If an element of force were used, the offender would be held accountable under another type of sexual assault statute (e.g., rape, sexual battery). If the victim is a child (typically defined as younger than age 12), the offender would be charged with a crime such as child molestation. In this way, statutory rape laws define and identify victims who have willingly engaged in sexual activity that the state deems they are not adequately prepared to participate in.

In some cases of statutory rape, the legally recognized "victim" does not express that she or he in fact feels victimized. Perhaps the most infamous case of statutory rape in the United States is the case of Mary Kay Letourneau and her sixth-grade student, Vili Fualaau. Letourneau, then a married mother of four, was a sixth-grade teacher in Washington when she met Fualaau in 1995. The two began an illicit affair, which was discovered later that year when Letourneau became pregnant with Fualaau's baby. Facing statutory rape charges, Letourneau pled guilty in exchange for a short term of incarceration (3 months) followed by a longer term of probation. In addition, she had to turn over custody of her daughter with Fualaau to Fualaau's mother. Once released on probation, Letourneau was banned from contacting her victim, who was then 14 years old. However, within a month, the two were found together in a compromising situation in Letourneau's vehicle. This violation led to additional charges, and Letourneau was sentenced to 7½ years in prison. While incarcerated, Letourneau announced that she was pregnant with Fualaau's second child, who was born in 1998 and released to the custody of Fualaau's mother. Letourneau was released from prison in 2005, and the no-contact order prohibiting her from seeing Fualaau was soon lifted. The two promptly rekindled their relationship and were wed (in a nationally televised ceremony) in 2005. Still married and raising two children as a family, Fualaau maintains that his love for Letourneau is sincere and not the result of any coercive or predatory behavior on the part of his former teacher. Despite multiple interventions by the legal system, the two were undeterred from their relationship. However, Fualaau's willingness to engage in sexual activity with his teacher was not recognized under the law because of his age status.

The Letourneau case made headlines for much of the 1990s and early 2000s because of the substantial age difference between the two partners, the fact that the perpetrator was a female and in a position of authority over the minor, and the repeat nature of the illegal trysts. Although the Letourneau/Fualaau affair was complicated, the law is simple. An adolescent cannot legally consent to engage in sexual activity that the government has defined as too potentially harmful. The wishes or desires of the victim are not relevant. When someone is below the legal age of consent, "no" means "no," and "yes" means "no."

History of Statutory Rape Laws in the United States

Statutory rape laws are not a recent legal construct; rather, they have a long history in the United States and elsewhere. The original intention of statutory rape laws in colonial America (imported from English common law) was to protect the chastity of young females. Virginity was a valuable financial asset, and the purpose of the laws was to discourage older males from devaluing females prior to marriage (Cocca, 2004). In short, females were viewed as property, and chaste females were valued more highly than females who had been sexually active. Even as the view of females as property faded, traditional views of gender still dictated the norms of sexual behavior and reactions to sexual activity. Legislators believed that the risk of pregnancy and social stigmatization were deterrence enough to prevent adolescent females from engaging in sexual activity. For men, however, legislators believed that legal intervention was necessary to deter sex with minor females (see, for example, the Supreme Court's discussion in *Michael M. v. Superior Court of Sonoma County*, 1981).

Early statutory rape laws set the age of consent as the approximate age of puberty: 10 or 12 (Bullough, 2004; Posner & Silbaugh, 1996). Thus, the age at which a minor began to transition to adulthood physically was approximately the age at which the minor's consent to engage in sexual activity was legally recognized. To a modern reader, setting the age of consent to sex at only 10 or 12 may seem outrageous. However, the social construction of childhood and adolescence are relatively recent developments. For hundreds of years, a high child mortality rate discouraged parents from becoming emotionally attached to their children, whom they saw as additional workers and providers for the family (Bullough). Infants and toddlers were obviously dependent on elders for food and other necessities. However, once able to participate in conversation and take care of basic needs, children were considered mature. Children were taught to work as soon as they were physically able (Feld, 1999). In other words, "people in western societies viewed young people after infancy as miniature adults, smaller versions of their parents, rather than as qualitatively different from their elders" (Feld, p. 17). Clearly, the physical and developmental views of children prior to the 1800s were very different from the views of today. As a result, in the early 20th century, the age of consent was raised across the United States and is now at least the age of 16 in every state.

Determining an Appropriate Age of Consent

Inconsistencies in determining an age of maturity (both across states and across acts, from driving a car to drinking alcohol) have been widely studied by psychologists, who have attempted to determine an appropriate age to declare individuals are mature. There is no clear consensus. Several studies of cognitive ability have compared groups of children, adolescents, and adults to determine whether or not differences exist among the three groups (Kaser-Boyd, Adelman, & Taylor, 1985; Neimark & Lewis, 1968; Weithorn & Campbell, 1982). In these studies, researchers administered similar tasks to members of the various age groups and then compared results between groups. None of these studies found statistically significant differences between the young adolescents and adults (Kaser-Boyd et al.; Neimark & Lewis; Weithorn & Campbell). Drawing on these and similar studies, the American Psychological Association (APA) submitted an amicus brief to the U.S. Supreme Court in the 1990 case of *Hodgson v. Minnesota.*[1] The brief argued that "the unvarying and highly significant findings of numerous scientific studies indicate that with respect to the capacity to understand and reason logically, there is no qualitative or quantitative difference between minors in mid-adolescence, i.e., about 14–15 years of age, and adults."

In addition to the research already mentioned, the brief discussed the process of formal operations, originally described by Piaget. This process, which is critical to the development of adult decision-making capacities, is characterized by the ability to carry out four primary tasks: (1) generating possible solutions to a problem, (2) identifying the possible consequences of each solution, (3) weighing the possible choices, and (4) making an informed decision. This process is typically completed by the age of 14 or 15, at which point the adolescent is able to make decisions in the same way as an adult would. The APA brief concluded that middle to late adolescents can make decisions as well as adults and should be treated as mature under the law.

The research used in the *Hodgson* brief was criticized and contradicted by other social scientists—specifically by those who argue that cognitive differences are only one half of the issue. Decision-making competence is sometimes measured in terms of the resulting consequences (Furby & Beyth-Marom, 1992). The fact that adolescents are overrepresented in terms of rates of premarital pregnancy, drug use, reckless driving, and driving under the influence has led researchers and lawmakers alike to conclude that adolescents are unable to make competent decisions (Arnett, 1992). However, some researchers have argued that the decisions that adolescents make and the consequences that follow them are not a good proxy for adolescents' decision-making competence (Furby & Beyth-Marom). That is, the cognitive process that adolescents use to reach a decision may be identical to that of adults, but psychosocial disparities cause them to reach different conclusions. Adolescents attach more weight to potentially positive consequences than they do to negative consequences in decision making and are less likely than adults to consider long-term consequences (Owen-Kostelnik, Repucci, & Meyer, 2006). Because of their focus on short-term consequences and the illusion of invulnerability to negative consequences, adolescents are likely to make choices that emphasize immediate gratification despite actual risk of danger, harm, or negative long-term consequences (Furby & Beyth-Marom). Adults who consider the same possible courses of action and consider the consequences of those actions may reach a different conclusion simply because their focus is different; they focus on long-term consequences and the negative risks involved in the situation (Furby & Beyth-Marom).

Recent research suggests that comparisons of adolescents to adults are not sufficient. In fact, there are significant differences between young adolescents and middle to late adolescents (Steinberg & Cauffman, 1996); therefore, it is erroneous to treat adolescents as a homogenous group. In a study of juveniles' understanding of Miranda rights, adolescents aged 15 and under showed significantly less understanding than did adults (Grisso, 1980). Adolescents younger than 16 performed worse than older adolescents on measures of competence and were more vulnerable to psychosocial influences such as peer pressure and risk perception (Grisso et al, 2003). In another study of adolescent decision making, older students were more likely than younger students to mention several important elements of a mature decision, such as consideration of potential consequences and seeking professional advice (Lewis, 1981). These differences may be attributable to an increase in decision-making experience that comes with age (Lewis).

In contrast to the earlier document, the 2004 amicus brief submitted by the APA in the case of *Roper v. Simmons*[2] argued that "at ages 16 and 17, adolescents, as a group, are not yet mature in ways that affect their decision-making." Specifically, the brief argued, adolescents are unable to effectively weigh possible courses of action and their various consequences. This argument opposed the position presented in the previous brief for *Hodgson v. Minnesota*, which argued that the process of formal operations was complete by the age of 14 or 15. The brief for *Roper* focused on cognitive development and the age at which the brain is fully developed, usually not before age 18. The portions of the brain necessary for impulse control, reasoning, and risk assessment are not fully developed during adolescence (Owen-Kostelnik et al., 2006). In one experiment in which young and old adolescents were provided with a brief counseling session on legal concepts, the young adolescents showed the least improvement (Viljoen, Odgers, Grisso, & Tillbrook, 2007). Given their possible cognitive disadvantage and their inability to restrain impulses, the APA argued that adolescents should not be held accountable for their actions until the age of 18.

Despite the divergent empirical results and the differing views of when an adolescent becomes mature, legislators in all 50 states have determined an age of consent to sexual activity. For pragmatic reasons, there must be a clear legal standard in place, and maturity cannot be assessed on a case-by-case basis. Current statutes define the age of consent as 16 in 29 states, 17 in 7 states, and 18 in 14 states (see the appendix to this chapter for age of consent by state).

Gendered Statutory Rape Laws

The age of consent was raised in the early 1900s in an effort to protect adolescent females, but this escalation had an unintended consequence: Adolescent males suffered greater risk of prosecution for consensual sexual activity. Furthermore, adolescent males were not protected by statutory rape legislation, which uniquely portrayed females as victims and males as perpetrators. These laws were challenged in the 1981 Supreme Court ruling in *Michael M. v. Superior Court of Sonoma County*, in which the Court upheld the gendered statute. The written decision provided by the Supreme Court stated three rationales for the constitutionality of statutory rape laws protecting only female victims of male perpetrators. First, the Supreme Court argued, as had early legislators, that males required a legal intervention to be deterred from adolescent sexual activity. Fear of stigmatization and pregnancy were sufficient, in the eyes of the Court, to deter females from such activity. Second, the potential physical harm to a female victim was believed to be more severe than the potential physical harm to a male victim. Third, female victims were more likely than male victims to suffer from emotional or psychological damage as a result of early sexual activity. Despite the *Michael M.* decision, all 50 states have expanded their statutory rape laws to protect minor male victims from statutory rape victimization as well as minor females (Cocca, 2004).

According to a major study of the prevalence of statutory rape convictions in the United States, using data from 1996 to 2000, the overwhelming majority of statutory rape cases (95%) still involve male perpetrators and female victims (Troup-Leasure & Snyder, 2005). These data also indicate that statutory rape prosecutions focus almost exclusively on heterosexual encounters (of those cases in which males were victimized, their perpetrator was female 94% of the time; of those cases in which females were victimized, their perpetrator was male 99% of the time; Troup-Leasure & Snyder).

Age Spans and Gradations Based on the Act

Most statutory rape convictions are *not* based on predatory sexual acts involving adults and teenagers but rather involve two teenagers or one teenager and one young adult (20 or 21 years old; Troup-Leasure & Snyder, 2005). To address the distinctly different nature of consensual sex acts between peers and predatory sex acts involving an older adult, most states have decreased criminal penalties for consensual sex between two teenagers. The primary mechanism for this decrease was the introduction of age spans (Cocca, 2004). Age spans provide a buffer zone above the age of consent such that for an individual to be guilty of statutory rape (at least at the felony level), he or she must have intercourse with someone who is below the age of consent *and also* a specified number of years younger than himself or herself. For example, the age of consent in Alabama is 16, but there is a protected age span of 2 years. Therefore, if a 15-year-old girl has sex with a 16-year-old classmate, despite the fact that she is below the age of consent, the act would not be considered statutory rape because the partner was within 2 years of the victim's age. If the same 15-year-old girl had sex with an 18-year-old, because the perpetrator is more than 2 years older and falls outside of the protected age span, this encounter could be prosecuted as a case of statutory rape.

The assumption of age-span laws is that sexual activity involving smaller age differences between partners is likely consensual rather than predatory. Thus, under this assumption, larger age spans are indicative of a coercive or predatory relationship that should be prohibited. Research on college students' perceptions of the appropriateness of adolescent sexual activity suggests that states' addition of age spans are in line with public perceptions (Koon-Magnin & Ruback, 2013). Two studies involving more than 1,000 undergraduates indicated that respondents were more critical of scenarios depicting the youngest victims and the oldest perpetrators. Above and beyond these effects, respondents were more critical of scenarios involving larger age spans between the partners (Koon-Magnin & Ruback). Lawmakers appear to perceive adolescent sexual activity in a similar way, reducing or eliminating penalties for sexual activity between adolescent peers but maintaining severe punishments for acts involving a substantially older partner.

Another form of gradation has also entered statutory rape legislation: The nature of the sexual act is now considered in the legal definitions of statutory rape. Generally, crimes involving penetration are punished more harshly than crimes involving sexual contact, but types of penetration are treated differently in many states. Vaginal intercourse is typically viewed as the most serious offense, followed by oral sex and sodomy. Nonpenetrative sexual contact is typically treated as the least serious offense.

The laws present in New York State, shown in the appendix, clearly illustrate the introduction of gradations based on both the age of the parties and the nature of the sexual act. There are three sets of statutes (Rape, Criminal Sexual Act, and Sexual Abuse), each with three degrees of severity. The difference among the three types of offenses is based on the sexual act engaged in: intercourse, oral/anal sex, or sexual contact. Within each type of offense, the degrees vary based on victim age. The highest degree of severity corresponds to crimes involving the youngest adolescents (younger than 13), and the lowest degree of severity is associated with the oldest adolescents (less than 17). Although all perpetrators must be 18 or older to be held accountable for these statutory rape offenses in New York, the state has also introduced age spans of 4 or 5 years for sexual acts involving older teens. For sexual acts involving the oldest teens (less than 17), perpetrators must be at least 21 years old to be prosecuted.

Recent additions to statutory rape legislation, specifically age spans and gradations based on the nature of the sexual act, are adaptations critical to the changing norms of adolescent sexuality. By permitting some forms of sexual contact prior to the age of consent for sexual intercourse, the legal system is acknowledging the fact that teens typically experiment with sexuality in a gradual way. The majority of sexually active teens are engaging in sexual behavior with peers (Leitenberg & Saltzman, 2000, 2003; Ompad et al. 2006). Age spans, therefore, afford some degree of sexual autonomy to many teens who previously could not have engaged in sexual activity without fear of prosecution.

It also seems that age spans may be achieving their goal of reducing the most predatory relationships, because research suggests that the age difference between partners is negatively related to the age of the female partner (Leitenberg & Saltzman, 2000). That is, the younger a female is at first intercourse, the larger the reported age difference between her and her partner. The older an adolescent female is at first intercourse, the smaller the reported age difference between her and her partner (Leitenberg & Saltzman). In one study, 93% of females who first had sex between the ages of 16 and 18 did so with a peer (someone within 5 years of their own age). Of those who first had sex between the ages of 13 and 15, 88% did so with a peer. However, among the youngest girls (those who first had sex at 11 or 12), slightly less than two thirds (64%) reported having sex with a peer, whereas more than one third (34%) reported having sex with a partner at least 5 years older than themselves. These statistics suggest that the younger a girl is at first intercourse, the more likely she is to have a significantly older partner (i.e., 5 or more years older). A second study by the same researchers focused retrospectively on women who had sex as young adolescents (Leitenberg & Saltzman, 2003). Consistent with the findings of the first study, girls who first had sex at age 13 (rather than 14 or 15) were more likely to do so with a significantly older partner. The authors attributed this trend to coercion and exploitation by predatory adults. In sum, the younger a girl is at the time of sexual intercourse, the more likely she is to have an older partner.

Research also suggests that statutory rape of male victims is more likely to involve large age spans than do similar cases with female victims (Troup-Leasure & Snyder, 2005). Based on 5 years of data, more than 70% of cases involving a male victim of statutory rape involved a perpetrator aged 21 or older, whereas less than half (45%) of cases involving female victims involved perpetrators who were 21 or older. Thus, it is clear that the majority of sexually active females are engaging in sexual activity with peers and that relationships involving larger age spans between partners are nonnormative for adolescent females. However, based on Troup-Leasure and Snyder's findings, it appears that the people who are in the most predatory relationships and perhaps in most need of government intervention are males. Ironically, these are also the victims who are least likely to receive government intervention, as fewer than 5% of all statutory rape cases involve male victims (Troup-Leasure & Snyder).

Statutory Rape Law Today

The form and function of statutory rape laws changed dramatically during the 20th century. The most important changes were the increased age of consent, the implementation of gender-neutral legislation, the creation of age spans, and the implementation of gradations of punishment based on the nature of the sexual act. Although there is still great variation among states' statutory rape legislation, there are also similarities. Every state has raised the age of consent to at least 16 and has implemented gender-neutral legislation. Nearly every state ($n = 48$) has introduced an age span to help distinguish truly predatory cases from cases of consensual sexual activity with a peer. The age span accomplishes this either through recognizing a protected number of years above/below the age of the victim or by declaring a minimum age requirement for prosecution of the perpetrator. Furthermore,

38 states have implemented gradations that account for the nature of the sexual act (e.g., vaginal intercourse, oral intercourse).

The chapter appendix shows the statutes prohibiting statutory rape in each state and the age spans associated with each. Across the 50 states, there is great variation in the number and nature of laws pertaining to adolescent sexual activity. Combined, 151 statutes govern adolescent sexual activity, with a range of 1 to 8 statutes per state. The most common age of consent in the United States is 16 ($n = 29$). However, in the most populous states (California, Florida, Illinois, New York, and Texas), the age of consent is either 17 or 18. Analysis of the age-of-consent statutes by state suggests that most American adolescents are living in states with an age of consent of 17 or 18 rather than the more common age of consent of 16.

There is substantial variation in age-span statutes across states. Some acts involving particularly young victims have no protected age span (for example, South Carolina's statute or Utah's sodomy statute). However, some sexual activity involving adolescents is protected by age spans of up to 11 years (i.e., Pennsylvania's statute), with several states providing age spans of up to 10 years for some acts (Colorado, Delaware, Maine, Massachusetts, Ohio, Tennessee, and Utah). Moreover, inspection of these statutes suggests that an age span of 2 to 4 years is typical.

It is clear, based on the fact that every state has at least one statute governing adolescent sexual activity, that controlling adolescent sexual activity is a priority for lawmakers. But some people question the appropriateness of government intervention in the private issue of sexual activity.

Is Governmental Regulation of Sexual Activity Warranted?

Two important concerns relate the prevalence of teen sex to governmental interests. First, the number of sexually active teens is large enough to constitute a public health problem. Nearly one half of those infected with STDs each year are between the ages of 15 and 24 (Centers for Disease Control and Prevention, 2007). Second, increased rates of sexual activity may also mean higher incidence of teen pregnancy. In 1996, to address the high correlation between teen pregnancy and welfare dependence, the U.S. Congress passed the Personal Responsibility and Work Opportunity Reconciliation Act (commonly known as the Welfare Reform Act). This Act called for "an effective strategy to combat teenage pregnancy . . . including statutory rape culpability and prevention" (§ 101.7). According to this act, states must develop and submit concrete plans for how to reduce "out-of-wedlock pregnancies, with special emphasis on teenage pregnancies" (§ 402.a.1.A).

Social science research suggests that sexual activity in early adolescence is associated with a greater number of sexual partners, having significantly older sexual partners, having sex more often, and using protection less frequently (Deardorff, Gonzales, Christopher, Roosa, & Millsap, 2005). Failure to use protection during intercourse increases the likelihood of both of the governmental concerns: teenage pregnancy and the spread of sexually transmitted infections.

Adolescent sexual activity is also highly correlated with substance use, particularly alcohol use (Deardorff et al., 2005). This association is troublesome because high levels of alcohol and marijuana use are associated with riskier sex practices and continued substance use in adulthood (Staton et al., 1999). Furthermore, adolescents with substance use problems are more likely to have early sex, have more sexual partners, and use condoms less often (Tapert, Aarons, Sedlar, & Brown, 2001).

In a national study of adolescent sexual behavior, researchers found that the context of the relationship (i.e., school status), not partner age difference, was the key predictor of other problem behaviors (Koon-Magnin, Kreager, & Ruback, 2010). That is, when adolescents who were both attending school were in relationships involving age differences of more than 3 years between the partners, the younger females were at no increased risk of engaging in sexual intercourse compared to teens who were not in a dating relationship. However, when the older partner had either graduated or dropped out of school, the risk of sexual activity increased, exposing the minor to negative health outcomes.

It is important to note that there is no evidence of a causal relationship between sexual activity and these negative outcomes. That is, teens who engage in more risk-taking behaviors such as substance abuse may be more likely to date and have sex with substantially older partners, who may be better able to provide them with opportunities to drink alcohol or obtain illegal drugs. In this way, it is reasonable to suspect that some teen girls are selecting relationships with older partners rather than becoming deviant as a result of the relationship with an older partner.

Frequency of Adolescent Sexual Activity

Despite the congressional call for a crackdown on premarital sex among teens, the frequency of this activity remains high. Furthermore, although the laws governing statutory rape vary substantially across states, adolescent sexual behavior does not, which suggests that these laws do not impact adolescents' sexual decisions (Koon-Magnin et al., 2010). By the time they enter the ninth grade, an estimated 30% of American girls and 40% of American boys have had sexual intercourse (Michels, Kropp, Eyre, & Halpern-Felsher, 2005). By the time they reach age 18, it is estimated that more than 50% of adolescent females in America have had sexual intercourse (Oberman, 2004). Other types of sexual activity are also prevalent, such as oral sex acts between adolescents. If statutory rape laws are strictly enforced, they may criminalize a nontrivial segment of the adolescent population of the United States.

The punishments associated with statutory rape convictions are more serious and long-term consequences than most offenders expect. In the news at the time of this writing (the summer of 2013) is the case of Kaitlyn Hunt, an 18-year-old Florida high school student who is accused of committing statutory rape against her then 14-year-old girlfriend. This is the first statutory rape case involving a same-sex couple to garner national attention. Hunt's parents started a petition to pressure the state to drop charges against their daughter—a petition that has been signed by more than 318,000 people within just a few months. Although she was offered a plea bargain, Hunt refused to plead guilty to an act that she does not view as predatory or criminal. The prosecution is proceeding with charges against Hunt, and—if convicted—she may be sentenced to a term of up to 15 years in prison. According to Hunt's lawyer, Julia Graves, the seriousness of these consequences is not proportional to the harm caused by the relationship. At a May 22, 2013, press conference, Graves stated, "High school relationships may be fleeting, but felony convictions are forever."

Genarlow Wilson knows the serious and lasting consequences of a statutory rape conviction. In 2003, Wilson—a popular honors student and high school football player in Georgia—attended a New Year's Eve party that changed his life forever. During the party, a 15-year-old female performed oral sex on Wilson, an act that was videotaped by another partygoer. When the video surfaced, Wilson was convicted of statutory rape and sentenced to 10 years in state prison. As a result of this case, Georgia lawmakers reassessed the legal treatment of statutory rape, and if Wilson were tried for the same act today, he would be sentenced to a maximum of 1 year in prison for a misdemeanor offense. However, because the law was not applied retroactively, Wilson had to fight for his freedom for almost 3 years before being released in 2007.

A felony conviction for the offense of statutory rape requires the offender to register as a sex offender, in accordance with the Adam Walsh Act's Sex Offender Registration and Notification Act (2006). This means that in addition to any period of incarceration, a statutory rapist may be subject to registration and community notification for the rest of his or her life. Although some states still consider statutory rape involving peers to be criminal, they have implemented age spans that reduce the level of the crime to a misdemeanor. Such age spans substantially reduce the penalty for teenage statutory rapists in that they prevent teenagers from being forced to register as sex offenders.

Although the frequency of enforcement has varied over time, current legislative activity in Mississippi suggests that lawmakers take statutory rape seriously and want to hold its perpetrators accountable. Legislation passed in 2013 requires that the medical professionals who deliver a baby for a girl under the age of 16 (with a partner who is suspected to be at least 21 years old) collect and preserve cord blood, which can then be used to identify the child's father for statutory rape prosecution (Coz, 2013). Mississippi currently has the highest rate of birth to teenage mothers, a fact that lawmakers pointed to when developing this new approach.

Adolescent sexual activity can have life-altering consequences for those who participate. Lawmakers from all 50 states have addressed the potential concerns associated with adolescent sexual activity by creating, modifying, and supporting statutory rape legislation. The federal government expressly promoted such legislation in the Personal Responsibility and Work Opportunity Reconciliation Act of 1996. However, if strictly and consistently implemented, statutory rape laws would criminalize a substantial segment of the adolescent population in the United States. At the same time that the case of Kaitlyn Hunt from Florida makes national headlines and rallies voices that oppose current statutory rape legislation, lawmakers in Mississippi pass new initiatives to crack down on the crime. The national conversation on statutory rape is not over, and as long as there is no consensus on the age at which an individual is mature enough to make a voluntary and knowledgeable decision about sexual activity, the debate will remain unresolved.

Conclusion

Statutory rape is a unique form of sexual assault in that no physical force is required. Sexual contact involving minors below the age of consent is believed to be predatory and is thus forbidden, regardless of whether the younger partner reports feeling like a victim. Statutory rape laws exist in many countries and have been in place for centuries (Cocca, 2004). However, the 20th century witnessed many important changes in statutory rape legislation in the United States. Specifically, statutory rape protections are now extended to male victims, most states now recognize protected age spans between partners, and the seriousness of the offense now typically corresponds to the sexual act engaged in (e.g., sexual intercourse, oral sex, sexual contact). The age of consent was also raised in the 1900s and is now 16 ($n = 29$ states), 17 ($n = 7$ states), or 18 ($n = 14$ states).

Despite these laws, many teens become sexually active prior to the age of consent, a fact that has concerned legislators. The federal government (in the Personal Responsibility and Work Opportunity Reconciliation Act) and various states (e.g., Mississippi's new requirement to keep the cord blood of infants born to mothers below the age of consent) continue to prioritize the prohibition of adolescent sexual activity through statutory rape legislation. Governmental concerns over both teenage pregnancy and the spread of sexually transmitted infections are primary motivations for the continued presence of statutory rape laws in the United States. As long as both of these issues remain, it is unlikely that statutory rape laws will be withdrawn.

Discussion Questions

1. Should there be an age of consent, or is adolescent sexual activity beyond the scope of the government's concern? If you believe that there should be an age of consent, what age do you view as appropriate? Why?

2. Is the existence of a protected age span for adolescent sexual activity a good idea? Why or why not?

3. Should parents have a say in whether their child's sexual partner faces statutory rape charges?

4. Do you think that age is the most important consideration in determining the risk associated with adolescent sexual relationships? Should other factors be considered in addition to or instead of age (e.g., student status, maturity level)?

Appendix

Statutes Governing Adolescent Sexual Activity in the United States

State	Statute	Name of Crime	Act	Age of Consent	Age of Victim	Age of Perp.	Age Span
Alabama	13A-6-61	Rape 1st Degree	Intercourse	16	< 12	≥ 16	
	13A-6-62	Rape 2nd Degree	Intercourse	16	12–16*	≥ 16	2 years
	13A-6-63	Sodomy 1st Degree	Deviate Intercourse	16	< 12	≥ 16	
	13A-6-64	Sodomy 2nd Degree	Deviate Intercourse	16	12–16*	≥ 16	
	13A-6-67	Sexual Abuse 2nd Degree	Sexual Contact	16	12–16*	≥ 19	
Alaska	11.41.434	Sex Abuse Minor 1st Degree	Penetration	16	< 13	≥ 16	
	11.41.436	Sex Abuse Minor 2nd Degree	Penetration	16	13–15	≥ 17	4 years
	11.41.436	Sex Abuse Minor 2nd Degree	Sexual Contact	16	< 13	≥ 16	
	11.41.438	Sex Abuse Minor 3rd Degree	Sexual Contact	16	13–15	≥ 17	4 years
	11.41.440	Sex Abuse Minor 4th Degree	Sexual Contact	16	< 13	< 16	3 years

(Continued)

State	Statute	Name of Crime	Act	Age of Consent	Age of Victim	Age of Perp.	Age Span
Arizona	13-1405	Sexual Conduct With a Minor	Intercourse	18	< 18		
	13-1405	Sexual Conduct With a Minor	Oral Sex	18	< 18		
	13-1405	Sexual Conduct With a Minor	Intercourse	18	≥ 15	< 19	2 years
	13-1405	Sexual Conduct With a Minor	Oral Sex	18	≥ 15	< 19	2 years
Arkansas	5-14-103	Rape	Intercourse	16	< 14		3 years
	5-14-125	Sexual Assault 2nd Degree	Sexual Contact	16	< 14	≥ 18	
	5-14-125	Sexual Assault 2nd Degree	Sexual Contact	16	12–13	< 18	4 years
	5-14-125	Sexual Assault 2nd Degree	Sexual Contact	16	< 12	≥ 18	
	5-14-125	Sexual Assault 2nd Degree	Sexual Contact	16	< 12	< 18	3 years
	5-14-126	Sexual Assault 3rd Degree	Intercourse or Deviate Intercourse	16	< 14	< 18	3 years
	5-14-127	Sexual Assault 4th Degree	Intercourse, Deviate Intercourse, or Sexual Contact	16	< 16	≥ 20	

State	Statute	Name of Crime	Act	Age of Consent	Age of Victim	Age of Perp.	Age Span
California	261.5	Unlawful Intercourse	Intercourse	18	< 18		3 years
	261.5	Unlawful Intercourse	Intercourse	18	< 16	≥ 21	
Colorado	18-3-402	Sexual Assault	Penetration	17	15–17*		10 years
	18-3-402	Sexual Assault	Penetration	17	< 15		4 years
	18-3-405	Sexual Assault on Child	Sexual Contact	17	< 15		4 years
Connecticut	53a-70	Sexual Assault 1st Degree	Intercourse	16	< 13		2 years
	53a-71	Sexual Assault 2nd Degree	Intercourse	16	13–16*		3 years
	53a-73	Sexual Assault 4th Degree	Sexual Contact	16	< 13		2 years
	53a-73	Sexual Assault 4th Degree	Sexual Contact	16	13–15*		3 years
Delaware	768	Unlawful Sex Conduct 2nd	Sexual Contact	18	< 18		
	770	Rape 4th Degree	Intercourse or Penetration	18	< 16		
	770	Rape 4th Degree	Intercourse	18	<18	≥ 30	
	771	Rape 3rd Degree	Intercourse	18	< 16		10 years
	771	Rape 3rd Degree	Intercourse	18	< 14	≥ 19	

(Continued)

(Continued)

State	Statute	Name of Crime	Act	Age of Consent	Age of Victim	Age of Perp.	Age Span
Delaware (continued)	772	Rape 2nd Degree	Penetration	18	< 12	≥ 18	
	773	Rape 1st Degree	Intercourse	18	< 12	≥ 18	
Florida	794.05	Unlawful Sexual Activity With Certain Minors	Oral, Anal, or Vaginal Penetration by a Sexual Organ	18	16 or 17	≥ 24	
Georgia	16-6-2	Sodomy	Oral/Anal Sodomy	16	13–16*	> 18	4 years
	16-6-3	Statutory Rape	Intercourse	16	< 16	< 21	
	16-6-3	Statutory Rape	Intercourse	16	< 16	≥ 21	
	16-6-3	Statutory Rape	Intercourse	16	14 or 15	≤ 18	4 years
Hawaii	707-730	Sexual Assault 1st Degree	Penetration	16	<14		
	707-730	Sexual Assault 1st Degree	Penetration	16	14–16*		5 years
	707-732	Sexual Assault 3rd Degree	Sexual Contact	16	< 14		
	707-732	Sexual Assault 3rd Degree	Sexual Contact	16	14–16*		5 years
Idaho	18-6101	Rape	Penetration	18	< 16	≥ 18	
	18-6101	Rape	Penetration	18	16 or 17		3 years

State	Statute	Name of Crime	Act	Age of Consent	Age of Victim	Age of Perp.	Age Span
Illinois	720 ILCS5/ 11-1.40	Predatory Sexual Assault of a Child	Penetration	17	< 13	≥ 17	
	720 ILCS5/ 11-1.50	Sexual Abuse	Penetration or Sexual Conduct	17	13–17*		5 years
	720 ILCS5/ 11-1.50	Sexual Abuse	Penetration or Sexual Conduct	17	9–17*	< 17	5 years
	720 ILCS5/ 11-1.60	Aggravated Sexual Abuse	Sexual Conduct	17	< 13	≥ 17	
	720 ILCS5/ 11-1.60	Aggravated Sexual Abuse	Penetration or Sexual Conduct	17	13–17*		5 years
Indiana	35-42-4-3	Child Molesting	Intercourse/ Deviate	16	< 14		
	35-42-4-3	Child Molesting	Intercourse/ Deviate	16	< 14	≥ 21	
	35-42-4-3	Child Molesting	Sexual Contact	16	< 14		
	35-42-4-3	Child Molesting	Sexual Contact	16	< 14	≥ 21	
	35-42-4-9	Sex Misconduct With a Minor	Intercourse/ Deviate	16	14–16*	≥ 18	
	35-42-4-9	Sex Misconduct With a Minor	Intercourse	16	14–16*	≥ 21	

(Continued)

State	Statute	Name of Crime	Act	Age of Consent	Age of Victim	Age of Perp.	Age Span
Indiana (continued)	35-42-4-9	Sex Misconduct With a Minor	Sexual Contact	16	14–16*	≥ 18	
	35-42-4-9	Sex Misconduct With a Minor	Sexual Contact	16	14–16*	≥ 21	
Iowa	709.4	Sexual Abuse 3rd Degree	Sex Act	18	12–14*		
	709.4	Sexual Abuse 3rd Degree	Sex Act	18	14–16*		4 years
	709.8	Lascivious Acts With a Child	Sexual Contact	18	< 18	< 16	
	709.12	Indecent Contact With a Child	Sexual Contact	18	< 18		
	709.12	Indecent Contact With a Child	Sexual Contact	18	< 18	16 or 17	5 years
Kansas	21-5503	Rape	Intercourse	16	< 14		
	21-5504	Criminal Sodomy	Sodomy	16	14–16*		
	21-5504	Aggravated Criminal Sodomy	Sodomy	16	< 14		
	21-5506	Indecent Liberties With a Child	Sexual Contact	16	14–16*		
	21-5506	Aggravated Indecent Liberties With a Child	Intercourse	16	14–16*		

State	Statute	Name of Crime	Act	Age of Consent	Age of Victim	Age of Perp.	Age Span
Kansas (continued)	21-5507	Unlawful Voluntary Sexual Relations	Intercourse	16	14–16*	< 19	4 years
	21-5507	Unlawful Voluntary Sexual Relations	Sodomy	16	14–16*	< 19	4 years
	21-5507	Unlawful Voluntary Sexual Relations	Sexual Contact	16	14–16*	< 19	4 years
Kentucky	510.050	Rape 2nd Degree	Intercourse	16	< 14	≥ 18	
	510.060	Rape 3rd Degree	Intercourse	16	< 16	≥ 21	
	510.080	Sodomy 2nd Degree	Deviate Intercourse	16	< 14	≥ 18	
	510.090	Sodomy 3rd Degree	Deviate Intercourse	16	< 16	≥ 21	
	510.110	Sexual Abuse 1st Degree	Sexual Contact	16	< 16	≥ 21	
	510.120	Sexual Abuse 2nd Degree	Sexual Contact	16	< 16	18–21*	
	510.120	Sexual Abuse 2nd Degree	Sexual Contact	16	14–16*	18–21*	5 years
	510.130	Sexual Abuse 3rd Degree	Sexual Contact	16	< 14	> 18	
Louisiana	14:43.1	Sexual Battery	Any Contact With Anus or Genitals	17	< 15		3 years

(Continued)

State	Statute	Name of Crime	Act	Age of Consent	Age of Victim	Age of Perp.	Age Span
Louisiana (continued)	14:43.3	Oral Sexual Battery	Oral Contact With Anus or Genitals	17	< 15		3 years
	14:80	Felony Carnal Knowledge of a Juvenile	Sexual Intercourse	17	13–17*	≥ 17	4 years
	14:80.1	Misdemeanor Carnal Knowledge of a Juvenile	Sexual Intercourse	17	13–17*	≥ 17	2 years
Maine	255-A	Unlawful Sexual Contact	Sexual Contact	16	< 14		3 years
	255-A	Unlawful Sexual Contact	Sexual Contact	16	< 12		3 years
	255-A	Unlawful Sexual Contact	Sexual Penetration	16	< 14		3 years
	255-A	Unlawful Sexual Contact	Sexual Penetration	16	< 12		3 years
	255-A	Unlawful Sexual Contact	Sexual Contact	16	14 or 15		10 years
	260	Unlawful Sexual Touching	Sexual Touching	16	14		5 years
	254	Sexual Abuse of a Minor	Sexual Act	16	14 or 15		5 years
	254	Sexual Abuse of a Minor	Sexual Act	16	14 or 15		10 years

State	Statute	Name of Crime	Act	Age of Consent	Age of Victim	Age of Perp.	Age Span
Maryland	3-304	Rape 2nd Degree	Intercourse	16	< 14		4 years
	3-306	Sex Offense 2nd Degree	Sexual Act	16	< 14		4 years
	3-307	Sex Offense 3rd Degree	Sexual Contact	16	< 14		4 years
	3-307	Sex Offense 3rd Degree	Sexual Act	16	14 or 15	≥ 21	
	3-307	Sex Offense 3rd Degree	Intercourse	16	14 or 15	≥ 21	
Massachusetts	272-4	Inducing Person Under 18 Into Sexual Intercourse	Intercourse	18			
	272-35	Unnatural Acts With a Child	Sexual Act	18			
	265-23A	Rape/Abuse of a Child	Intercourse	18	< 12		5 years
	265-23A	Rape/Abuse of a Child	Intercourse	18	12–16*		10 years
Michigan	750.520b	Criminal Sex Conduct 1st	Penetration	16	< 13		
	750.520c	Criminal Sex Conduct 2nd	Sexual Contact	16	< 13		
	750.520d	Criminal Sex Conduct 3rd	Penetration	16	13–16*		

(Continued)

123

(Continued)

State	Statute	Name of Crime	Act	Age of Consent	Age of Victim	Age of Perp.	Age Span
Michigan (continued)	750.520e	Criminal Sex Conduct 4th	Sexual Contact	16	13–16*		5 years
Minnesota	609.342	Sexual Conduct 1st	Sexual Contact	16	< 13		3 years
	609.342	Sexual Conduct 1st	Penetration	16	< 13		3 years
	609.343	Sexual Conduct 2nd	Sexual Contact	16	< 13		4 years
	609.344	Sexual Conduct 3rd	Penetration	16	< 13		3 years
	609.344	Sexual Conduct 3rd	Penetration	16	13–16*		2 years
	609.345	Sexual Conduct 4th	Sexual Contact	16	< 13		3 years
	609.345	Sexual Conduct 4th	Sexual Contact	16	13–16*		4 years
Mississippi	97-3-65	Rape	Intercourse	18	< 14	≥ 18	
	97-3-65	Rape	Intercourse	18	< 14	13–17	
	97-3-67	Rape	Intercourse	18	14–18*		
Missouri	566.032	Statutory Rape 1st Degree	Intercourse	17	< 14		
	566.034	Statutory Rape 2nd Degree	Intercourse	17	< 17	≥ 21	
	566.062	Statutory Sodomy 1st	Deviate Intercourse	17	< 14		
	566.064	Statutory Sodomy 2nd	Deviate Intercourse	17	< 17	≥ 21	
Montana	45-5-502	Sexual Assault	Sexual Contact	16	< 16		3 years

124

State	Statute	Name of Crime	Act	Age of Consent	Age of Victim	Age of Perp.	Age Span
Montana (continued)	45-5-503	Intercourse Without Consent	Intercourse	16	< 16		4 years
Nebraska	28-319	Sexual Assault 1st Degree	Penetration	16	12–16*	≥ 19	
	28-319.01	Sexual Assault of a Child 1st Degree	Penetration	16	12–16*	≥ 25	
	28-320.1	Sexual Assault of a Child 2nd or 3rd Degree	Sexual Contact	16	< 14	≥ 19	
Nevada	200.368	Statutory Sexual Seduction	Penetration	16	< 16	18–20	
	200.368	Statutory Sexual Seduction	Penetration	16	< 16	≥ 21	
New Hampshire	632-A:3	Felonious Sexual Assault	Penetration	16	13–16*		4 years
	632-A:4	Sexual Assault	Sexual Contact	16	13–16*		5 years
	632-A:4	Sexual Assault	Penetration	16	13–16*		4 years
New Jersey	2c:14-2	Sexual Assault	Penetration	16	13–16*		4 years
	2c:14-3	Criminal Sexual Contact	Sexual Contact	16	13–16*		4 years
New Mexico	30-9-11	Criminal Sexual Penetration 4th Degree	Penetration	16	13–16*	≥ 18	4 years
New York	130.35	Rape 1st Degree	Intercourse	17	< 13	≥ 18	

(Continued)

(Continued)

State	Statute	Name of Crime	Act	Age of Consent	Age of Victim	Age of Perp.	Age Span
New York (continued)	130.30	Rape 2nd Degree	Intercourse	17	< 15	≥ 18	4 years
	130.25	Rape 3rd Degree	Intercourse	17	< 17	≥ 21	
	130.50	Criminal Sexual Act 1st	Oral or Anal Sex	17	< 13	≥ 18	
	130.45	Criminal Sexual Act 2nd	Oral or Anal Sex	17	< 15	≥ 18	4 years
	130.40	Criminal Sexual Act 3rd	Oral or Anal Sex	17	< 17	≥ 21	
	130.60	Sexual Abuse 1st Degree	Sexual Contact	17	< 13	≥ 21	
	130.55	Sexual Abuse 3rd Degree	Sexual Contact	17	14–16*		5 years
North Carolina	14-27.2	Rape 1st Degree	Vaginal Intercourse	16	< 13	≥ 12	4 years
	14-27.4	Sexual Offense 1st	Sexual Act	16	< 13	≥ 12	4 years
	14-27.7A	Statutory Rape	Intercourse or Sexual Act	16	13–15*		6 years
	14-27.7A	Statutory Rape	Intercourse or Sexual Act	16	13–15*		4–6* years
North Dakota	12.1-20-03	Gross Sexual Imposition	Sexual Act	18	< 15		
	12.1-20-03	Gross Sexual Imposition	Sexual Act	18	< 15	≥ 22	

State	Statute	Name of Crime	Act	Age of Consent	Age of Victim	Age of Perp.	Age Span
North Dakota (continued)	12.1-20-03	Gross Sexual Imposition	Sexual Contact	18	< 15		
	12.1-20-03.1	Continuous Sexual Abuse of a Child	Sexual Contact	18	< 15		
	12.1-20-03.1	Continuous Sexual Abuse of a Child	Sexual Contact	18	< 15	≥ 22	
	12.1-20-05	Corruption of a Minor	Sexual Act/ Contact	18	15–18*	18–21	3 years
	12.1-20-05	Corruption of a Minor	Sexual Act/ Contact	18	15–18*	≥ 22	3 years
	12.1-20-07	Sexual Assault	Sexual Contact	18	15–18*	18–21	3 years
	12.1-20-07	Sexual Assault	Sexual Contact	18	15–18*	≥ 22	3 years
Ohio	2907.04	Unlawful Sexual Conduct With a Minor	Sexual Conduct	16	13–16*	≥ 18	
	2907.04	Unlawful Sexual Conduct With a Minor	Sexual Conduct	16	13–16*	≥ 18	4 years
	2907.04	Unlawful Sexual Conduct With a Minor	Sexual Conduct	16	13–16*	18	10 years
Oklahoma	21-1114	Rape 1st Degree	Intercourse	16	< 14	≥ 18	
	21-1111	Rape	Vaginal or Anal Intercourse	16	< 16		

(Continued)

(Continued)

State	Statute	Name of Crime	Act	Age of Consent	Age of Victim	Age of Perp.	Age Span
Oklahoma (continued)	21-1111	Rape	Vaginal or Anal Intercourse	16	14–16*	≥ 18	
Oregon	163.355	Rape 3rd Degree	Intercourse	18	< 16		3 years
	163.365	Rape 2nd Degree	Intercourse	18	< 14		3 years
	163.385	Sodomy 3rd Degree	Deviate Intercourse	18	< 16		3 years
	163.395	Sodomy 2nd Degree	Deviate Intercourse	18	< 14		3 years
	163.415	Sexual Abuse 3rd Degree	Sexual Contact	18	< 18		3 years
	163.425	Sexual Abuse 2nd Degree	Sexual Contact	18	< 18	≥ 21	3 years
	163.427	Sexual Abuse 1st Degree	Sexual Contact	18	< 14		3 years
	163.435	Contrib. Delinq. of Minor	Intercourse	18	< 18	18	3 years
Pennsylvania	3122.1	Statutory Sexual Assault	Intercourse	16	< 16		4 years
	3122.1	Statutory Sexual Assault	Intercourse	16	< 16		4–8* years
	3122.1	Statutory Sexual Assault	Intercourse	16	< 16		8–11* years
	3122.1	Statutory Sexual Assault	Intercourse	16	< 16		11 years

State	Statute	Name of Crime	Act	Age of Consent	Age of Victim	Age of Perp.	Age Span
Pennsylvania (continued)	3123	Involuntary Deviate Sexual Intercourse	Deviate Intercourse	16	< 16		4 years
	3125	Aggravated Indecent Assault	Penetration	16	< 16		4 years
Rhode Island	11-37-6	Sexual Assault 3rd	Penetration	16	14 or 15	≥ 18	
South Carolina	16-3-655	Criminal Sexual Conduct With a Minor 2nd Degree	Sexual Battery	16	11–14		
South Dakota	22-22-1	Rape	Penetration	16	13–16*		3 years
	22-22-7	Sexual Contact With Child	Sexual Contact	16	< 16	≥ 16	
	22-22-7	Sexual Contact With Child	Sexual Contact	16	13–16*	≥ 16	5 years
Tennessee	39-13-506	Mitigated Statutory Rape	Penetration	18	15–18*		4–5* years
	39-13-506	Statutory Rape	Penetration	18	13 or 14		4–10* years
	39-13-506	Statutory Rape	Penetration	18	15–18*		5–10* years
	39-13-506	Aggravated Statutory Rape	Penetration	18	13–18*		10 years
Texas	22.021	Aggravated Sexual Assault	Penetration	17	< 14		

(Continued)

(Continued)

State	Statute	Name of Crime	Act	Age of Consent	Age of Victim	Age of Perp.	Age Span
Texas *(continued)*	22.011	Sexual Assault	Penetration	17	< 17		
	22.011	Sexual Assault	Penetration	17	14–16*		3 years
Utah	76-5-401	Unlawful Sexual Activity With a Minor	Intercourse	18	14–16*		4 years
	76-5-401.1	Sexual Abuse of Minor	Sexual Contact	18	14–16*		
	76-5-401.2	Unlawful Sexual Conduct With a 16 or 17	Any Sexual Act	18	16–18*		7 years
	76-5-401.2	Unlawful Sexual Conduct With a 16 or 17	Any Sexual Act	18	16–18*		10 years
	76-5-401.2	Unlawful Sexual Conduct With a 16 or 17	Any Sexual Act	18	16–18*		4 years
	76-5-403	Sodomy	Any Sexual Act	18	≥ 14		
	76-5-403.1	Sodomy on a Child	Any Sexual Act	18	< 14		
Vermont	3252	Sexual Assault	Sexual Act	16	< 16		
	3252	Sexual Assault	Sexual Act	16	15	≥ 19	
	3253	Aggravated Sex Assault	Sexual Act		< 13	≥ 18	
Virginia	18.2-61	Rape	Intercourse	18	< 13		3 years

State	Statute	Name of Crime	Act	Age of Consent	Age of Victim	Age of Perp.	Age Span
Virginia (continued)	18.2-63	Carnal Knowledge of a Child Between 13 and 15	Intercourse	18	13–15*		
	18.2-63	Carnal Knowledge of a Child Between 13 and 15	Intercourse	18	13–15*	≥ 18	3 years
	18.2-63	Carnal Knowledge of a Child Between 13 and 15	Intercourse	18	13–15*	< 18	3 years
	18.2-67.4.2	Sexual Abuse of a Child Under 15	Sexual Abuse	18	13–15*	≥ 18	
	18.2-371	Causing Acts Rendering Children Delinquent	Intercourse	18	15–18*	≥ 18	
Washington	9A.44.073	Rape of Child 1st Degree	Intercourse	16	< 12		2 years
	9A.44.076	Rape of Child 2nd Degree	Intercourse	16	12–14*		3 years
	9A.44.079	Rape of Child 3rd Degree	Intercourse	16	14–16*		4 years
	9A.44.083	Child Molestation 1st Degree	Sexual Contact	16	< 12		3 years
	9A.44.086	Child Molestation 2nd Degree	Sexual Contact	16	12–14*		3 years

(Continued)

(Continued)

State	Statute	Name of Crime	Act	Age of Consent	Age of Victim	Age of Perp.	Age Span
Washington (continued)	9A.44.089	Child Molestation 3rd Degree	Sexual Contact	16	14–16*		4 years
West Virginia	61-8B-3	Sexual Assault 1st Degree	Intercourse/Intrusion	16	< 12	≥ 14	
	61-8B-3	Sexual Assault 1st Degree	Intercourse/Intrusion	16	< 12	≥ 18	
	61-8B-5	Sexual Assault 3rd Degree	Sexual Intrusion	16	< 16	≥ 16	4 years
	61-8B-7	Sexual Abuse 1st Degree	Sexual Contact	16	< 12	≥ 14	
	61-8B-7	Sexual Abuse 1st Degree	Sexual Contact	16	< 12	≥ 18	
	61-8B-9	Sexual Abuse 3rd Degree	Sexual Contact	16	< 16	≥ 16	4 years
Wisconsin	948.02	2nd Degree Sexual Assault of a Child	Sexual Contact	18	< 16		
	948.09	Sexual Intercourse With a Child Age 16 or Over	Intercourse	18	16 or 17		
Wyoming	6-2-314	Sex Abuse Minor 1st	Sexual Intrusion	17	< 13	≥ 16	

132

State	Statute	Name of Crime	Act	Age of Consent	Age of Victim	Age of Perp.	Age Span
Wyoming (continued)	6-2-315	Sex Abuse Minor 2nd	Sexual Intrusion	17	13–15	≥ 17	4 years
	6-2-315	Sex Abuse Minor 2nd	Sexual Contact	17	< 13	≥ 16	
	6-2-316	Sex Abuse Minor 3rd	Sexual Contact	17	13–15	≥ 17	4 years
	6-2-316	Sex Abuse Minor 3rd	Sexual Intrusion	17	< 13	< 16	3 years
	6-2-316	Sex Abuse Minor 3rd	Indecent Liberties	17	< 17	≥ 17	4 years
	6-2-317	Sex Abuse Minor 4th	Sexual Contact	17	< 13	< 16	3 years

Note: When an age range is followed by an asterisk (*), it indicates that the age range is not inclusive of the higher number. That is, the statute states that a person must be "at least" the first age provided in the range but "less than" the second age provided in the range.

Notes

1. In *Hodgson v. Minnesota*, the Supreme Court held that parental notification laws regarding abortion are constitutional, so long as a judicial alternative is available.

2. In *Roper v. Simmons*, the Supreme Court held it unconstitutional to impose the death penalty on anyone who was under the age of 18 at the time of the crime.

References

Adam Walsh Child Protection and Safety Act, Pub. L. 109-248 (2006).

Arnett, J. (1992). Reckless behavior in adolescence: A developmental perspective. *Developmental Review, 12*(4), 339–373.

Bullough, V. L. (2004). Age of consent: A historical overview. *Journal of Psychology & Human Sexuality, 16*(2/3), 25–42.

Centers for Disease Control and Prevention (CDC). (2007). *Sexually transmitted disease surveillance, 2006.* Retrieved from http://www.cdc.gov/std/stats06/

Cocca, C. (2004). *Jailbait: The politics of statutory rape laws in the United States.* Albany: State University of New York Press.

Coz, E. L. (2013). Mississippi aims to curb teen pregnancy with umbilical blood law. Reuters. Retrieved from http://www.reuters.com/article/2013/06/07/us-usa-mississippi-babies-idU.S.BRE9560SL20130607

Deardorff, J., Gonzales, N. A., Christopher, F. S., Roosa, M. W., & Millsap, R. E. (2005). Early puberty and adolescent pregnancy: The influence of alcohol use. *Pediatrics, 116*(6), 1451–1456.

Feld, B. C. (1999). *Bad kids: Race and the transformation of the juvenile court.* New York, NY: Oxford University Press.

Furby, L., & Beyth-Marom, R. (1992). Risk taking in adolescence: A decision-making perspective. *Developmental Review, 12*(1), 1–44.

Grisso, T. (1980). Juveniles' capacities to waive Miranda rights: An empirical analysis. *California Law Review, 68*(6), 1134–1166.

Grisso, T., Steinberg, L., Woolard, J., Cauffman, E., Scott, E., Graham, S., . . . Schwartz, R. (2003). Juveniles' competence to stand trial: A comparison of adolescents' and adults' capacities as trial defendants. *Law and Human Behavior, 27*(4), 333–363.

Hodgson v. State of Minnesota, 497 U.S. 502 (1990).

Kaser-Boyd, N., Adelman, H. S., & Taylor, L. (1985). Minors' ability to identify risks and benefits of therapy. *Professional Psychology: Research and Practice, 16*(3), 411–417.

Koon-Magnin, S., Kreager, D. A., & Ruback, R. B. (2010). Partner age differences, educational contexts and adolescent female sexual activity. *Perspectives on Sexual and Reproductive Health, 42*(3), 206–213.

Koon-Magnin, S., & Ruback, R. B. (2013). The perceived legitimacy of statutory rape laws: The effects of victim age, perpetrator age, and age-span. *Journal of Applied Social Psychology, 43*(9), 1918–1930.

Lewis, C. C. (1981). How adolescents approach decisions: Changes over grades seven to twelve and policy implications. *Child Development, 52*(2), 538–544.

Leitenberg, H., & Saltzman, H. (2000). A statewide survey of age at first intercourse for adolescent females and age of their male partners: Relation to other risk behaviors and statutory rape implications. *Archives of Sexual Behavior, 29*(3), 203–215.

Leitenberg, H., & Saltzman, H. (2003). College women who had sexual intercourse when they were underage minors (13–15): Age of their male partners, relation to current adjustment, and statutory rape implications. *A Journal of Research and Treatment, 15*(2), 135–147.

Michael M. v. Superior Court of Sonoma County, 450 U.S. 464 (1981).

Michels, T. M., Kropp, R. Y., Eyre, S. L., & Halpern-Felsher, B. L. (2005). Initiating sexual experiences: How do young adolescents make decisions regarding early sexual activity. *Journal of Research on Adolescence, 15*(4), 583–607.

Neimark, E. D., & Lewis, N. (1968). Development of logical problem solving: A one-year retest. *Child Development, 39*(2), 527–536.

Oberman, M. (2004). Turning girls into women: Re-evaluating modern statutory rape law. *DePaul Journal of Health Care Law, 8,* 4–19.

Ompad, D. C., Strathdee, S. A., Celentano, D. D., Latkin, C., Poduska, J. M., Kellam, S. G., & Ialongo, N. S. (2006). Predictors of early initiation of vaginal and oral sex among urban young adults in Baltimore, Maryland. *Archives of Sexual Behavior, 35*(1), 53–65.

Owen-Kostelnik, J., Reppucci, N. D., & Meyer, J. R. (2006). Testimony and interrogation of minors: Assumptions about maturity and morality. *American Psychologist, 61*(4), 286–304.

Personal Responsibility and Work Opportunity Reconciliation Act of 1996, Pub. L. 104-193, 912, 110 Stat. 2353–2354 (1997).

Posner, R. A., & Silbaugh, K. B. (1996). *A guide to America's sex laws.* Chicago, IL: The University of Chicago Press.

Roper v. Simmons, 543 U.S. 551 (2005).

Staton, M., Leukfeld, C., Logan, T. K., Zimmerman, R., Lynam, D., Milich, R., . . . Clayton, R. (1999). Risky sex behavior and substance use among young adults. *Health and Social Work, 24*(2), 147–154.

Steinberg, L., & Cauffman, E. (1996). Maturity of judgment in adolescence: Psychosocial factors in adolescent decision making. *Law and Human Behavior, 20*(3), 249–272.

Tapert, S. F., Aarons, G. A., Sedlar, G. R., & Brown, S. A. (2001). Adolescent substance use and sexual risk-taking behavior. *Journal of Adolescent Health, 28*(3), 181–189.

Troup-Leasure, K. H., & Snyder, N. (2005, August). Statutory rape known to law enforcement. *Juvenile Justice Bulletin* (NCJ 208803). Retrieved from https://www.ncjrs.gov/pdffiles1/ojjdp/208803.pdf

Viljoen, J. L., Odgers, C., Grisso, T., & Tillbrook, C. (2007). Teaching adolescents and adults about adjudicative proceedings: A comparison of pre- and post-teaching scores on the MacCAT-CA. *Law and Human Behavior, 31*(5), 419–432.

Weithorn, L. A., & Campbell, S. B. (1982). The competency of children and adolescents to make informed treatment decisions. *Child Development, 53*(6), 1589–1598.

8

Sexual Victimization Online

Kelsey Becker and Catherine D. Marcum

The world has never before seen such amazing advances in technology, which allow humans to do things they never before thought possible. But with these advances come problems, especially when it comes to the accessibility of information and material on the Internet. The Internet provides an environment where criminals can act anonymously, sheltered from potential repercussions. It also creates an atmosphere in which sexual materials can be easily accessed by anyone able to use a computer. Users of the Internet can effortlessly search for pornographic materials or even stumble upon such websites. With such ease of access to materials of a sexual nature, crimes involving child pornography and sexual solicitation have soared. This chapter aims to first present the legislative definitions of child pornography, the categories of materials, and the offenders who use it. Various laws and policies that have been enacted to protect the victims of child pornography will also be discussed. A description of offenders and victims of sexual solicitation will be given along with an explanation of policies implemented against crimes of sexual solicitation.

Child Pornography

The presence of adult pornography online is not illegal, though it is not authorized for access and viewing by individuals under the age of 18. However, it is child pornography that poses the most danger to minors, who can often be unintentional victims of exposure to child pornography. When young adolescents make search errors, open up spam emails, or receive pop-up ads, they may unintentionally be exposed to sexual images or videos (Jones, Mitchell, & Finkelhor, 2012). Jones et al. found that the percentage of users who experience unwanted exposure to pornographic materials has actually decreased from 34% in 2005 to 23% in 2010. This decrease, while surprising at first glance, may have been caused by the use of more effective anti-spamware, pop-up blockers, and filters along with better education of children about the potential consequences of opening unidentified emails or links. However, while instances of unwanted exposure to explicit sexual material are declining, a large number of children are still being victimized as the subjects of pornography. The next section will define what constitutes child pornography.

THE DEFINITION OF CHILD PORNOGRAPHY

There is much controversy over what constitutes a "child," and that can often make defining the term *child pornography* difficult (Gillespie, 2011). The majority of states declare that 16 years old is the age of consent to participate in sexual relationships or, in some states, get married. However, U.S. federal law gives the base definition of child pornography as any material that is sexually explicit in nature and involves individuals younger than 18 years of age. Since the 1980s, the Supreme Court has spent much time debating the exact definition of child pornography (Marcum, Higgins, Ricketts, & Freiburger, 2011).

The first major landmark case in this area was *New York v. Ferber* (1982), in which the Supreme Court ruled that child pornography, because it involves the sexual abuse of children, is not protected under the First Amendment. It was also ruled that to be considered child pornography, the material must visually portray children younger than a certain age engaged in sexual activities. The children in the images much be actual children, as the production and possession of virtual child pornography, or digitally created images, is not considered illegal under the rulings of *Ashcroft v. Free Speech Coalition* (2002). That is because real children are not harmed in the production of virtual child pornography. It is, however, illegal to pander these virtual images (*United States v. Williams*, 2008). In other words, selling digitally created images under the pretense that the images are of real individuals is prohibited in the United States.

Pornographic images of children have been in production far longer than the Internet has been in existence. Traditionally, people would receive through the mail magazines or videos depicting sexually explicit material involving children. This system of distributing child pornography made it extremely easy for offenders to be apprehended. With the advent of the Internet, child pornography became a "hybrid" crime (Wall, 2007), or a crime that falls on a continuum between traditional crimes and true cybercrimes. Since child pornography can be found both offline and online, it is considered a hybrid crime. The Internet has simply created a setting where offenders can easily access materials, thus expanding the crime beyond the realm of the physical world.

CATEGORIES OF CHILD PORNOGRAPHY OFFENSES

The crimes of child pornography offenders can be broken down into three categories based on the offenders' level of involvement: production, dissemination or distribution, and possession. Each of these three categories results in different criminal charges. In regard to production, 18 U.S.C. § 2251 criminalizes usage, persuasion, inducement, incitement of a minor to engage in, or assistance in engaging in sexual conduct for the purpose of producing a still or live depiction of the conduct. The law also considers advertisements about the access or sale of pornography to be a form of production. Furthermore, 18 U.S.C. § 2251 claims that parents or guardians allowing children to be used for child pornography production should be charged as well. It is important to note that in order for an individual to be charged with the production or possession of child pornography, he or she must deliberately receive, disseminate, transport, ship, or have child pornography in his or her possession ("Child Pornography," 2009).

The illegal dissemination or distribution of child pornography involves the mailing or transporting of images or videos (18 U.S.C. § 2252A[a][1]). This includes email and other methods of spreading images and videos, along with the physical transportation of materials. Distributing pornographic materials to a minor is a separate offense and can increase an offender's sentence. *United States v. Goff* (2005) further stated that if the prosecution could prove an email originated from an offender's account, that was evidence enough to convict, even if the image could not be located on the hard drive of the offender's computer.

The possession of child pornography is another offense criminals can be charged with. Possession includes the act of consciously accessing images or videos with the intent to view them for any purpose. Possession is defined as "holding or having something (material or immaterial) as one's own, or in one's control" (*United States v. Tucker*, 2002, p. 1204). According to *United States v. Shiver* (2008), deleting images is also considered control or possession of child pornography. Therefore, individuals are unable to simply delete pornographic images off their computers to protect themselves from criminal punishment. The *mens rea* of the individual, or the intent of the person to commit a crime, must be determined to see whether the person knowingly and intentionally accessed child pornography.

A person cannot be charged with possession of child pornography if he or she can demonstrate several different things (18 U.S.C. § 2252; "Child Pornography," 2009). The suspect must demonstrate that he or she did not intentionally obtain pornographic material of children, that the image was immediately destroyed upon receipt, and that it was reported to the authorities as soon as possible. Furthermore, the individual must have no more than three images in his or her possession and must refuse to present or grant access of the image to anyone but the authorities. If an individual can meet these criteria, he or she cannot be charged with possession of child pornography.

CATEGORIES OF CHILD PORNOGRAPHY AND USERS

There are many ways to classify images and videos depicting sexual conduct of children. Based on its legal definition, child pornography can be categorized into three main types: indicative, indecent, and obscene (Gillespie, 2011). Indicative child pornography involves images or film of clothed minors displaying an interest in children sexually. Material involving naked children and a suggested sexual interest in children falls into the indecent category of child pornography. Lastly, material exhibiting children conducting sexual activities is placed in the obscene category. This is, however, a very simple method for classifying child pornography. Much more detailed and in-depth classifications exist. One example is a classification system created by the COPINE unit (Table 8.1) based on a 10-point scale determining the type of victimization experienced in the image (Taylor, Holland, & Quayle, 2001). This scale involves a progression from less serious images in which no physical harm is done to the child to more serious images in which aspects of torture are involved. This is one of the most widely used and recognized scales of child pornography.

The topic of child pornography is not an easy one to think about, especially when it comes to considering who views it and why people access it. There is no simple answer to why people do the things they do or like the things they like. Creating a profile of the type of individuals who use child pornography is also not straightforward. However, the typical users of pornographic material of children

Table 8.1   Scale of Pornographic Images as Categorized by the COPINE Unit

Level	Name	Description
1	Indicative	Nonerotic pictures of children featured in underwear, bathing suits, etc.
2	Nudist	Seminaked or naked pictures of children in appropriate nudist settings
3	Erotica	Secretively taken pictures of children in nudist settings
4	Posing	Deliberate posing of partially naked or entirely naked children
5	Erotic posing	Deliberate posing of children partially clothed or entirely naked in sexual poses
6	Explicit erotic posing	Emphasis of genital areas with partially clothed or naked children
7	Explicit sexual activity	Involvement of touching, masturbation, oral sex, and intercourse with another child
8	Assault	Children subject to sexual assault by an adult
9	Gross assault	Obscene pictures of children subject to sexual assault, sex, masturbation, or oral sex with an adult
10	Sadistic/ bestiality	Depiction of child being tied, bound, beaten, or whipped to inflict pain *or* involvement with an animal and sexual behavior

Source: Taylor, Holland, & Quayle, 2001.

are white males between the ages of 25 and 50 years old, more than half of whom are in romantic relationships (Bourke & Hernandez, 2009; Burke, Sowerbutts, Blundell, & Sherry, 2002; Webb, Craissatti, & Keen, 2007). Users are also typically employed and are fairly intelligent. This profile is not very beneficial for attempting to predict or find child pornography offenders because many, many people fit this profile in the United States.

Determining why people view child pornography is as difficult as attempting to create a profile of those who do. There are several main reasons why individuals access child pornography, but many other reasons could be present as well. The main reason people use pornographic material of children is for sexual arousal (Sheldon & Howitt, 2007). Individuals may download and fill folder after folder on their computers with pornographic images and videos specially chosen to meet their specific tastes and needs. Many child pornography offenders are very selective about the types of images they want to view. Attempting to avoid life by leaving behind reality and expectations is another key motive offenders have for downloading pornographic material of children. The stresses of life and lack of acceptance for their behaviors makes them desire an environment that they themselves can control. Another reason offenders access this type of material is to satisfy their collecting behaviors. Collecting images helps users evade the reality of their crimes by making the behavior seem as normal as collecting coins or baseball cards. Lastly, child pornography is used to help the cultivation of relationships in society. In the hope of being accepted by others, many offenders visit websites and join groups where they can communicate and trade images.

SEXTING AS A FORM OF CHILD PORNOGRAPHY

It is becomingly increasingly common to witness children and young adolescents talking on their own personal cell phones. It has been estimated that 52% of young adolescents in the United States own cell phones (Blair & Fletcher, 2011, p. 156). Because of this increase in children and teenagers owning cell phones and accessing the Internet with them, the occurrence of sexting has become a major issue. Using cellular phones and/or the Internet to post or send sexual images and messages is referred to as *sexting*, a term that originated in the United Kingdom (Levick & Moon, 2010; Parker, 2009). A recent study found that 17% of the student participants admitted to sexting behavior, with this behavior steadily increasing with age (Dake, Price, Maziarz, & Ward, 2012, p. 7). For example, 3% of 12-year-olds admitted to sexting, while 32% of 18-year-olds claimed that they had sent or posted sexual images or messages. The study also found that higher rates of sexting correlated with higher rates of substance use, sexual behaviors, and emotional health problems such as depression and thoughts of suicide. There are many reasons why teenagers sext, but often, it is not of their own accord. Twenty-three percent of teenagers who sext do so because they are pressured by their friends, while 51% of female teenagers sext because they are pressured by boys. Furthermore, 61% of young adolescents send sexual messages or pictures because they are coerced. This shockingly high number of adolescents being coerced into sending sexual images or messages displays just how immense the issue of sexting has become.

Sexting is a form of "self-produced child pornography" and can be as simple as a minor sending pictures of himself or herself to a boyfriend or girlfriend. It can also be as complex as a minor being coerced into sending pictures to an individual who is impersonating someone else to acquire sexual images (Leary, 2010). People who sext can be classified in three tiers based on how many people they sext and how often. The first tier describes minors who send one picture to one person who does not forward the image to anyone else (Ostrager, 2010). These sexters can be sending a sexual picture just to their boyfriend or girlfriend. Individuals who are mass sexters, meaning those who send a sexual image to up to 10 people, make up the second tier. A female, for example, in this tier may send a naked picture of herself to several male friends. The third and final tier includes mass sexters who send images to over 11 people or minors who participate in mass sexting multiple times within a month.

It is hard for young adolescents to understand the dangers sexting can present, especially because it is so common for individuals to participate in sexting behaviors. First of all, because sexting involves minors, it is considered child pornography and can lead to criminal sanctions against the producers and possessors of images (Mitchell, Finkelhor, Jones, & Wolak, 2012). Sexters, by creating sexual images and posting them online where they cannot be deleted, may also put their futures at risk if family members, academic institutions, and possible employers are able to access the images. Furthermore, individuals who send sexual images of themselves to others may experience extreme distress, embarrassment, or fear because of their behavior. For all these reasons, sexting is becoming an extremely problematic phenomenon.

LEGISLATION AND POLICIES AGAINST CHILD PORNOGRAPHY

Many steps have been taken to combat the rising rates of sexual victimization online, including the enactment of various laws aimed at protecting children and punishing offenders. In 1977, the Protection of Children Against Sexual Exploitation Act was passed, becoming one of the first steps of legislation taken to help prevent child pornography (Simon, 1999). According to this act, it is illegal to create a visual production of sexually explicit behavior using an individual under the age of 16 years; this age was later raised to 18 years (McCabe, 2000). The 1986 Child Sexual Abuse and Pornography Act made the production and advertising of pornographic material of children illegal (Mota, 2002). Next, using a computer to transport, disseminate, and receive child pornography became illegal in 1988 under the Child Protection and Obscenity Enforcement Act. Further, punishments for intentionally creating, soliciting, or transmitting sexually explicit images to anyone younger than 18 years of age were created under the Communications Decency Act of 1996. In that year, a federal court struck down a portion of the act, stating that it was too broad in regard to standards of indecency. Further, the Supreme Court upheld the decision made in *Reno v. ACLU* that the indecency provisions were too broad, both because they did not did not allow parents to decide what material was acceptable for children and because "patently offensive" was not well defined well as it had no prior legal meaning. It was later made clear that companies such as telephone and Internet providers were not liable for pornographic material that was not within their ability to control.

To protect children while using school computers, the Children's Internet Protection Act (CIPA) of 2000 was enacted (Federal Communications Commission, 2006). This act attempted to prevent children from being able to access pornographic materials online by requiring schools to have blocking and filtering software installed on each of their computers. In 2006, the National Sex Offender Registry was expanded, and penalties for child abusers were also increased with the implementation of the Adam Walsh Child Protection Act (Marcum, 2008). This act also created a National Child Abuse Registry and made it more challenging for predators to access children online. Recent legislation includes the Child Protection Act of 2012. This act called for an increase in penalties for individuals involved in the trafficking of child pornography and an increase in prison sentences to 20 years for people who are caught in possession of sexual images or videos depicting children 12 years old or younger.

Sexual Solicitation Online

With the advent of the Internet came several new means of meeting people and making friends: chat rooms, social networking websites, and many other online locations. The Internet also became a new avenue for child predators to find their next targets and for individuals to solicit others for sexual activities. Sexual solicitation takes place when a user of the Internet persuades an individual to partake in sexual behaviors, either online or offline, including discussing the topic of sex and receiving inappropriate and unwanted sexual information about the user (Mitchell, Finkelhor, & Wolak, 2007; Stahl & Fritz, 2002). The act of persuading youth to participate in online masturbation or cybersex, view videos of a pornographic nature, or look at images they receive that are sexually explicit is considered a form of sexual solicitation (Bryce, 2010).

THE PREVALENCE OF ONLINE SEXUAL SOLICITATION

Comprehending the true prevalence of online sexual solicitation can be extremely difficult. This is partly because adolescents might not be able to recognize sexual solicitation when they experience it. Because adolescents have the tendency to use the Internet more often than people in other age groups and because they are the group with the fastest growing user rate, adolescents are usually the individuals involved in sexual solicitation (Jones & Fox, 2009; Rainie, 2006; Wolak, Mitchell, & Finkelhor, 2006).

One of the largest studies analyzing the occurrence of sexual solicitation online is the Youth Internet Safety Survey (Jones et al., 2012). This survey attempts to assess the prevalence of online sexual solicitation, unwanted exposure to pornography, and experiences of harassment online. The data for the study were taken in the years 2000, 2005, and 2010, and the study involved a sample of 1,500 users of the Internet who were between 10 and 17 years old at the time. The results of the study demonstrated that there had been a 50% decrease in online sexual solicitation between the years 2000 and 2010. In the year 2000, rates of unwanted online sexual solicitation were at approximately 19%, while in the year 2010, the rate had decreased to 9%. Rates of unwanted pornography exposure also decreased from 34% in 2005 to 23% in 2010. The researchers claim that there are several reasons why this decrease in both sexual solicitation and exposure to pornography may have occurred. First, an increase in the use of anti-spamware and filters on computers may be preventing pornographic pop-ups and the opening of spam containing pornographic content. Second, chat rooms are becoming less popular than social networking sites. On social networking sites such as Facebook and Twitter, adolescents interact mainly with people they already know, as opposed to meeting new people in chat rooms. Young individuals have also become more aware of the dangers of the Internet and are being more cautious while online. Furthermore, with more offenders being punished and having their cases covered in the news media, people may be deterred from committing a similar crime. All of these reasons may help explain why rates of online sexual solicitation and exposure to pornography have been steadily declining. The Youth Internet Safety Survey also showed that, despite these declining rates of sexual solicitation and unwanted pornography exposure, rates of online harassment increased from 6% in 2000 to 11% in 2010 (Jones et al., 2012). This may potentially be due to a shifting of bullying from the physical world to the Internet.

Ybarra and Mitchell (2008) conducted a study with 1,588 participants between the ages of 10 and 15 using the Growing Up With Media Survey. Fifteen percent of the young adolescents had experienced a form of unwanted sexual solicitation in the past 6 months, with 4% reporting that the experience had occurred while they were on a social networking site. The study also found that the most common locations for sexual solicitations are instant messaging sites and chat rooms. Approximately 43% claimed that they had been solicited through instant messaging, and 32% were solicited through chat rooms.

Studies have also compared rates of sexual solicitation between high school age groups and college age groups along with between males and females. A study by Marcum (2008) found that 9.6% of freshmen in college had experienced sexual solicitation, with 0.8% actually claiming to have sent a sexual solicitation to someone else. Another study found that 12% of high school senior females and 10.8% of high school senior males experience forms of sexual solicitation (Marcum, Higgins, & Ricketts, 2010). The prevalence of sexual solicitation appears to decrease as individuals enter college, where males begin to experience sexual solicitation more than females. Male college freshmen reported experiencing sexual solicitation at a rate of 7.7%, while only 5.5% of female college freshmen experienced it.

SEXUAL SOLICITATION OFFENDER
CHARACTERISTICS AND MOTIVATIONS

People struggle to understand why others do the things they do, especially when crimes with children are involved. Knowing what types of people sexually solicit others online and why they resort to this behavior is important for determining how to prevent it. It seems, however, that no one specific profile can describe all offenders. Many studies have attempted to distinguish individuals who are more likely than others to sexually solicit people online.

First of all, the majority of sexual solicitation offenders are males (Baumgartner, Valkenburg, & Peter, 2010). Because these predators use the Internet to find their victims, they are able to create their own identity and pretend to be teenagers without having to reveal their physical appearance (Durkin & Bryant, 1999). In other words, offenders can remain anonymous while communicating with their targets. Furthermore, not all sexual solicitations are classified as aggressive sexual solicitations, or those requesting that individuals meet offline. Some sexual solicitations are only for cybersexual behaviors. Predators who communicate solely online and never attempt to arrange a meeting with an individual for sexual activities will often rationalize their behaviors and desires by declaring that no child is physically harmed if they maintain only online communication (Durkin & Bryant).

Attempting to create a general profile for sexual solicitation offenders has proven difficult. A study by Malesky (2007) found that 71% of the sample of 31 sexual solicitation offenders had prior sexual offense contact history and that 52% had sent potential victims pornographic images of children. Most of these offenders met minors using chat rooms and engaged children in conversations involving sexually explicit information. More than half of the offenders in the study made an attempt to meet with their targets for sex. Surprisingly, only 29% of the offenders lied about their age hoping to seduce minors to engage in sexual behaviors with them. However, this study contradicts another study conducted by Young (2005). That study relied on 22 cases of sexual solicitation and found that not a single offender in the sample had any prior criminal history. Furthermore, child pornography was in the possession of only 3 of the 22 offenders. Because Yang's results are so different from Malesky's, it can be seen that creating a general profile for sexual solicitation offenders is no easy feat.

Many researchers still attempt to determine the general characteristics of sexual solicitation offenders. Characteristics might include the following: experiencing abuse during their lifetime, being unable to form and maintain close relationships with others their age, participating in sexual behaviors and sustaining attitudes about sex that are considered deviant, and having a feeling of entitlement (Leigh Baker, as cited in Henderson, 2005). Grooming techniques are common among sexual solicitation offenders (Marcum, 2007). Offenders use these techniques to gain the trust of the target so that the individual will partake in sexual behaviors with the offender. While every offender conducts the grooming process differently, several techniques are often used. A commonly used grooming technique is to compliment a target on his or her appearance or on how smart he or she is. Expressing a desire for a loving and intimate relationship along with showing adoration toward the individual are also well-used grooming techniques. Essentially, it is the same process as forming a legitimate, romantic relationship between two teenagers or adults, but an adult is attempting to inappropriately seduce a minor.

It is difficult for society to comprehend why adults would have the desire to sexually solicit a minor. A pathway model was proposed to help predict sexual exploitation of children in the physical world (Ward & Siegert, 2002). The model can be easily used for instances of online sexual solicitation as well and is one of the more contemporary methods used to understand the motivations of online sex offenders. This model claims that there are five pathways, each with a dysfunctional mechanism, that cause an offender to behave the way he or she does toward children (Middleton, Elliot, Mandeville-Norden, & Beech, 2006). The first pathway is categorized by intimacy deficits and involves offenders who target children because they are easier to manage than adults, whom the offender would prefer to have relationships with. Offenders from this pathway find it difficult to form close adult relationships due to rejections from childhood attachments that were insecure. The second pathway deals with distorted sexual scripts; these offenders are emotionally similar to children and identify with children. To these offenders, children can be trusted more than adults and are more likely to agree to try various sexual activities. Emotional dysregulation, the third pathway, involves offenders having difficulty controlling any negative emotions they possess. Sex becomes a coping mechanism. The fourth pathway is based on antisocial cognitions that cause offenders to experience impulsivity, high self-esteem, and feelings of superiority over children. These individuals maintain a desire to dominate children. The final pathway is called the multiple dysfunction pathway. Offenders from this pathway experience all of the dysfunctions of the other pathways. Because these offenders feel that children are ideal sex partners, they are known as "pure pedophiles." Middleton et al. (2006) conducted a study showing that only half of offenders could be described by the pathway model, while others may be affected by other factors.

CHARACTERISTICS AND BEHAVIORS OF VICTIMS

Like other types of victimization, victimization by sexual solicitation does not discriminate by sex, age, or race. Some characteristics, however, make individuals more likely to become targets of online predators. Many studies have focused on these traits in an attempt to predict which individuals may become victims. The individuals who are most vulnerable to sexual solicitation are adolescents (Baumgartner et al., 2010). Adolescents use the Internet more than do adults, especially for leisure activities. Spending so much time online makes young teens prime targets for predators. Furthermore, adolescents perceive the benefits of online sexual behavior much more easily than they see the risks. Therefore, adolescents have a tendency to overestimate the benefits produced by online sexual behavior while underestimating or failing to see the possible dangers that their behavior poses. In other words, some adolescents perceive themselves to be safer with digital sex than with physical sex since no physical contact is necessary.

Biological sex also plays a large role in determining which individuals are more likely to fall victim to sexual solicitation offenders. Twenty-seven percent of female adolescents have experienced an incident of sexual solicitation, as opposed to 12% of males (Baumgartner et al., 2010). In other words, it is more likely for a female to be victimized than a male. Females are also more likely to be the recipients of aggressive sexual solicitations where an individual attempts to arrange offline contact, as are all individuals who use chat rooms and who talk to people they do not know online, especially about sexual topics (Mitchell, Ybarra, & Finkelhor, 2007).

Individuals who participate in risky online behaviors are also more likely to become victims of sexual solicitation. Examples of risky behaviors include providing personal information, discussing sex with someone met while online, and harassing other individuals online. Significantly higher rates of online sexual solicitation are experienced by individuals who talk about sex with people they do not actually know and who meet people online (Ybarra & Mitchell, 2008). Also more likely to be sexually solicited online are high school seniors who give personal information to people they do not know, who visit chat rooms, and who are not monitored by adults when they use the Internet (Marcum et al., 2010). For college freshmen, using email and instant messaging increased their likelihood for being sexually solicited more than did use of chat rooms.

Other vulnerable individuals are those experiencing any of a wide variety of psychological problems. For example, sexual solicitation by pedophiles is more likely for emotionally vulnerable or socially disconnected adolescents (O'Connell, 2003). Depression, suicidal thoughts, self-destructive behaviors, and other forms of psychopathology cause individuals to be more likely to be sexually victimized online (Schrock & Boyd, 2009). Victims of sexual solicitation also often have low self-esteem. Offenders gain the trust of a victim who has low self-esteem by praising and seducing him or her.

EFFECTS OF SEXUAL SOLICITATION ON VICTIMS

When adolescents are presented with a situation of sexual solicitation, they may experience several negative consequences that may have long-lasting effects. According to Dombrowski, LeMasney, Ahia, and Dickson (2004), "sexual abuse robs children of their dignity, threatens their social-emotional integrity, and places them at great developmental disadvantage" (p. 65). It's easy to see that sexual solicitation can be a traumatic experience for anyone who falls victim to it. Sexual victimization offline is associated with problems such as anxiety, delinquent behavior, depression, and substance abuse (Saunders, 2003). One can assume that these problems would also occur in situations of online sexual solicitation. Another study produced similar results and found that sexual victimization also leads to eating disorders, problems with relationships, and thoughts of suicide (Dombrowski et al).

Furthermore, people who had experienced sexual solicitation were 3 times more likely to have symptoms of depression than those who had not experienced sexual solicitation (Mitchell, Ybarra, & Finkelhor, 2007). Victims are also 1.8 times more likely to have delinquent tendencies and 2.6 times more likely to resort to substance abuse.

Online sexual solicitation can have many negative effects that greatly influence the victims. This sad reality makes it all the more important to find a way to stop this behavior.

PROGRAMS AND POLICIES TO FIGHT ONLINE SEXUAL VICTIMIZATION

As long as the Internet is in existence, cybercrime will be a problem, especially crime involving sexual victimization. People all over the world have access to computers and the Internet, meaning people all over the world have the ability to be victims of online sexual victimization or to be offenders. The dangers of the Internet are immense for children and adolescents and will probably continue to grow. Therefore, fighting online sexual victimization has become an important aspect of the criminal justice system. With the expansion of Internet usage has come the expansion of programs and policies attempting to protect the users.

Many police departments have their own designated cybercrime task force that focuses on investigating online sexual victimization (Broadhurst, 2006; Hinduja, 2004). These task forces are often referred to as computer emergency response teams, or CERTs. The task forces follow tips provided by citizens and delve into the systems of Internet service providers looking for sexually explicit material. A similar program created as a part of the FBI's Cyber Crimes Program is called the Innocent Images National Initiative. This multiagency operation strives to combat sexual crimes involving children. Because of the initiative, the number of cases opened and the number of arrests have increased by 2,062% and 1,401%, respectively. These increases demonstrate amazing progress toward protecting children.

In 1998, the Office of Juvenile Justice and Delinquency Prevention created the Internet Crimes against Children (ICAC) Task Force Program. The goal of ICAC was to aid law enforcement, both local and state, in the construction of programs that will be better able to handle crimes involving both sexual solicitation and child pornography. Yet another program is Project Safe Childhood, which attempts to prevent children from experiencing abuse online (U.S. Department of Justice, 2006). It also aims to help residents protect themselves by increasing the public's knowledge about the dangers of the Internet.

Conclusion

It is not abnormal to see weekly media reports of trusted community members who have been arrested for possession, dissemination, or production of child pornography.

Teachers, Sunday school teachers, and day care workers—all entrusted with the care of children—have been thrust into the public spotlight for their violation of young people. While the Internet provides humans with the ability to communicate at the speed of light and to access information efficiently, it has also become a playground of availability for persons looking to access child pornography. Protecting innocent Internet users has become a major challenge for law enforcement and the criminal justice system in general, and both are working daily to combat child pornography's presence online.

This chapter documents how the criminal justice system has attacked the explosion of the presence of child pornography online, as well as the setbacks experienced. The purpose of this chapter is not only to demonstrate the continuum of how the criminal justice system has handled this form of criminality but also to show how child pornography's uses have changed over the years. Today, not only pedophiles are looking for and using child pornography, but, in fact, minors are disseminating this material without understanding the true consequence of their actions. Surely, the next 10 years of technology development will bring more changes, good and bad, to all facets of the criminal justice system and its offenders.

Discussion Questions

1. Despite the Supreme Court's ruling in *Ashcroft v. Free Speech Coalition* (2002), should digitally created images of children be considered child pornography?

2. Should individuals be punished differently based on the types of material they possess and the harm such material causes to the victim(s)?

3. Should sexting be considered a criminal behavior or simply a deviant act? Why?

References

Adam Walsh Child Protection and Safety Act, 42 U.S.C. § 16911 (2006).

Ashcroft v. Free Speech Coalition, 535 U.S. 234 (2002).

Baumgartner, S. E., Valkenburg, P. M., & Peter, J. (2010). Unwanted online sexual solicitation and risky sexual online behavior across the lifespan. *Journal of Applied Developmental Psychology, 31*(6), 439–447. doi:10.1016/j.appdev.2010.07.005

Blair, B. L., & Fletcher, A. C. (2011). "The only 13-year-old on planet earth without a cell phone": Meanings of cell phones in early adolescents' everyday lives. *Journal of Adolescent Research, 26*(2), 155–177. doi:10.1177/0743558410371127

Bourke, M., & Hernandez, A. (2009). The "Butner Study" redux: A report of the incidence of hands-on child victimization by child pornography offenders. *Journal of Family Violence, 24,* 183–191. doi:10.1007/s10896-008-9219-y

Broadhurst, R. (2006). Developments in the global law enforcement of cyber-crime. *Policing: An International Journal of Police Strategies & Management, 29*(3), 408–433. doi: 10.1108/1363 9510610684674

Bryce, J. (2010). Online sexual exploitation of children and young people. In Y. Jewkes & M. Yar (Eds.), *Handbook of Internet crime* (pp. 320–342). Portland, OR: Willian.

Burke, A., Sowerbutts, S., Blundell, B., & Sherry, M. (2002). Child pornography and the Internet: Policing and treatment issues. *Psychiatry, Psychology and Law, 9*(1), 79–84. doi:10.1375/1321871027 60196925

Child pornography, the Internet, and the challenge of updating statutory terms. (2009). *Harvard Law Review, 122*(8), 2206–2227.

Child Protection Act, Pub. L. No. 112-206 (2012).

Child Protection and Obscenity Enforcement Act, 18 U.S.C. 2251 (1988).

Children's Internet Protection Act, Pub. L. No. 106-554 (2000).

Child Sexual Abuse and Pornography Act, 18 U.S.C. 2251 (1986).

Dake, J. A., Price, J. H., Maziarz, L., & Ward, B. (2012). Prevalence and correlates of sexting behavior in adolescents. *American Journal of Sexuality Education, 7*(1), 1–15. doi:10.1080/15546128.201 2.650959

Dombrowski, S. C., LeMasney, J. W., Ahia, C. E., & Dickson, S. A. (2004). Protecting children from online sexual predators: Technological, psychoeducational, and legal considerations. *Professional Psychology: Research and Practice, 35*(1), 65–73. doi:10.1037/0735-7028.35.1.65

Durkin, K. F., & Bryant, C. D. (1999). Propagandizing pederasty: A thematic analysis of the on-line exculpatory accounts of unrepentant pedophiles. *Deviant Behavior, 20*(2), 103–127. doi: 10.1080/ 016396299266524

Federal Communications Commission. (2006). *Children's Internet Protection Act.* Retrieved from http://www.fcc.gov/cgb/consumerfacts/cipa.html

Gillespie, A. (2011). *Child pornography: Law and policy.* New York, NY: Routledge.

Henderson, H. (2005). *Internet predators.* New York, NY: Facts on File.

Hinduja, S. (2004). Perceptions of local and state law enforcement concerning the role of computer crime investigative teams. *Policing: An International Journal of Police Strategies & Management, 27*(3), 341–357. doi: 10.1108/13639510410553103

Jones, S., & Fox, S. (2009). Generations online in 2009. *Pew Internet & American Life Project.* Retrieved from http://www.pewinternet.org/Reports/2009/Generations-Online-in-2009.aspx

Jones, L. M., Mitchell, K. J., & Finkelhor, D. (2012). Trends in youth Internet victimization: Findings from three youth Internet safety surveys 2000–2010. *Journal of Adolescent Health, 50*(2), 179–186. doi:10.1016/j.jadohealth.2011.09.015

Leary, M. (2010). Sexting or self-produced child pornography? The dialog continues—structured prosecutorial discretion within a multidisciplinary response. *Virginia Journal of Social Policy and the Law, 17*(3), 486–566.

Levick, M., & Moon, K. (2010). Prosecuting sexting as child pornography: A critique. *Valparaiso University Law Review, 44*(4), 1035–1054.

Malesky, L. (2007). Predatory online behavior: Modus operandi of convicted sex offenders in identifying potential victims and contacting minors over the Internet. *Journal of Child Sexual Abuse, 16*(2), 23–32. doi: 10.1300/J070v16n02_02

Marcum, C. D. (2007). Interpreting the intentions of Internet predators: An analysis of online predatory behavior. *Journal of Child Sexual Abuse, 16*(4), 99–114.

Marcum, C. D. (2008). Identifying potential factors of adolescent online victimization in high school seniors. *International Journal of Cyber Criminology, 2*(2), 346–367.

Marcum, C. D., Higgins, G. E., & Ricketts, M. L. (2010). Potential factors of online victimization of youth: An examination of adolescent online behaviors utilizing Routine Activities Theory. *Deviant Behavior, 31*(5), 381–410. doi:10.1080/01639620903004903

Marcum, C. D., Higgins, G. E., Ricketts, M. L., & Freiburger, T. L. (2011). An assessment of the training and resources dedicated nationally to the investigation of the production of child pornography. *Policing: A Journal of Policy & Practice, 5*(1), 23–32.

McCabe, K. (2000). Child pornography and the Internet. *Social Science Computer Review, 18*(1), 73–76.

Middleton, D., Elliot, L., Mandeville-Norden, R., & Beech, A. R. (2006). An investigation into the applicability of the Ward and Siegert pathways model of child abuse with Internet offenders. *Psychology, Crime and Law, 12,* 589–603. doi: 10.1080/10683160600558352

Mitchell, K. J., Finkelhor, D., Jones, L. M., & Wolak, J. (2012). Prevalence and characteristics of youth sexting: A national study. *Pediatrics, 129*(1), 13–20. doi:10.1542/peds.2011–1730

Mitchell, K. J., Finkelhor, D. & Wolak, J. (2007). Online requests for sexual pictures from youth: Risk factors and incident characteristics. *Journal of Adolescent Health, 41*(2), 196–203.

Mitchell, K. J., Ybarra, M., & Finkelhor, D. (2007). The relative importance of online victimization in understanding depression, delinquency, and substance use. *Child Maltreatment, 12*(4), 314–324.

Mota, S. A. (2002). The U.S. Supreme Court addresses the Child Pornography Prevention Act and Child Online Protection Act in *Ashcroft v. Free Speech Coalition* and *Ashcroft v. American Civil Liberties Union. Federal Communications Law Journal, 55*(1), 85–98.

New York v. Ferber, 458 U.S. 747 (1982).

O'Connell, R. (2003). *A typology of cybersexpolitation and online grooming practices.* Retrieved from http://www.jisc.ac.uk/uploaded_documents/lis_PaperJPrice.pdf

Ostrager, B. (2010). SMS. OMG! LOL! TTYL: Translating the law to accommodate today's teens and the evolution from texting to sexting. *Family Court Review, 48*(4), 712–726. doi: 10.1111/j.1744-1617.2010.01345.x

Parker, M. R. (2009). *Kids these days: Teenage sexting and how the law should deal with it.* Retrieved from http://works.bepress.com/michael_parker/1/

Protection of Children Against Sexual Exploitation Act, 18 U.S.C. § 2251 (1977).

Rainie, L. (2006, March). *Life online: Teens and technology and the world to come.* Speech to the annual conference of the Public Library Association, Boston, MA. Retrieved from http://www.pewinternet.org (no longer available online)

Saunders, B. (2003). Understanding children exposed to violence: Toward an integration of overlapping fields. *Journal of Interpersonal Violence, 18*(4), 356–376.

Schrock, S., & Boyd, D. (2009). Online threats to youth: Solicitation, harassment, and problematic content; A review by the Research Advisory Board of the Internet Safety Technical Task Force. Retrieved from http://www.danah.org/papers/ISTTF-RABLitReview.pdf

Sheldon, K., & Howitt, D. (2007). *Sex offenders and the Internet.* Chichester, UK: John Wiley & Sons.

Simon, B. (1999). United States v. Hilton. *Berkeley Technology Law Journal, 14*(1), 385–401.

Stahl, C., & Fritz, N. (2002). Internet safety: Adolescents' self-report. *Journal of Adolescent Health, 31*(1), 7–10.

Taylor, M., Holland, G., & Quayle, E. (2001). Typology of paedophile picture collections. *Police Journal, 74,* 97–107.

United States v. Goff, 155 Fed.Appx. 773 (5th Cir. 2005).

United States v. Shiver, 305 Fed.Appx. 640 (11th Cir.2008 (2008).

United States v. Tucker, 305 F.3d 1193 (10th Cir. 2002).

United States v. Williams, 583 U.S. 285 (2008).

U.S. Department of Justice. (2006). *Project Safe Childhood.* Retrieved from http://www.project safechildhood.gov

Wall, D. (2007). *Cybercrime: The transformation of crime in the information age.* Cambridge, MA: Polity.

Ward, T., & Siegert, R. (2002). Toward a comprehensive theory of child sexual abuse: A theory knitting perspective. *Psychology, Crime & Law, 8*(4), 319–351. doi:10.1080/1068316020 8401823

Webb, L., Craissati, J., & Keen, S. (2007). Characteristics of internet child pornography offenders: A comparison with child molesters. *Sexual Abuse: A Journal of Research and Treatment, 19*(4), 449–465. doi: 10.1007/s11194-007-9063-2

Wolak, J., Mitchell, K. J., & Finkelhor, D. (2006). *Online victimization of youth: Five years later.* Washington, DC: National Center for Missing & Exploited Children.

Ybarra, M., & Mitchell, K. (2008). How risky are social networking sites? A comparison of places online where youth sexual solicitation and harassment occur. *Pediatrics, 121*(2), 350–357. doi: 10.1542/peds.2007-0693

Young, K. (2005). Profiling online sex offenders, cyber-predators, and pedophiles. *Journal of Behavioral Profiling, 5*(1), 1–18.

9

Victimization of the Vulnerable

Tammy Garland and Christina Policastro

"**V**ulnerability refers to the ease of being victimized and the impact the crime has upon the victim" (Doerner & Lab, 2008, p. 293). Although all populations may experience some type of sexual victimization, it is those who are deemed vulnerable that are placed at a heightened risk. Sexually vulnerable populations are not limited by age (e.g., children and the elderly); others may be considered at risk due to mental illness or disabilities as well as situational and lifestyle factors such as homelessness or incarceration. However, for the purposes of this chapter, child, elderly, and inmate sexual victimization will be examined.

Those who are at a greater dependency or are under the direct care of others are at risk of being forced or coerced into sexual relationships. While some of these relationships may be beneficial to both parties, the problem inherently lies in "the fundamental asymmetry of the relationship" (Finkelhor, 1979, p. 695). As in sexual harassment cases where quid pro quo harassment exists, the inability to fully understand the consequences of such behaviors warrants concern (see Chapter 4). For instance, staff/inmate consensual sexual relationships do occur within prison settings (see Worley, Marquart, & Mullings, 2003); however, the power differential within these relationships causes problems, and as a result the relationships are deemed policy violations or illegal. While there are exceptions, sexual victimization is often motivated by power and control, such that one individual preys upon another. Perpetrators are, in essence, able to use power imbalances to capitalize on the relative helplessness of a victim, thus allowing them to either force or coerce their victim into engaging in a sexual relationship. While this power may not be used in a forceful manner, the power to manipulate an individual (e.g., a child) into compliance regardless of method does long-lasting harm to the victim.

In instances of childhood sexual abuse, a power imbalance is implicit simply due to the nature of the construct (Jinich et al., 1998). As noted by Finkelhor (1979, 1984), a child lacks power and knowledge regarding the act; therefore, the child does not have the ability to give consent. "Because they are children; they can never consent. . . . For true consent to occur, two conditions must prevail. A person must know what it is that he or she is consenting to, and a person must be free to say yes or no" (1979, p. 694). Although Finkelhor's argument was initially used to explain child sexual victimization, it can be applied equally to specific adult populations, especially those who are under the care and control of others such as the incarcerated and dependent elderly. Studies on adult populations are more concerned with the idea of the ability to consent. While the victimization of adults does not garner as much sympathy as child victims, it still poses a significant problem in society. Sexual abuse, regardless of the age of the victim, is a question of power, albeit one that is often ignored. Society continues to blame victims for their abuse, especially victims who are not considered completely helpless or incapacitated. However, as Finkelhor noted, people must "have *true freedom* to say yes or no" in order to give consent (1979, p. 694).

Not all instances of sexual relationships with vulnerable populations are a result of an offender seeking power and control. Cognitively impaired offenders cannot be considered rational in their victimization others. Additionally, peer-on-peer child sexual victimizations are not always about control, as some instances may involve modeling behaviors rather than intentional victimization. Regardless of the reason, all sexual violence, whether motivated by the intent to control or not, harms the victim. Since certain populations are at a distinct disadvantage for resisting sexually aggressive behaviors, it is up to caregivers or others responsible for the vulnerable individuals to ensure their safety.

Child Sexual Abuse

While child sexual abuse (CSA) has always existed and is neither an isolated nor rare incident, as it occurs across all cultures and socioeconomic statuses, the topic remains one of the most disconcerting issues to address when examining the literature on sexual victimization (Belknap, 2007; Pereda, Guilera, Forns, & Gómez-Benito, 2009). While CSA covers a wide range of acts and has been noted to have definitional problems due to an inability to agree upon the consensuality of certain crimes (e.g., peer victimization) and certain cultural norms (Finkelhor, 1994), most scholars are in agreement that CSA may include contact or noncontact forms of victimization. As noted by the Child Abuse and Prevention Treatment Act (CAPTA), childhood sexual abuse is defined as

> the employment, use, persuasion, inducement, enticement, or coercion of any child to engage in, or assist any other person to engage in, any sexually explicit conduct of simulation of such conduct for the purpose of producing

a visual depiction of such conduct; or the rape, and in cases of caretaker or inter-familial relationships, statutory rape, molestation, prostitution, or other form of sexual exploitation of children, or incest with children. (42 U.S.C. § 5106g[4][A–B])

In general, forms of child sexual abuse include fondling, penetration, incest, rape, sodomy, indecent exposure, and exploitation through prostitution or the production of pornographic material (Child Welfare Information Gateway [CWIG], 2013). While CSA may not be obvious, victims may present signs of abuse both physically and behaviorally. Physical signs may include injury to the genital area, difficulty sitting or walking, pregnancy, and presence of a sexually transmitted disease. Fear of being alone with adults, knowledge of sexual relations inappropriate for the child's age, running away from home, and sexual victimization of other children are common behavioral indicators of CSA (CWIG).

Measuring childhood victimization has proven to be very difficult due to the nature of the crime, and data collected on CSA are often combined with instances of physical abuse and neglect. Additionally, while data on CSA are collected by organizations such as the National Incidence Study of Child Abuse and Neglect (NIS), child protective services, and criminal justice agencies, most instances of CSA do not come to the attention of these agencies as they remain unreported; most victims do not report their victimization until adulthood (Belknap, 2007). Because CSA is a hidden offense, as are most forms of sexual victimization, obtaining an accurate count of the victims is virtually impossible (Belknap; Finkelhor, 1994). Regardless, the extant literature has shown that youths are disproportionately at increased risk of being victims of sexual violence (Tjaden & Thoennes, 2006). In 1995, approximately 1.8 million youths between the ages of 12 and 17 reported being a victim of sexual assault. Notably, these statistics do not address youth under 12 years of age, reflecting a consistent problem in data collection. Studies have, however, reported rates of sexual abuse that are greater than those of adults; approximately 70% of all reported sexual assaults are against children under the age of 17 (Snyder, 2000). Although substantiated reports of childhood sexual abuse have consistently declined over the past two decades (Finkelhor, Ormrod, Turner, & Hamby, 2010), CSA continues to remain a problem.

A recent metaanalysis found that 7.5% of male and 25.3% of female youths had experienced CSA (Pereda et al., 2009). While boys are prone to be victims of CSA, the nature of these crimes remains very gendered (Belknap, 2007). Without question, the sexual victimization of young males cannot be ignored; however, studies have repeatedly shown girls to be at a greater risk of childhood sexual violence than boys (Finkelhor & Dziuba-Leatherman, 1994; Finkelhor et al., 2005; MacMillan, Tanaka, Duku, Vaillancourt, & Boyle, 2013). As Finkelhor's (1994) study reported, the ratio for prevalence of CSA typically represents 1 man for every 3 women. A decade later, using data from the Second National Incidence Studies of Missing, Abducted, Runaway, and Thrownaway Children (NISMART-2), Finkelhor, Hammer, and Sedlak (2008) found that 285,400 youths were victims of sexual assault; girls represented approximately 89% of these cases. Another study conducted by Kilpatrick, Saunders, and Smith (2003) found that girls were more likely to be victims of sexual assault (13%) than boys (3.4%). While girls do make up the majority of CSA cases, when examining cases of childhood rape, males are at a greater risk of being raped at younger ages. Tjaden and Thoennes (2006) found that over half of female victims and almost three quarters of male victims reported that they were raped prior to their 18th birthday; male sexual victimization decreases with age. Of those sampled, 48% of men reported their first rape occurring prior to the age of 12 in comparison to 2.16% of women. Women were more likely to report that they had first experienced rape between the ages of 12 and 17. According to Finkelhor & Dziuba-Leatherman (1994), girls, especially in instances of sexual abuse, become more vulnerable as they age. While the peak age for CSA is between 9 and 13 (Finkelhor, 1994), data indicate that teenagers, especially girls, are disproportionately represented as rape victims when compared to the general adolescent population. This can largely be attributed to peer-on-peer violence. Other factors that may place youth at risk are physical and mental disabilities, broken or nontraditional homes, parental drug and alcohol abuse, and a prior history of victimization (APA, 2013).

CONSEQUENCES OF CHILD SEXUAL ABUSE

Without question, CSA is a traumatic experience that may lead to severe and long-term negative psychological and physical outcomes for its victims. Dependent on the extent of victimization, no symptoms may manifest in abnormal behavior (Browne & Finkelhor, 1986; Kendall-Tackett, Williams, & Finkelhor, 1993); however, in many cases, victims often experience short- and long-term effects. Initial responses to CSA may include bed-wetting, eating disorders, feelings of guilt, sleep disturbances, and behavioral problems at home or school. Some studies have shown that physical problems, such as chronic pelvic pain and nonepileptic seizures, may manifest. Additionally, other studies have shown that victims of CSA are likely to experience a number of psychological disorders over the long term, including depression, anxiety, separation anxiety, low self-esteem, fear, withdrawal, insomnia, posttraumatic stress disorder (PTSD), sexual dysfunction, aggressive behavior, self-injury, and other self-destructive behaviors such as alcohol and drug abuse or acting out in a promiscuous manner (APA, 2013; Browne & Finkelhor; Kendall-Tackett, Williams, & Finkelhor). Much of the research has indicated that victims of CSA are more likely to experience psychological problems than nonvictims and for longer periods of time. For instance, victims of CSA are not only likely to suffer from depression as youths, but survivors of CSA have been found to suffer a lifetime risk of depression (Thomas, DiLillo, Walsh, & Polusny, 2011) in which they are 4 times more likely to suffer from depression as those who were not exposed to CSA.

Previous literature has also shown a link between CSA and adult sexual assault revictimization (see Filipas & Ullman, 2006). Consistent with findings from the

National Violence Against Women Survey (NVAWS), Tjaden and Thoennes (2006) found that women who had been raped as minors were 2 times as likely to be raped as adults. These individuals were also more likely to engage in maladaptive coping strategies to manage past victimizations, thus placing them at risk for future victimization. Filipas and Ullman found that individuals who were revictimized were more likely to use drugs and alcohol, suffer from withdrawal, be more sexually promiscuous, and experience more PTSD-related symptoms. While it is evident that CSA may pose a risk for subsequent victimization, other factors such as poverty and sexual orientation should not be overlooked. Further research examining and controlling for these issues is needed (Tjaden & Thoennes).

PREVENTING CSA

In 1994, the Jacob Wetterling Crimes Against Children and Sexually Violent Offender Act (Jacob Wetterling Act) was passed requiring states to implement a sex-offender registration program or forfeit federal funds granted by the Department of Justice. After the death of Megan Kanka, state legislatures expanded their laws to include mandatory community notification; these laws became known as Megan's Laws (Doerner & Lab, 2008; Terry & Ackerman, 2009). A decade later, the Adam Walsh Child Protection and Safety Act of 2006 was used to implement uniform requirements for sex offender registration. With the increased focus on CSA, all 50 states have enacted sex offender registration laws as a means to track prior sex offenders; methods of tracking and restrictions vary depending on the state (Terry & Ackerman). The laws, however, have come under scrutiny due to the broad interpretation applied to such violations, including public urination and peer sexual relations. While this legislation allows communities to identify convicted sex offenders living in the area, it does little to protect youths against those who have not been identified, or the majority of sex offenders. As noted throughout this text, sexual predators are often known to the victim, and sexual violence often remains unreported as a result.

All U.S. states and territories have statutes identifying persons who are required to report child abuse; however, these laws vary in scope (see CWIG, 2012). For instance, under Texas law, professionals (i.e., teachers, doctors, nurses, child day care workers) must make a verbal report of suspected CSA within 48 hours; failure to do so is punishable by imprisonment for up to 180 days and/or a fine of up to $2,000 (Texas Family Code, § 261.101). Most states specify professional groups that must report; however, states such as New Jersey and Wyoming require all persons to report suspected cases of child abuse, including CSA. While failure to report CSA is classified as a misdemeanor, many often fail to do so even though disclosure is immune from criminal and/or civil liability under the "good faith" doctrine (CWIG, 2012). Many individuals do not want to get involved in personal family matters and thus take a noninterventionist approach.

While there is no surefire way to prevent CSA, as victims have little choice in the violence perpetrated against them, it is possible to educate society about how to identify and report CSA. However, education efforts have proven to be more difficult than expected. Currently, most programs target children and families in prevention strategies. Programs targeting youths and CSA prevention have been found to be beneficial, as researchers have consistently found that these programs increase youths' knowledge about the issue, increase self-protective skills, lead to an earlier disclosure of abuse, and increase positive feelings about self. Long-term programs that incorporate repetitive practice skills and engage children are seemingly more successful than one-time events (NSVRC, 2011b). Regardless, as with most preventative training, it appears that the children are tasked with protecting themselves from sexual abuse. While educating potential victims is important, there must be more comprehensive measures that protect children from victimization.

Although it should be intuitive that educating parents and caregivers about the dangers of CSA would prevent these acts from occurring, the literature has found that education efforts do not necessarily increase parents' knowledge about CSA and their willingness to discuss these issues with their children. As a result, the effects of prevention efforts aimed toward parent education and lowering the rate of CSA are unclear (NSVRC, 2011b). Thus, it becomes necessary for professionals (e.g., teachers, child care workers, and medical doctors) to be able to identify and respond to reports of CSA, especially when the victimization was perpetrated by a family member. While professionals who work with children are often required to attend annual training on CSA, as they are likely to be tasked with the identification and reporting of CSA, state requirements vary with respect to the time that must be spent in training and the material covered. These aspects also vary across different organizations and locales (e.g., rural vs. metropolitan). The literature has shown that professionals are not always able to identify signs of CSA. Hibbard and Zollinger (1990) found that approximately 20% of 902 professionals attending training were not knowledgeable about key CSA material; this lack of knowledge could impede the legal and medical investigation of a case. Research has also indicated that those tasked with obtaining information from suspected victims (e.g., law enforcement officers, social workers, and medical doctors) are often untrained or use inappropriate techniques. One study found that police officers received less training than other professional staff, such as child protective services and mental health providers, even though they were often tasked with similar interviewing and investigating techniques (Daly, 2004). While urban areas are not as impacted by this because child protective teams investigate claims of CSA, rural areas are at a significant disadvantage when law enforcement officers are not equipped to conduct such investigations (Daly). In addition, Korkman, Santtila, Drzewiecki, and Sandnabba (2008) found that the language used in interviewing suspected victims of CSA exceeded the cognitive level of the child interviewed, which does little to obtain credible information for prosecution. Failure to identify CSA, investigate claims, and use proper investigative techniques does not assist victims and almost ensures that justice will not be served. Thus, it is necessary to ensure effective training at all levels of CSA investigation, regardless of agency and jurisdiction.

Elder Sexual Abuse

Sexual abuse of older adults has received very little attention in the broader sexual abuse literature or in empirical studies of elder abuse. This inattention has been linked to several factors, including misperceptions about the sexuality of older adults, rape myth acceptance, and generational values/beliefs that lead many elders to view sex and victimization as private matters (Benbow & Haddad, 1993; Vierthaler, 2008). Consequently, our understanding of the extent, consequences, and causes of elder sexual abuse is very limited. Elder sexual abuse can be considered to fall within the broader scope of physical elder abuse, but it is often differentiated from other forms of physical abuse due to the distinct nature and consequences of sexual victimization. The National Center on Elder Abuse (NCEA, 2013) defined elder sexual abuse as any nonconsensual contact of a sexual nature with an elderly individual. This type of abuse encompasses a diverse range of harmful acts and behaviors that can occur in both institutional settings (e.g., nursing homes, hospitals, assisted-living facilities) and community environments such as the victim's home. To capture the wide variety of sexually abusive experiences reported by older adults, Ramsey-Klawsnik (1996) outlined three types of elder sexual abuse: hands-on behavior, hands-off behavior, and harmful genital practices.

Hands-on behavior involves direct contact between the offender and victim such as rape and fondling. In comparison, hands-off behavior refers to situations where the offender does not have direct-contact with the victim yet behaves in a sexually abusive way. This type of sexual abuse includes acts such as exhibitionism, voyeurism, unwanted sexualized comments, forcing the elder to view pornography, and nonconsensual sexually explicit photography (NCEA, 2013; Ramsey-Klawsnik & Brandl, 2009). The last type of elder sexual abuse, harmful genital practices, refers to "painful, intrusive, or unnecessary procedures that are committed during the provision of personal care" to a dependent elder (Ramsey-Klawsnik & Brandl, p. 1). Examples of harmful genital practices include the inappropriate application of creams, medications, and enemas, as well as genital or rectal penetration while bathing the elder (Ramsey-Klawsnik, 1996).

The extant literature suggests that elder sexual abuse is less common than other forms of elder abuse. For instance, Acierno and colleagues (2010) found that less than 1% (0.6%) of the 5,777 community-dwelling elders included in the National Elder Mistreatment Study (NEMS) reported that they had experienced sexual abuse in the year prior to the survey. In comparison, NEMS participants reported a past-year prevalence of 4.6% for emotional abuse, 1.6% for physical abuse, 5.9% for potential neglect, and 5.2% for financial abuse. The NEMS findings confirmed results reported by Tatara (1998) based on data derived from the National Elder Mistreatment Study, which indicated that sexual abuse comprised the smallest category of elder abuse cases reported to adult protective services (APS) during 1996. Similarly, using data from all patient abuse cases reported to Medicaid Fraud Control Units (MFCUs) between 1987 and 1992, Payne and

Cikovic (1995) found that only 9% of elder abuse occurring in nursing homes involved sexual abuse.

As with sexual victimization in general, underreporting is considered to significantly impact prevalence estimates of sexual abuse among the elderly, with some scholars suggesting that sexual abuse may be the most underreported form of elder abuse (see Mickish, 1993; Teaster & Roberto, 2003, 2004). Focusing on all types of elder abuse, Tatara (1998) reported that only 1 out of every 5 cases of elder abuse is reported to authorities. Pillemer and Finkelhor (1988) suggested that an even greater proportion of cases escape detection, estimating that only 1 out of every 14 cases is reported. Existing prevalence rates most likely underestimate the true extent of elder sexual abuse. When considering elder sexual abuse, a number of potential barriers may prevent elderly victims from reporting that they have been victimized. Like younger victims, elderly sexual abuse victims may not report their victimization because of feelings of shame, as well as fear retaliation by the offender (Benbow & Haddad, 1993; Vierthaler, 2008). Aging, however, poses unique obstacles for many older sexual abuse victims, including cognitive impairments such as Alzheimer's disease and limited mobility associated with declines in physical functioning. Impaired elders may encounter problems accessing transportation and access to service agencies, as well as difficulty communicating to others that they have been victimized (Vierthaler).

CONSEQUENCES OF ELDER ABUSE

Studies of reported cases of elder sexual victimization indicate that elderly victims experience a number of negative consequences associated with their victimization. Comparing female sexual assault victims, ages 55 and older, to female sexual assault victims between the ages of 18 and 45, Muram, Miller, and Cutler (1992) established that older victims were more likely than their younger counterparts to sustain genital injury as a result of the sexual assault. Further, 28% of the elderly victims who experienced genital injuries required surgery to address their injuries. More recently, Poulos and Sheridan (2008) reviewed seven studies of sexual assault among postmenopausal women and concluded that genital injuries were more common and more serious among older female sexual assault victims than among younger female victims.

Evidence suggest that elder sexual abuse results not only in physical injuries but also in psychological trauma, with studies identifying symptoms of PTSD, increased anxiety, and high levels of confusion and fear among older sexual abuse victims (Burgess, Dowdell, & Prentky, 2000; Burgess & Phillips, 2006; Ramsey-Klawsnik, 2004). Findings from Burgess and colleagues' examination of 20 elder sexual abuse cases suggest that sexual victimization may also influence life expectancy among elderly victims. Specifically, 11 of the sexual abuse victims included in the study were deceased within a year of their victimization incident (Burgess et al.). Although their findings seem to suggest a link between mortality and sexual victimization, Burgess and colleagues acknowledged that they could not determine whether the 11 deaths were a direct result of the victimization or related to other factors. Over half of the deceased victims were between the ages of 80 and 99 when they were sexually abused; thus, it is possible that their deaths were due to the natural process of aging (Burgess et al., 2000). More research is needed to clarify the link between elder sexual abuse and mortality rates, as well as other possible consequences of sexual victimization among the elderly.

TARGETING ELDERLY VICTIMS

As previously mentioned, the study of elder sexual abuse is relatively new and, thus, the majority of elder sexual abuse research is descriptive in nature. The existing literature, however, identifies several key patterns of victimization and offending risk that provide some insight into the dynamics of this form of sexual victimization. With regard to victimization risk, research consistently suggests an association between victim vulnerability and increased risk of sexual abuse. Specifically, elder sexual abuse victims are predominately females characterized by cognitive and physical impairments (Brozowski & Hall, 2010; Burgess et al., 2000; Burgess & Phillips, 2006; Holt, 1993; Ramsey-Klawsnik, 1991; Teaster & Roberto, 2003, 2004; Teaster, Roberto, Duke, & Kim, 2001). Research indicates that older male sexual abuse victims, like their female counterparts, are generally low functioning, both cognitively and physically (Teaster et al., 2007). According to Ramsey-Klawsnik (2004), sexual abuse offenders are likely to target impaired elders whom offenders can readily intimidate, overpower, and control. Further contributing to their vulnerability, impaired elders are believed to be less likely to report their victimization and, if they do report, less likely to be viewed as reliable sources (Ramsey-Klawsnik, 2004; Vierthaler, 2008). The overwhelming majority of offenders who sexually abuse older adults are male (Holt, 1993; Ramsey-Klawsnik, 1991; Ramsey-Klawsnik, Teaster, Mendiondo, Marcum, & Abner, 2008; Teaster & Roberto, 2003, 2004; Teaster et al., 2007). The elder sexual abuse research is much less clear with regard to the relationship between the victim and offender, with the literature suggesting that the type of sample used, whether institutional or community, is likely to influence the types of perpetrators identified. For example, Teaster and Roberto (2004) examined reported cases of elder sexual abuse occurring in both the community and institutional environments. They found that offenders who sexually abused community-dwelling elders were as likely to be family members as nonrelatives. In comparison, other residents comprised the largest category of offenders who sexually abused residents of care facilities (Teaster & Roberto). It appears that offenders target victims to whom they have the most access, and this access consequently creates more opportunities for sexual victimization to occur (Ramsey-Klawsnik et al., 2008). Very few studies have focused on characteristics of elder sexual abuse offenders beyond basic demographics and the victim-offender relationship, yet preliminary evidence suggests these offenders tend to suffer from substance abuse problems and/or mental illness (Ramsey-Klawsnik et al., 2008; Teaster & Roberto, 2003, 2004).

PREVENTING ELDERLY SEXUAL ABUSE

Currently, every state in the United States has implemented some form of legislation that extends protections, as well as services to the elderly and other vulnerable adults (e.g. disabled individuals over the age of 18; Ehrlich & Anetzberger, 1991; Wolf, 1996). In general, legislative responses to elder abuse have included the establishment of APS agencies, as well as mandatory reporting laws. Statutory definitions of elder abuse vary considerably from state to state (Jogerst et al., 2003; Payne, 2011). Examining elder abuse laws for all 50 states and the District of Columbia, Daly and Jogerst (2003) found 38 statutes that included terms that described sexual abuse of older adults. They concluded that *sexual abuse* is among one of the most frequently used terms included in statutory definitions of elder abuse (Daly & Jogerst). Interestingly, findings from a study conducted by Payne, Berg, and Byars (1999) indicate that professionals often exclude sexual abuse from their definitions of elder abuse. Payne and colleagues asked 54 nursing home directors, 132 nursing home employees, 64 police chiefs, and 127 university students to provide a definition of elder abuse. Only 11.1% of nursing home directors, 3.8% of nursing home employees, and 1.6% of students included sexual abuse in their definitions. None of the police chiefs included sexual abuse in their definition of elder abuse. This is problematic considering that police officers and health care employees are often in a key position to intervene in cases of elder abuse and are typically designated as mandatory reporters in states with mandatory reporting laws.

Despite the inclusion of sexual abuse in statutory definitions of elder abuse, very few services exist to serve elderly victims of sexual violence, and the official response to elder sexual abuse is often inadequate (Vierthaler, 2008). Studies of reported elder sexual abuse cases indicate that offenders are rarely arrested and prosecuted, with many cases citing lack of sufficient evidence as a major barrier to prosecution (Ramsey-Klawsnik et al., 2008; Teaster et al., 2001; Teaster & Roberto, 2003, 2004). Further, older individuals typically do not utilize or are even referred to rape and sexual assault crisis services (Vierthaler, 2008). Multiple agencies, including law enforcement, APS, and regulatory agencies, are responsible for responding to elder sexual abuse, and professionals from different fields often receive vastly different training (Payne, 2011; Ramsey-Klawsnik et al.). Given the recent recognition of elder sexual abuse, many professionals do not have sufficient training on how to effectively identify and respond to suspected abuse, nor do they understand how other agencies respond to abuse. Scholars have suggested that improving the ability of professionals to recognize and report elder sexual abuse, as well as collaboration and cross-training with other agencies, is essential to crafting a more effective response (Ramsey-Klawsnik et al.; Vierthaler). Research is needed to determine the efficacy of training programs designed to increase awareness of sexual abuse among the elderly.

Sexual Victimization of Inmates

According to the Prison Rape Elimination Act (PREA), prison rape is defined as "the rape of an inmate in the actual or constructive control of prison officials" (Worley, Worley, & Mullings, 2010, p. 66). Factors that are taken into consideration when determining sexual violence include whether the act was forcible or against the victim's will and whether the victim was incapable of consent due to age, mental or physical incapacity, or threat of violence (PREA, 2003; Worley et al., 2010). Although rape is only one form of sexual victimization that occurs in prisons, sexual victimization in prisons tends to be defined as rape and not as including other offenses. Like sexual victimizations experienced by other populations, inmate sexual abuse is not simply a matter of penetration but may include all types of sexual activity, including inappropriate touching (Beck, Harrison, Berzofsky, Caspar, & Krebs, 2010).

Using data from the 2008–2009 National Inmate Survey (NIS-2), Beck and colleagues (2010) found that of the 76,249 inmates participating in the study, 2,861 reported experiencing one or more incidents of sexual victimization in the past 12 months. Thus, approximately 4.4% of prison inmates and 3.1% of jail inmates were victims of sexual violence. As noted in the literature, there are two types of sexual victimization in correctional facilities: inmate-on-inmate and staff-on-inmate (Hensley, Eigenberg, & Gibson, 2013). While consensual sexual relationships do occur between inmates within the prison setting, this chapter is concerned with the nonconsensual sexual victimization of prisoners; all staff-on-inmate sexual relationships are considered nonconsensual due to the legal definitions of such behavior.

INMATE-ON-INMATE SEXUAL VICTIMIZATION

Studies of inmate-on-inmate sexual victimization have been ongoing since the late 1960s. Interviewing 3,304 prisoners in the Philadelphia jail system, Davis (1968) determined that approximately 3% of inmates had been victims of rape during incarceration. More expansive studies conducted in the federal prison system found that less than 1% of inmates reported being a victim of sexual violence; however, 11% of the sample reported being targets of attempted sexual assaults (Nacci & Kane, 1984). Similar findings have been found in examinations of state prisons. Maitland and Sluder (1998) surveyed inmates at a midwestern prison and determined that less than 1% of the population sampled had been a victim of sexual violence. Another study of Oklahoma prisoners found that while 13.8% of inmates had been "sexually threatened," only 1.2% of the inmates sampled had reported being raped by another inmate at any time during incarceration (Hensley, Tewksbury, & Castle, 2003).

As noted by Hensley and colleagues (2013), some studies have produced higher sexual victimization rates. Struckman-Johnson and colleagues (1996) found that 22% of male inmates in Nebraska prisons had been forced or coerced into engaging in sexual activity with another inmate. Similar results were found by Struckman-Johnson and Struckman-Johnson (2000) in their examination of seven midwestern prisons; 21% of study participants had been coerced or sexually victimized at least once. An examination of 6,964 New Jersey inmates found that approximately 4% of male inmates had been victims of sexual violence by another inmate (Wolff, Blitz, Bachman, Shi, & Siegel, 2006). Other recent studies have produced similar results. Jenness, Maxson, Matsueda, and Sumner (2007) found that about 4.4% of sampled California inmates had experienced a sexual assault while incarcerated, and approximately 6% of sampled inmates in Ohio and Texas indicated being victims of sexual violence (Warren, Jackson, Loper, & Burnette, 2010). National survey data collected by the Bureau of Justice Statistics (BJS) also revealed that approximately 2% of male inmates self-reported at least one incident of sexual victimization within the last 12 months (Beck et al., 2010).

Female inmates are not immune to inmate-on-inmate sexual victimization. Hensley, Castle, and Tewksbury (2003) found that approximately 4% of female inmates had been a victim of sexual coercion by another female inmate. Wolff et al. (2006) found that while only 4% reported being a victim of a nonconsensual act, 21% admitted some type of sexual victimization committed by another inmate. Another study found that while 17% of female respondents reported a sexual victimization in prison, only 3% reported a completed sexual assault (Blackburn, Mullings, & Marquart, 2008); however, as noted by Hensley et al. (2013), "this study failed to distinguish between staff and inmate perpetrated assault, making it difficult to determine the nature and context of these incidents" (p. 248). Similarly, the most recent BJS study found low rates of inmate-on-inmate sexual victimization; 3% of female victims reported being a victim of sexual violence by another inmate over the prior 12 months (Beck et al., 2010).

Most inmate-on-inmate sexual assaults occur on average between 1 and 5 months of being incarcerated (Hensley, Koscheski, & Tewksbury, 2005; Hensley, Tewksbury, & Castle, 2003; Nacci & Kane, 1984). The risk of being victimized by another inmate has been attributed to a number of factors. White inmates are more likely to be targets of sexual violence in comparison to black inmates, who often make up the majority of perpetrators (Austin, Fabelo, Gunter, & McGinnis, 2006; Beck et al., 2010; Hensley et al., 2005; Hensley, Tewksbury, & Castle, 2003; Struckman-Johnson et al., 1996). Those who enter prison at a younger age are more likely to be targeted; the research has found that victims are on average 3 years younger than their perpetrators (Austin et al., 2006). Additionally, those with a college degree (Beck et al., 2010), who had a mental impairment (Austin et al., 2006), or were married (Hensley et al., 2005) were more likely to experience sexual victimization in prison. Most notably, the literature has found that those who identify as bisexual or homosexual are more apt to be a victim of inmate-on-inmate sexual violence (Beck et al., 2010; Hensley et al., 2005). Consistent with other studies, Hensley and colleagues (2005) suggested that "perceived vulnerability is a major predictor of possible sexual targeting" (p. 675). As a result, those who identify as homosexual are considered feminine and weak and are thus labeled as such, leaving them susceptible to sexual victimization. This may also explain why those who have been victimized before entering prison are more likely to be victimized during incarceration (Beck et al., 2010). Institutional factors such as barrack housing, solid cell fronts, and lax security have been implicated in increased sexual victimization of prisoners (Austin et al., 2006; Struckman-Johnson & Struckman-Johnson, 2000).

STAFF-ON-INMATE SEXUAL VICTIMIZATION

Staff sexual victimization against inmates varies among inmate populations. While many of these sexual encounters are believed to be consensual, consensual sexual relationships between prison staff and inmates are prohibited due to the inherent power differentials within such relationships and are thus deemed non-consensual by law (PREA, 2003). Regardless of gender, there appears to be no differences in the rate of staff-perpetrated sexual violence against inmates in male and female correctional facilities (Wolff et al., 2006). Beck and colleagues (2010) found that 2.9% of male state and federal prisoners and 2.1% of male jail inmates reported being victims of staff sexual misconduct. In comparison, 2.1% of female prison inmates and 1.9% of females housed in jails were victims of staff-on-inmate sexual violence. Staff-on-inmate sexual encounters are typically perpetrated by members of the opposite sex. For instance, Beck and colleagues found that approximately 69% of all male prison respondents reporting staff-on-inmate sexual misconduct indicated that their sexual encounters had been with female staff. While there are similar rates of victimization in male and female institutions, female inmates are often exposed to numerous types of sexual violence, with deleterious effects. Female prisoners often "face extensive problems with sexual harassment, molestation during strip searches, coercive sexual fondling, and pressured and forced sexual intercourse, most likely perpetrated by prison staff" (Struckman-Johnson & Struckman-Johnson, 2002, p. 217). Baro (1997) examined 38 cases of staff sexual misconduct in a Hawaii correctional facility and found that the custodial abuse resulted in forced sexual contact, unwanted pregnancies, and prostitution.

Factors that place inmates at risk of being victimized by prison staff are similar to those involved in inmate-on-inmate sexual victimization. Older prisoners (over the age of 25) are less likely to be victimized; however, there is a lower victimization rate among white inmates (Beck et al., 2010). Additionally, those who have experienced victimization before incarceration are more likely to be victimized by prison staff (Baro, 1997; Beck et al.).

CONSEQUENCES OF INMATE SEXUAL VICTIMIZATION

While many have blamed inmates for their own victimization, the reality remains that prisoners are not only at risk of being victimized but are also likely to experience negative outcomes as a result (Hensley et al., 2013). Sexual violence against prisoners has been associated with numerous psychological problems, including anxiety, depression, suicidal ideation, substance abuse, and PTSD (Dumond & Dumond, 2002; McGuire, 2005). Prison victims are also exposed to physical harm (Beck & Harrison, 2007). "Where threats or fear are insufficient to induce submission, victims may be seriously beaten, suffering concussions, broken bones, lacerations, and other physical injuries—not to mention the injuries associated with forced sexual penetration" (McGuire, p. 83). Victims of sexual violence are also placed at a great risk for contracting sexually transmitted diseases, including HIV/AIDS (Dumond & Dumond). Some studies have linked prison sex to other forms of prison violence; sexual violence or fear of sexual violence has been linked to an increase in violence among inmates (Struckman-Johnson & Struckman-Johnson, 2000). Furthermore, the fear or actual experience of sexual victimization is not conducive to the rehabilitation process (Hensley et al., 2013; Worley et al., 2010) and may also result in future violence. Another consequence may be increased racism, since these assaults are often interracial (McGuire).

PREVENTING PRISON RAPE

In an attempt to address the issue of sexual violence against inmates under the custody of correctional facilities, the Prison Rape Elimination Act (PREA) was passed in 2003. PREA (2003) mandated that states implement a zero tolerance policy toward prison rape and punish those engaging in such behaviors. To do this, the legislation instituted specific provisions. First, PREA required the BJS to conduct an annual comprehensive review of statistical data to analyze the incidence and effects of prison rape. Secondly, the National Institute of Corrections (NIC) was tasked with constructing a clearinghouse of information and to provide training and education for all federal, state, and local administrators. Additionally, the law provided funding for states to comply and allowed the federal government to withhold funds from states that fail to meet the requirements.

PREA has in theory made it easier to report sexual violence in prisons, yet sexual victimization remains a problem. The majority of sexual victimization incidents that are known to prison authorities are a result of victim reporting (Austin et al., 2006). While victims often tell someone (e.g., a friend, family member, or another inmate) about their victimization, formal disclosure remains problematic, as prison culture often prevents victims from talking with correctional authorities (Fowler, Blackburn, Marquart, & Mullings, 2010; Struckman-Johnson & Struckman-Johnson, 2006; Struckman-Johnson et al., 1996). As noted by Fowler and colleagues (2010), many of the reasons for not reporting sexual violence are similar to real-world explanations: shame, lack of proof, ineffective officials, fear of reprisal, reluctance to be placed in protective custody, and being labeled a snitch (Jenness et al., 2007; Struckman et al., 1996). To combat prison cultural norms and dismissive treatment by correctional officers, many states have enacted policies to increase reporting, including toll-free hotlines, the ability to make anonymous written complaints, and educational efforts that teach victims how to file a report (Fowler et al.).

Although most states have adhered to the spirit of PREA and have implemented numerous policies to prevent prison rape, some have embraced a "wait and see approach" toward the policy (see Thompson, Nored, & Cheeseman Dial, 2008, p. 432). As a result, special interest groups have criticized the government for failing to act and for funding programs that are ineffective. Despite the inherent problems that persist within the system, it is apparent that correctional facilities are being challenged to implement the policies established in PREA. The ability of administrators to prevent individuals from engaging in sexual violence in prisons is limited, yet they do have control over the organizational structure of the prison. Increased supervision of cell blocks, single cells, and better screening and classification procedures have been identified as methods that may lead to a reduction in inmate-on-inmate sexual victimization (Austin et al., 2006; Hensley et al., 2013). Additionally, implementing programs that focus on education and training of correctional officers are critical for reducing and responding to sexual violence. Although the literature has addressed the lack of training for years (Nacci & Kane, 1984), it has become apparent that training is a key factor in preventing the sexual victimization of prisoners (Hensley et al., 2013). More recent literature has noted an increase in training activities since the passage of PREA (Thompson et al., 2008). However, the quality and content of the training are unknown. Further research is needed to examine the effects of training on safety and sexual violence prevention in prisons (see Hensley et al., 2013).

Conclusion

Power differentials in sexual relationships are problematic even when consent exists; however, when individuals such as children, the elderly, and prison inmates are exposed to an imbalance of power, consent cannot occur due to the nature of the sexual relationship. As noted, it is the asymmetry of these relationships and the inability to fully comprehend the consequences of these actions that prevents consent from being given by the subordinate. Additionally, many instances of rape and sexual assault are not coercive but are rather a forced act. Regardless of the method, victims are still blamed for the sexual violence perpetrated against them. The notion that victims could have refused sexual advances or protected themselves against sexual violence remains pervasive, but it is not a viable rationale even when victims are adults.

While both state and federal laws have begun to recognize the risk that persons deemed "vulnerable" face, current strategies have failed to keep these individuals safe. As with all victims of sexual violence, the sexual victimization of these populations remains invisible. For instance, CSA has been recognized as a social problem since the 1980s (Belknap, 2007). While strides have been made, current strategies to protect youths and prosecute offenders have not been successful since there is no standard for training and investigation. Indeed, no standard has been implemented to protect those who are deemed "vulnerable," especially when the victims are deemed culpable. Even more disconcerting is the realization that the legal system has seemingly ignored elderly and imprisoned victims. While elder and inmate sexual abuse has been identified as a major problem, little has been done to combat it. Elder sexual abuse has only recently been identified as a major health issue. Similarly, PREA (2003) was supposed to protect inmates from sexual violence; however, the research indicates that many states have failed to take these measures seriously. Greater attention needs to be paid to these groups to identify procedures and safeguards that work to protect the "vulnerable."

Discussion Questions

1. Why are victims of childhood sexual assault less likely to be blamed for their own victimization than adult victims such as the elderly and prison inmates?

2. How do power differentials affect the ability to consent in sexual relationships? Please give examples of these among children, the elderly, and inmates.

3. Why is it so difficult to measure the victimization of "vulnerable" populations? Please give examples.

4. What are the consequences for individuals in "vulnerable" populations who experience sexual victimization? Please discuss how members of each "vulnerable" group may be affected.

References

Acierno, R., Hernandez, M. A., Amstadter, A. B., Resnick, H. S., Steve, K., Muzzy, W., & Kilpatrick, D. G. (2010). Prevalence and correlates of emotional, physical, sexual, and financial abuse and potential neglect in the United States: The national elder mistreatment study. *American Journal of Public Health, 100*(2), 292–297.

Adam Walsh Child Protection and Safety Act (AWA), 42 U.S.C. § 16911 (2006).

American Psychological Association (APA). (2013). *Child sexual abuse.* Retrieved from http://www.apa.org/pi/families/resources/child-sexual-abuse.aspx

Austin, J., Fabelo, T., Gunter, A., & McGinnis, K. (2006). *Sexual violence in the Texas prison system.* Washington, DC: The JFA Institute.

Baro, A. L. (1997). Spheres of consent: An analysis of the sexual abuse and sexual exploitation of women incarcerated in the state of Hawaii. *Women and Criminal Justice, 8*(3), 61–84.

Beck, A. J., & Harrison, P. M. (2007, December). Sexual victimization in state and federal prisons reported by inmates, 2007. *Bureau of Justice Statistics Special Report.* Retrieved from http://www.bjs.gov/content/pub/pdf/svsfpri07.pdf

Beck, A. J., Harrison, P. M., Berzofsky, M., Caspar, R., & Krebs, C. (2010). *Sexual victimization in prisons and jails reported by inmates, 2008–2009* (NCJ 231169). Washington, DC: Bureau of Justice Statistics. Retrieved from http://www.bjs.gov/content/pub/pdf/svpjri0809.pdf

Belknap, J. (2007). *The invisible woman: Gender, crime, and justice* (3rd ed.). Belmont, CA: Wadsworth.

Benbow, S. M., & Haddad, P. M. (1993). Sexual abuse of the elderly mentally ill. *Postgraduate Medical Journal, 69*(816), 803–807.

Blackburn, A. G., Mullings, J. L., & Marquart, J. W. (2008). Sexual assault in prison and beyond: Toward an understanding of lifetime sexual assault among incarcerated women. *The Prison Journal, 88*(3), 351–377.

Browne, A., & Finkelhor, D. (1986). The impact of child sexual abuse: A review of the research. *Psychological Bulletin, 99*(1), 66–77.

Brozowski, K., & Hall, D. R. (2010). Aging and risk: Physical and sexual abuse of elders in Canada. *Journal of Interpersonal Violence, 25*(7), 1183–1199.

Burgess, A. W., Dowdell, E. B., & Prentky, R. A. (2000). Sexual abuse of nursing home residents. *Journal of Psychosocial Nursing & Mental Health Services, 38*(6), 10–18.

Burgess, A. W., & Phillips, S. L. (2006). Sexual abuse, trauma, and dementia in the elderly: A retrospective study of 284 cases. *Victims & Offenders: An International Journal of Evidence-based Research, Policy, and Practice, 1*(2), 193–204.

Child Abuse and Prevention Treatment Act (CAPTA), Pub. L. No. 111-320 (2010). Retrieved from http://www.acf.hhs.gov/sites/default/files/cb/capta2010.pdf

Child Welfare Information Gateway (CWIG). (2012). *Mandatory reporters of child abuse and neglect.* Retrieved from https://www.childwelfare.gov/systemwide/laws_policies/statutes/manda.pdf

Child Welfare Information Gateway (CWIG). (2013). *What is child abuse and neglect? Recognizing the signs and symptoms.* Retrieved from https://www.childwelfare.gov/pubs/factsheets/whatiscan.pdf

Daly, L. W. (2004). Factors contributing to inadequate training. *Issues in Child Abuse Accusations, 14*(1), 6–11.

Daly, J. M., & Jogerst, G. (2003). Statute definitions of elder abuse. *Journal of Elder Abuse & Neglect, 13*(4), 39–57.

Davis, A. J. (1968). Sexual assaults in the Philadelphia prison system and sheriff's vans. *Trans-action, 6*(2), 8–16.

Doerner, W. G., & Lab, S. P. (2008). *Victimology* (5th ed.). Cincinnati, OH: LexisNexis.

Dumond, R. W., & Dumond, D. A. (2002). The treatment of sexual assault victims. In C. Hensley (Ed.), *Prison sex: Practice & policy.* Boulder, CO: Lynne Reiner.

Ehrlich, P., & Anetzberger, G. (1991). Survey of state public health departments on procedures for reporting elder abuse. *Public Health Reports, 106*(2), 151–154.

Filipas, H. H., & Ullman, S. E. (2006). Child sexual abuse, coping responses, self-blame, posttraumatic stress disorder, and adult sexual revictimization. *Journal of Interpersonal Violence, 21*(5), 652–672.

Finkelhor, D. (1979). What's wrong with sex between adults and children. *American Journal of Orthopsychiatry, 49*, 692–697.

Finkelhor, D. (1984). *Child sexual abuse: New theory and research.* New York, NY: Free Press.

Finkelhor, D. (1994). Current information on the scope and nature of child sexual abuse. *The Future of Children, 4*(2), 31–53.

Finkelhor, D., & Dziuba-Leatherman, J. (1994). Children as victims of violence: A national survey. *Pediatrics, 4*(Part 1), 413–420.

Finkelhor, D., Hammer, H., & Sedlak, A. (2008). *Sexually assaulted children: National estimates and characteristics.* Washington, DC: Department of Justice. Retrieved from https://www.ncjrs.gov/pdffiles1/ojjdp/214383.pdf

Finkelhor, D., Ormrod, R., Turner, H., & Hamby, S. L. (2005). The victimization of children and youth: A comprehensive, national survey. *Child Maltreatment, 10*(5), 5–25.

Fowler, S. K., Blackburn, A. G., Marquart, J. W., & Mullings, J. L. (2010). Would they officially report an in-prison sexual assault? An examination of inmate perceptions. *The Prison Journal, 90*(2), 220–243.

Hensley, C., Castle, T., & Tewksbury, R. (2003). Inmate-to-inmate sexual coercion in a prison for women. *Journal of Offender Rehabilitation, 37*(2), 77–87.

Hensley, C., Eigenberg, H., & Gibson, L. (2013). Gay and lesbian inmates: Sexuality and sexual coercion behind bars. In L. Gideon (Ed.), *Special needs: Offenders in correctional institutions* (pp. 233–252). Los Angeles, CA: Sage.

Hensley, C., Koscheski, M., & Tewksbury, R. (2005). Examining the characteristics of male sexual assault targets in a Southern maximum-security prison. *Journal of Interpersonal Violence, 20*(6), 667–679.

Hensley, C., Tewksbury, R., & Castle, T. (2003). Characteristics of prison sexual assault targets in male Oklahoma correctional facilities. *Journal of Interpersonal Violence, 18*(6), 595–606.

Hibbard, R. A., & Zollinger, T. W. (1990). Patterns of child sexual abuse: Knowledge among professionals. *Child Abuse and Neglect, 14*(3), 347–355.

Holt, M. (1993). Elder sexual abuse in Britain: Preliminary findings. *Journal of Elder Abuse & Neglect, 5*(2), 63–71.

Jacob Wetterling Crimes Against Children and Sexually Violent Offender Registration Act (Jacob Wetterling Act), 42 U.S.C. § 14071 (1994).

Jenness, V., Maxson, C. L., Matsuda, K. N., & Sumner, J. M. (2007). Violence in California correctional facilities: An empirical examination of sexual assault. *The Bulletin of the Center for Evidence-Based Corrections, 2*(2). Retrieved from http://ucicorrections.seweb.uci.edu/files/2013/06/BulletinVol2Issue2.pdf

Jinich, S., Paul, J. P., Stall, R., Acree, M., Kegeles, S., Hoff, C., & Coates, T. J. (1998). Childhood sexual abuse and HIV risk-taking behavior among gay and bisexual men. *AIDS and Behavior, 2*(1), 41–51.

Jogerst, G. J., Daly, J. M., Brinig, M. F., Dawson, J. D., Schmuch, G. A., & Ingram, J. G. (2003). Domestic elder abuse and the law. *American Journal of Public Health, 93*(12), 2131–2136.

Kendall-Tackett, K. A., Williams, L. M., & Finkelhor, D. (1993). Impact of sexual abuse on children: A review and synthesis of recent empirical studies. *Psychological Bulletin, 113*(1), 164–180.

Kilpatrick, D. G., Saunders, B. E., & Smith, D. W. (2003). *Youth victimization: Prevalence and implications.* Washington, DC: National Institute of Justice. Retrieved from https://www.ncjrs.gov/pdffiles1/nij/194972.pdf

Korkman, J., Santtila, P., Drzewiecki, T., & Sandnabba, N. K. (2008). Failing to keep it simple: Language use in child sexual abuse interviews with 3–8-year-old children. *Psychology, Crime & Law, 14*(1), 41–60.

MacMillan, H. L., Tanaka, M., Duku, E., Vaillancourt, T., & Boyle, M. H. (2013). Child physical and sexual abuse in a community sample of young adults: Results from the Ontario Child Health Study. *Child Abuse and Neglect, 37*(1), 14–21.

Maitland, A. S., & Sluder, R. D. (1998). Victimization and youthful prison inmates: An empirical analysis. *The Prison Journal, 78*(1), 55–73.

McGuire, D. M. (2005). The impact of prison rape on public health. *Californian Journal of Public Health Promotion, 3*(2), 72–83.

Mickish, J. (1993). Abuse and neglect: The adult and elder. In B. Byers & J. E. Hendricks (Eds.), *Adult protective services: Research and practice* (pp. 33–60). Springfield, IL: Charles C Thomas.

Muram, D., Miller, K., & Cutler, A. (1992). Sexual assault of the elderly victim. *Journal of Interpersonal Violence, 7*(1), 70–76.

Nacci, P. L., & Kane, T. R. (1984). Sex and sexual aggression in federal prisons: Inmate involvement and employee impact. *Federal Probation, 48*(1), 46–53.

National Center on Elder Abuse (NCEA). (2013). *Types of abuse.* Retrieved from http://www.ncea.aoa.gov/FAQ/Type_Abuse/index.aspx

National Sexual Violence Resource Center (NSVRC). (2011a). *Child sexual abuse prevention and risk reduction: Literature review for parents and guardians.* Retrieved from http://www.nsvrc.org/sites/default/files/Publications_NSVRC_LiteratureReview_Child-Sexual-Abuse-Prevention-and-Risk-Reduction-review-for-parents.pdf

National Sexual Violence Resource Center (NSVRC). (2011b). *Child sexual abuse prevention: Programs for children.* Retrieved from http://www.nsvrc.org/sites/default/files/Publications_NSVRC_Guide_Child-Sexual-Abuse-Prevention-programs-for-children.pdf

Payne, B. K. (2011). *Crime and elder abuse: An integrated perspective* (3rd ed.). Springfield, IL: Thomas.

Payne, B. K., Berg, B. L., & Byars, K. (1999). A qualitative examination of the similarities and differences of elder abuse definitions among four groups: Nursing home directors, nursing home employees, police chiefs and students. *Journal of Elder Abuse & Neglect, 10*(3–4), 63–85.

Payne, B. K., & Cikovic, R. (1995). An empirical examination of the characteristics, consequences, and causes of elder abuse in nursing homes. *Journal of Elder Abuse & Neglect, 7*(4), 61–74.

Pereda, N., Guilera, G., Forns, M., & Gómez-Benito, J. (2009). The prevalence of child sexual abuse in community and student samples: A meta-analysis. *Clinical Psychology Review, 29*(4), 328–338.

Pillemer, K., & Finkelhor, D. (1988). The prevalence of elder abuse: A random sample survey. *The Gerontologist, 28*(1), 51–57.

Poulos, C. A., & Sheridan, D. J. (2008). Genital injuries in postmenopausal women after sexual assault. *Journal of Elder Abuse & Neglect, 20*(4), 323–335.

Prison Rape Elimination Act (PREA), 42 U.S. § 15601 (2003).

Ramsey-Klawsnik, H. (1991). Elder sexual abuse: Preliminary findings. *Journal of Elder Abuse & Neglect, 3*(3), 73–90.

Ramsey-Klawsnik, H. (1996). Assessing physical and sexual abuse in health care settings. In L. A. Baumhover & S. C. Beall (Eds.), *Abuse, neglect, and exploitation of older persons: Strategies for assessment and intervention* (pp. 67–87). Baltimore, MD: Health Professions Press.

Ramsey-Klawsnik, H. (2004). Elder sexual abuse within the family. *Journal of Elder Abuse & Neglect, 15*(1), 43–58.

Ramsey-Klawsnik, H., & Brandl, B. (2009). *Sexual abuse in later life.* Kingston, NJ: Civic Research Institute. Retrieved from http://www.ncall.us/sites/ncall.us/files/resources/SAR1206-SA2-SexualAbuseLaterinLife.pdf

Ramsey-Klawsnik, H., Teaster, P. B., Mendiondo, M. S., Marcum, J. L., & Abner, E. L. (2008). Sexual predators who target elders: Findings from the first national study of sexual abuse in care facilities. *Journal of Elder Abuse & Neglect, 20*(4), 353–376.

Snyder, H. (2000). *Sexual assault of young children as reported to law enforcement: Victim, incident, and offender characteristics* (NCJ 182990). Washington, DC: U.S. Department of Justice. Retrieved from http://www.bjs.gov/content/pub/pdf/saycrle.pdf

Struckman-Johnson, C., & Struckman-Johnson, D. (2000). Sexual coercion rates for seven midwestern prisons for men. *The Prison Journal, 80*(4), 379–390.

Struckman-Johnson, C., & Struckman-Johnson, D. (2002). Sexual coercion reported by women in three midwestern prisons. *Journal of Sex Research, 39*(3), 217–227.

Struckman-Johnson, C., Struckman-Johnson, D., Rucker, L., Bumby, K., & Donaldson, S. (1996). Sexual coercion reported by men and women in prison. *Journal of Sex Research, 33*(3), 67–76.

Tatara, T. (1998). *The national elder abuse incidence study: Final report.* Retrieved from http://aoa.gov/AoA_Programs/Elder_Rights/Elder_Abuse/docs/ABuseReport_Full.pdf

Teaster, P. B., Ramsey-Klawsnik, H., Mendiondo, M. S., Abner, E., Cecil, K., & Tooms, M. (2007). From behind the shadows: A profile of the sexual abuse of older men residing in nursing homes. *Journal of Elder Abuse & Neglect, 19*(1–2), 29–45.

Teaster, P. B., & Roberto, K. A. (2003). Chapter 7: Sexual abuse of older women living in nursing homes. *Journal of Gerontological Social Work, 40*(4), 105–119.

Teaster, P. B., & Roberto, K. A. (2004). Sexual abuse of older adults: APS cases and outcomes. *The Gerontologist, 44*(6), 788–796.

Teaster, P. B., Roberto, K. A., Duke, J. O., & Kim, M. (2001). Sexual abuse of older adults: Preliminary findings of cases in Virginia. *Journal of Elder Abuse & Neglect, 12*(3–4), 1–16.

Terry, K. J., & Ackerman, A. R. (2009). A brief history of major sex offender laws. In R. G. Wright (Ed.), *Sex offender laws: Failed policies and new directions* (pp. 65–98). New York, NY: Springer.

Texas Family Code, § 261.101. Retrieved from http://www.statutes.legis.state.tx.us/Docs/FA/htm/FA.261.htm

Thomas, R., DiLillo, D., Walsh, K., & Polusny, M. A. (2011). Pathways from child sexual abuse to adult depression: The role of parental socialization of emotions and alexithymia. *Psychology of Violence, 1*(2), 121–135.

Thompson, R. A., Nored, L. S., & Cheeseman Dial, K. (2008). The Prison Rape Elimination Act (PREA): An evaluation of policy compliance with illustrative excerpts. *Criminal Justice Policy Review, 19*(4), 414–437.

Tjaden, P., & Thoennes, N. (2006). *Extent, nature, and consequences of rape victimization: Findings from the National Violence Against Women Survey* (NCJ 210346). Washington, DC: National Institute of Justice. Retrieved from https://www.ncjrs.gov/pdffiles1/nij/210346.pdf

Vierthaler, K. (2008). Best practices for working with rape crisis centers to address elder sexual abuse. *Journal of Elder Abuse & Neglect, 20*(4), 306–322.

Warren, J. I., Jackson, S. L., Loper, A. B., & Burnette, M. L. (2010). *Risk markers for sexual predation and victimization in prison.* Washington, DC: Department of Justice. Retrieved from https://www.ncjrs.gov/pdffiles1/nij/grants/230522.pdf

Wolf, R. S. (1996). Understanding elder abuse and neglect. *Aging, 367,* 4–9.

Wolff, N., Blitz, C. L., Shi, J., Bachman, R., & Siegel, J. A. (2006). Sexual violence inside prisons: Rates of victimization. *Journal of Urban Health, 83*(5), 835–848.

Worley, R., Marquart, J. W., & Mullings, J. L. (2003). Prison guard predators: An analysis of inmates who established inappropriate relationships with prison staff, 1995–1998. *Deviant Behavior, 24*(2), 175–194.

Worley, V. B., Worley, R. M., & Mullings, J. L. (2010). Rape lore in correctional settings: Assessing inmates' awareness of sexual coercion in prison. *Southwest Journal of Criminal Justice, 7*(1), 65–86.

10

Same-Sex Victimization and the LGBTQ Community

Xavier Guadalupe-Diaz

The general discussion on sexual violence in the United States has primarily focused on those victimizations occurring within the context of opposite-sex or heterosexual perpetration. As a result of the focus on sexual violence, rape, and sexual assault of women perpetrated by men, defining same-sex sexual violence has been problematic. Definitions of sexual violence serve multiple purposes, whether they are academic and research based, service oriented, legal, or criminal, and have therefore resulted in varying conceptualizations. For example, for the vast majority of American history, men were systematically excluded as potential rape victims in the legal definitions; it was not until the 1980s when states' statutory provisions began to include men as potential victims of rape by law (Weiss, 2008). Across the United States, the only recognition of same-sex sexual violence came in the form of sodomy laws, which were inherently homophobic as they criminalized all same-sex sexual behaviors, primarily those involving men, including those that were consensual. Sodomy laws were often so broad, they even criminalized anal and oral sexual behaviors between opposite-sex partners. In 2003, the U.S. Supreme Court overturned the remaining sodomy laws in *Lawrence v. Texas*.

A broader and more encompassing definition of same-sex sexual violence involves both the physical and psychological elements of forced or coerced sexual contact that is not limited to vaginal, oral, or anal penetration. Much of the existing literature of and discussion about same-sex sexual violence has been limited to child sexual victimization or sexual victimization in prisons or other institutional settings (Stermac, Del Bove, & Addison, 2004). While these contributions are essential, far fewer scholars have examined sexual violence between same-sex individuals in the context of dating, intimate, or acquaintance relationships. More specifically, little research has addressed sexual violence within the lesbian, gay, bisexual, transgender, and queer (LGBTQ) community. In recent decades, research on intimate-partner violence has expanded to include same-sex relationships and the LGBTQ community. However, research has not focused enough on same-sex sexual violence victimization or perpetration between LGBTQ partners, strangers, or acquaintances. Some scholars have stated that the "discussion of same-sex domestic violence is fifteen to twenty years ahead of discussion of same-sex sexual violence" (Girshick, 2002, p. 54).

Victims of same-sex sexual violence face unique realities when compared to their opposite-sex counterparts. In addition to the historical limitations of the law and how rape and sexual violence has been defined, LGBTQ victims of same-sex sexual violence face heterosexist, homophobic, and genderist discriminations. The heterosexist and gendered narrative that constructs an assumed male perpetrator and a female victim may undermine the experiences of many LGBTQ survivors (Erbaugh, 2007). Beyond the personal struggles these survivors may face with identifying victimization, homophobic and heterosexist responses by the criminal justice system often revictimize those LGBTQ victims seeking help. This chapter examines the nature and extent of same-sex sexual violence and the challenges faced by victims and the criminal justice system.

The Extent of Same-Sex Sexual Violence

Obtaining estimates for the prevalence of same-sex sexual violence presents several unique challenges. To date, no single method of measuring same-sex sexual violence has been utilized across time and in consecutive assessments (Peterson, Voller, Polusny, & Murdoch, 2010). The inconsistencies in measurements result in a wide range of prevalence rates and make it difficult to obtain an accurate picture of the problem. Commonly used measures of sexual violence—the Sexual Experiences Survey and the revised Conflict Tactics Scale—have been modified to include male victims of sexual assault, but neither has resulted in strong assessments of either male sexual victimization or same-sex female victimization. Regarding male experiences with sexual violence, Peterson et al. noted that there "are no well-validated instruments specifically designed to measure men's experiences with sexual assault" (p. 2). The same could be said for measures assessing female-to-female sexual victimization (Girshick, 2002; Wang, 2011).

While not unique to same-sex sexual violence research, a contributing factor to measurement issues is the wide range of definitions for what constitutes sexual violence. Researchers examining female sexual violence, specifically in opposite-sex victimizations, have often been able to rely on legal definitions of rape for studies or could utilize government-reported data. These measurements of rape often include gender-specific language such as "vaginal penetration," which encompasses only female victimization. As a result, male sexual violence victimization data have often been scarce and inconsistent (Todahl, Linville, Bustin, Wheeler, & Gau, 2009).

Self-report studies, such as the National Violence Against Women Survey (NVAWS), have been inclusive of same-sex relationships, including male sexual violence victims (Tjaden & Thoennes, 2000). While the NVAWS showed that sexual victimization was far more common for females than it was for males, it illustrated that 2.8 million men are sexually victimized at some point in their life (p. 1). The authors found that the majority of male sexual violence victimizations occurred before the age 18, while for women, approximately 50% of experiences with sexual violence occurred before age 18. Those women who were partnered with other women were less likely to have experienced sexual violence, while those men who were partnered with other men were more likely than their heterosexual counterparts to have experienced sexual violence. Self-report studies of sexual violence allow for a broader examination of same-sex sexual violence. While all participants may feel reluctant to disclose sexual violence victimizations, homophobia may make LGBTQ victims of same-sex sexual violence even less likely to report their victimizations. Beyond the difficulty in disclosing these victimizations, many LGBTQ survivors may fear misrepresentation of their community and feel as if reporting these victimizations could further homophobic discrimination against them (Balsam, Rothblum, & Beauchaine, 2005; Girshick, 2002; National Coalition of Anti-Violence Projects [NCAVP], 2011; Renzetti, 1992, 1996, 1997).

Self-report studies continue to be a common method of obtaining prevalence estimates of same-sex sexual violence. Since 1997, the NCAVP has released annual reports detailing incidents of intimate-partner, sexual, and hate-motivated violence experienced by the LGBTQ community. The NCAVP gathers information from 19 participating organizations that work directly with LGBTQ populations in 23 states. The report relies on survivors who contact these organizations and disclose victimizations. In 2012, the NCAVP estimated that approximately 5.1% of incidents of intimate-partner violence within the LGBTQ community involved acts of sexual violence (NCAVP, 2011). Among its findings, the NCAVP estimated that those who identified as transgender were nearly 2 times as likely to have reported sexual violence as those who were not transgender. Furthermore, those who identified as queer, a more fluid nonheterosexual sexual orientation, were almost 3 times more likely to have reported sexual violence than those who did not identify as queer.

As a result of the various methods and definitions used to collect information on same-sex sexual violence, estimated prevalence rates may range widely. In an evaluation of 75 articles on sexual violence within the LGBTQ community, Rothman, Exner, & Baughman (2011) concluded that the range of sexual violence victimization among gay and bisexual men was between 12% and 54%. They found an even wider range for lesbian and bisexual women, 16% to 85%. The authors concluded that these wide ranges are a result of varying methodologies, sampling strategies, definitions of sexual violence and sexual orientation, and other measures. The majority of the available studies utilized non-probability-based methods, given the difficulty of obtaining truly representative data on LGBTQ populations. Those studies that utilized non-probability-based methods found higher rates of sexual violence than those that used a probability-based sampling method. The authors noted that the vast majority of studies on same-sex sexual violence focused on childhood victimization. For example, regarding lesbian and bisexual women in particular, they found twice as many studies on childhood sexual victimization than on adult victimization. It can be argued that the emphasis on researching same-sex sexual violence in childhood among LGBTQ populations has been fueled by homophobic and erroneous notions that this form of abuse "causes" same-sex desire. As Rothman et al. stated, while there is a greater need for attention to same-sex childhood victimizations, "the relative dearth of information about adult experiences of sexual assault and the impact of sexual assault across the life-course should be considered" (p. 62). This calls attention to the serious lack of information on adult sexual victimization among LGBTQ individuals. Compounding this problem, many of the available estimates of intimate partner sexual victimization and other adult sexual victimizations within the LGBTQ community do not report on the sex or gender of the perpetrator (Rothman et al.; Waldner-Haugrud, & Gratch, 1997).

While no available estimates have consistently defined the problem of same-sex sexual violence or found a consistent estimate of its prevalence, its existence as a problem is well documented and merits further investigation. The complex dynamics of same-sex sexual violence require an understanding of how homophobia and heterosexism contextualize these victimizations. These systematic oppressions silence victims and are reflected in the institutional response to those who seek both legal and social services.

LGBTQ Populations and Same-Sex Sexual Violence

For victims of same-sex sexual violence, the powerful narratives that define "appropriate" victims and perpetrators contextualize these experiences. The prevailing cultural explanations for sexual violence victimization often point to structural factors that explain female victimization by male perpetrators. Further, the gendered construction of the categories of "victim" (or "survivor") and "perpetrator" assume much about masculinity and femininity in a way that ignores male victimization and female perpetration. For male survivors of same-sex sexual violence, the intense homophobia that polices dominant notions of masculinity perpetuates myths that men can't be raped or that they must be "homosexual" if they are victimized by other men (Coxell & King, 1996). In addition, female victims of same-sex sexual violence are faced with established cultural beliefs that women cannot possibly rape (Girshick, 2002; Renzetti, 1997; Ristock, 2002). Persons who identify as LGBTQ face broader narratives that view homosexuality negatively. The larger homophobic culture views homosexuality as deviant, sexual assault as a cause of homosexuality, and same-sex relationships as generally unhealthy. The acceptance of these stereotypes of and negative associations with homosexuality, otherwise known as internalized homophobia, has been documented as a prominent mental health concern among LGBTQ individuals (Herek, Gillis, Cogan, & Glunt, 1997; Otis & Skinner, 1996; Shidlo, 1994). Hostile and homophobic environments also foster acts of same-sex sexual violence in the form of hate-motivated crimes. As Scarce (1997) noted, "rigidly traditional forms of hegemonic masculinity portray gay men as weak, feminine, and fit only for punishment and humiliation in the most dehumanizing way possible" (p. 171). The following sections examine how homophobia and heterosexism contextualize experiences of same-sex sexual violence victimization.

MALE SAME-SEX SEXUAL VIOLENCE

Theorists who examine gender as a social construct often argue that cultural expectations of masculinity foster or reward aggressive and violent behavior (Connell, 1996; Kimmel, 2002). In a patriarchal society, men are encouraged to be in control and domineering while also remaining independent and stoic or unemotional. These assumptions about and expectations of masculine display socialize boys and men into a limited form of self-expression and identity. Behaviors that deviate from these dominant masculine expressions are socially condemned as effeminacy. Under this customary notion of masculinity, homophobia functions to maintain rigid constructs of masculinity. As homosexuality is constructed as effeminate and "unmanly," the threat of being perceived as a homosexual fuels hatred against gay and bisexual men. Regardless of their own sexual orientation, the fear male victims of same-sex sexual violence feel about disclosing victimization is often rooted in homophobia.

Cultural narratives pertaining to hegemonic masculinity often assume that men are constantly seeking sexual interactions and experiences; in particular, gay and bisexual men are especially thought of as hypersexual. These assumptions place a certain burden of guilt on gay and bisexual male victims of same-sex sexual violence. Gay and bisexual male victims often face assumptions that they wanted to engage in sexual activity and that any type of sex is ultimately an enjoyable experience. Additionally, physiological responses to sexual victimization may confuse male victims. For example, the belief exists that men cannot experience erections if they do not wish to engage in sexual activity. While this myth is rarely a debate in contemporary literature, older studies have shown that men may in fact experience both erections and ejaculations regardless of whether the sexual activity was forced or even frightening to the victim (Coxell & King, 1996; Gonsiorek, 1994). Experiencing erection and/or ejaculation during sexual victimizations may lead gay and bisexual male victims to question whether an assault was an "actual" violent action. Damaging stereotypes revolving around gay and bisexual male hypersexuality often shape experiences of sexual violence as simply acts of sex or desire. Further, as much of the study of male same-sex sexual violence has focused on these actions as committed by "homosexuals," it has framed these crimes as driven by sexual attraction. Hickson et al. (1994) stated that "early commentators on sexual assault assumed that because the act was sexualized, it was primarily sexual because it involved two men, it was necessarily (and by definition), homosexual" (p. 282). These conventions failed to address the more contemporary feminist critiques, which frame sexual violence as actions intended to "assert power, release aggression, and control feelings of helplessness" (Hickson et al., p. 282).

Compounding these narratives, men are rarely constructed as "defenseless" or even proper "victims" of sexual violence (Connell, 1995; Connell & Messerschmidt, 2005). While women are thought of as weaker and more easily "victimized," men are expected to fight back. Especially in the face of an emasculating victimization such as sexual violence, men are expected to resist aggressively and maintain control (Weiss, 2008).

While relatively few studies have examined same-sex sexual violence among gay and bisexual male populations, generally these victimizations occur within the context of an intimate relationship, that is, between friends or acquaintances, lovers, or dates (Hickson et al., 1994; Todahl et al., 2009; Weiss, 2008). Though this is a commonly reported fact in cases of opposite-sex sexual violence, stranger perpetration of same-sex sexual violence among men has been found to be more commonly experienced by men than by heterosexual women (Stermac et al., 2004; Stermac, Sheridan, Davidson, & Dunn, 1996). This distinction in itself is not a consistent finding, but for gay and bisexual men, meeting others in the community may often involve meeting and interacting with strangers.

Far fewer studies have explored differences in types of sexual violence victimizations among gay and bisexual men. In one example, Hickson et al. (1994) examined a sample of 930 gay and bisexual men and found that approximately 27.6% of this sample had experienced nonconsensual sexual activity; this was mostly perpetrated by someone known to the victim. In comparative analyses, the authors found relationships between the types of sexual violence experienced and the relationship of the victim to the offender. While the most common forms of sexual violence committed involved forced stimulation of the victim, masturbation, fellatio, and genital manipulation, in 75.8% of cases in which the victim was regularly seeing the perpetrator as a casual sex partner, anal penetration of the victim occurred. However, in an analysis of 3,635 male victims of adult sexual violence, 94% of which was perpetrated by men, Isely and Gehrenbeck-Shim (1997) found that their sample most commonly experienced forced anal penetration. The majority of that sample knew their assailants, but they mostly self-identified as heterosexual. More recently, Stermac et al. (2004) examined stranger and acquaintance sexual victimization of men and compared varying outcomes in characteristics. The authors found that sexual victimizations of men by strangers were more likely to have involved weapons and to have occurred outside the home. Within the context of intimate relationships, or at least in relationships in which gay and bisexual men know the perpetrator, coerced or forced sexual activity could be more elusive than that perpetrated by strangers (Todahl et al., 2009).

As homophobia and rigid expectations of masculinity silence victims of male same-sex sexual violence, for gay and bisexual male survivors, negative attitudes about homosexuality may construct the notion that this form of violence is normal or deserved. The internalization of negative assumptions about male homosexuality constructs expectations that aggressive hypersexuality is simply a part of being a gay or bisexual man. Gold, Marx, and Lexington (2007) stated that often, many aspects of internalized homophobia are directly related to sexual assault narratives. One common misconception is that sexual violence is often presumed as a causal factor of homosexuality; that is, that men become gay as a result of a same-sex rape or sexual assault (Arey, 1995; Gold et al.). This misled belief places sexual violence at the center of the source of male homosexuality. Often, internalized homophobia creates beliefs of inferiority such that victims expect sexual violence to be an inseparable part of being a gay or bisexual male. These beliefs perpetuate the notion that LGBTQ people are somehow deserving of violence as a result of their deviance (Balsam, 2003; Gold et al.).

The severity of same-sex male sexual violence has been compared to the severity of female same-sex sexual violence. In some studies, male survivors of same-sex sexual violence have been found to experience severe physical injury in comparison to female same-sex sexual violence victims (Struckman-Johnson & Struckman-Johnson, 2006). Men are typically seen as having the ability to hurt more or cause more severe injuries than women.

However, this has not been a consistent finding across studies. Light and Monk-Turner (2009) examined a subsample of 219 men in the Violence and Threats of Violence Against Women and Men in the United States Survey and found that 89% of their sample had reported no physical injuries as a result of their experiences. For gay and bisexual men, force or injury may not be part of the experience of sexual victimization when the perpetrator is a well-known acquaintance or intimate partner. On the other hand, Waldner-Haugrud and Gratch (1997) found that sexual coercion or forced persuasion of sexual activity was a common experience in their sample of 162 gay men. In particular, Waldner-Haugrud (1999) emphasized that sexual coercion in male same-sex relationships is an important concern when considering HIV infection rates. Sexual coercion between men may often entail unprotected practices that could place victims at higher risk for HIV or other sexually transmitted infections (Kalichman & Rompa, 1995).

More commonly, psychological outcomes illustrate that victims of male same-sex sexual violence may, like other victims of sexual violence, experience severe posttraumatic stress disorder (PTSD), depression, and anxiety (Heidt, Marx, & Gold, 2005; Hickson et al., 1994). Among gay men, self-esteem measures have illustrated that sexual violence has a negative impact on self-concept and is linked to bouts of depression (Kalichman & Rompa). Men in particular are socialized to hold back emotions and not reach out to others for help, and these inhibitions may intensify negative psychological outcomes. Regardless of sexual orientation, male survivors often internalize the need to settle things on their own accord without freely expressing their feelings (Scarce, 1997).

FEMALE SAME-SEX SEXUAL VIOLENCE

While male-perpetrated acts of sexual violence would commonly be viewed as a serious crime or violation, female-on-female perpetration of sexual violence continues to challenge heteronormative conceptions of what constitutes rape and sexual assault. Much as assumptions or social constructs of masculinity silence male victims, assumptions about femininity work to stifle victims of female same-sex sexual violence. While it is commonly accepted that men commit acts of sexual violence, whether they be same-sex or opposite-sex, female perpetration is, at best, culturally taboo and largely ignored. The cultural narratives surrounding sexual violence often invoke ideas of aggressive force or even penile penetration. These narratives of what constitutes "legitimate rape" stand in contradiction to the perpetration of female same-sex sexual violence.

In direct contrast to constructs of hegemonic masculinity, femininity—or what it means to be an "appropriate" woman—assumes the complete lack of masculinity. That is, masculinity is everything femininity is not. Among the attendant expectations is that women are more delicate and less physically violent and aggressive than men. In the consideration of sexual violence, these dominant perspectives essentially erase any possibility of female perpetration of rape and sexual assault. Further, they also serve to trivialize or undermine the experiences of victims of female-perpetrated sexual violence. Because women are considered weaker, female perpetration of sexual violence may seem less threatening or damaging. The victim–perpetrator binary invokes the dominant notion that perpetrators must be men, as sexual violence requires force and may assume penile penetration. For female-to-female sexual violence, this heterosexist construct of perpetration stifles an inclusive dialogue that would address issues of lesbian rape and sexual assault.

The misconception that women cannot rape or commit acts of sexual violence is often internalized within the lesbian community itself. In the groundbreaking work on woman-to-woman sexual violence, Girshick (2002) addressed what she termed the myth of a lesbian utopia. Heterosexist assumptions about rape are not simply external to the lesbian community. Rather there exists the internalized belief that lesbian relationships are free from sexual violence. Girshick argued that the

> mythology of women's nonviolence and lesbian egalitarianism has proved to be a formidable block to admitting and dealing with same-sex sexual violence perpetrated by women. It is not only that others in the community believe in the utopian vision; survivors of this abuse internalize the myths and want to believe that they are safe from other women. (p. 49)

Similarly, other authors have argued that lesbian communities actively foster tight-knit groups in which reliance on other lesbian women is pivotal (Renzetti, 1998; Rich, 1980; Risktock, 2002). In the face of a male-centered, patriarchal culture, lesbian women are often at the margins of history. Lesbianism fosters a woman-centered collective that actively resists this oppression and a sisterhood that, although it serves to cultivate community, may render lesbian violence invisible.

Over recent decades, a growing body of research has addressed female same-sex sexual violence. The overwhelming majority of these studies have focused on lesbian sexual violence within the context of an intimate, acquaintance, or dating relationship. As mentioned earlier in the chapter, the estimated prevalence of lesbian sexual violence ranges widely, with between 16% and 85% of lesbian samples reporting victimization across 75 recent studies from 1989 to 2009

(Rothman et al., 2011). As sexual violence is generally understood, female same-sex sexual violence has been framed as acts of forced and unwanted sexual activity used not to fulfill sexual desires but rather to assert control, power, and dominance over a victim (Campbell, 2008; Girshick, 2002; Hart, 1986; Renzetti, 1992). Despite the narrow conceptions of sexual violence as inherently male acts or that penile penetration is an essential component of rape, perpetration of female same-sex sexual violence involves a wide spectrum of abuses. King and Evans (1999) stated that in woman-to-woman sexual violence, "a woman rapist might use a fist, a finger, a dildo, or other external objects in an assault, although this type of assault may or may not involve penetration" (p. 71). In a much broader conceptualization of perpetration of female same-sex sexual violence, Girshick included "any unwanted sexual activity" not limited to "touching parts of the body, kissing, vaginal penetration by objects, vaginal penetration by fingers, oral sex, anal sex, rubbing and being forced to do things to yourself" (p. 19).

Early studies in the 1980s and 1990s had previously indicated mixed findings in rates of sexual abuse in lesbian samples when compared to both gay male and heterosexual women (Duncan, 1990; Lie, Schilit, Bush, Montagne, & Reyes, 1991; Waterman, Dawson, & Bologna, 1989). In Duncan's work, a comparison of gay, lesbian, and heterosexual students revealed that approximately 31% of lesbian students had been forced to engage in sexual activity as opposed to 12% of gay male students. Illustrating similarly higher rates, Lie et al. compared the sexual victimizations in a sample of 174 lesbian women by women or men and found higher victimization by female partners than by male partners (56.8% versus 41.9%). Contrary to these findings, Brand and Kidd (1986) compared lesbian women to heterosexual women and found that only 7% of lesbian women had reported being raped by a same-sex perpetrator as opposed to 9% of heterosexual women having reported being raped by a male perpetrator. Similarly, Waldner-Hagrud and Gratch (1997) utilized a sample of 306 LGB respondents to examine events of sexual coercion in same-sex relationships and found that, overall, lesbian women were less likely than gay men to experience acts of forced or coerced sex.

Since then, a number of critiques have illustrated that these estimates may have been inflated either by not first controlling for the number of sexual victimizations lesbian women may have experienced by male partners or not examining statistical significance (Waldner-Hagrud, 1999). By not excluding those opposite-sex experiences, some early estimates of lesbian sexual victimization were counting any experience of sexual violence, including opposite-sex victimizations. Further, the use of convenience samples makes it impossible to conclusively generalize findings.

More recently, research has illustrated that while reports of sexual victimization among lesbian women is high, when opposite-sex abuses are excluded, lesbians tend to report lower sexual victimization than do heterosexual women (Rothman et al, 2011). In addition, larger national samples of lesbian women illustrate lower rates of sexual victimization than studies relying on smaller, convenience-based samples (Rothman et al.). For example, Morris and Balsam (2003) utilized a large, national sample and acquired responses from 2,431 lesbian women, of whom 20% reported sexual victimization. These findings echoed other, similar studies that found nearly the same victimization rate (Bradford, Ryan, & Rothblum, 1994; Hughes, Johnson, & Wilsnack, 2001).

The context of female same-sex sexual violence is uniquely compounded by issues of sexism, heterosexism, internalized homophobia, and social isolation. To effectively capture the complexities of these experiences, Girshick (2002) examined the stories of 70 women who had experienced same-sex sexual violence. Through in-depth interviews, Girshick found emerging patterns across experiences with female same-sex sexual violence that brought attention to the impact of gender, homophobia, and the internalization of myths regarding lesbian rape on the lives of the survivors of her sample. Throughout the accounts, Girshick noted that social and cultural assumptions about women, femininity, and violence had directly affected how women experienced sexual violence by another woman. To female survivors of same-sex sexual violence, the idea that women could or do rape contradicts assumptions about women. In particular, lesbian women form a sense of community in which the external world may seem hostile, while the safest place is among other women. Those women victimized by same-sex partners face a barrier that challenges their beliefs about how women are socialized. Among lesbian women in particular, it is believed that no greater egalitarian relationship could exist outside of a loving, intimate partnership between two women. After all, women are taught to be self-expressive, nurturing, kind, and loving—not aggressive or violent. Girshick stated,

> But it is the myth that women aren't violent because of their socialization and that two women together have egalitarian, loving, and passionate relationships that is the more insidious belief leading to the denial of violence between women in same-sex relationships. (p. 55)

This belief in the "lesbian utopia" may be one of the most significant barriers to the discussion of sexual violence within lesbian communities. Further, similar to aspects of internalized homophobia experienced by male survivors of same-sex sexual violence, women may struggle with acceptance of violence due to marginalization or internalizing the belief that deviant lifestyles are deserving of violence. Others' perceived homophobia may also silence lesbian survivors of sexual violence, who feel as if exposing the acts would reflect negatively on the community as a whole.

Simply speaking or addressing the problem of female same-sex sexual violence presents a wider range of challenges when considering the dominant language around rape. Discourse, language, and the meaning behind words work to foster the domination of individuals through subjective interaction. In its application to sexual violence crimes, the "language of the court or law expresses and institutionalizes the domination of individuals by social institution" (Bernard, Vold, Snipes, & Gerould, 2010, p. 278). More specifically, to call an act "rape" is not simply to define it legally but rather to invoke a narrative about what is considered a legitimate rape. Regarding female same-sex sexual violence, to articulate the word *rape* or name an act rape inherently assumes a male perpetrator. Scholars have argued that this linguistic construct of what constitutes rape has been a major factor in the silencing of female survivors of same-sex sexual violence (Campbell, 2008; Girshick, 2002; Renzetti, 1998; Ristock 2002).

This perpetual cycle of silence is damaging not only to the survivors themselves but also to the broader lesbian community, because it stifles preventative discussions of sexual violence. Perpetrators may go from victim to victim without ever having their actions accounted for and confronted as sexual violence. Female survivors of same-sex sexual violence suffer many of the same psychological affects as do other victims of adult sexual violence, including PTSD, anxiety, low self-esteem, and depression. In contrast, the extent of physical injuries may be very different for these victims than for those assaulted by male perpetrators. For example, in many cases of male-perpetrated sexual violence, it is possible to obtain DNA evidence should prosecution be sought. For female victims of penetrative same-sex sexual violence, it may be more likely that objects were used, which tend to leave less conclusive DNA evidence than do body parts.

TRANSGENDER SEXUAL VIOLENCE

Under the broader discussion of same-sex sexual violence, transgender experience with sexual violence is a largely unexplored area of scholarly inquiry. The term *transgender*, often rendered as *trans* for short, refers to those individuals who fall under the larger umbrella of gender variance. Specifically, a transgender individual's gender identities and expressions exist outside of the person's socially assigned physical sex and/or gender (Bornstein, Fawcett, Sullivan, Senturia, & Shiu-Thornton, 2006; Feinberg, 1998). While trans experiences with sexual violence may not necessarily be accurately described as "same-sex," given the range in possible sex identifications, it is still crucial to address the sexual violence victimization that occurs within the transgender community.

While few estimates are available to measure the extent of sexual violence experienced by transgender individuals, available estimates indicate very high prevalence rates across the community. One of the few examples of research in this area comes from the 1998 Gender, Violence, and Resource Access Survey in which 50% of respondents reported having been raped or sexually assaulted by a romantic partner (Courvant & Cook-Daniels, 2003). Another study that examined lifetime experiences with violence in a large transgender sample found that 14% had experienced rape or sexual abuse (Lombardi, 2001). The most recent NCAVP estimates indicate that transgender individuals are 1.81 times more likely to be sexually victimized than are those who do not identify as transgender (NCAVP, 2011).

Several distinct factors place trans populations at higher risk for sexual violence than their cisgender (nontransgender) counterparts. Transphobia, or the feeling of unease or revulsion toward those who express nonnormative expressions of gender identity and expression, may foster intense hatred toward trans individuals and/or foster acceptance of sexual violence as an unavoidable aspect of being transgender (Lombardi, 2001). Istar-Lev and Lev (2000) stated that "transgender people are often sexually targeted specifically because of their transgendered status. The sexual perpetrator will stalk them, or attack them, infuriated by their cross-gender behavior" (p. 1). In cases of sexual violence that occurs within intimate relationships, transphobia plays a key role in the oppression and silencing of trans victims. Intimate-partner perpetrators of sexual violence may utilize transphobia to justify sexual violence against trans victims, often reminding the victims of their vulnerabilities in a transphobic culture and thereby entrapping them in a cycle of violence. As one scholar has stated, "perpetrators are acutely aware of the individual and institutional vulnerabilities faced by trans people and these vulnerabilities feature explicitly in the abuse tactics and harm done" (Brown, 2011, p. 162). The ridiculing of trans identities may leave many trans victims of intimate-partner sexual violence feeling that they should tolerate their victimization or settle for abusive partners out of fear of being alone. Transgender individuals, particularly male-to-female (MTF) individuals, may also be at higher risk for participation in sex work, which may place them at higher risk for sexual victimization (Clements-Nolle, Marx, Guzman, & Katz, 2001)

There remains a need for further research and scholarly inquiry into the unique realities of transgender victims of sexual violence. The complexities faced by these victims of sexual violence require an examination of the dynamics and types of sexual abuse experienced. Comparative research is needed to analyze the varying contexts of sexual violence experienced by trans populations. Further, the consequences and repercussions of sexual victimization, an understanding of which is needed to assist with resource allocation, remain largely unexamined in the trans community.

Barriers to Resources and the Criminal Justice System

Just as homophobia, transphobia, heterosexism, and heteronormativity shape and contextualize the experiences with and dynamics of same-sex sexual violence, so too do they influence formal help-seeking avenues. Sexual assault response organizations, shelters, law enforcement, and the criminal justice system offer counseling, housing, and legal advocacy for victims of sexual violence. However, perceived and actual prejudices in formal help avenues may prevent victims of same-sex sexual violence from seeking much needed advocacy and mental health services. Service providers and law enforcement personnel may often be perpetrators of homophobic discrimination, sometimes denying services, refusing to promote inclusive policies, or undermining experiences of same-sex sexual violence. Historically, state and federal laws have not recognized acts of same-sex sexual violence, only acknowledging rape as being perpetrated by men on female victims. This long history continues to deter and curb help-seeking opportunities for LGBTQ survivors, despite recent progress toward inclusion of same-sex victimization in services, laws, and policies.

Rape advocacy organizations and shelters developed in response to the activism of feminists of the late 1960s and 1970s. These organizations were tailored for heterosexual, cisgender women who had been domestically abused and were cultivated by a larger social movement that framed sexual violence as a result of a patriarchal power structure that fostered sexual violence against women. While these efforts brought public attention to a previously private matter, they created a foundation of resources for sexual violence that were entirely based of the experiences of female victims of male-perpetrated acts.

Research has established that negative experiences with shelter staff, resources, and policies have resulted in many victims of same-sex sexual violence not following through with programs or not seeking formal help at all (Island & Letellier, 1991; Merrill & Wolfe, 2000; Renzetti, 1992; Scherzer, 1998). Seeking help from formal resources—such as a rape advocacy or domestic violence shelter—is among the least taken avenues for LGBTQ victims of sexual and domestic violence. In fact, studies have consistently shown that LGBTQ survivors overwhelming rely on informal resources, such as friends and family, rather than seek professional or legal assistance (Guadalupe-Diaz & Yglesias, in press; McClennen, Summers, & Vaughn, 2002; Turell, 2000). In particular, male survivors of same-sex sexual violence may be less likely than their female counterparts to seek any form of help (Masho & Alvanzo, 2009).

Victims of same-sex sexual violence often find that available staff and resources are not equipped to deal with the unique dynamics and legalities of their victimization. Regarding lesbian survivors, Renzetti (1992) stated that the "most common reason [for not going to shelters] was that they considered the shelter services for heterosexual women, and they feared they would be rejected or uncomfortable there because they are lesbians" (p. 93). In actuality, rape advocacy staff are trained and prepared to address only instances of male-to-female rape and are not adequately prepared to address same-sex sexual violence. In addition, scholars have documented that homophobia is a prominent issue among shelter staff (Irvine, 1990; NCAVP 2011; Renzetti). Many staff in shelter and rape advocacy programs may trivialize same-sex sexual violence and undermine victims' experiences. In 2011, the NCAVP estimated that 62% of LGBTQ victims of sexual and domestic violence were denied assistance in shelters and rape advocacy programs in part because those organizations did not offer space for these individuals or programs for their needs.

Another important aspect of help seeking for survivors of same-sex sexual violence is the ability or willingness to reach out to the criminal justice system. While reporting sexual violence to law enforcement may be among the least common reactions to sexual violence among all victims, LGBTQ survivors may be even less likely than their heterosexual counterparts to involve law enforcement. Liang, Goodman, Tummala-Narra, and Weintraub (2005) mentioned that homophobic stereotyping by police fuels reluctance to involve the criminal justice system in cases of same-sex partner abuse or sexual violence. In a key study that explored the help-seeking behaviors of gay male intimate-partner violence victims, Merrill and Wolfe (2000) reported that "battered gay and bisexual men, like their lesbian counterparts, have difficulty enlisting appropriate response from the police" (p. 7). While not specific to sexual violence, previous studies have found that LGB victims of partner violence consistently have negative experiences with the police or negative perceptions of the police that influenced reporting (Berrill, 1992; McClennan, 2005; Renzetti, 1992). Merrill and Wolfe mentioned that for gay men in particular, there exists a "long history of harassing" (p. 7). This historical homophobic discrimination by law enforcement continues to be a prominent issue in the LGBTQ community. Recent estimates illustrate that among LGB, the police are still largely viewed as homophobic and discriminatory in dealing with cases of same-sex violence (Guadalupe-Diaz & Yglesias, in press; Hickson et al., 1994; NCAVP, 2011).

Perceived homophobia by law enforcement is a key factor in the underreporting of same-sex sexual violence. Beyond initial contact with police, victims of same-sex sexual violence are confronted with systemic homophobia in courtrooms and legal proceedings. As Kramer (1998) stated, "any discussion of how the criminal justice system can best cope with cases of same-sex rape must take anti-gay bias into consideration" (p. 311). The NCAVP (2011) estimated that in 2011, 55% of LGBTQ survivors of some form of partner violence (not limited to sexual violence) were denied protective orders. Existing within a broader homophobic culture, criminal justice staff are not immune to biases against homosexuality that may negatively influence justice system proceedings. Victims of same-sex sexual violence who are not LGBTQ face assumptions of homosexuality. These victims may fear disclosure of their stories or misrepresentations of who they are during criminal proceedings. Even for those victims who are LGBTQ, fear of disclosing sexual orientation and publicly coming out in criminal proceedings may deter reporting or create hostile courtroom environments.

For those LGBTQ survivors of same-sex sexual violence who do proceed with criminal prosecution, issues of blame attribution are documented to work against their accounts of victimization. Blame attribution is the amount of responsibility that is placed on victims of crime for their victimization. Of interest to researchers is how gender and race influence how much blame is attributed to victims of sexual violence in general; women and racial minority survivors are often viewed as more responsible for their victimizations (Foley, Evancic, Karnik, King, & Parks, 1995; Schneider, Ee, & Aronson, 1994). For gay and lesbian victims of sexual violence, similar prejudices in blame attribution have been found. In one example, Mitchell, Hirschman, and Nagayama Hall (1999) asked a sample of participants questions about blame attribution for male victims of same-sex stranger rape. They found that when participants were told a victim was gay, they attributed significantly more blame to the victim than if the victim were a heterosexual male. Similarly, Wakelin and Long (2003) asked a sample of 221 college students to report their perceptions of different crime scenarios of same-sex rape. The researchers found that victims who were gay men received more blame for their victimization than did their heterosexual counterparts and even more than did lesbian women. Further, participants held gay and lesbian victims as having significantly more responsibility to avoid the violent situation than did heterosexual victims of sexual violence.

Similar attitudes may permeate criminal proceedings in which the victim's sexual orientation becomes part of the victim-blaming narrative. Homophobic stereotyping may lead lawyers, judges, and juries to attribute much more responsibility to victims of same-sex violence by assuming that the victim wanted or deserved the assault. That is, lesbian and gay victims of same-sex sexual violence may be seen as unconsciously desiring the victimization or feeling sexual attraction to the perpetrator (Davies & McCartney, 2003; Mitchell et al., 1999; Wakelin & Long, 2003). For transgender victims of sexual violence, transphobia plays a major factor in blame attribution, and studies have indicated that trans status is significantly related to the victim blaming of trans survivors of sexual violence; in particular, a strong bias exists against male-to-female transgender victims (Davies, 2000; Davies & Hudson, 2011).

Victims of same-sex sexual violence require advocacy programs that are conscious of the unique factors that affect their reporting and legal recourses. More and more, police departments are incorporating LGBTQ sensitivity training and building LGBTQ–police liaison teams to respond to incidents of same-sex sexual and domestic violence. Various voluntary bar associations, such as the Gay and Lesbian Lawyers Association of Los Angeles and the Central Florida Gay and Lesbian Law Association, work to bring attention to these and other legal issues affecting the LGBTQ community while often also providing a wide range of services. On college campuses, victim services units have increasingly moved toward inclusive services for victims of dating violence, rape, harassment, and sexual assault.

Legislative Progress and Same-Sex Sexual Violence

Very recently, major federal legislative progress has been made to ensure that victims of same-sex sexual and domestic violence have better access to services and legal recourse. In addition, new legislation has made it easier to keep track of the perpetration of same-sex sexual violence in federal databases. While many states had already begun to include statistics on reported same-sex sexual violence, offer protective orders regardless of gender, and expand rape and domestic violence laws to include victims of same-sex sexual violence, several states had remained rigid in their heterosexist laws. In particular, the 2013 reauthorization of the 1994 Violence Against Women Act (VAWA) included a new wave of LGBTQ protections.

Until early 2012, national crime statistics collected by the Federal Bureau of Investigation's (FBI) Uniform Crime Report (UCR) did not include male victims of rape, female victims of same-sex rape, or acts of anal or oral penetration in the definition of forcible rape. The traditional definition of forcible rape included gendered language that stated "the carnal knowledge of a female, forcible and against her will" and mentioned forcible vaginal penetration by a penis (Savage, 2012, p. 1). In addition, this previous definition did not account for acts of sexual violence that were not physically forced. Part of the new definition includes "the penetration, no matter how slight, of the vagina or anus with any body part or object, or oral penetration by a sex organ of another person, without the consent of the victim" (FBI, 2012; Savage, 2012).

The 2013 reauthorization of VAWA addressed disparities in services for LGBTQ survivors of violence. Activists, service providers, advocates, and scholars had long challenged the existing system that left many LGBTQ survivors without legal recourse or appropriate services. The expansions of the law provided three major advances for LGBTQ survivors. First, VAWA acknowledged the LGBTQ community as an underserved population. This designation now allows organizations that serve LGBTQ victims to apply for and receive grants from programs that are specifically in place for underserved populations. Second, for the first time VAWA now includes language that specifically contains a nondiscrimination clause categorizing sexual orientation and gender identity as protected statuses. This means that all organizations receiving any VAWA related funding can no longer turn away victims on the basis of sexual orientation or gender identity. This affects mainly shelters and some rape advocacy groups that serve victims of sexual and domestic violence. Finally, the VAWA reauthorization now provides states with the opportunity to direct grants toward initiatives that improve the criminal justice response to LGBTQ sexual and domestic violence.

Conclusion

As funds become available, new policies and programs will protect victims of same-sex sexual violence in ways not previously available. While these protections will represent progress, a strong effort should be made in community and educational outreach to LGBTQ populations to disseminate this new information among a population that has historically been disenfranchised by systemic responses to violence. A stronger and more thorough examination of the dynamics and nature of same-sex sexual violence is needed to ensure the highest quality of services and appropriate criminal justice responses. Finally, a continued effort is needed to ensure that new policies are implemented and work efficiently toward their intended purposes.

Discussion Questions

1. How did past rape legislation limit the prosecution of offenders of same-sex sexual victimization?

2. What psychological and emotional conflicts do male victims experience that may affect their decision to report their victimization?

3. What is the myth of the lesbian utopia, and how does it affect the perception of female-on-female sexual victimization?

4. What factors place transgender individuals at a higher risk for sexual victimization?

References

Arey, D. (1995). Gay males and sexual child abuse. In L. A. Fontes (Ed.), *Sexual abuse in nine North American cultures: Treatment and prevention* (pp. 200–235). Thousand Oaks, CA: Sage.

Balsam, K. F. (2003). Traumatic victimization in the lives of lesbian and bisexual women: A contextual approach. *Journal of Lesbian Studies, 7*(1), 1–14.

Balsam, K. F., Rothblum, E. D., & Beauchaine, T. P. (2005). Victimization over the life span: A comparison of lesbian, gay, bisexual, and heterosexual siblings. *Journal of Consulting and Clinical Psychology, 73*(3), 477–487.

Bernard, T. J., Vold, G. B., Snipes, J. B., & Gerould, A. L. (2010). *Vold's theoretical criminology* (6th ed.). New York, NY: Oxford University Press.

Berrill, K. T. (1992). Anti-gay violence and victimization in the United States: An overview. In G. M. Herek & K. Berrill (Eds.), *Hate crimes: Confronting violence against lesbians and gay men* (pp. 19–44). Thousand Oaks, CA: Sage.

Bornstein, D. R., Fawcett, J., Sullivan, M., Senturia, K. D., & Shiu-Thornton, S. (2006). Understanding the experiences of lesbian, bisexual and trans survivors of domestic violence: A qualitative study. *Journal of Homosexuality, 51*(1),159–181.

Bradford, J., Ryan, C., & Rothblum, E. D. (1994). National Lesbian Health Care Survey: Implications for mental health care. *Journal of Consulting and Clinical Psychology, 62*(2), 228–242.

Brand, P. A., & Kidd, A. H. (1986). Frequency of physical aggression in heterosexual and female homosexual dyads. *Psychological Reports, 59*, 1307–1313.

Brown, N. (2011). Holding tensions of victimization and perpetration: Partner abuse in trans communities. In J. L. Ristock (Ed.), *Intimate partner violence in LGBTQ lives* (pp. 153–168). New York, NY: Routledge.

Campbell, P. P. (2008). *Sexual violence in the lives of lesbian rape survivors.* St. Louis, MO: St. Louis University.

Clements-Nolle, K., Marx, R., Guzman, R., & Katz, M. (2001). HIV prevalence, risk behaviors, health care use, and mental health status of transgender persons: Implications for public health intervention. *American Journal of Public Health, 91*(6), 915–921.

Connell, R. W. (1995). *Masculinities.* Berkeley: University of California Press.

Connell, R. W. (1996). *Gender and power: Society, the person, and sexual politics.* Cambridge, MA: Polity Press.

Connell, R. W., & Messerschmidt, J. W. (2005). Hegemonic masculinity: Rethinking the concept. *Gender & Society, 19*(6), 829–859.

Courvant, D., & Cook-Daniels, L. (2003). Trans and intersex survivors of domestic violence: Defining terms, barriers and responsibilities. Retrieved from http://www.survivorproject.org/defbarresp.html

Coxell, A. W., & King, M. B. (1996). Male victims of rape and sexual abuse. *Sexual and Marital Therapy, 11*(3), 297–308.

Davies, M. (2000, July). *When a friend has a sex change: Investigating attitudes towards transsexuality.* Paper presented at the British Psychological Society Psychology of Women Section Conference, University of Dundee, Scotland.

Davies, M., & Hudson, J. (2011). Judgments toward male and transgendered victims in a depicted stranger rape. *Journal of Homosexuality, 58*(2), 237–247.

Davies, M., & McCartney, S. (2003). Effects of gender and sexuality on judgments of victim blame and rape myth acceptance in a depicted male rape. *Journal of Community & Applied Social Psychology, 13*(5), 391–398.

Duncan, D. F. (1990). Prevalence of sexual assault victimization among heterosexual and gay/lesbian university students. *Psychological Reports, 66*(1), 65–66.

Erbaugh, E. (2007). Queering approaches to intimate partner violence. In L. L. O'Toole, J. R. Schiffman, & M. L. Kilter Edwards (Eds.), *Gender violence: Interdisciplinary perspectives* (2nd ed., pp. 451–459). New York: New York University Press.

Federal Bureau of Investigation (FBI). (2012). *Preliminary semiannual uniform crime report, January–June 2012.* Retrieved from http://www.fbi.gov/about-us/cjis/ucr/crime-in-the-u.s/2012/preliminary-semiannual-uniform-crime-report-january-june-2012

Feinberg, L. (1998). *Stone butch blues: A novel.* Ithaca, NY: Firebrand Books.

Foley, L. A., Evancic, C., Karnik, K., King, J., & Parks, A. (1995). Date rape: Effects of race of assailant and victim and gender of subjects on perceptions. *Journal of Black Psychology, 21*(1), 6–18.

Girshick, L. B. (2002). *Woman-to-woman sexual violence: Does she call it rape?* Boston, MA: Northeastern University Press.

Gold, S. D., Marx, B. P., & Lexington, J. M. (2007). Gay male sexual assault survivors: The relations among internalized homophobia, experiential avoidance, and psychological symptom severity. *Behaviour Research and Therapy, 45*(3), 549–562.

Gonsiorek, J. C. (1994). A critique of current models in sexual abuse. In J. C. Gonsiorek, W. H. Bera, & D. LeTourneau (Eds.), *Male sexual abuse: A trilogy of intervention strategies* (pp. 21–36). Thousand Oaks, CA: Sage.

Guadalupe-Diaz, X., & Yglesias, J. (In press). "Who's protected?" Exploring perceptions of domestic violence law by lesbians, gays, and bisexuals. *Journal of Gay and Lesbian Social Services.*

Hart, B. (1986). Lesbian battering: An examination. In K. Lobel (Ed.), *Naming the violence: Speaking out about lesbian battering* (pp. 173–189). Seattle, WA: Seal Press.

Heidt, J. M., Marx, B. P., & Gold, S. D. (2005). Sexual revictimization among sexual minorities: A preliminary study. *Journal of Traumatic Stress, 18*(5), 533–540.

Herek, G. M., Gillis, J. R., Cogan, J. C., & Glunt, E. K. (1997). Hate crime victimization among lesbian, gay, and bisexual adults. *Journal of Interpersonal Violence, 12*(2), 195–215.

Hickson, F. C., Davies, P. M., Hunt, A. J., Weatherburn, P., McManus, T. J., & Coxon, P. (1994). Gay men as victims of nonconsensual sex. *Archives of Sexual Behavior, 23*(3), 281–294.

Hughes, T. L., Johnson, T., & Wilsnack, S. C. (2001). Sexual assault and alcohol abuse: A comparison of lesbians and heterosexual women. *Journal of Substance Abuse, 13*(4), 515–532.

Irvine, J. (1990). Lesbian battering: The search for shelter. In P. Elliot (Ed.), *Confronting lesbian battering: A manual for the battered women's movement* (pp. 25–30). St. Paul: Minnesota Coalition for Battered Women.

Isely, P. J., & Gehrenbeck-Shim, D. (1997). Sexual assault of men in the community. *Journal of Community Psychology, 25*(2), 159–166.

Island, D., & Letellier, P. (1991). *Men who beat the men who love them: Battered gay men and domestic violence.* New York, NY: Haworth Press.

Istar Lev, A., & Lev, S. (2000). Sexual assault in the transgender communities. *FORGE, 4*(1). Retrieved from http://my.execpc.com/~dmmunson/Nov99_7.htm

Kalichman, S. C., & Rompa, D. (1995). Sexually coerced and noncoerced gay and bisexual men: Factors relevant to risk for human immunodeficiency virus (HIV) infection. *Journal of Sex Research, 32*(1), 45–50.

Kimmel, M. (2002). "Gender symmetry" in domestic violence: A substantive and methodological research review. *Violence Against Women, 8*(11), 1332–1363.

King, A., & Evans, J. L. (1999). Same-sex abuse. In M. Carter (Ed.), *Support for survivors: Training for sexual assault counselors* (pp. 71–72). Sacramento: California Coalition Against Sexual Assault.

Kramer, E. (1998). When men are victims: Applying rape shield laws to male same-sex rape. *New York University Law Review, 73*, 293–332.

Lawrence v. Texas, 539 U.S. 558 (2003).

Liang, B., Goodman, L., Tummala-Narra, P., & Weintraub, S. (2005). A theoretical framework for understanding help-seeking processes among survivors of intimate partner violence. *American Journal of Community Psychology, 36*(1–2), 71–84.

Lie, G-Y., Schilit, R., Bush, J., Montagne, M., & Reyes, L. (1991). Lesbians in currently aggressive relationships: How frequently do they report aggressive past relationships? *Violence and Victims, 6*(2), 121–135.

Light, D., & Monk-Turner, E. (2009). Circumstances surrounding male sexual assault and rape: Findings from the National Violence Against Women Survey. *Journal of Interpersonal Violence, 24*(11), 1849–1858.

Lombardi, E. (2001). Enhancing transgender health care. *American Journal of Public Health, 91*(6), 869–872.

Masho, S. W., & Alvanzo, A. (2010). Help-seeking behaviors of men sexual assault survivors. *American Journal of Men's Health, 4*(3), 237–242.

McClennen, J. C. (2005). Domestic violence between same-gender partners: Recent findings and future research. *Journal of Interpersonal Violence, 20*(2), 149–154.

McClennen, J. C., Summers, A. B., & Vaughan., C. (2002). Gay men's domestic violence: Dynamics, help-seeking behaviors, and correlates. *Journal of Gay and Lesbian Social Services, 14*(1), 23–49.

Merrill, G. S., & Wolfe, V. A. (2000). Battered gay men: An exploration of abuse, help-seeking and why they stay. *Journal of Homosexuality, 39*(2), 1–30.

Mitchell, D., Hirschman, R., & Nagayama Hall, G. C. (1999). Attributions of victim responsibility, pleasure and trauma in male rape. *Journal of Sex Research, 36*(4), 369–373.

Morris, J. F., & Balsam, K. F. (2003). Lesbian and bisexual women's experiences of victimization: Mental health, revictimization, and sexual identity development. *Journal of Lesbian Studies, 7*(4), 67–85.

National Coalition of Anti-Violence Projects (NCAVP). (2011). Lesbian, gay, bisexual, transgender, queer and HIV-affected intimate partner violence 2010. Retrieved from http://www .standingfirmswpa.org/docs-all/IPV-LGBTQH.pdf

Otis, M. D., & Skinner, W. F. (1996). The prevalence of victimization and its effect on mental well-being among lesbian and gay people. *Journal of Homosexuality, 30*(3), 93–121.

Peterson, Z. D., Voller, E. K., Polusny, M. A., & Murdoch, M. (2010). Prevalence and consequences of adult sexual assault of men: Review of empirical findings and state of the literature. *Clinical Psychology Review, 31*(1), 1–24.

Renzetti, C. M. (1992). *Violent betrayal: Partner abuse in lesbian relationships.* Newbury Park, CA: Sage.

Renzetti, C. M. (1996). The poverty of services for battered lesbians. *Journal of Gay & Lesbian Social Services, 4*(1), 61–68.

Renzetti, C. M. (1997). Violence and abuse among same-sex couples. In A. P. Cardarelli (Ed.), *Violence between intimate partners: Patterns, causes, and effects* (pp. 70–89). Boston, MA: Allyn & Bacon.

Renzetti, C. M. (1998). Violence and abuse in lesbian relationships: Theoretical and empirical issues. In R. K. Bergen (Ed.), *Issues in intimate violence* (pp. 117–128). Thousand Oaks, CA: Sage.

Rich, A. (1980). Compulsory heterosexuality and lesbian existence. *Signs, 5*(4) 631–660.

Ristock, J. I. (2002). *No more secrets: Violence in lesbian relationships.* New York, NY: Routledge.

Rothman, E., Exner, D., & Baughman, A. (2011). The prevalence of sexual assault against people who identify as gay, lesbian, or bisexual in the United States: A systematic review. *Trauma, Violence, & Abuse, 12*(2), 55–66.

Savage, C. (2012, January 6). U.S. to expand its definition of rape in statistics. *The New York Times.* Retrieved from http://www.nytimes.com/2012/01/07/us/politics/federal-crime-statistics-to-expand-rape-definition.html

Scarce, M. (1997). Same-sex rape of male college students. *Journal of American College Health, 45*(4), 171–173.

Scherzer, T. (1998). Domestic violence in lesbian relationships: Findings of the Lesbian Relationships Research Project. *Journal of Lesbian Studies, 2*(1), 29–47.

Schneider, L. J., Ee, J. S-C., & Aronson, H. (1994). Effects of victim gender and physical vs. psychological trauma/injury on observer's perceptions of sexual assaults and its aftereffects. *Sex Roles, 30*(11–12), 793–808.

Shidlo, A. (1994). Internalized homophobia: Conceptual and empirical issues in measurement. In B. Greene & G. M. Herek (Eds.), *Lesbian and gay psychology: Theory, research, and clinical applications* (pp. 176–205). Thousand Oaks, CA: Sage.

Stermac, L., del Bove, G., & Addison, M. (2004). Stranger and acquaintance sexual assault of adult males. *Journal of Interpersonal Violence, 19*(8), 901–915.

Stermac, L., Sheridan, P. M., Davidson, A., & Dunn, S. (1996). Sexual assault of adult males. *Journal of Interpersonal Violence, 11*(1), 52–64.

Struckman-Johnson, C., & Struckman-Johnson, D. (2006). A comparison of sexual coercion experiences reported by men and women in prison. *Journal of Interpersonal Violence, 21*(12), 1591–1615.

Tjaden, P., & Thoennes, N. (2000). Full report of the prevalence, incidence, and consequences of violence against women: Findings from the National Violence Against Women Survey. Washington, DC: U.S. Department of Justice. Retrieved from https://www.ncjrs.gov/pdffiles1/nij/183781.pdf

Todahl, J. L., Linville, D., Bustin, A., Wheeler, J., & Gau, J. (2009). Sexual assault support services and community systems: Understanding critical issues and needs in the LGBTQ community. *Violence Against Women, 15*(8), 952–976.

Turell, S. C. (2000). A descriptive analysis of same-sex relationship violence for a diverse sample. *Journal of Family Violence, 15*(3), 281–293.

Violence Against Women Act (VAWA) reauthorization, Pub. L. 113-4 (2013).

Wakelin, A., & Long, K. M. (2003). Effects of victim gender and sexuality on attributions of blame to rape victims. *Sex Roles, 49*(9–10), 477–487.

Waldner-Haugrud, L. K. (1999). Sexual coercion in lesbian and gay relationships: A review and critique. *Aggression and Violent Behavior, 4*(2), 139–149.

Waldner-Haugrud, L. K., & Gratch, L. V. (1997). Sexual coercion in gay/lesbian relationships: Descriptives and gender differences. *Violence and Victims, 12*(1), 87–98.

Wang, Y. W. (2011). Voices from the margin: A case study of a rural lesbian's experience with woman-to-woman sexual violence. *Journal of Lesbian Studies, 15*(2), 166–175.

Waterman, C. K., Dawson, L. J., & Bologna, M. J. (1989). Sexual coercion in gay male and lesbian relationships: Predictors and implications for support services. *Journal of Sex Research, 26*(1), 118–124.

Weiss, K. G. (2008). Male sexual victimization: Examining men's experiences of rape and sexual assault. *Men and Masculinities, 12*(3), 275–298.

11

Sexual Victimization in the U.S. Military

Jamie A. Snyder and Heidi L. Scherer

One of the many issues that face young men and women in the U.S. military is sexual victimization. In 2012, 3,374 incidents of sexual victimization were reported according to the U.S. Department of Defense (DoD), an increase over the number of incidents reported in 2011. In fact, since 2004, the number of sexual victimizations reported by the DoD has nearly doubled (DoD, 2013b). Additionally, in a recent survey, over 1 in 5 women reported experiencing sexual victimization by someone in the military since entering service (DoD, 2013a). These official numbers, coupled with findings from self-report surveys, suggest that sexual victimization in the U.S. military is a continuing problem that warrants further attention. In addition to concern over the number of sexual victimizations, there has also been substantial interest in the process for handling these incidents, as well as the possible negative effects of victimization. Victims have expressed a range of negative outcomes, including disillusionment with the military and the intention to leave their positions, combined with other mental or physical effects (Magley, Waldo, Drasgow, & Fitzgerald, 1999; Williams, Fitzgerald, & Drasgow, 1999). Estimates of large-scale underreporting, media attention focused on the outcomes of cases, and the military judicial process add to the increasing scrutiny on the military to respond to this issue. These concerns have led to a number of efforts to collect data and develop strategies to prevent sexual victimization, including processes to manage the current problem.

This chapter has three main objectives. First, it will discuss the nature of sexual victimization in the military, providing estimates of its occurrence and research on possible negative mental and physical health outcomes. Second, the process for prosecution and punishment of military personnel in military courts, along with criticisms of the process, will be examined. Finally, the reporting of sexual victimization and the issues surrounding it will be discussed as will possible influences on reporting, including power differentials and the culture of the military. It should be noted that in this chapter, *sexual victimization* refers to multiple types of victimization, including unwanted sexual contact, sexual assault, and attempted/completed rape. Sexual harassment will be discussed separately unless otherwise noted.

Prevalence of Sexual Victimization in the Military

Estimating the number of sexual victimizations that occur in the U.S. military or in other populations, such as the general public, is difficult. Estimates of the prevalence of sexual victimization in the military vary depending on the source, definitions used, sample taken, and other methodological factors. Despite these difficulties, several efforts have been made to obtain this data. Typically, estimates are calculated through two major sources: official reports from the military or surveys collected by military that are either disseminated by the military or analyzed and reported by other researchers. Currently, the military uses both official reports and victim surveys to estimate the number of victimizations that occur each year.

Official reports provide insight into the number of sexual victimizations that are reported each year along with pertinent information on perpetrators, military responses, and outcomes of reported incidents. This information is collected for active duty men and women as well as individuals attending the military academies. However, this method of documentation does not account for sexual victimizations that are not reported in an official capacity. Sexual victimization has been found to be widely underreported across victims, including victims who are in the military (Culbertson & Rosenfeld, 1994; Fisher, Cullen, & Turner, 2000). To examine the nature of underreporting and better estimate the number of sexual victimizations that may occur, the military also conducts several surveys that include questions on sexual victimization and sexual harassment. These surveys produce data on the number of sexual victimizations that may go unreported, providing improved information on the possible "true" number of victimizations. Further, they examine reasons why individuals may not report their victimizations.

An additional source of estimates is data collected or analyzed by researchers outside the military. These surveys often examine veterans or individuals who are no longer in the military by asking them about their past experiences while in the military, or they analyze data collected by the military to provide more detailed information than officially released reports. Typically, this type of data collection and/or analysis provides more nuanced and contextualized results than officially released reports and includes information on the potential negative outcomes of sexual victimization. Each of these types of information provides unique insights into sexual victimization in the military. The remainder of this section will discuss each of these data sources in terms of trends and estimations of the prevalence of sexual victimization.

OFFICIAL REPORTS

In 2005, the Sexual Assault Prevention and Response (SAPR) program was established to combat sexual victimization, increase reporting, and provide victims with needed assistance (DoD, 2013b). The SAPR also established a yearly reporting system that provides information on incidents of sexual victimization in the military. This document indicates the number of incidents of sexual victimization that was reported to the military in the past year for U.S. Army, Navy, Air Force, and Marine Corps. As noted at the beginning of this chapter, 3,374 incidents of sexual victimization were reported to the military in 2012. The most common type of sexual victimization reported was wrongful sexual contact (35% of incidents), followed by aggravated sexual assault (28% of incidents) and rape (27% of incidents). The report also indicated that the majority (62%) of the victimizations reported were service member on service member (DoD). In other words, most of the victims had been victimized by a fellow service member, not by someone outside of the military.

The annual report also provides information on sexual victimization by each branch of the military. The U.S. Army accounted for the majority of the incidents reported in 2012 (42%), followed by the Air Force (23%), Navy (23%), and Marines (12%). For both the Navy and Marines, aggravated assault was the most commonly reported incident, while wrongful sexual contact was the most common type of sexual victimization for the Army. Rape was the most common type of incident reported for the Air Force (DoD, 2013b).

Similarly to its official reporting on active military personnel, the DoD also reports official incidents of sexual victimization for cadets and midshipmen currently attending a military academy. Data are reported for the U.S. Army, Navy, and Air Force academies. In 2012, there were 80 reports of sexual victimization, nearly 2 times the number of reports in 2006 (42; DoD, 2012b). However, these numbers should be interpreted with caution, as they may reflect an increase in reporting and not an increase in the number of sexual victimizations that occurred. Rape was the most common type of sexual victimization reported (DoD). Additionally, these numbers only include incidents that were reported and likely highly underestimate the true rate of sexual victimization in the military academies.

Characteristics of victims of sexual violence in the military mirror those in other populations such as college students (e.g., Fisher et al., 2000). Specifically, victims were most likely to be female and young (age 20–24). In addition, most military victims were victimized by someone who was also in the military (DoD, 2012b). This pattern is found for both active duty individuals and those currently enrolled in an academy. In other words, the majority of sexual victimizations that are reported by either active duty or academy members involve both perpetrators and victims who are in the military. Additionally, the majority of incidents involve a victim and perpetrator who are of similar rank (DoD). In particular, most individuals who are sexually victimized in the military are not victimized by a superior.

MILITARY SURVEYS

While official reports are important in the understanding of the nature and extent of sexual victimization in the military, the surveying of men and women in the military about their sexual victimization experiences provides a deeper look into the problem. These surveys provide varying estimates depending on the type of victimization examined, length of the reference period (e.g., since entering the military vs. last 12 months), and definition type. According to a recent review of the literature by Turchik and Wilson (2009), an estimated 22% to 84% of women experienced some type of sexual victimization or sexual harassment while in the military. Fewer studies have focused on males, but the limited research suggests that up to three quarters experienced at least sexual harassment while in the military (Turchik & Wilson). While these estimates provide insight into the big picture of sexual victimization in the military, more detailed estimates broken down by type of victimization and examined over a shorter reference period also supply useful information. Since 2004–2005, the military has been collecting information every 1 or 2 years using several major surveys, including the Service Academy Gender Relations Survey (SAGR) and the Survey of Health Related Behaviors Among Active Duty Military Personnel (HRB).

The SAGR is a congressionally mandated survey conducted every 2 years by the DoD that asks men and women currently attending a military academy (U.S. Military, U.S. Naval, U.S. Air Force) about their experiences with sexual victimization and sexual harassment in the past year, among several other questions. This effort began in 2004 as a part of an attempt to combat sexual victimization and provide victims with guidelines on what actions to take if they are victimized. The HRB, which began in 1980 and was expanded in 2005, collects information on various health-related behaviors, including drug and alcohol use, stress, and victimization.

In 2012, nearly 11% of women and 2% of men reported they had experienced unwanted sexual contact in the past year (DoD, 2013b). Unwanted sexual contact includes attempted and completed rape and other unwanted sexual touching. Over half (54%) of unwanted sexual contacts were reported as completed or attempted rapes (DoD). These numbers are similar to estimates of sexual victimization among active duty military. It was reported that in 2012, a little over 12% of women and 2% of men experienced unwanted sexual contact in the past year (DoD). These numbers are also consistent with other research conducted using veteran samples or through the further analysis of military data by researchers outside the military (e.g., Skinner et al., 2000).

For example, Skinner and colleagues (2000) found that nearly a quarter (23%) of women experienced sexual assault at some point duing their military tenure. These estimates are also consistent with research conducted on men and women who were deployed. One study found that 15% of women and 1% of men veterans who were deployed during Operation Enduring Freedom or Operation Iraqi Freedom reported some form of military sexual trauma (Kimerling et al., 2010). These findings suggest that even men and women who are deployed do not escape the risk of sexual victimization. Finally, of the few studies that have examined sexual assault in males, it has been reported that as many as 12% of males may experience sexual assault while in the military (Turchik & Wilson, 2009).

Several studies have also attempted to estimate the occurrence of rape through the use of samples of veterans or more detailed analysis of data collected by the military. For example, Snyder, Fisher, Scherer, and Daigle (2012) reported that 5% of females and 2.5% of males reported experiencing attempted or completed rape in the past year. Additionally, in a study of veterans, Sadler, Booth, Nielson, and Doebbeling (2000) found that 11% of women had experienced attempted rape while 19% had experienced a completed rape during their military tenure. These numbers are similar to those found by Murdoch, Pryor, Polusny, and Gackstetter (2007), who reported that nearly 11% of women experienced either an attempted or completed rape while serving in the military. Overall, rates of rape experienced over a military career are reported to be as high as 33% for women (Turchik & Wilson, 2009).

As a point of comparison, one may consider the general population. A study using a nationally representative sample of adult women found that less than 1% (0.07%) of women reported experiencing rape in the past year (Kilpatrick, Edmunds, & Seymour, 1992). In another, more recent study, Tjaden and Thoennes (2006) reported that 0.03% of women reported experiencing attempted or completed rapes in the past 12 months. These estimates suggest that women in the military experience attempted and completed rapes at higher rates than does the general population of women. However, it should be noted that it is difficult to compare estimates across studies due to differences in definitions of sexual victimization, the types of behaviors that are included, and the samples utilized.

Aside from sexual assault and rape, military personnel are also asked about their experiences with sexual harassment (i.e., crude and offensive behavior, unwanted sexual attention, and sexual coercion). In 2012, about half of cadets and midshipmen reported they had experienced some form of sexual harassment in the past year (DoD, 2012a). The 2012 DoD report produced similar numbers for active duty military. Specifically, 51% of active duty women and 10% of active duty men reported being sexual harassed (DoD, 2013b). These estimates are similar, although somewhat lower, than those of other studies that have examined sexual harassment.

For example, Snyder and colleagues (2012) reported that 82% of females and 38% of males currently enrolled in a U.S. military academy had experienced sexual harassment in the past year. Rosen and Martin (1998) found that 84% of women and 74% of male military members had experienced at least one form of sexual harassment in the past year. Estimates of sexual harassment during one's time in the military are exceedingly high. Brubaker (2009) reported that 96% of women had experienced sexist behavior while in the military. More concerning are reports that sexual harassment is a repeated and often serious issue for individuals in the military. According to Street, Stafford, Mahan, and Hendricks (2008), 60% of women and close to a third of men experienced repeated or severe sexual harassment while in the military.

Overall, estimates of the prevalence of sexual victimization and sexual harassment in the military based on data collected by the military and other sources suggest a significant problem. While it is difficult to pinpoint the actual number of sexual victimizations that occur due to inconsistencies in measurement, methods, sample sizes, definitions, and other methodological issues, surveys and official reports provide important information about this continuing challenge. However, military samples are often difficult to access, and there is little consistency across measures used by the military to examine sexual victimization (Turchik & Wilson, 2009). Regardless of the data source and methodology, research nonetheless consistently demonstrates that sexual victimization and sexual harassment are pervasive in the military.

Effects of Military Sexual Victimization

Many negative effects of sexual victimization have been identified from studies of military personnel. These studies indicate that the consequences of military sexual victimization are multifaceted and have wide-reaching effects on victims, influencing their mental and physical health as well as their personal and professional lives (Magley et al., 1999; Williams, Fitzgerald, & Drasgow, 1999). While females experience a disproportionate amount of sexual victimization in the military, the consequences of victimization have been found to transcend gender lines and adversely influence both sexes (Culbertson & Rosenfeld, 1994; Fitzgerald, Drasgow, & Magley, 1999; Zinzow, Grubaugh, Frueh, & Magruder, 2008). Further, the negative effects of military sexual trauma and its various forms have been found to affect all members of the military regardless of rank or position, including academy cadets and midshipmen, active duty enlisted, and ranking officers (Buchanan, Settles, & Woods, 2008; Culbertson & Rosenfeld). The scope and nature of these consequences highlight the critical need for the U.S. military to prevent sexual victimization.

One of the most well-established research findings regarding the consequences of sexual victimization among this population is that it can negatively impact the psychological well-being of victims. On average, victims of sexual harassment in the military have reported poorer psychological well-being and greater distress and other emotional problems than their counterparts who did not experience sexual harassment or unwanted gender-related behaviors (Buchanan et al., 2008; Culbertson & Rosenfeld, 1994; Fitzgerald et al., 1999; Harned, Ormerod, Palmieri, Collinsworth, & Reed, 2002; Magley et al., 1999; Street, Gradus, Stafford, & Kelly, 2007; Williams et al., 1999). Poor psychological and mental health outcomes also have been associated with experiencing more serious forms of sexual victimization in the military, including sexual assault and rape. From their analyzes utilizing both official and unofficial data sources, Chang, Skinner, and Boehmer (2001); Harned et al.; Surìs, Lind, Kashner, and Borman (2007); and Zinzow et al. (2008) each reported that victims of sexual assault and trauma were more likely to report poorer mental health functioning and higher levels of emotional problems than those who did not report sexual assault in the military.

Further, these adverse mental health effects of sexual harassment and assault have been found among both male and female samples, indicating that both sexes experience negative consequences of sexual victimization (Culbertson & Rosenfeld, 1994; Fitzgerald et al., 1999, Magley et al., 1999; Street et al. 2007; Williams et al., 1999; Zinzow et al., 2008). While both genders were susceptible to developing psychological distress as a result of victimization, research indicated that the effect may be stronger for females than males (Culbertson & Rosenfeld; Magley et al.; Zinzow et al.). A similar pattern existed for rank: Both officers and enlisted individuals reported experiencing negative mental health outcomes as a result of sexual harassment, yet the effect appeared to be stronger for enlisted military personnel (Buchanan et al., 2008; Culbertson & Rosenfeld).

In addition to examining the relationship between sexual victimization and general indicators of mental health, several studies have examined more specific psychological impacts of sexual harassment and assault among the military population. One specific psychological outcome that has been associated with sexual victimization in the military is depression. Studies on female and male military and reservist samples have indicated that victims of sexual harassment and assault in the military are more likely to experience depression than their counterparts who have not experienced victimization (Chang et al., 2001; Gradus, Street, Kelly, & Stafford, 2008; Hankin et al., 1999; Surìs et al., 2007). Related to the onset of depressive symptoms, Zinzow et al. (2008) found that both male and female victims of military sexual assault were approximately 4 times more likely than nonvictims to have reported suicidal thoughts. Elevated levels of stress have also been reported among military victims of sexual harassment (U.S. General Accounting Office [GAO], 1994). In addition, Luterek, Bittinger, and Simpson (2011) found that symptoms of extreme stress were higher in female victims of military sexual assault than in females who had experienced no trauma or had experienced other forms of trauma in childhood and adulthood.

Alcohol dependency and abuse are other detrimental consequences that have been associated with military sexual victimization. On average, victims of sexual harassment and assault have reported higher rates of alcohol abuse than those who report no history of military sexual victimization (Frayne et al., 1999; Gradus et al., 2008; Hankin et al., 1999; Kimerling et al., 2010; Maguen et al., 2012; Surìs et al., 2007).

In comparison to their nonvictim counterparts, victims of sexual assault and harassment while in the military have been found to have more diagnoses for psychiatric disorders, including anxiety disorders (Kimerling et al., 2010; Maguen et al., 2012; Zinzow et al., 2008), adjustment disorders (Kimerling et al.), eating disorders (Maguen et al.), and mood disorders (Zinzow et al.). Another adverse mental health outcome of sexual victimization concerns the relationship between victimization and posttraumatic stress disorder (PTSD). A growing body of research indicates that military sexual victimization, particularly sexual assault, increases a victim's likelihood of developing PTSD (Kimerling et al.; Luterek et al., 2011; Maguen et al.; Smith et al., 2011; Street et al., 2007, 2008; Zinzow et al.). Kang, Dalager, Mahan, & Ishii (2005) reported that male and female victims of sexual assault were 5 and 6 times, respectively, more likely to develop PTSD than were nonvictims, even after controlling for combat status. Similarly, both Yaeger, Himmelfarb, Cammack, and Mintz (2006) and Wolfe and colleagues (1998) found that military sexual assault had a stronger relationship to PTSD compared to other trauma, including combat exposure.

Military sexual victimization has also been associated with consequences for physical health. Several studies have found that victims of sexual harassment and assault, including both males and females, are more likely to have reported lower satisfaction with their physical health than their nonvictim counterparts (Fitzgerald et al., 1999; Harned et al., 2002; Magley et al., 1999; Williams et al., 1999). Additionally, both Magley et al. and Street et al. (2008) reported that sexual victimization during military tenure is associated with a greater number of reported medical conditions and physical health problems. More specifically, Frayne and colleagues (1999) found that military sexual assault victims are more likely than those with no history of military sexual assault to have experienced negative respiratory, cardiac, and reproductive conditions. Further, Frayne, Skinner, Sullivan, and Freund (2003) reported that female victims of sexual assault have a greater number of cardiac risk factors, including obesity, smoking, alcohol consumption, and a less active lifestyle than do nonvictims. Smith et al. (2011) also found lower physical health among victims, represented by more frequent headaches; abdominal, muscular, or joint pain; and sexual discomfort. Additionally, there appears to be interplay between physical and mental health: Smith and colleagues found that PTSD symptomology resulting from military sexual assault independently influences victims' physical health.

In addition to the psychological and medical consequences of sexual military victimization, sexual harassment and assault experienced by military personnel have been associated with negative impacts on victims' personal lives. For instance, Pryor (1995) found that victims of sexual harassment are more likely than their nonvictim counterparts to have reported lower-quality relationships with spouses and family members. Frayne and colleagues (1999) also asserted that military sexual assault could have adverse effects on victims. They found that in comparison to women with no history of sexual assault, victims are more likely to have reported that their military experience has had an effect on their desire or ability to have children. McCall-Hosenfeld, Liebschutz, Spiro, and Seaver (2009) stated that military sexual assault adversely impacts female victims' sexual satisfaction and that victims report lower satisfaction in intimate relationships than do nonvictims. Research by Strauss, Marz, Weitlauf, Stechuchak, and Straits-Tröster (2011) also indicated that military sexual trauma can affect women's sexual relationships. They reported that female victims who experience sexual assault while enlisted are significantly more likely than those with no victimization history to have engaged in sex trade (i.e., the exchange of unprotected sex for something). While the effects of military sexual victimization on the personal domains of victims have not been as extensively examined as other consequences, the evidence suggests that sexual victimization experienced in the military leads to serious and long-term impacts on victims' personal and family lives.

The effects of sexual victimization have also been found to impact the professional lives of victims, broadly influencing their decisions regarding their military career as well as their perception of the military organization. Several studies have indicated that victims of military sexual harassment and assault report lower levels of job satisfaction (Antecol & Cobb-Clark, 2006; Fitzgerald et al., 1999; Harned et al., 2002; Magley et al., 1999; Williams et al., 1999), coworker satisfaction (Fitzgerald et al.; Harned et al.; Magley et al.; Settles, Buchanan, & Colar, 2012; Williams et al.), and supervisor satisfaction (Harned et al.; Magley et al.; Snyder et al., 2012; Williams et al.) than do their counterparts who did not experience victimization while in the military. In addition to overall poorer job-related satisfaction, victims of military sexual harassment also have reported lower productivity than those who have not experienced such unwanted gender-related behaviors (Magley et al.; Pryor, 1995; Settles et al.; Williams et al.).

One of the more well-established relationships between military sexual victimization and career outcomes regards victims' intentions to leave the military. Antecol and Cobb-Clark (2006); Rosen and Martin (1998); Sadler et al. (2000); and Sims, Drasgow, and Fitzgerald (2005) all reported that victims of military sexual victimization are more likely to have left the military early or express intentions to leave the military. Further, sexual harassment was found to reduce commitment to the military (Magley et al., 1999; Williams et al., 1999) and lead to poorer attitudes toward the organization (Pryor, 1995). These negative effects have also been found among military academy cadets and midshipman. Students who experienced sexual victimization at one of the military academies are more likely than nonvictims to consider leaving the military (DoD, 2012a; GAO, 1994) and less likely to have considered the military for a career (GAO). The DoD (2012a) also reported that student victimization has negative impacts on victims' academic performance.

In sum, a wide range of research studies have demonstrated that military sexual victimization, including both harassment and sexual assault, is associated with a variety of adverse consequences. These negative impacts affect the mental and physical health of victims and extend to both the victims' personal and professional lives. Given the seriousness and extent of these outcomes, programs focusing on reducing sexual victimization in the military could be critical for retaining military personnel and fostering their overall health and well-being.

Responses to Sexual Victimization in the Military

THE MILITARY JUDICIAL SYSTEM AND PUNISHMENT

One of the many responses the military has undertaken to combat sexual victimization is to use the military judicial system. In contrast to civilians, military personnel are subject to the Uniform Code of Military Justice (UCMJ). The UCMJ outlines the laws and regulations to which every military individual is held accountable. These regulations include incidents of sexual victimization. In other words, when an incident of sexual victimization in the military occurs, it is not processed through the civilian court system; it is instead handled by the military judicial system. Once an incident of sexual victimization is reported by an individual in the military, the commanding officer (CO) decides whether to move forward with the report and open an investigation or to dismiss the report. The large amount of discretion a CO has in forwarding a case has received much scrutiny. Critics argue that if the perpetrator is the CO, then the victim may feel he or she has few options for reporting and may abstain from the entire process (Nelson, 2002). Further, many victims may be concerned about the possible relationship between their CO and the perpetrator if they are from the same unit. Other victims express concern about being taken seriously by their CO and retaliation as the result of reporting (Bergman et al., 2002).

If the CO decides to move forward with the incident, it is then referred to the Military Criminal Investigation Organization (MCIO) where an investigation is opened and the incident is categorized by type of victimization (e.g., rape). Once the investigation is completed, the findings are presented to the CO, who has a number of options. These options consist of no action, some sort of administrative action, nonjudicial punishment, or court-martial (GAO, 2011). If the decision is to proceed, the incident is eligible for trial in a military court.

In 2012, 2,661 cases of sexual assault were eligible to be processed in the military judicial system (DoD, 2013b). Of these cases, close to 14% were dismissed due to the allegations being unfounded, and another 22% fell outside of the DoD legal jurisdiction. Of the remaining 1,714 cases that were eligible for court-martial, only 13% of defendants were convicted of their charges (133 cases were still awaiting disposition at the end of 2012). The low number of cases that proceed to successful prosecution is a major concern for victims and the effort to deter future sexual victimization. Lankford (2012) found that in 2009, only 5.4% of cases resulted in a court-martial during the same year the victimization was reported. While the number of cases that are successfully prosecuted has increased, it still remains relatively low.

Once an individual is convicted of sexual assault, several forms of punishment may be administered. Common punishments include confinement, reductions in rank, discharge/dismissal, fines, and extra duties. Individuals who are convicted of sexual assault often receive several different punishments. For example, of the individuals convicted in 2012, 74% received confinement, 76% received a reduction in rank, 66% received a fine, 56% were discharged, and 8% received extra duties (DoD, 2013b).

While considerable efforts have been made to increase punishments and accountability for sexual victimization, there are still many criticisms. First, the lengthy time to process cases may lead to victim/observer perceptions that the perpetrator is "getting away with it." Further, it may send the message that sexual victimization is not a serious concern of the military and may foster perceptions of tolerance (Pryor, La Vite, & Stoller, 1993). When asked about their perceptions of the military judicial process, many victims expressed frustration and dissatisfaction. In 2012, 48% of victims expressed dissatisfaction with the amount of information they were receiving about their case, and 34% stated they were dissatisfied with the process overall (DoD, 2013b).

The wide discretion given to a CO—including what charges to file, whether charges should be filed, jury selection, and nonjudicial forms of punishment—is also subject to much scrutiny. Several critics have suggested that the system be modified to reduce some of the discretion held by COs, with responsibility distributed to nonmilitary entities or other military individuals outside of the COs unit (Nelson, 2002). Defenders argue that the uniqueness of military life and the importance of discipline in the military make a "separate" and "special" system necessary (Hillman, 1999). However, it is this "uniqueness" of military culture that often adds complexity to addressing victimization.

Finally, another criticism often levied against the military judicial system is the use of the "good solider" defense. The most famous example of this defense is the case of Army Sergeant Major Gene McKinney. McKinney was accused of several counts of sexual misconduct and sexual harassment, which led to a military trial. During his trial, six women testified against him, each relating her own experiences (Hillman, 2009; Nelson, 2002). Aside from allowing testimony from victims, military trials also allow for individuals to testify on behalf of the accused. McKinney produced several individuals, including former superiors and subordinates, who testified to his good character (Hillman). The purpose of this defense was to convince the jury that individuals of very high rank would not have made it to their current position unless they are good people, implying that the military only advances individuals who have sound character (Nelson). In other words, individuals with "good character" do not commit actions such as sexual assault and harassment. Based heavily on testimony about McKinney's "good character," he was subsequently acquitted of all charges (Nelson). This case raises many concerns for victims and suggests that the power afforded by higher rank may undermine the successful prosecution of cases and discourage victims from pursuing judicial forms of punishment. Additionally, it sends a message that individuals who have long served in the military are immune from prosecution and punishment (Hillman). Finally, it discourages victims from reporting their experiences, a major issue faced by the military.

REPORTING IN THE MILITARY

Along with using the military judicial system, the military has also sought to "increase the climate of victim confidence associated with reporting" (DoD, 2013b, p. 28). While estimates vary across samples, evidence indicates that less than 20% of sexual victimization is reported through official channels. That is, approximately only 1 of every 5 victims reports his or her experiences (Culbertson & Rosenfeld, 1994; DoD, 2012a). Culbertson and Rosenfeld found that reporting sexual harassment victimization to the military is the least likely action taken by victims. They stated that no more than 25% of victims notify immediate supervisors of the incident and an even smaller number, less than 10%, file a formal grievance against the perpetrator. Low levels of reporting were also found among military cadets and midshipmen. According to the DoD (2012a), while some minor differences exist across the military academies, fewer than 20% of sexual assault and harassment victims report their victimization incidents to the military authority or organization. Further, when cadets and midshipmen were asked about their perceptions of sexual victimization reporting, the majority of students reported that they believed that a large extent of sexual victimization at the academy went unreported (DoD). These findings indicate that the majority of sexual victimization in the military is not being brought to the attention of the organization, and, in turn, they raise questions regarding why many victims choose to remain anonymous.

Many factors are taken into consideration when deciding whether to report a sexual victimization. Within the military domain, evidence suggests that these decisions are largely influenced by the victim's fear of reprisal or backlash from superiors and coworkers. For instance, Culbertson and Rosenfeld (1994) reported that approximately 40% of women in their sample would not report sexual harassment because they felt that doing so would make their work situation unpleasant, while about 30% of the women felt that the military chain of command would do nothing. Cadets and midshipmen at the military academy have expressed similar sentiments. For instance, Bastian, Lancaster, and Reyst (1996) reported that as many as 40% to 60% of female students would be hesitant to report sexual harassment out of fear of some type of reprisal. Further, females at the academy expressed concerns that the reporting of sexual harassment and assault would cause other students to gossip about them, shun them, or label them "crybabies" (Pershing, 2003; DoD, 2012b; GAO, 1994, 1995). Cadets and midshipmen also conveyed hesitation in reporting sexual victimization because of the view that they would receive no support from the military chain of command and that their supervisors would do nothing about the incident (Pershing; GAO, 1995). Unfortunately, there is evidence to demonstrate that these perceptions are based on reality in some cases. For instance, according to the DoD (2012a), a significant proportion of female victims from the academy who reported victimization experiences stated that the incident was either discounted or not taken seriously and that they suffered some form of retaliation.

Given the extent of the underreporting of sexual victimization in the military and the negative perceptions associated with reporting through official channels, in 2004 the DoD issued a mandate to develop a sexual assault policy that would provide victims with improved care and accountability (Friedman, 2005). This mandate resulted in the development of the SAPR program and the introduction of a two-pronged reporting system for victims. This system provides victims with the option to submit a victimization incident as either a restricted or unrestricted report. Under unrestricted reporting, the traditional reporting method, a victim reports sexual victimization through the military chain of command, which in turn initiates a formal investigation (DoD, 2012c). On the other hand, under restricted reporting, the new reporting method, victims can report the sexual victimization to a victim care or medical organization and remain anonymous.

Restricted reporting allows victims to gain access to treatment yet avoid prompting an official investigation (DoD). Restricted reporting moves beyond the old system by providing crucial assess to victim services that would have only been available in the past with the initiation of a formal report (Friedman). While there is concern that this restricted reporting system could allow perpetrators to go unpunished and thus put others at risk, since the implementation of this new policy, some evidence suggests that it is meeting its intended purpose through the increased reporting of sexual victimization and improved services for victims (Friedman; DoD).

Along with making changes in reporting options, the military has also undertaken several training efforts and attempts at organizational change with the hope of encouraging victims to report their experiences. However, it is important to recognize that the characteristics of the military culture and its organizational structure play a central role in shaping the occurrence of sexual victimization within the military as well as the ways in which victims choose to respond to the incidents. One characteristic that is particularly influential is a male-dominated culture in the military and military academies. This culture heavily promotes values such as masculinity, strength, dominance, and aggression, and it associates those who do not meet these criteria (i.e., women) with weakness. In addition to these core values, the military's male-dominated culture is perpetuated through the underrepresentation of female personnel in the military compared to their representation in the general population. For instance, while females comprise roughly half of the U.S. population, they constitute approximately 15% of active military personal and 10% of cadets and midshipman (Pershing, 2003; VA, 2012). Together these two factors create an environment in which women are often viewed as outsiders or as existing on the periphery. In turn, the sexual victimization of women is often discounted and marginalized, and any victim, regardless of sex, is often viewed as weak and nonmasculine.

Another cultural value related to the military that shapes the prevalence of sexual victimization and its reporting is the military's informal code of silence (Pershing, 2003). This culture prompts secrecy and loyalty to peers and, in turn, strongly discourages the reporting of any incidents through formal channels. The failure to maintain this code of silence has serious implications and can result in victims being ostracized, alienated, and potentially retaliated against (Pershing). Among military cadets and midshipmen, violation of this code has been found to greatly influence the likelihood to report victimization experiences. For instance, two of the most common reasons females in the academy identify for not reporting unwanted sexual contact and harassment are that they do not want people gossiping about them and they do not want anyone to know about the incident (DoD, 2012b).

An organizational characteristic that has been found to have an influence on the prevalence and reporting of sexual victimization concerns the power differentials that exist within the military. As a hierarchical system, the military chain of command is central to decision making and the execution of orders within the organization, yet it results in significant differentials of power across enlisted military personnel and ranking officers. Research has indicated that these differentials often have an adverse influence on sexual victimization. For instance, traditional reporting methods (i.e., unrestricted reporting) require that victims report incidents through the military chain of command. In cases where the perpetrator is a ranking officer, it is possible that nonranking victims perceive reporting sexual victimization as either futile or potentially harmful due to the perpetrator's position. Research from studies on military personnel and students support the idea that personnel often perceive their supervisors as having no interest in addressing sexual victimization incidents (Culbertson & Rosenfeld, 1994; DoD, 2012a).

Taken together, these three key factors greatly influence sexual victimization in the military and the cultivation of a culture that allows victimization both to occur and to remain hidden. Significant reductions in sexual victimization among this population will not be possible unless the military culture itself changes to value all members of the organization and recognize the need to break down both informal and formal barriers to reporting sexual victimization.

VICTIM SERVICES AND CARE

While many of the efforts made by the military to address the problem of sexual victimization have been heavily criticized, the military has outlined several positive steps. Specifically, two of the military's priorities are a focus on increasing victim care and building relationships outside of the military to improve knowledge and awareness. Other priorities mainly focus on providing these types of information and services. For example one major priority outlined by the military is to "improve sexual assault response" in terms of providing adequate services and care to victims (DoD, 2013b, p. 38). This priority provides several types of services to victims. Examples of these services include a helpline for victims, survivor summits, and collaborative training efforts. Responder training is also provided for individuals who investigate and handle sexual assault cases (DoD).

Another major priority identified by the military is "improving system account-ability" (DoD, 2013b, p. 49). This priority focuses on collecting data, reporting, and improving the types of information the military analyzes related to sexual victim-ization. In the past, it has been difficult to compare data across surveys due to little consistency in the types of victimization examined and definitions used (Turchik & Wilson, 2009). This priority hopes to establish a precedent for definitions used across data collection efforts.

Finally, a last priority highlighted by the military is "improving stakeholder knowledge and understanding of sexual assault prevention and response" (DoD, 2013b, p. 57). The goal of this priority is to reach out to community members and other organizations outside the military to seek out suggestions and collaborations that may improve strategies to combat sexual victimization. Taken collectively, these priorities can be seen as positive efforts to prevent and address sexual victim-ization, suggesting that despite much criticism of the military's response, the insti-tution has made some progress toward increasing accountability and providing better care for victims.

Conclusion

Sexual victimization in the U.S. military is a continuing problem. Recent estimates of the prevalence of sexual victimization suggest that men and women in the military experience sexual victimization at high rates. Victims may experience a wide range of mental and physical health effects as a result of their victimization, including PTSD, leaving the military, and depression. Several efforts undertaken to address this issue are training, encouraging reporting, and prosecuting perpetrators. However, research and official reports suggest that underreporting is very common and the majority of incidents are not successfully prosecuted through the military judicial system. These issues, coupled with the stigma associated with victimization and the large amount of discretion given to COs, suggest the need for further prevention efforts and a more detailed examination of the current process.

Discussion Questions

1. What percent of military sexual victimization is reported through official channels? Why do you think that this number has been historically low? What characteristics of the military culture may play a role in influencing the likelihood that victims will report their experiences officially? What could the U.S. military do to increase the official reporting of sexual assaults and harassment?

2. Identify some of the consequences of military sexual victimization on the mental/emotional health, physical health, and personal/professional lives of victims. How does the SAPR program's two-pronged reporting system address these negative outcomes? What could administrators in the military and the military academies do to provide better service to victims? Is the U.S. military adequately addressing victims' needs?

3. Discuss the advantages and disadvantages of the military judicial process. Do you think the military judicial system should more closely mirror the civilian judicial system? Why or why not? Should more changes to the military judicial process be made?

4. The U.S. military has proposed several priorities or strategies aimed at combating the problem of sexual victimization. Which of these priorities or strategies do you think will be most effective? Why? Which strategies you do think will be least effective? Why? Are there other strategies or priorities the military should be focusing on in terms of combating sexual victimization?

References

Antecol, H., & Cobb-Clark, D. (2006). The sexual harassment of female active-duty personnel: Effects of job satisfaction and intentions to remain in the military. *Journal of Economic Behavior & Organization, 61*(1), 55–80.

Bastian, L. D., Lancaster, A. R., & Reyst, H. E. (1996). *Department of Defense: 1995 Sexual Harassment Survey.* Arlington, VA: Defense Manpower Data Center.

Bergman, M. E., Langhout, R. D., Palmieri, P. A., Cortina, L. M., & Fitzgerald, L. F. (2002). The (un)reasonableness of reporting: Antecedents and consequences of reporting sexual harassment. *Journal of Applied Psychology, 87*(2), 230–242.

Brubaker, S. J. (2009). Sexual assault prevalence, reporting and polices: Comparing college and university campuses and military service academies. *Security Journal, 22*(1), 56–72.

Buchanan, N. T., Settles, I. H., & Woods, K. C. (2008). Comparing sexual harassment subtypes among black and white women by military rank: Double jeopardy, the jezebel, and the cult of true womanhood. *Psychology of Women Quarterly, 32*(4), 347–361.

Chang, B., Skinner, K. M., & Boehmer, U. (2001). Religion and mental health among women veterans with sexual assault experience. *International Journal of Psychiatry in Medicine, 31*(1), 77–95.

Culbertson, A. L., & Rosenfeld, P. (1994). Assessment of sexual harassment in the active-duty Navy. *Military Psychology, 6*(2), 69–93.

Fisher, B. S., Cullen, F. T., & Turner, M. G. (2000). *The sexual victimization of college women.* Washington, DC: U.S. Department of Justice, National Institute of Justice.

Fitzgerald, L. F., Drasgow, F., & Magley, V. J. (1999). Sexual harassment in the armed forces: A test of an integrated model. *Military Psychology, 11*(3), 329–343.

Frayne, S. M., Skinner, K. M., Sullivan, L. M., & Freund, K. M. (2003). Sexual assault while in the military: Violence as a predictor of cardiac risk? *Violence and Victims, 18*(2), 219–225.

Frayne, S. M., Skinner, K. M., Sullivan, L. M., Tripp, T. J., Hankin, C. S., Kressin, N. R., & Miller, D. R. (1999). Medical profile of women Veterans Administration outpatients who report a history of sexual assault occurring while in the military. *Journal of Women's Health & Gender-Based Medicine, 8*(6), 835–845.

Friedman, J. (2005). Reporting sexual assault of women in the military. *Cardozo Journal of Law & Gender, 14*, 375–399.

Gradus, J. L., Street, A. E., Kelly, K., & Stafford, J. (2008). Sexual harassment experiences and harmful alcohol use in a military sample: Differences in gender and the mediating role in depression. *Journal of Studies on Alcohol and Drugs, 69*(3), 348–351.

Hankin, C. S., Skinner, K. M., Sullivan, L. M., Miller, D. R., Frayne, S., & Tripp, T. J. (1999). Prevalence of depressive and alcohol abuse symptoms among women VA outpatients who report experiencing sexual assault while in the military. *Journal of Traumatic Stress, 12*(4), 601–612.

Harned, M. S., Ormerod, A. J., Palmieri, P. A., Collinsworth, L. L., & Reed, M. (2002). Sexual assault and other types of sexual harassment by workplace personnel: A comparison of antecedents and consequences. *Journal of Occupational Health Psychology, 7*(2), 174–188.

Hillman, E. L. (1999). The "good soldier" defense: Character evidence and military rank at courts-martial. *The Yale Law Journal, 108*(4), 879–911.

Hillman, E. L. (2009). Front and center: Sexual violence in U.S. military law. *Politics and Society, 37*(1), 101–129.

Kang, H., Dalager, N., Mahan, C., and Ishii, E. (2005). The role of sexual assault on the risk of PTSD among Gulf War veterans. *Annals of Epidemiology, 15*(3), 191–195.

Kilpatrick, D. G., Edmunds, C. N., & Seymour, A. K. (1992). *Rape in America: A report to the nation.* Arlington, VA: National Victim Center.

Kimerling, R., Street, A. E., Pavao, J., Smith, M. W., Cronkite, C., Holmes, T. H., & Frayne, S. M. (2010). Military-related sexual trauma among Veterans Health Administration patients returning from Afghanistan and Iraq. *American Journal of Public Health, 100*(8), 1409–1412.

Lankford, A. (2012). An analysis of sexual assault in the U.S. military, 2004–2009. *Journal of Military and Strategic Studies, 14*(2), 1–21.

Luterek, J. A., Bittinger, J. N., & Simpson, T. L. (2011). Posttraumatic sequelae associated with military sexual trauma in female veterans enrolled in VA outpatient mental health clinics. *Journal of Trauma & Dissociation, 12*(3), 261–274.

Magley, V. J., Waldo, C. R., Drasgow, F., & Fitzgerald, L. F. (1999). The impact of sexual harassment on military personnel: Is it the same for men and women? *Military Psychology, 11*(3), 283–302.

Maguen, S., Cohen, B., Ren, L., Bosch, J., Kimerling, R., & Seal, K. (2012). Gender differences in military sexual trauma and mental health diagnoses and Iraq and Afghanistan veterans with posttraumatic stress disorder. *Women's Health Issues, 22*(1), 61–66.

McCall-Hosenfeld, J. S., Liebschutz, J. M., Spiro, A., & Seaver, M. R. (2009). Sexual assault in the military and its impact on sexual satisfaction in women veterans: A proposed model. *Journal of Women's Health, 18*(6), 901–909.

Murdoch, M., Pryor, J. B., Polusny, M. A., & Gackstetter, G. D. (2007). Functioning and psychiatric symptoms among military men and women exposed to sexual stressors. *Military Medicine, 172,* 718–725.

Nelson, T. S. (2002). *For the love of country: Confronting rape and sexual harassment in the U.S. military.* Binghamton, NY: Haworth Press.

Pershing, J. L. (2003). Why women don't report sexual harassment: A case study of an elite military institution. *Gender Issues, 21*(4), 3–30.

Pryor, J. B. (1995). The psychosocial impact of sexual harassment on women in the U.S. military. *Basic and Applied Social Psychology, 17*(4), 581–603.

Pryor, J. B., La Vite, C. M., & Stoller, L. M. (1993). A social psychological analysis of sexual harassment: The person/situation interaction. *Journal of Vocational Behavior, 42,* 68–83.

Rosen, L. N., & Martin, L. (1998). Incidence and perceptions of sexual harassment among male and female U.S. Army soldiers. *Military Psychology, 10*(4), 239–257.

Sadler, A. G., Booth, B. M., Nielson, D., & Doebbeling, B. N. (2000). Health-related consequences of physical and sexual violence: Women in the military. *Obstetrics & Gynecology, 96*(3), 473–480.

Settles, I. H., Buchanan, N. T., & Colar, B. K. (2012). The impact of race and rank on the sexual harassment of black and white men in the U.S. military. *Psychology of Men & Masculinity, 13*(3), 256–263.

Sims, C. S., Drasgow, F., & Fitzgerald, L. F. (2005). The effects of sexual harassment on turnover in the military: Time-dependent modeling. *Journal of Applied Psychology, 90*(6), 1141–1152.

Skinner, K. M., Kressin, N., Frayne, S., Tripp, T. J., Hankin, C. S., Miller, D. R., & Sullvian, L. M. (2000). The prevalence of military sexual assault among female Veterans' Administration outpatients. *Journal of Interpersonal Violence, 15*(3), 291–310.

Smith, B. N., Shipherd, J. C., Schuster, J. L., Vogt, D. S., King, L. A., & King, D. W. (2011). Posttraumatic stress symptomatology as a mediator of the association between military sexual trauma and post-deployment physical health in women. *Journal of Trauma & Dissociation, 12*(3), 275–289.

Snyder, J. A., Fisher, B. S., Scherer, H. L., & Daigle, L. E. (2012). Unsafe in the camouflage tower: Sexual victimization and perceptions of military academy leadership. *Journal of Interpersonal Violence, 27*(16), 3171–3194.

Strauss, J. L., Marz, C. E., Weitlauf, J. C., Stechuchak, K. M., & Straits-Tröster, K. (2011). Is military sexual trauma associated with trading sex among women veterans seeking outpatient mental health care? *Journal of Trauma & Dissociation, 12*(3), 290–304.

Street, A. E., Gradus, J. L., Stafford, J., & Kelly, K. (2007). Gender differences in experiences of sexual harassment: Data from a male-dominated environment. *Journal of Consulting and Clinical Psychology, 75*(3), 464–474.

Street, A. E., Stafford, J., Mahan, C. M., & Hendricks, A. (2008). Sexual harassment and assault experienced by reservists during military service: Prevalence and health correlates. *Journal of Rehabilitation Research & Development, 45*(3), 409–420.

Suris, A., Lind, L., Kashner, T. M., & Borman, P. D. (2007). Mental health, quality of life, and health functioning in women veterans: Differential outcomes associated with military and civilian sexual assault. *Journal of Interpersonal Violence, 22*(2), 179–197.

Tjaden, P., & Thoennes, N. (2006). *Extent, nature, and consequences of rape victimization: Findings from the national violence against women survey.* Washington, DC: National Institute of Justice.

Turchik, J. A., & Wilson, S. M. (2009). Sexual assault in the U.S. military: A review of the literature and recommendations for the future. *Aggression and Violent Behavior, 15,* 267–277.

U.S. Department of Defense (DoD). (2012a). *2012 service academy gender relations survey.* Washington, DC: Office of the Secretary of Defense, Sexual Assault and Prevention Response Office.

U.S. Department of Defense (DoD). (2012b). *Annual report on sexual harassment and violence at the military service academies: Academic program year 2011–2012.* Washington, DC: Office of the Secretary of Defense, Sexual Assault and Prevention Response Office.

U.S. Department of Defense (DoD). (2012c). *Department of Defense annual report on sexual assault in the military: Fiscal year 2011.* Washington, DC: Office of the Secretary of Defense, Sexual Assault and Prevention Response Office.

U.S. Department of Defense (DoD). (2013a). *2011 health related behaviors survey of active duty military personnel.* Washington, DC: Department of Defense, Lifestyle Assessment Program.

U.S. Department of Defense (DoD). (2013b). *Department of Defense annual report on sexual assault in the military: Fiscal year 2012.* Washington, DC: Office of the Secretary of Defense, Sexual Assault and Prevention Response Office. Retrieved from http://www.sapr.mil/public/docs/reports/FY12_DoD_SAPRO_Annual_Report_on_Sexual_Assault-VOLUME_ONE.pdf

U.S. Department of Veterans Affairs (VA). (2012). *Strategies for servicing our women veterans.* Washington, DC: U.S. Department of Veterans Affairs.

U.S. General Accounting Office (GAO). (1994). *DoD service academies: More action needed to eliminate sexual harassment.* Washington, DC: U.S. General Accounting Office.

U.S. General Accounting Office (GAO). (1995). *DoD service academies: An update on extent of sexual harassment.* Washington, DC: U.S. General Accounting Office.

U.S. General Accounting Office (GAO). (2011). *Military justice: Oversight and better collaboration needed for sexual assault investigations and adjudications.* Washington, DC: U.S. General Accounting Office.

Williams, J. H., Fitzgerald, L. F., & Drasgow, F. (1999). The effects of organizational practices on sexual harassment and individual outcomes in the military. *Military Psychology, 11*(3), 303–328.

Wolfe, J., Sharkansky, E. J., Read, J. P., Dawson, R., Martin, J. A., & Ouimette, P. C. (1998). Sexual harassment and assault as predictors of PTSD symptomatology among U.S. female Persian Gulf War military personnel. *Journal of Interpersonal Violence, 13*(1), 40–57.

Yaeger, D., Himmelfarb, N., Cammack, A., & Mintz, J. (2006). DSM-IV diagnosed posttraumatic stress disorder in women veterans with and without military sexual trauma. *Journal of General International Medicine, 21*(S3), S65–S69.

Zinzow, H. M., Grubaugh, A. L., Frueh, B. C., & Magruder, K. M. (2008). Sexual assault, mental health, and service use among male and female veterans seen in Veterans Affairs primary care clinics: A multi-site study. *Psychiatry Research, 159*(1–2), 226–236.

12

Sexual Victimization and the Disputed Victim

Joan A. Reid

Deep schisms and sharp debates surround sexual victimization of individuals connected to the legal or illegal commercial sex industry. The commercial sex industry, built upon the buying and selling of sexual activity, is fiercely disputed as either benignly beneficial or expansively exploitive. This chapter focuses on several types of individuals involved in the commercial sex industry, giving greatest attention to those engaging in prostitution—a key form of commercial sexual activity. First, the chapter highlights the shifting depiction of prostituted minors who are U.S. citizens or legal permanent residents, from juvenile delinquents routinely arrested and adjudicated on prostitution charges to domestic minor sex-trafficking victims legally guaranteed protection from prosecution. Next, the chapter reviews the central arguments in the scholarly discourse regarding prostitution of adults and the difficulties encountered in disentangling forced from nonforced prostitution. Lastly, the chapter examines the tenuous status of illegal immigrants in the United States as well as vulnerable populations along the U.S.–Mexican border, emphasizing the perilous circumstances commonly affecting child and adult international sex-trafficking victims.

Child Prostitute Versus Domestic Minor Sex-Trafficking Victim

DISPARATE LABELING AND MISIDENTIFICATION: VICTIM VERSUS DELINQUENT

Over the past decade, contradictory labels have been applied to minors illegally exploited in prostitution, from child/juvenile/teen prostitute or sex worker to

211

domestic minor sex-trafficking victim (Annitto, 2011; Mitchell, Finkelhor, & Wolak, 2010; Reid, 2010). The more contemporary term, *domestic minor sex trafficking*, is commonly used interchangeably with *commercial sexual exploitation of children* by U.S. advocates and policy makers, based on recent federal legislation (Annitto). These two terms are also used interchangeably in this chapter.

In an informative study using language analysis, researchers examined and described the subtle influence of inaccurate labeling of sexually exploited minors by the media (Goddard, De Bortoli, Saunders, & Tucci, 2005). Positioning labels commonly used to describe sexually exploited minors on a continuum, Goddard et al. reported that

> as "child prostitution" inherits the adult prostitution discourse, it moves along the continuum and away from the concepts of child sexual abuse and victimization. The child is constructed as an accomplice to his or her own sexual abuse, the effect of which is a redefinition of the offence and the offender. (p. 286)

The label *child prostitute* omits and obscures the exploitive roles of the buyers of sex and sex traffickers. Such inaccurate "textual abuse" by the media results in collective societal exploitation of child victims through the minimization of their victimization and the denial of the crimes committed against them (Goddard et al.). Similarly, the *Trafficking in Persons Report 2008* strongly advised against the continued use of inaccurate labels that had previously been assigned to child victims of commercial of sexual exploitation, contending that "terms such as 'child sex worker' are unacceptable because they falsely sanitize the brutality of this exploitation" (U.S. Department of State [DOS], 2008, p. 24). In sum, inaccurate labeling seriously obscures the exploitation experienced by minors illegally used in the commercial sex industry, thereby decreasing the likelihood of any public outcry for child protection, intervention, and justice.

Even more tragically, disparity in labeling results in the commercial exploitation of children being treated as a public nuisance crime and minors being arrested for prostitution rather than being treated as victims of commercial sexual exploitation or sex trafficking (Adelson, 2008; Halter, 2010; Mitchell et al., 2010; Reid & Jones, 2011; DOS, 2011). A national survey of local law enforcement found that 40% of minors picked up for involvement in prostitution were treated as juvenile delinquents and 60% were treated as victims (Halter). The misidentification of victims as juvenile prostitutes severely impedes the criminal investigation of sex trafficking, the successful prosecution of traffickers, and victim restoration (U.S. General Accounting Office [GAO], 2007; Reid, 2013).

Some argue that detention of these minors protects them from sex traffickers and gives law enforcement personnel the leverage needed to pressure minors into assisting with the investigation and prosecution of sex traffickers (Annitto, 2011). However, federal investigations of human trafficking have shown that taking a victim-centered approach results in a greater likelihood of victims choosing to cooperate with prosecutions (Adams, Owens, & Small, 2010; Annitto; Farrell et al., 2012; Reid, 2013; GAO, 2007). Sex traffickers typically lie to vulnerable and previously maltreated minors, convincing them that the traffickers alone are trustworthy. Arresting exploited minors reinforces these lies and further deepens the victims' mistrust of authority. Moreover, victims of domestic minor sex trafficking who are erroneously identified or mislabeled as juvenile delinquents do not have access to the best treatment available for victims of crime in their communities (Reid, 2010) and are often placed in juvenile detentions centers that do not provide adequate services or appropriate shelter for these highly victimized and vulnerable youth (Annitto).

MYTHS AND MISCONCEPTIONS: SEXUAL EXPLOITATION VERSUS SEX WORK

Within the United States, minors exploited in prostitution are commonly assimilated into the adult commercial sex industry (Estes & Weiner, 2005; Kreston, 2000). Minors exploited in prostitution are not commodified and sold in response to a unique market demand created by pedophiles who specifically seek to buy sex with minors. On the contrary, most of those who buy sex with minors are opportunistic offenders who also buy sex with adults (Estes & Weiner; Kreston). Sex traffickers may choose to exploit younger victims due to the ease of manipulating and controlling minors in comparison to adults (Brayley, Cockbain, & Laycock, 2011; Reid & Jones, 2011) or because they can accrue greater profit margins when exploiting minor victims because many buyers of sex are willing to pay more for sex with younger victims (Reid, 2013). Nevertheless, in general, minors exploited in prostitution are integrated with adults and are exploited by sex traffickers who also sell sex with adults.

Due to this integration, widely propagated and commonly accepted beliefs regarding prostitution are erroneously applied to minors by sex traffickers and buyers of sex, justifying the sexual exploitation of minors (Kreston, 2000). Due to these widely held myths, minors exploited in prostitution are among the most overlooked and underserved child sex crime victims (Annitto, 2011; Estes & Weiner, 2005; Kreston). As a result, the tragedy of domestic minor sex trafficking victims remains virtually invisible within a society reluctant to relinquish myths regarding prostitution, even if it involves minors (Kreston; Whitehead, 2008).

In 2000, Kreston detailed the commonly held myths and misconceptions that have been effectively propagated by those who profit from the commercial sexual exploitation of minors:

1. Prostitution, even when involving minors, is a victimless crime and, therefore, no harm comes from it.

2. Minors freely choose prostitution, and they retain power and control in the situation.

3. Prostitution is a glamorous and exciting life that offers wealth or at least employment to the prostituted child.

Kreston argued that until these myths and misconceptions are successfully refuted, minors will continue to be victimized by the illegal commercial sex industry, and their plight will be ignored by society.

Since Kreston (2000) enumerated these myths regarding the commercial sexual exploitation of minors, scholarly research has provided evidence that challenges these popular myths and misconceptions. First, in response to the misconception that commercial sexual exploitation is a victimless crime and no harm is done, researchers, clinicians, and social service providers have repeatedly documented pervasive and lasting consequences suffered by minors as a result of being sexually exploited in prostitution, highlighting physical injuries, psychological harm, and social impairments (for review, see Reid, 2012). Frequently observed physical or medical problems include sexually transmissible infections, unwanted and high-risk teen pregnancies, physical injuries resulting from beatings and rapes, mal-nourishment, and drug-related difficulties. Documented psychological damage covers an extensive list of severe mental health disorders, such as depression, anxi-ety, dissociative disorders, substance abuse, suicidal ideations and gestures, and posttraumatic stress disorder (PTSD). In addition, low self-esteem, guilt, and shame are often mentioned as lasting emotional consequences. Common social consequences associated with commercial sexual exploitation are interpersonal relationship problems, behavioral problems, poor life skills, lack of education, and long-term marginalization. These extensively documented consequences compel-lingly contest the misconception that the commercial sexual exploitation or sex trafficking of minors is a victimless crime and minors are not harmed.

Countering the misconception that minors freely choose prostitution, findings from developmental and neurobiological research indicate that, due to biological and psychological immaturity, minors are highly impressionable and easily manip-ulated and they inherently have a propensity to make poor, short-sighted decisions (Gardner & Steinberg, 2005; Steinberg & Scott, 2003). As a result, minors are treated differently than adults and are legally protected as a particularly vulnerable population. Certain feminists have warned that casting doubt on the ability of minors to choose prostitution may be construed as an attack on their capability to make choices involving reproductive health (Annitto, 2011). These concerns are unfounded, as varying levels of legal protection have traditionally been afforded to minors to protect them from all types of exploitation. A myriad of federal and state statutes provide minors with special legal protection from physical, psychological, and financial harm (Reid & Jones, 2011). These protections include statutory rape laws and regulations prohibiting minors' involvement in commercial sexual activ-ity (for reviews, see Reid & Jones, 2011; Shared Hope International, 2011).

Furthermore, researchers have found that the majority of minors exploited in prostitution are among the most vulnerable of youth with histories marred by extensive physical and sexual abuse as well as neglect and abandonment (Estes & Weiner, 2005; Reid, 2012). Sex traffickers often prey on vulnerable youth and are skilled at manipulating maltreated youth by promising to rescue them and provide them with a better life (Albanese, 2007; Annitto, 2011; Hanna, 2002). Gang members have coined a term for this manipulative recruitment technique, *love bombing*

(Dorias & Corriveau, 2009). Gang members purposefully use promises of love and a better life to seduce young girls and then persuade these vulnerable youth to earn money for the gang via prostitution (Dorias & Corriveau). Annitto quoted a convicted sex trafficker as stating, "With young girls, you promise them heaven, and they'll follow you to hell" (p. 14). This comment was evidently lifted from a musical that glamourized the pimp lifestyle, its lyrics bragging: "Weave your magic spell. Promise her a piece of heaven. And, she'll follow you to hell" (Coleman, 1996, track 7).

Once they have become dependent on a sex trafficker, minors are often further manipulated through romantic gestures while being systematically terrorized into conformity (Brayley et al., 2011; Kennedy, Klein, Bristowe, Cooper, & Yuille, 2007; Raphael, Reichert, & Powers, 2010; Spidel et al., 2006). Intermittent positive attention combined with violence and degradation produces intense loyalty, almost worshipful fear, and trauma bonding (commonly referred to as Stockholm syndrome; Reid, Haskell, Dillihunt-Aspilliga, & Thor, 2013). In this way, sex traffickers create what appears to the untrained eye to be a willing victim (Herman, 1992). These colluding dynamics—the cardinal features of adolescence, namely malleability and immaturity; a childhood filled with abuse and abandonment; and the deceitfulness and manipulation of sex traffickers—cast doubt on the ability of any minor to "freely choose" prostitution or maintain power and control in the situation.

Another argument typically made by those who claim that minors freely choose prostitution is that minors say they do so. Many minors take full responsibility for their involvement in prostitution by projecting a tough-girl or boy persona and denying that they were, are, or ever will be victims. Child victims of sex trafficking are commonly confused about their culpability in the crime being committed against them and fail to recognize that they are being exploited (Kennedy et al., 2007; Reid, 2010). Kennedy et al. detailed such a response by a young woman who assumed responsibility for her initiation into street prostitution although this had occurred when she was only 10 years old. She stated, "I turned myself out. It was just me. It was me. I'm responsible" (p. 15). Kennedy et al. noted the implausibility of the absence of external forces influencing this young woman when she was a girl—fortunately, "many 10-year-olds do not know that street prostitution exists" (p. 15). The assumption of personal responsibility by child sex-trafficking victims parallels a typical response of children who have been sexually abused. Long after the abuse has ended and even into adulthood, many survivors of childhood sexual abuse maintain that they were responsible for the abuse rather than assigning blame on the adult abuser (Jülich, 2005). Theorized by Summit (1983), the child sexual abuse accommodation syndrome explains this false assumption of responsibility by child victims as an attempt to rectify feelings of moral badness cultivated by the manipulation of the molester. Spidel et al. (2006) noted that sex traffickers/pimps "are also likely to deny the sexual nature of their offense, and transfer responsibility" to the victims (p. 197). Consequently, the child victim subscribes to a complete reversal of adult and child responsibility. The child creates and believes in a self-contrived reconstruction of reality, in which the abuser is good and they are bad, thereby attaining a fabricated sense of control over the abuse (Summit, 1983).

Countering the last of the misconceptions, that prostitution is a glamorous and exciting life offering wealth to the prostituted child, researchers consistently report that minors rarely keep any of the money earned from buyers of sex (Kennedy et al., 2007; Nixon, Tutty, Downe, Gorkoff, & Ursel, 2002; Raphael et al., 2010; Williamson & Cluse-Tolar, 2002) . In sharp contrast to this myth, studies show that sex traffickers create financial indebtedness via drug dependence (either from a preexisting condition or from drug addiction facilitated by the trafficker), by demanding reimbursement for primping the minors for prostitution (i.e., buying lingerie, manicures, hairstyling), or through other cunning bait-and-switch cons (Kennedy et al.; Raphael et al. 2010; Reid, 2010). Subsequently, sex traffickers use the fraudulently created financial indebtedness to threaten and coerce involvement in prostitution as the only way for minors to pay off their "debt." Based on these findings, rather than creating wealth for minors, sex traffickers commonly entrap minors in prostitution via trickery and debt bondage.

SHIFTS IN CRIMINAL JUSTICE RESPONSE

Although significant statutory and attitudinal shifts have occurred based on U.S. federal legislation, the debate about whether U.S. minors involved in prostitution are victims of sex trafficking or juvenile delinquents continues to smolder within the criminal justice system (Adams et al., 2010; DOS, 2011). The changing legal response to minors involved in prostitution can best be understood by first reviewing the treatment of this crime against children within the international, federal, and local contexts.

Child Sex Trafficking and International Law

Child sex trafficking is classified within the general crime category of trafficking in persons or human trafficking. First and foremost considered an acute human rights issue, human trafficking deprives thousands of men, women, and children of their fundamental rights to human dignity and personal freedoms (Farrell & Fahy, 2009; Gallagher, 2010; Kelly, 2005; Lehti & Aromaa, 2007; Wheaton, Schauer, & Galli, 2010). Human trafficking occurs in many industries. Men, women, and children can be exploited in domestic servitude, in service industries such as tourism and health care, in migrant farmwork or construction, in the drug trade, in mail-order bride ruses, in a diamond mine, or in a warlord's army (Graycar & McCusker, 2007; DOS, 2008, 2011). While there may be variation in form and location, at the core, human trafficking is profit-driven exploitation through the use force, fraud, or coercion (Bales, 2007). Frequently, victims are fraudulently promised one job and eventually forced or coerced into another, or they are significantly deceived about the working conditions (Goździak & Collett, 2005; Kim, 2007; Shelley, 2010). Among international human rights advocates, sex trafficking of children is considered an especially inexcusable form of human trafficking due to children's inherent physical and psychological vulnerabilities (International Labour Organization [ILO], n.d., 2005).

Despite widespread concern and concerted efforts of the international community to end child sex trafficking, in some underdeveloped countries, the lives of children are sacrificed for short-term economic benefit because the prostitution of children contributes significantly to gross national product (Farr, 2005; Leth, 2005). Beyond violating human rights of thousands of children, sex trafficking fosters corruption and violence by generating enormous financial profits for organized crime (Farr; Wheaton et al., 2010). Child sex trafficking also contributes to the transmission of disease, creating overwhelming health costs to local communities, and ultimately sustains poverty by hindering economic and social development (Acharya, 2010; Agrusa, 2003; Hynes & Raymond, 2002; Leung, 2003; Silverman et al., 2006, 2007). In sum, child sex trafficking is a problem with many dimensions and deep social impacts that extend far beyond the lives of its child victims (Shelley, 2010; Shlyk, 2007).

Considered one of the most successful international conventions in terms of quick and prevalent ratification, The Worst Forms of Child Labour Convention (No. 182) was adopted in 1999 and has been ratified by 177 of 185 member countries of the International Labour Organization, including the United States. Each member country that ratified this convention agreed to take immediate and effective measures to prohibit and eliminate the worst forms of child labor, including using, procuring, or offering a child for prostitution or pornography. This international convention defines a child as any individual under the age of 18, and this definition of a child is considered binding regardless of existing national legislation. In other words, even if a country has legalized prostitution, it must prohibit and strive to eliminate the use of any individual under the age of 18 years old in commercial sexual activity (ILO, n.d.).

Federal Response to Child Sex Trafficking

Aligning with the international movement to combat human trafficking, the Trafficking Victims Protection Act (TVPA) was passed in 2000 by the U.S. Congress. This groundbreaking federal legislation defines all minors under the age of 18, both U.S. citizens and foreign nationals, engaged in any type of commercial sex activity as victims of a severe form of human trafficking (TVPA, 2000). Commercial sexual activity is defined by the TVPA as profiting in any way from prostitution, pornography, nude dancing, or live sex shows. More specifically, the profit gained from sexual activity can take the form of payment or settlement in money, services, products, or "anything of value" (TVPA, Sec. 103[3]). The TVPA provides protection from prosecution for trafficking victims even if victims are entangled in illegal activities, stating that "victims . . . of trafficking should not be inappropriately incarcerated, fined, or otherwise penalized solely for unlawful acts committed as a direct result of being trafficked" (TPVA, Sec. 102).

Sex trafficking of minors is a major emphasis of the TVPA. While the main objective of the TVPA of 2000 was to protect international victims trafficked into the United States, it was not intended to exclude the protection of victims who are U.S. citizens or legal permanent residents (Adelson, 2008). Due to the conventional meaning of the term *trafficking*, one widespread misconception is that human trafficking always involves the clandestine movement of individuals across international borders (Logan, Walker, & Hunt, 2009). In reality, many victims exploited in sex trafficking are not trafficked into or out of foreign countries but rather are trafficked domestically within their home country (Acharya, 2009, 2010; Brayley et al., 2011; Reid, 2012). Vulnerable and exploited individuals are not only trafficked from war-ravished or impoverished countries; within the United States there also exists an ample quantity of vulnerable individuals susceptible to exploitation by sex traffickers (Shelley, 2010). U.S. legislators recognized that sex trafficking may occur internationally or domestically, and in legislative deliberations, they noted that the TVPA could "make a difference for many American girls, mostly runaways, who are then victimized by traffickers" (statement by Rep. Smith, quoted in Adelson, p. 101).

Minors are not required to show that "force, fraud, or coercion" was involved in their entrapment in sex trafficking (TVPA, 2000, Sec. 103). Similar to statutory rape laws, which obviate the need to prove coercion, the TVPA provides protection for minors who become involved in prostitution without being coerced or forced. This enhanced protection was intended to assist U.S. minors who become involved in prostitution due to disadvantaged circumstances or abandonment (Adelson, 2008; DOS, 2011).

State and Local Criminal Justice Response to Domestic Minor Sex Trafficking

Criminal justice professionals treat U.S. minors involved in prostitution in very incongruent ways, with responses fluctuating from arresting minors as prostitutes to providing prosecutorial protection to them as domestic minor sex-trafficking victims (Adams et al., 2010; Adelson, 2008; Halter, 2010; Mitchell et al., 2010). Adding to the controversy and confusion, states generally consider sexual acts with a person under the age of consent, which varies by state, as statutory rape or lewd and lascivious battery regardless of whether the act was consensual. Yet minors arrested for prostitution are being criminalized despite the fact that they are often legally too young to consent to sexual activity (Annitto, 2011; Reid & Jones, 2011).

According to the previously mentioned national survey of local law enforcement, U.S. minors picked up due to involvement in prostitution who cooperated with law enforcement by identifying sex traffickers and who did not have a prior record were more likely to be treated as victims, while other youth were more likely to be treated as delinquents (Halter, 2010). This study highlights the need for clearer state legislation regarding domestic minor sex trafficking. According to the TVPA, if a victim is under the age of 18 years old, cooperation with law enforcement is not a prerequisite for receiving victim status and protection. According to U.S. Citizenship and Immigration Services (ICE),

> if under the age of 18 at the time of the victimization, or if you are unable to cooperate with a law enforcement request due to physical or psychological

trauma, you may qualify for the T nonimmigrant visa without having to assist in investigation or prosecution. (ICE, 2010, "How Do You Become Eligible")

In a parallel legislative development, "safe harbor" laws have been passed in several states, including Florida, Illinois, Massachusetts, Minnesota, New York, Ohio, Vermont, and Washington (Shared Hope International, 2011). These acts encourage nonpunitive, protective processes that appropriately identify sexually exploited youth as victims of sex trafficking and oversee the provision of social services and safe shelter instead of the traditional punitive juvenile justice response (Shared Hope International). However, not all of the safe harbor laws are consistent with the federal TVPA. For example, the Safe Harbor Act passed in New York allows a minor involved in prostitution to avoid adjudication on prostitution charges and receive crime victim services only if the victim aids in the prosecution of the sex trafficker (Reid & Jones, 2011; Shared Hope International). As noted earlier, this requirement is not consistent with the provisions of the TVPA (2000), which exempts minors from this requirement and allows minors to receive victim status and all the associated benefits regardless of whether or not they assist law enforcement.

As evidenced by this brief review of state statutes and inconsistent treatment of minors exploited in prostitution, there exists a critical disconnect between state and federal laws. While the federal statutes and initiatives specify that all individuals under the age of 18 who become involved in prostitution are vulnerable victims of a severe form of sex trafficking, state and local systems continue to identify and treat many of them as juvenile delinquents (Albanese, 2007; Annitto, 2011; Halter, 2010; Reid & Jones, 2011).

Prostitution and Sex Trafficking of Adults

Perhaps no issue has been as passionately debated by feminist scholars as arguments regarding prostitution and forced prostitution, which is also referred to as sex trafficking. Briefly stated, some see prostitution as a manifestation of objectification, sexual exploitation, and subjugation regardless of whether prostitution is a product of force and intimidation, the absence of alternative methods to earn financial support, or other disadvantaged circumstances. Others endorse prostitution as a benign form of wage labor that may even be an expression of empowerment and freedom, with the criminalization of prostitution considered one more way in which patriarchal societies preserve power and control.

CRIMINALIZATION VERSUS LEGALIZATION OF PROSTITUTION

Four positions on the legalization of prostitution emerge from these two opposing, underlying assumptions regarding prostitution: (a) the *complete criminalization* position, in which all aspects of sex work are criminalized so that all involved—prostitutes or sellers of sex, buyers of sex, and third parties such as pimps/traffickers or brothel keepers—can be prosecuted and punished; (b) the *abolitionist or partial decriminalization* position, in which the activities of prostitutes or sellers of sex alone are decriminalized but the activities of all others are criminalized; (c) the *complete decriminalization* schema, which envisions the repeal of any specific criminalization of activities related to the commercial sex industry; and (d) the *legalization* position, which involves total decriminalization plus the creation of supplemental legislation regulating aspects of the commercial sex industry such as zoning and licensing statutes. For an overview of theoretical positions, relevant research, and supporting arguments, see Farley (2003, 2004); Halley, Kotiswaran, Thomas, and Shamir (2006); Jeffreys (2009); and Weitzer (2009).

Across the United States, *complete criminalization of prostitution* has historically been the most prominently supported legal position. Currently, prostitution is illegal except within eight rural counties of Nevada. These rural areas exclude all of the state's major metropolitan areas (Las Vegas, Reno, and Carson City). Reflecting the *legalization of prostitution* position, prostitution is only legal within approximately 30 regulated and licensed brothels located in rural counties throughout the state. With the passing of the TVPA (2000), the *abolitionist or partial decriminalization* position, built upon the conviction that those involved in prostitution are vulnerable victims, gained significant legal support. Closely aligning with this position, federal efforts to combat human trafficking have focused on three key objectives: the prevention of human trafficking; the prosecution of traffickers; and the protection of victims, including protection from prosecution even if victims are entangled in illegal activities (TPVA, 2000, Sec. 102; DOS, 2008). In 2000, the passage of the TVPA emphasized the resolve of the federal government to provide protection for international victims trafficked into the United States. With the passage of the Trafficking Victims Protection Reauthorization Act (TVPRA) in 2005, new attention was directed toward the plight of U.S. citizens, whether minors or adults, exploited in prostitution on the streets of the United States. The TVPRA highlighted the vulnerability of certain U.S. populations, such as teenage runaways, and allocated additional resources for victim assistance programs working with U.S. citizens exploited by human trafficking.

While the scholarly debate continues regarding prostitution, all agree that forced prostitution or sex trafficking is harmful (Farley, 2009). Exposure to life-threatening health risks, the development of psychological problems, and the possibility of long-term social stigmatization are among the detrimental consequences commonly associated with commercial sexual exploitation, sex trafficking, and prostitution (Farley, 2004; Farley & Kelly, 2000; Ross, Farley, & Schwartz, 2004). Tragically, rapes, sexual assaults, and other types of victimizations committed against those involved in prostitution are callously considered "part of the job description" and doubted or disregarded by law enforcement (Coy, 2009; Farley, 2004). Most poignantly, distinguishing between nonforced and forced prostitution/sex trafficking has turned out to be extremely difficult.

DIFFICULTIES DISENTANGLING
FORCED FROM NONFORCED PROSTITUTION

Federal legislation, in the form of the TVPA (2000), provides protection for both adult and child victims of sex trafficking. Specifically, the TVPA defines a severe form of trafficking as "sex trafficking in which a commercial sex act is induced by force, fraud or coercion, or in which the person induced to perform such act is under 18 years of age" (TVPA, Sec. 103[8]). Based on the definitions in the TVPA, identifying adult victims of sex trafficking poses a special set of challenges because, unlike minors, adult victims must prove that they were forced, tricked, or coerced into prostitution in order to receive victim status. The U.S. Department of Health and Human Services (HHS; 2012) defines force, fraud, and coercion as follows:

> *Force* can involve the use of physical restraint or serious physical harm. Physical violence, including rape, beatings, and physical confinement, is often employed. . . .
>
> *Fraud* involves false promises regarding employment, wages, working conditions, or other matters. . . .
>
> *Coercion* can involve threats of serious harm to or physical restraint against any person; any scheme, plan or pattern intended to cause a person to believe that failure to perform an act would result in serious harm to or physical restraint against any person; or the abuse or threatened abuse of the legal process ("How Victims Are Trafficked").

Clarifying that a person who initially consented to prostitution may still be classified as a sex-trafficking victim, the directives of the U.S. Office to Monitor and Combat Trafficking in Persons state, "When an adult is coerced, forced, or deceived into prostitution—or maintained in prostitution through one of these means after initially consenting—that person is a victim of trafficking" (DOS, 2012, "Sex Trafficking"). Prosecutors of sex-trafficking cases involving adult victims report difficulties proving these elements, particularly coercion, in the courtroom to judges and juries (Farrell et al., 2012). Members of juries are uninformed about the psychological effects of exposure to prolonged trauma and interpersonal violence and thus fail to grasp victims' fear and inability to leave (Farrell et al.). Acknowledging the difficulty of identifying and proving coercion in court before judges and juries, The U.S. House of Representatives Report on the William Wilberforce Act listed specific examples of psychological coercion "including but not limited to isolation, denial of sleep and punishments, or preying on mental illness, infirmity, drug use or addictions (whether pre-existing or developed by the trafficker)" (Berman, 2008, p. 36).

The difficulty encountered when attempting to verify sex trafficking in cases involving adult victims is evidenced by the substantially lower proportion of suspected human-trafficking incidents involving adult victims in prostitution that are confirmed by law enforcement as compared to the proportion of those involving child victims. Between January 2008 and June 2009, only 18.6% (108 out of 581 incidents) of suspected human-trafficking incidents involving adult prostitution were confirmed as human trafficking by highly efficient human-trafficking task force personnel, with the remaining incidents either closed as unconfirmed or pending confirmation (Banks & Kyckelhahn, 2011). During the same time period, 47.3% (164 of 347 cases) of suspected incidents of human trafficking involving minors exploited in prostitution were confirmed as human trafficking (Banks & Kyckelhahn). Thus, suspected incidents of sex trafficking involving minors were 2.5 times more likely to be confirmed as human trafficking than were suspected incidents involving adults.

Challenges to identifying adult sex-trafficking victims and establishing the use of force, fraud, and coercion by sex traffickers arise from the dynamics of sex trafficking, which often affect victims' behavior and willingness to cooperate with authorities (Herman, 1992; Reid et al., 2013). A number of scholars have highlighted the similarities between victim–abuser dynamics in intimate-partner violence and those in sex trafficking, noting that in both situations, the victim is isolated from outside support and controlled physically and emotionally (Farley et al., 2003; Kennedy et al., 2007; Stark & Hodgson, 2003). Batterers and sex traffickers both typically manipulate victims via isolation, terrify victims through the use of physical and sexual violence, control victims' money and work, and produce pornography to blackmail and shame victims (Stark & Hodgson). Sex traffickers commonly threaten to harm victims and their families if victims fail to comply with the demands of the trafficker or if they cooperate with law enforcement (Farrell et al., 2012; Kennedy et al.).

Additionally, researchers have noted that the majority of adults involved in prostitution initially became involved during adolescence (Kennedy et al., 2007; Nixon et al., 2002). These findings cast doubt on whether such adults ever freely chose to engage in prostitution or if, instead, disadvantaged circumstances extending from childhood sexual exploitation may have kept them entrapped them in a life that they would leave behind if given the opportunity. Farley (2009) noted that research collected from nine countries indicated that "89% of all those in prostitution said that they were in prostitution because they had no alternatives for economic survival and that they saw no means of escape" (p. 311). Numerous studies have documented multiple problematic barriers—such as lack of education and job skills, mental health and drug problems, and trafficking/pimp intimidation—that hinder those attempting to exit street prostitution, with few succeeding despite making numerous attempts to exit (Baker, Dalla, & Williamson, 2010; Dalla, 2000, 2006; Murphy, 2010).

Further complicating the issue of forced versus nonforced prostitution, questions emerge regarding the long-term physical and psychological effects of experiencing excessive violence. Approximately 50% of women interviewed for a study on violence in prostitution reported traumatic brain injuries (TBI) due to "violent assaults with baseball bats, crowbars, or from having their heads slammed against the wall or against car dashboards" (Farley et al., 2003, p. 59). Patients with TBI may have difficulty with concentration, often feel confused, struggle with problem solving, and demonstrate poor judgment (Jackson, Philip, Nuttall, & Diller, 2002). In addition, terrorized individuals may appear as amenable to and compliant with the demands of their exploiters, not as forced or coerced. In the case of sex trafficking, brutalized by rape and violence, passed from trafficker to trafficker, and sold again and again in prostitution, these women are often broken by the force that has been used against them—it would be a grave injustice to mistake their submission for consent. It is not consent, but it makes force, fraud and coercion very difficult to prove. (Neuwirth, 2008, para. 3)

International Victims of Sex Trafficking

The last section of the chapter highlights unique vulnerabilities of foreign nationals, both those who are trafficked into the United States as well as foreign nationals sexually exploited along the U.S.–Mexican border. North America's intersection of extreme wealth and extreme poverty contributes to the problem of human trafficking in the region. The United States receives the second largest number of international victims of sex trafficking in the world (Mizus et al., 2003). Mexico is primarily considered a sending and transiting country for trafficking of persons into the United States (Goh, 2009). In Mexico, widespread poverty and a practically nonexistent social safety net push many individuals to pursue precarious ways of meeting basic survival needs, creating heightened susceptibility to entrapment in sex trafficking (Acharya, 2010; Estes, Azaola, & Ives, 2005; Shelley, 2010). For example, near the U.S.–Mexican border, popular tourist destinations flourish where organized groups profiting from the commercial sex industry recruit displaced and vulnerable children and adults to fill the thriving demand for commercial sex fueled by wealthy American tourists (Acharya, 2009, 2010; Azaola, 2000).

UNIQUE VULNERABILITIES AND CHALLENGES ENCOUNTERED BY FOREIGN NATIONALS

Being a foreigner, even for those legally migrating to the United States with a U.S. visa, severely elevates the likelihood of experiencing various types of victimization. Although migration heightens the risk of victimization for all, women and children are at greatest risk (Erez & Ammar, 2003; Walters & Davis, 2011). Women and children are often reliant on spouses, boyfriends, employers, visa sponsors, and other immigrants. Laws and government authorities that generally provide protection and reduce the likelihood of victimization either are not accessible or are feared by many victimized foreign nationals living in the United States.

Challenges unique to international sex-trafficking victims commonly revolve around their tenuous immigration status in the United States, such as being in the country without proper documentation, having travel documents or a visa that is sponsored by a trafficker or trafficker-owned agency, or having expired travel documents (Goh, 2009; Hepburn & Simon, 2010; Logan et al., 2009). Traffickers often use these problems to frighten victims and enforce their compliance. Problems related to proper documentation often stem from widespread corruption in the victims' home countries. For example, fraudulent travel and employment agencies deceive victims about the true conditions of their travel or employment abroad (Acharya, 2010; Goh, 2009; Raymond & Hughes, 2001). International trafficking victims are easily coerced, as they have a particular fear of police and immigration enforcement personnel due to both previous exploitation by corrupt officials in their home countries and a belief they will be deported, arrested, or further victimized by U.S. authorities. Furthermore, language and cultural barriers can result in isolation, increasing vulnerability to exploitation by traffickers and decreasing access to protection and support (Logan et al.; Raymond & Hughes).

INTERNATIONAL CHILD SEX-TRAFFICKING VICTIMS IN THE UNITED STATES

Estes and Wiener (2005) estimated that there were 17,000 international child sex-trafficking victims in the United States. The most commonly cited estimate of the number of both children and adults trafficked into the United States every year is 14,000 to 17,500 (HHS, 2005). Few regard these estimates as accurate, and several associated figures support the assumption that these estimates are too low. First, approximately 100,000 unaccompanied children are apprehended by the U.S. Border Patrol every year (Goździak & Bump, 2008; Haddal, 2007). These apprehended youth originate primarily from Mexico or Central America (Barnett, 2004). The majority of the children state that they are traveling to the United States to join distant relatives, who are already living in the United States legally or illegally (Barnett). Other children report traveling to the United States in search of a better life, as coming to the United States seems to be "the only hope for 'street children' in Central America" (Barnett, p. 4).

Most of these apprehended children, particularly if they are from Mexico, are immediately returned to their country of origin, while approximately 7,000 to 10,000 are detained annually in U.S. federal custody (Goździak & Bump, 2008; Haddal, 2007). Very little is known about the circumstances surrounding the movement of these minors across international borders, such as whether they were victims of trafficking and in danger of further victimization by traffickers (Barnett, 2004; Goździak & Bump). Moreover, perhaps an even greater number of minors cross U.S. borders completely undetected. So, while estimates of the number of international child sex victims in the United States are relatively low, many more child victims may be undetected.

CHILD SEX TOURISM ALONG THE U.S.–MEXICAN BORDER

While not technically considered international child sex-trafficking victims in the United States because these victims are not trafficked across international borders, much of domestic or internal sex trafficking of children in Mexico is linked to child sex tourism driven by visitors from the United States. Within Mexico, many urban areas are economically supported by the commercial sex industry; these areas include centers of sex tourism located near the U.S.–Mexican border (Acharya, 2009; Azaola, 2000; Hepburn & Simon, 2010; Zhang, Pacheco-McEvoy, & Campos, 2011). Within these high-risk communities, the presence of various types of transient males, including tourists, sex tourists, and international military personnel, heightens the demand for sex-trafficking victims (Estes et al., 2005; Zhang et al.).

Both boys and girls are exploited in child sex trafficking in Mexico; Azaola (2000) examined six localities in Mexico and found that the proportion of boys or girls sexually exploited varied considerably in each location based on the characteristics of the market demand. Girls, as young as 12 years old, are typically kept in brothels or massage parlors, having sex with dozens of "Northern" men or men from the United States every day (Walters & Davis, 2011). Along the Mexican–U.S. border, organized networks also actively recruit boys for sex crime rings to meet the demand of U.S. sex tourists (Estes et al., 2005; Walters & Davis).

Wealthy sex tourists who buy sex with impoverished children abroad justify their sexual exploitation by stating that, in this way, they are providing for children and their families who have no other means of earning money for food or other basic necessities (Fraley, 2005; Walters & Davis, 2011). One retired school teacher from Orlando, Florida, traveling in Latin America stated:

> If they don't have sex with me, they may not have enough food. If someone has a problem with me doing this, let UNICEF feed them. I've never paid more than $20 to these young women, and that allows them to eat for a week. (cited in Fraley, p. 450)

Those who sexually exploit children also propagate other myths or rationalizations to justify their behavior, including the incorrect notions that the exploited children are nothing more than chattel and entirely impervious to the abusive experience, that younger children will not remember the abuse, and that the exploited children take pleasure in the sexual experience (Cooper, 2005; Farr, 2005). Justifying the sexual exploitation of children in other countries, child sex tourists also depict foreign children as less sexually inhibited and surmise that other cultures do not have social prohibitions against sex with children (Fraley; Walters & Davis).

To combat the problem of sexual exploitation through child sex tourism by U.S. citizens, the federal government passed the Protect Act of 2003, which supports the prosecution of U.S. citizens or legal permanent residents who engage in sexual exploitation of minors while abroad. Under the Protect Act of 2003, U.S. citizens or residents who engage in sexual activity abroad with a child under the age of 18 can be sentenced to a maximum of 30 years in prison. Several investigations and prosecutions of U.S. citizens have been successful, yet more needs to be done to combat this problem (Fraley, 2005; Steinman, 2002). Supplementary legal remedies have been recommended, such as not issuing passports to U.S. citizens who have previously been convicted of a sex offense to prevent them from victimizing individuals in other countries in order to victimize others (Hall, 2011).

Conclusion

This chapter described ongoing debates surrounding sexual victimization of individuals involved in the commercial sex industry. Widely held misconceptions regarding the commercial sexual exploitation of minors in prostitution were refuted based on current research findings. The documentation of severe health consequences, lasting psychological problems, and long-term social marginalization of minors who have been sexually exploited in prostitution contradicts the misconception that the prostitution of minors is a victimless crime. A review of the common dynamics involved in the commercial sexual exploitation of minors, including the malleability and immaturity of minors, childhood histories often marred by abuse and abandonment, and the cunning manipulation of sex traffickers, cast doubt on the ability of any minor to "freely choose" prostitution or maintain power and control over the situation. Additionally, rather than involvement in prostitution creating wealth for minors, sex traffickers commonly entrap minors in prostitution through trickery and debt bondage.

Federal legislation, specifically the TVPA (2000), provides blanket legal protection for minors involved in any type of commercial sexual activity. However, exploited adults must prove that force, fraud, or coercion was involved to gain protection as victims of sex trafficking. The difficulty of disentangling nonforced prostitution from forced prostitution reduces the effectiveness of the federal legislation in protecting adult sex-trafficking victims and limits the successful prosecution of sex traffickers who exploit adults.

Foreign nationals trafficked into the United States or living along the U.S.–Mexican border face perilous circumstances. They lack access to police protection. In addition, stronger legislation is needed to protect disadvantaged populations from being exploited in sex trafficking and in child sex tourism. Justifications of sexual exploitation made by wealthy sex offenders, including notions that they are helping impoverished children by paying for sex with them, parrot hollow justifications commonly used by all types of sex offenders to justify and excuse criminal behavior.

Discussion Questions

1. Are there differences between prostitution involving minors and prostitution involving adults? If yes, what are the differences?

2. Can legalized prostitution ever be safe and free of exploitation? Or should laws against prostitution remain?

3. Should the United States police the actions of its citizens when they travel abroad or use the Internet and digital technology to sexually exploit children living in other countries? Why or why not?

4. How would you respond to those who buy sex with children and rationalize this behavior by saying that they are supporting children and giving them money they need to pay for food?

References

Acharya, A. K. (2009). The dynamic of internal displacement, forced migration, and vulnerable to trafficking in Mexico. *Journal of Human Ecology, 27*(3), 161–170. Retrieved from http://www.krepublishers.com

Acharya, A. K. (2010). Feminization of migration and trafficking of women in Mexico. *Revista de cercetare si interventie sociala (Review of Research and Social Intervention), 30,* 19–38. Retrieved from http://www.rcis.ro/images/documente/rcis30_02.pdf

Adams, W., Owens, C., & Small, K. (2010, July). Effects of federal legislation on the commercial exploitation of children. *Juvenile Justice Bulletin* (NCJ 228631). Washington, DC: Office of Juvenile Justice and Delinquency Protection. Retrieved from http://www.ncjrs.gov/pdffiles1/ojjdp/228631.pdf

Adelson, W. J. (2008). Child prostitute or victim of trafficking. *University of St. Thomas Law Journal, 6,* 96–127. Retrieved from LexisNexis Academic.

Agrusa, J. F. (2003). AIDS and tourism: A deadly combination. In T. G. Bauer & B. McKercher (Eds.), *Sex and tourism: Journeys of romance, love, and lust* (pp. 167–180). Binghamton, NY: Haworth Hospitality Press.

Albanese, J. (2007). *Commercial sexual exploitation of children: What do we know and what do we do about it?* (NCJ 215733). Washington, DC: National Institute of Justice. Retrieved from http://www.ncjrs.gov/pdffiles1/nij/215733.pdf

Annitto, M. (2011). Consent, coercion, and compassion: Emerging legal responses to the commercial sexual exploitation of minors. *Yale Law & Policy Review, 30*(1), 1–70. Retrieved from LexisNexis.

Azaola, E. (2000). *Boy and girl victims of sexual exploitation in Mexico.* Mexico City: United Nations Children's Fund (UNICEF). Retrieved from http://www.sp2.upenn.edu/restes/Mexico_Final_Report_001015.pdf

Baker, L. M., Dalla, R. L., & Williamson, C. (2010). Exiting prostitution: An integrated model. *Violence against women, 16*(5), 579–600. doi: 10.1177/1077801210367643

Bales, K. (2007). What predicts global trafficking? *International Journal of Comparative and Applied Criminal Justice, 31,* 269–280. doi: 10.1080/01924036.2007.9678771

Banks, D., & Kyckelhahn, T. (2011). *Characteristics of suspected human trafficking incidents, 2008–2010* (NCJ 233732). Washington, DC: U.S. Department of Justice, Office of Justice Programs, Bureau of Justice Statistics. Retrieved from http://bjs.gov/content/pub/pdf/cshti0810.pdf

Barnett, D. (2004). No child left behind: New rules for unaccompanied minor illegal aliens. *Backgrounder, 13,* 1–6. Washington, DC: Center for Immigration Studies.

Berman, H. L. (2008, December 10). William Wilberforce Trafficking Victims Protection Reauthorization Act of 2008. *Congressional Record 154*(185), 20–36. Retrieved from LexisNexis.

Brayley, H., Cockbain, E., & Laycock, G. (2011). The value of crime scripting: Deconstructing internal child sex trafficking. *Policing, 5,* 132–143. doi:10.1093/police/par024

Coleman, C. (1996). "Don't Take Much" [Recorded by Chuck Cooper]. On *The life: The new musical, original Broadway cast* [CD recording]. New York, NY: Sony Music Entertainment.

Cooper, S. W. (2005). A brief history of child sexual exploitation. In S. W. Cooper, R. J. Estes, A. P. Giardino, N. D. Kellogg, & V. I. Vieth (Eds.), *Medical, legal & social science aspects of child sexual exploitation: A comprehensive review of child pornography, child prostitution and Internet crimes against children* (pp. 1–24). St. Louis, MO: GW Medical.

Coy, M. (2009). Invaded spaces and feeling dirty: Women's narratives of violation in prostitution and sexual violence. In M. Horvath & J. Brown (Eds.), *Rape: Challenging contemporary thinking* (pp. 184–206). Collumpton, England: Willan.

Dalla, R. L. (2000). Exposing the pretty woman myth: Qualitative examination of the lives of female street-walking prostitutes. *Journal of Sex Research, 37,* 344–353. doi:10.1080/002244 90009552057

Dalla, R. L. (2006). "You can't hustle all your life": An exploratory investigation of the exit process among street-level prostituted women. *Psychology of Women Quarterly, 30,* 276–290. doi: 10.1111/j.1471-6402.2006.00296.x

Dorias, M., & Corriveau, P. (2009). *Gangs and girls: Understanding juvenile prostitution.* Montreal, Canada: McGill-Queen's University Press.

Erez, E., & Ammar, N. (2003). *Violence against immigrant women and systemic responses: An exploratory study* (Report submitted to the National Institute for Justice). Retrieved from https://www.ncjrs.gov/pdffiles1/nij/grants/202561.pdf

Estes, J. R., Azaola, E., & Ives, N. (2005). The commercial sexual exploitation of children in North America. In S. W. Cooper, R. J. Estes, A. P. Giardino, N. D. Kellogg, & V. I. Vieth (Eds.), *Medical, legal & social science aspects of child sexual exploitation: A comprehensive review of child pornography, child prostitution, and Internet crimes against children* (pp. 297–336). St. Louis, MO: GW Medical.

Estes, J. R., & Weiner, N. A. (2005). The commercial sexual exploitation of children in the United States. In S. W. Cooper, R. J. Estes, A. P. Giardino, N. D. Kellogg & V. I. Vieth (Eds.), *Medical, legal & social science aspects of child sexual exploitation: A comprehensive review of child pornography, child prostitution, and Internet crimes against children* (pp. 95–128). St. Louis, MO: GW Medical.

Farley, M. (2003). *Prostitution, trafficking and traumatic stress.* Binghamton, NY: Haworth Press.

Farley, M. (2004). Bad for the body, bad for the heart: Prostitution harms women even if legalized or decriminalized. *Violence Against Women, 10,* 1087–1125. doi: 10.1177/1077801204268607

Farley, M. (2009). Theory versus reality: Commentary on four articles about trafficking for prostitution. *Women's Studies International Forum, 32*(4), 311–315.

Farley, M., Cotton, A., Lynne, J., Zumbeck, S., Spiwak, F., Reyes, M. E., . . . Sezgin, U. (2003). Prostitution and trafficking in nine countries: An update on violence and posttraumatic stress disorder. In M. Farley (Ed.), *Prostitution, trafficking and traumatic stress* (pp. 33–74). Binghamton, NY: Haworth.

Farley, M., & Kelly, V. (2000). Prostitution: A critical review of the medical and social sciences literature. *Women & Criminal Justice, 11*(4), 29–64. doi:10.1300/J012v11n04_04

Farr, K. (2005). *Sex trafficking: The global market in women and children.* New York, NY: Worth.

Farrell, A., & Fahy, S. (2009). The problem of human trafficking in the U.S.: Public frames and policy responses. *Journal of Criminal Justice, 31,* 617–626. doi: 10.1016/j.jcrimjus.2009.09.010

Farrell, A., McDevitt, J., Pfeffer, R., Fahy, S., Owens, C., Dank, M., & Adams, W. (2012). *Identifying challenges to improve the investigation and prosecution of state and local human trafficking cases* (NCJ 238795). Washington, DC: National Institute of Justice. Retrieved from https://www.ncjrs .gov/pdffiles1/nij/grants/238795.pdf

Fraley, A. (2005). Child sex tourism legislation under the Protect Act: Does it really protect? *St. John's Law Review, 79,* 445–484. Retrieved from LexisNexis.

Gallagher, A. T. (2010). *The international law of human trafficking.* New York, NY: Cambridge University Press.

Gardner, M., & Steinberg, L. (2005). Peer influence on risk taking, risk preference, and risky decision making in adolescence and adulthood: An experimental study. *Developmental Psychology, 41,* 625–635. doi: 10.1037/0012-1649.41.4.625

Goddard, C., De Bortoli, L., Saunders, B. J., & Tucci, J. (2005). The rapist's camouflage: "Child prostitution." *Child Abuse Review, 14,* 275–291. doi: 10.1002/car.894

Goh, J. P. L. (2009). Deterritoialized women in the global city: An analysis of sex trafficking in Dubia, Tokyo, and New York. *Intersections, 10,* 271–324. Retrieved from http://depts.washington.edu/

chid/intersections_Spring_2009/Janice_Phaik_Lin_Goh_Deterritorialized_Women_in_the_Global_City.pdf

Goździak, E. M., & Bump, M. N. (2008). *Victims no longer: Research on child survivors of sex trafficking for sexual and labor exploitation* (Research report submitted to the U.S. Department of Justice). Retrieved from https://www.ncjrs.gov/pdffiles1/nij/grants/221891.pdf

Goździak, E. M., & Collett, E. A. (2005). Research on human trafficking in North America: A review of literature. *International Migration 43*, 99–128. doi: 10.1111/j.0020-7985.2005.00314.x

Graycar, A., & McCusker, R. (2007). Transnational crime and trafficking in persons: Quantifying the nature, extent and facilitation of a growing phenomenon. *International Journal of Comparative and Applied Criminal Justice, 31*, 147–166. doi: 10.1080/01924036.2007.9678766

Haddal, C. C. (2007). *Unaccompanied alien children: Policies and issues* (RL33896). Washington, DC: Congressional Research Service. Retrieved from http://assets.opencrs.com/rpts/RL33896_20070301.pdf

Hall, J. A. (2011). Sex offenders and child sex tourism: The case for passport revocation. *Virginia Journal of Social Policy and the Law, 18*(2), 153–169. Retrieved from LexisNexis.

Halley, J. E., Kotiswaran, P., Thomas, C.; & Shamir, H. (2006). From the international to the local in feminist legal responses to rape, prostitution/sex work, and sex trafficking: Four studies in contemporary governance feminism. *Harvard Journal of Law & Gender, 29*, 335–360. Retrieved from LexisNexis.

Halter, S. (2010). Factors that influence police conceptualization of girls involved in prostitution in six U.S. cities: Child sexual exploitation victims or delinquents? *Child Maltreatment, 15*, 152–160. doi:10.1177/1077559509355315

Hanna, C. (2002). Somebody's daughter: Domestic trafficking of girls for the commercial sex industry and the power of love. *William and Mary Journal of Women and Law, 9*, 1–29. Retrieved from LexisNexis.

Hepburn, S., & Simon, R. J. (2010). Hidden in plain sight: Human trafficking in the United States. *Gender Issues, 27*, 1–26. doi: 10.1007/s12147-010-9087-7

Herman, J. L. (1992). *Trauma and recovery*. New York, NY: Basic Books.

Hynes, H. P., & Raymond, J. G. (2002). Put in harm's way: The neglected health consequences of sex trafficking in the United States. In J. Silliman & A. Bhattacharjee (Eds.), *Policing the national body: Sex, race, and criminalization* (pp. 197–229). Cambridge, MA: South End Press.

International Labour Organization (ILO). (n.d.). *Commercial sexual exploitation of children and adolescents: The ILO's response*. Geneva, Switzerland: International Programme on the Elimination of Child Labour (IPEC). Retrieved from http://www.ilo.org/ipecinfo/product/download.do?type=document&id=9150

International Labour Organization (ILO). (2005). *A global alliance against forced labour*. Geneva, Switzerland: International Labour Office. Retrieved from http://www.ilo.org/public/english/standards/relm/ilc/ilc93/pdf/rep-i-b.pdf

Jackson, H., Philip, E., Nuttall, R. L., & Diller, L. (2002). Traumatic brain injury: A hidden consequence for battered women. *Professional Psychology: Research and Practice, 33*(1), 39–45. doi:10.1037/0735-7028.33.1.39

Jeffreys, S. (2009). *The industrial vagina: The political economy of the global sex trade*. New York, NY: Routledge.

Jülich, S. (2005).Stockholm syndrome and child sexual abuse. *Journal of Child Sexual Abuse, 14*(3), 107–129. doi:10.1300/J070v14n03_06

Kelly, L. (2005). "You can find anything you want": A critical reflection on research on trafficking in persons within and into Europe. *International Migration, 43*, 235–265. doi: 10.1111/j.0020-7985.2005.00319

Kennedy, M. A., Klein, C., Bristowe, J. T. K., Cooper, B. S., & Yuille, J. C. (2007). Routes of recruitment: Pimps' techniques and other circumstances that lead to street prostitution. *Journal of Aggression, Maltreatment & Trauma, 15*(2), 1–19. doi: 10.1300/J146V15n02_01

Kim, K. (2007). Psychological coercion in the context of modern-day involuntary labor: Revisiting *United States v. Kozminski* and understanding human trafficking. *University of Toledo Law Review, 37*, 941–972. Retrieved from LexisNexis.

Kreston, S. (2000, November/December). Prostituted children: Not an innocent image. *The Prosecutor, 34*(6), 37–41.

Lehti, M., & Aromaa, K. (2007). Trafficking in women and children for sexual exploitation: The European context. *International Journal of Comparative and Applied Criminal Justice, 31*, 123–146.

Leth, I. (2005). Child sexual exploitation from a global perspective. In S. W. Cooper, R. J. Estes, A. P. Giardino, N. D. Kellogg, & V. I. Vieth (Eds.), *Medical, legal & social science aspects of child sexual exploitation* (pp. 59–84). St. Louis, MO: GW Medical.

Leung, P. (2003). Sex tourism: The case of Cambodia. In T. G. Bauer & B. McKercher (Eds.), *Sex and tourism: Journeys of romance, love, and lust* (pp. 181–195). Binghamton, NY: Haworth Hospitality Press.

Logan, T. K., Walker, R., & Hunt, G. (2009). Understanding human trafficking in the United States. *Trauma, Violence, & Abuse, 10*, 3–30. doi: 10.1177/1524838008327262

Mitchell, K. J., Finkelhor, D., & Wolak, J. (2010). Conceptualizing juvenile prostitution as child maltreatment: Findings from the National Juvenile Prostitution Study. *Child Maltreatment, 15*, 18–36. doi: 10.1177/1077559509349443

Mizus, M., Moody, M., Privado, C., Douglas, C. A., Collins, J. M., Mata, E., . . . Stachowski, R. (2003, July/August). Germany, U.S. receive most sex-trafficked women. *Off Our Backs, 33*(7/8), 4. doi: 10.2307/20837856

Murphy, L. S. (2010). Understanding the social and economic contexts surrounding women engaged in street-level prostitution. *Issues in Mental Health Nursing, 31*(12), 775–784. doi:10.3109/0161 2840.2010.524345

Neuwirth, J. (2008, June 11). *Statement of Jessica Neuwirth, President of Equality Now, to the New York City Council 6/11/08.* Retrieved from http://www.equalitynow.org/node/954/

Nixon, K., Tutty, L., Downe, P., Gorkoff, K., & Ursel, J. (2002). The everyday occurrence violence in the lives of girls exploited through prostitution. *Violence against women, 8*(9), 1016–1043. doi: 10.1177/107780120200800902

Raphael, J., Reichert, J., & Powers, M. (2010). Pimp control and violence: Domestic sex trafficking of Chicago women and girls. *Women & Criminal Justice, 20*, 89–104.

Raymond, J. G., & Hughes, D. M. (2001). *Sex trafficking of women in the United States: International and domestic trends.* North Amherst, MA: Coalition Against Trafficking in Women. Retrieved from http://www.uri.edu/artsci/wms/hughes/sex_traff_us.pdf

Reid, J. A. (2010). Doors wide shut: Barriers to the successful delivery of victim services for domestically trafficked minors in a southern U.S. metropolitan area. *Women and Criminal Justice, 20*(1), 147–166. doi: 10.1080/08974451003641206

Reid, J. A. (2012). *A girl's pathway to prostitution: Linking caregiver adversity to child susceptibility.* El Paso: TX: LFB Scholarly.

Reid, J. A. (2013). Rapid assessment exploring impediments to successful prosecutions of sex traffickers of U.S. minors. *Journal of Police and Criminal Psychology, 28*, 75–89. doi: 10.1007/s11896-012-9106-6

Reid, J. A., Haskell R. A., Dillahunt-Aspillaga, C., & Thor, J. A. (2013). Trauma bonding and interpersonal violence. In T. van Leeuwen & M. Brouwer (Eds.), *Psychology of Trauma*, Hauppauge, NY: Nova Science.

Reid, J. A., & Jones, S. (2011). Exploited vulnerability: Legal and psychological perspectives on child sex trafficking victims. *Victims & Offenders, 6,* 207–231. doi:10.1080/15564886.2011.557327

Ross, C. A., Farley, M., & Schwartz, H. L. (2004). Dissociation among women in prostitution. *Journal of trauma practice, 2*(3–4), 199–212. doi:10.1300/J189v02n03_11

Shared Hope International. (2011). *The Protected Innocence Challenge: State report cards on the legal framework of protection for the nation's children.* Vancouver, WA: Shared Hope International. Retrieved from http://sharedhope.org/wp-content/uploads/2012/10/PIC_ChallengeReport_ 2011.pdf

Shelley, L. (2010). *Human trafficking: A global perspective.* New York, NY: Cambridge University Press.

Shlyk, S. (2007). Criminal sex trade: System aspects and tendencies. *International Journal of Comparative and Applied Criminal Justice, 31,* 245–268. doi:10.1080/01924036.2007.9678770

Silverman, J. G., Decker, M. R., Gupta, J., Maheshwari, A., Patel, V., & Raj, A. (2006). HIV prevalence and predictors among rescued sex-trafficked women and girls in Mumbai, India. *Journal of Acquired Immune Deficiency Syndromes, 43,* 588–593. doi: 10.1097/01 .qai.0000243101.57523.7

Silverman, J. G., Decker, M. R., Gupta, J., Maheshwari, A., Willis, B. M., & Raj, A. (2007). HIV prevalence and predictors of infection in sex-trafficked Nepalese girls and women. *JAMA, 298,* 536–542. doi:10.1001/jama.298.5.536

Spidel, A., Greaves, C., Cooper, B. S, Hervé, H. F., Hare, R. D., & Yuille, J. C. (2006). The psychopath as pimp. *Canadian Journal of Police and Security Services, 4,* 193–199. Retrieved from http:// www.hare.org/references/SpideletalCJPSS2006.pdf

Stark, C., & Hodgson, C. (2003). Sister oppressions: A comparison of wife battering and prostitution. In M. Farley (Ed.), *Prostitution, trafficking and traumatic stress* (pp. 17–32). Binghamton, NY: Haworth Press.

Steinberg, L., & Scott, E. S. (2003). Less guilty by reason of adolescence: Developmental immaturity, diminished responsibility, and the juvenile death penalty. *American Psychologist, 58,* 1009–1018. doi: 10.1037/0003-066X.58.12.1009

Steinman, K. J. (2002). Sex tourism and the child: Latin America's and the United States' failure to prosecute sex tourists. *Hastings Women's Law Journal, 13,* 53–74. Retrieved from LexisNexis

Summit, R. C. (1983). The child sexual abuse accommodation syndrome. *Child Abuse and Neglect, 7*(2), 177–193. doi:10.1016/0145-2134(83)90070-4

Trafficking Victims Protection Act of 2000 (TVPA), 22 U.S.C. §7105(b)(1)(E)(u)[2000]).

Trafficking Victims Protection Reauthorization Act of 2005 (TVPRA), Pub. L. No. 109-164, 119 Stat. 3558 (2006). (Current version at 22 U.S.C. §§7101–7106 [2008])

U.S. Citizenship and Immigration Services (ICE). (2010). Questions and answers: Victims of human trafficking, T nonimmigrant status. Retrieved from http://www.uscis.gov/portal/site/uscis/men uitem.5af9bb95919f35e66f614176543f6d1a/?vgnextoid=a53dc7f5ab548210VgnVCM 100000082ca60aRCRD&vgnextchannel=02ed3e4d77d73210VgnVCM100000082ca60aRCRD

U.S. Department of Health and Human Services (HHS). (2005, November 16). Campaign launched in Houston to identify, assist victims of human trafficking (press release). Retrieved from http:// archive.acf.hhs.gov/trafficking/rescue_restore/press_houstonrelease.htm

U.S. Department of Health and Human Services (HHS). (2012). Fact sheet: Human trafficking. Retrieved from http://www.acf.hhs.gov/programs/orr/resource/fact-sheet-human-trafficking

U.S. Department of State (DOS). (2008). *Trafficking in persons report 2008.* Retrieved from http:// www.state.gov/g/tip/rls/tiprpt/2008/

U.S. Department of State (DOS). (2011). *Trafficking in persons report 2011.* Retrieved from http:// www.state.gov/g/tip/rls/tiprpt/2011/

U.S. Department of State (DOS). (2012). What is modern slavery? Retrieved from http://www.state .gov/j/tip/what/index.htm

U.S. General Accounting Office (GAO). (2007). *Human trafficking: A strategic framework could help enhance the interagency collaboration needed to effectively combat trafficking crimes.* Washington, DC: U.S. GAO. Retrieved from http://www.gao.gov/new.items/d07915.pdf

Walters, J., & Davis, P. H. (2011). Human trafficking, sex tourism, and child exploitation on the southern border. *Journal of Applied Research on Children, 2*(1), Article 6. Retrieved from http:// digitalcommons.library.tmc.edu/childrenatrisk/vol2/iss1/6/

Weitzer, R. (Ed.). (2009). *Sex for sale: Prostitution, pornography, and the sex industry.* New York, NY: Routledge.

Wheaton, E. M., Schauer, E. J., & Galli, T. V. (2010). Economics of human trafficking. *International Migration, 48*, 114–141. doi:10.1111/j.1468-2435.2009.00592.x

Whitehead, J. W. (2008, July 29). Children of the night: Child prostitution is America's dirty little secret. *Huffington Post.* Retrieved from http://www.huffingtonpost.com/john-w-whitehead/ children-of-the-night-chi_b_115348.html

Williamson, C., & Cluse-Tolar, T. (2002). Pimp-controlled prostitution: Still an integral part of street life. *Violence Against Women, 8*(9), 1074–1092. doi: 10.1177/107780102401101746

Zhang, S. X., Pacheco-McEvoy, R., & Campos, R. (2011). Sex trafficking in Latin America: Dominant discourse, empirical paucity, and promising research. *Global Crime, iFirst* online, doi:10.1080/ 17440572.2011.632504

Index

About the Editors

Tara N. Richards is an Assistant Professor in the School of Criminal Justice at the University of Baltimore. Dr. Richards earned her PhD in criminology from the University of South Florida in 2011. Her major research interests include violence against women; mental health, substance abuse, and trauma/violence; and evaluation research. Some of her most recent published work appears in *Crime & Delinquency, Violence Against Women, Journal of Interpersonal Violence*, and *Women & Criminal Justice*. She is the recipient of the 2011 American Society of Criminology Division on Women and Crime's Graduate Scholar Award and was honored by the University of South Florida's Department of Criminology with an Outstanding Criminology Ambassador Alumni Award for her policy-relevant scholarship concerning intimate-partner violence and her service to dating-violence prevention efforts among adolescents in the Tampa Bay, Florida, area.

Catherine D. Marcum is an Assistant Professor of Justice Studies at Appalachian State University. She received her PhD in criminology from Indiana University of Pennsylvania in 2008. Her research interests and areas of publication include cybercrime victimization and offending, correctional issues, and sexual victimization.

About the Contributors

Kelsey Becker is an honors undergraduate at Appalachian State University, obtaining her BS in criminal justice. She is planning to pursue her graduate studies in criminal justice and research in the area of cybercrime.

Amanda Burgess-Proctor is an Assistant Professor of Criminal Justice at Oakland University. She received her PhD from the Michigan State University School of Criminal Justice in 2008. Her primary research interests include feminist criminology, criminological theory, intimate-partner abuse, and U.S. crime and drug policy. Her research has appeared in *Justice Quarterly*, *Journal of Crime & Justice*, *Feminist Criminology*, *Violence Against Women*, and *Violence and Victims*.

Shelly Clevenger is an Assistant Professor at Illinois State University. Her research area includes sexual offenses, the experiences of sexual-assault victims and significant others in the criminal justice system, and victims' rights. Dr. Clevenger teaches courses on victimology, sex offenders, and crime and behavior.

Tammatha L. Clodfelter is an Assistant Professor at Appalachian State University. She earned her PhD in public policy with a concentration in justice policy from the University of North Carolina at Charlotte. Dr. Clodfelter's current research interests include interpersonal violence, the relationship between drug and alcohol consumption and crime, and policing.

Leah E. Daigle is an Associate Professor in the Department of Criminal Justice at the Andrew Young School of Policy Studies at Georgia State University. She received her PhD in criminal justice from the University of Cincinnati. Her most recent research has centered on repeat sexual victimization of college women and the development and continuation of victimization across the life course. Dr. Daigle is coauthor of *Criminals in the Making: Criminality Across the Life Course* (second edition) and *Unsafe in the Ivory Tower: The Sexual Victimization of College Women*, which was awarded the 2011 Outstanding Book Award by the Academy of Criminal Justice Sciences. She is also author of *Victimology: A Text/Reader*. Her research has appeared in peer-reviewed journals, including *Justice Quarterly, Victims & Offenders, Journal of Quantitative Criminology,* and *Journal of Interpersonal Violence*.

Bonnie S. Fisher is a Professor in the School of Justice at the University of Cincinnati. She earned her PhD at Northwestern University. She was awarded the 2012 George Rieveschl Jr. Award for Creative and/or Scholarly Works from the University of Cincinnati. Dr. Fisher has coedited and coauthored a number of books, including *Encyclopedia of Victimology and Crime Prevention* (Sage, 2010);

The Dark Side of the Ivory Tower: Campus Crime as a Social Problem; Unsafe in the Ivory Tower: The Sexual Victimization of College Women (Sage, 2010), which won the 2011 Outstanding Book Award from the Academy of Criminal Justice Sciences; and *Campus Crime: Legal, Social and Policy Perspectives,* now in its third edition. She also serves on the National Academy of Sciences panel on Measuring Rape and Sexual Assault in Bureau of Justice Statistics Household Surveys. Her more than 150 published articles and book chapters span the field of victimology, and her primary research area has been violence against women—from domestic violence to sexual assault—with an emphasis on college women.

Tammy Garland is an Associate Professor at the University of Tennessee at Chattanooga, where she teaches courses in victimology, juvenile justice, media and crime, and drugs and crime. She received a PhD in criminal justice from Sam Houston State University in 2004. Dr. Garland's current research emphasis includes victimization of the homeless, women, and children; popular culture; and drug policy issues. Her publications can be found in *American Journal of Criminal Justice, Criminal Justice Policy Review, Criminal Justice Studies,* and *Journal of Poverty.*

Lane Kirkland Gillespie is an Assistant Professor in the Department of Criminal Justice at Boise State University. She earned her PhD in criminology from the University of South Florida. Her research focuses on violence and victimization, including the relationship between gender and crime, intimate-partner violence, corporate victimization, and the role of the victim in criminal justice processes. Dr. Gillespie has recently been recognized by the Department of Criminology at the University of South Florida as an outstanding criminology ambassador. Her publications can be found in *Feminist Criminology, Violence Against Women,* and *Homicide Studies.*

Xavier Guadalupe-Diaz is an Assistant Professor in the Department of Sociology at Framingham State University. He received his PhD in sociology from the University of Central Florida and his MS in sociology from Virginia Commonwealth University. His primary research focuses on various aspects of intimate-partner violence (IPV) within the lesbian, gay, bisexual, transgender, and queer (LGBTQ) communities. Much of his work involves the community, including various stakeholders such as service organizations, providers, advocates, and activists. His dissertation research explored transgender experiences with IPV. This project sought to empower trans voices that have been historically marginalized or largely absent from the IPV literature and provided new insight into the unique realities of these survivors. His most recent publications have examined LGB perceptions of domestic violence law and the help-seeking behaviors of LGB victims of violence.

Laura King is an Assistant Professor of Criminal Justice at Boise State University, where she teaches courses primarily in research methods, statistical analysis, and victimization. She completed her PhD in criminology at Indiana University of Pennsylvania. The majority of her research interests focus on sexual offending and victimization, with an emphasis on system responses to sex crimes, female sex offenders, sexual violence in correctional facilities, public opinion, advocacy, and underserved populations. Much of this research has been survey based and has been published in peer-reviewed journals or presented at national conferences. Dr. King conducts workshops on sexual violence as a part of Victims' Rights Week at Boise State University and for the Idaho Victim Assistance Academy, a statewide training program for criminal justice professionals.

Sarah Koon-Magnin is an Assistant Professor at the University of South Alabama. She earned her PhD in crime, law, and justice from Pennsylvania State University in 2011. Her research interests include multiple aspects of sexual violence but focus primarily on the legal response to sexual offending and the victimization experience.

Sadie Mummert is currently pursuing her PhD in criminal justice and criminology at Georgia State University. Her main research areas are sexual victimization, victims' rights, and intimate-partner violence. Her work has been published in *Journal of Interpersonal Violence, Journal of Criminal Justice Education,* and *International Criminal Justice Review.*

Christina Policastro is an Assistant Professor at Georgia Southern University. She received her PhD from Georgia State University in 2013. Dr. Policastro's research interests include elder abuse, intimate-partner violence, and victimization.

Joan A. Reid is an Assistant Professor in the School of Criminology and Justice Studies at the University of Massachusetts Lowell. She earned her PhD in criminology from the University of South Florida in 2010. Her research concerns include human trafficking, sexual violence, child maltreatment, victimology, and the recovery of crime victims. For 10 years, Joan has counseled individuals recovering from sexual trauma, including youth in foster care and detained in juvenile justice facilities. She maintains her license as a mental health counselor as well as national certifications as a clinical mental health counselor and a rehabilitation counselor. Her research on human trafficking, sexual victimization, and child maltreatment has appeared in journals such as *Child Maltreatment, Victims & Offenders, Criminal Justice and Behavior,* and *Violence and Victims.*

Lauren Restivo is a master's degree student in the School of Criminal Justice at the University of Baltimore, where she also serves as a research assistant. She earned her BA in criminology from the University of Maryland in 2011. Lauren's research interests include intimate-partner violence, corrections, and the intersection of mental health and criminal justice.

Heidi L. Scherer an Assistant Professor in the Department of Sociology & Criminal Justice at Kennesaw State University. She is currently working on research related to victimization risk of college students with disabilities. Dr. Scherer has worked on research projects related to victimization in the workplace, intimate-partner victimization among college students, and place-based management practices at apartment complexes. Her work has appeared in peer-reviewed publications including *Journal of Interpersonal Violence, Women & Criminal Justice,* and *WORK: A Journal of Prevention, Assessment & Rehabilitation.*

Jamie A. Snyder is an Assistant Professor in the Department of Criminal Justice at the University of West Florida. Dr. Snyder is currently working on research into the victimization of college students. Dr. Snyder has also been involved in research focusing on sexual harassment and victimization in the workplace, intimate-partner violence among college students, disabilities and victimization, and sexual victimization in the military. Her current research interests include victimization, college students, crime prevention, criminology, and problem-oriented policing.

Christopher G. Urban is a first-year law student at Wayne State University. He received his BA in sociology from Oakland University in 2012.

⑤SAGE research**methods**

The essential online tool for researchers from the world's leading methods publisher

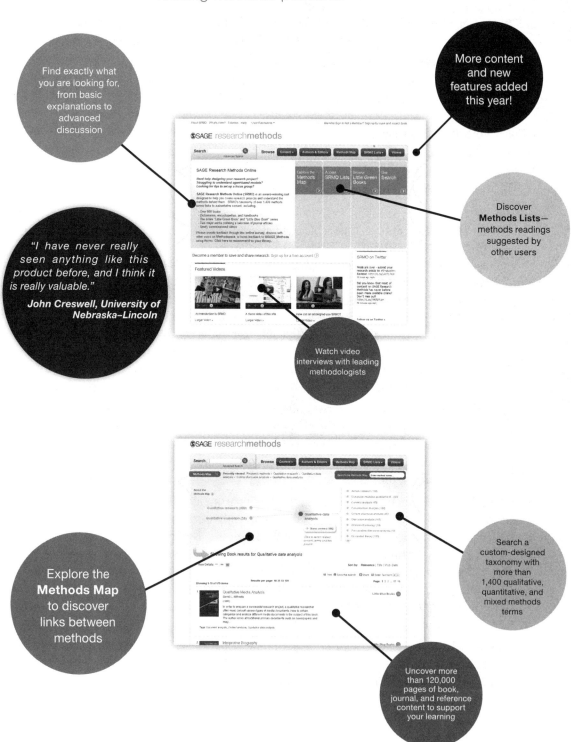

Find exactly what you are looking for, from basic explanations to advanced discussion

More content and new features added this year!

"I have never really seen anything like this product before, and I think it is really valuable."

John Creswell, University of Nebraska–Lincoln

Discover **Methods Lists**— methods readings suggested by other users

Watch video interviews with leading methodologists

Explore the **Methods Map** to discover links between methods

Search a custom-designed taxonomy with more than 1,400 qualitative, quantitative, and mixed methods terms

Uncover more than 120,000 pages of book, journal, and reference content to support your learning

Find out more at
www.sageresearchmethods.com